BLENDED LEARNING

Blended learning, which combines the strength of face-to-face and technology-enhanced learning, is increasingly being seen as one of the most important vehicles for education reform today. Blended learning allows both teacher and learner access to radically increased possibilities for understanding how we transmit and receive information, how we interact with others in educational settings, how we build knowledge, and how we assess what we have taught or learned.

Blended Learning: Research Perspectives, Volume 2 provides readers with the most current, in-depth collection of research perspectives on this vital subject, addressing institutional issues, design and adoption issues, and learning issues, as well as an informed meditation on future trends and research in the field. As governments, foundations, schools, and colleges move forward with plans and investments for vast increases in blended learning environments, a new examination of the existing research on the topic is essential reading for all those involved in this educational transformation.

Anthony G. Picciano is a Professor and Executive Officer in the PhD Program in Urban Education at the Graduate Center of the City University of New York (CUNY).

Charles D. Dziuban is Director of the Research Initiative for Teaching Effectiveness at the University of Central Florida.

Charles R. Graham is a Professor of Instructional Psychology & Technology at Brigham Young University. He also currently serves as the Associate Dean for the David O. McKay School of Education.

"*Blended Learning: Research Perspectives, Volume 2* is an important and needed contribution to updating our understanding and practice of blended learning. The range of relevant blended learning applications and issues addressed in this book provides invaluable insights into the continued development of blended learning."—Dr. Randy Garrison, Professor, Faculty of Education, University of Calgary, Co-author of *Blended Learning in Higher Education*

"Blended learning is an important choice for students, educators, and institutions. The research explored in this volume, spanning engagement, pedagogical practice, and learning outcomes will ensure that blended learning is well understood and of high quality. Changing to blended learning is an important choice. This book ensures the choice is a well-informed one."—Diana Oblinger, President and CEO, EDUCAUSE

"Cyberspace and real space are no longer a dichotomy, but rather a continuum of ever-expanding possibilities. Tony Picciano, Chuck Dziuban, and Charles Graham have brought together a diverse set of voices whose research areas and insightful conclusions will be of crucial help in designing blended learning for an increasingly blended world."—Gardner Campbell, Ph.D., Director, Center for Innovation in Learning, Virginia Tech

"Blended learning is rapidly becoming the standard approach to undergraduate education for a majority of students. It is essential to articulate and conduct research that describes the impact of different implementations of blended learning on the learner, the instructor, and the institution. This compilation does just that, laying the foundation for the 'new norm' in education." —Phillip D. Long, Professor, University of Queensland

"Blended learning has become a lynchpin in higher education, a vehicle to help institutions achieve a variety of strategic curricular goals. Research into best practices in blended learning is therefore of the highest importance to higher education. Edited by a team of leading researchers, this book will serve as an important reference and guide in the years ahead."—Malcolm Brown, Director, EDUCAUSE Learning Initiative

"Blending learning environments are the future for education at all levels. Research-based, this book goes beyond opinion and advice and provides insights from those who have studied the blended learning both broadly and finely. A most important contribution to the scholarship of teaching and learning with technology."—A. Frank Mayadas, President Emeritus, The Sloan Consortium

"Nontraditional learning is the new norm. As blended learning has evolved from the project of a small interest group to the mainstream, scholars must take a step back to document the progress that has been made, discuss recent developments, and chart a path for the future. The thoughtful essays in this book do just that, highlighting the myriad choices as well as challenges that instructors and learners face each day as they utilize web-based tools."—Curt Bonk, President of CourseShare, LLC, and Professor of Instructional Systems Technology in the School of Education at Indiana University, USA

BLENDED LEARNING

Research Perspectives

Volume 2

Edited by

*Anthony G. Picciano, Charles D. Dziuban,
and Charles R. Graham*

Routledge
Taylor & Francis Group
NEW YORK AND LONDON

First published 2014
by Routledge
711 Third Avenue, New York, NY 10017

and by Routledge
2 Park Square, Milton Park, Abingdon, Oxon OX14 4RN

Routledge is an imprint of the Taylor & Francis Group, an informa business

© 2014 Taylor & Francis

Library of Congress Cataloging in Publication Data
Blended learning : research perspectives / edited by Anthony G. Picciano,
Charles D. Dziuban, Charles R. Graham.
    pages cm
  Includes bibliographical references and index.
  1. Blended learning.   2. Blended learning.   I. Picciano, Anthony G.
  II. Dziuban, Charles D.   III. Graham, Charles R.
  LB1028.5.B568 2013
  371.3—dc23

                                                          2013018913

ISBN: 978–0–415–63250–8 (hbk)
ISBN: 978–0–415–63251–5 (pbk)
ISBN: 978–1–315–88031–0 (ebk)

Typeset in Bembo
by RefineCatch Limited, Bungay, Suffolk

Printed and bound in the United States of America by Publishers Graphics,
LLC on sustainably sourced paper.

To those individual researchers who study technology in education in an effort to improve how teachers teach and learners learn.

CONTENTS

SECTION II
Evaluation   71

SECTION III
Faculty Issues   159

ABOUT THE EDITORS

Anthony G. Picciano is a Professor and Executive Officer of the Ph.D. Program in Urban Education at the Graduate Center of the City University of New York. He is also a member of the faculty in the graduate program in Education Leadership at Hunter College, the doctoral certificate program in Interactive Pedagogy and Technology at the City University of New York Graduate Center, and CUNY Online BA Program in Communication and Culture. In 1998, Dr. Picciano co-founded CUNY Online, a multi-million dollar initiative funded by the Alfred P. Sloan Foundation, which provides support services to faculty using the Internet for course development. He was a founding member and continues to serve on the Board of Directors of the Sloan Consortium. Dr. Picciano's major research interests are school leadership, education policy, Internet-based teaching and learning, and multimedia instructional models. Dr. Picciano has conducted three major national studies with Jeff Seaman on the extent and nature of online and blended learning in American K–12 school districts. He has authored or edited 14 books including *Educational Leadership and Planning for Technology, 5th Edition* (2010, Pearson), *Data-Driven Decision Making for Effective School Leadership* (2006, Pearson), *Distance Learning: Making Connections across Virtual Space and Time* (2001, Pearson), and *Educational Research Primer* (2004, Continuum). He has just completed a new book entitled *The Great Education-Industrial Complex*, co-authored with Joel Spring, which was published by Routledge/Taylor & Francis. In 2010, Dr. Picciano received the Sloan Consortium's National Award for Outstanding Achievement in Online Education by an Individual. Visit Dr. Picciano's website at: http://anthonypicciano.com

Charles D. Dziuban is Director of the Research Initiative for Teaching Effectiveness at the University of Central Florida (UCF), where he has been a faculty member since 1970 teaching research design and statistics, as well as the founding Director of the university's Faculty Center for Teaching and Learning. He received his Ph.D. from the University of Wisconsin. Since 1996, he has directed the impact evaluation of UCF's distributed learning initiative, examining student and faculty outcomes as well as gauging the impact of online, blended, and lecture capture courses on the university. Chuck has published in numerous journals, including *Multivariate Behavioral Research, The Psychological Bulletin, Educational and Psychological Measurement, The American Education Research Journal, The Phi Delta Kappan, The Internet in Higher Education, The Journal of Asynchronous Learning Networks,* and *The Sloan-C View.* His methods for determining psychometric adequacy have been featured in both the SPSS and the SAS packages. He has received funding from several government and industrial agencies including the Ford Foundation, Centers for Disease Control, National Science Foundation, and the Alfred P. Sloan Foundation. In 2000, Chuck was named UCF's first ever *Pegasus Professor* for extraordinary research, teaching, and service, and in 2005 received the honor of *Professor Emeritus* as well as the Sloan Consortium award for *Most Outstanding Achievement in Online Learning by an Individual.* In 2007, he was appointed to the National Information and Communication Technology (ICT) Literacy Policy Council. Chuck has co-authored, co-edited, or contributed to numerous books and chapters on blended and online learning and is a regular invited speaker at national and international conferences and universities. In 2011, UCF established the Chuck D. Dziuban award for excellence in online teaching.

Charles R. Graham is a Professor of Instructional Psychology and Technology at Brigham Young University with interest in technology-mediated teaching and learning. Charles studies the design and evaluation of blended learning environments and the use of technology to enhance teaching and learning. Charles has authored articles in over two dozen journals. He has also published work related to online and blended learning environments in edited books including *Online Collaborative Learning: Theory and Practice, Blended Learning: Research Perspectives, The Encyclopedia of Distance Learning,* and the *AECT Handbook of Research on Educational Communications and Technology.* Charles also co-edited the *Handbook of Blended Learning: Global Perspectives, Local Designs* which contains 39 chapters with examples of blended learning in higher education, corporate, and military contexts from around the world. His research publications can be found online at: https://sites.google.com/site/charles-rgraham/

LIST OF CONTRIBUTORS

Dylan Barth is a Learning Technology Consultant at the University of Wisconsin–Milwaukee.

William Bloemer does research for the Center for Online Learning, Research and Service at the University of Illinois Springfield.

D. Christopher Brooks is a Research Associate for Academic Technology Support Services at the University of Minnesota.

Thomas B. Cavanagh is Associate Vice President of Distributed Learning at the University of Central Florida.

Kara Chesal is the Chief of Staff for the Deputy Chief in the Office of Innovation at the New York City Department of Education.

Elizabeth Ciabocchi is Associate Vice President of Information Technology and Faculty Development at Long Island University.

Sarah Cosgrove is Associate Professor of Economics at UMass Dartmouth.

Kent C. Dolasky is the outgoing Commandant of JSOFSEA and an adjunct professor for University of the Incarnate Word.

Laurie P. Dringus is Professor in the Graduate School of Computer and Information Sciences at Nova Southeastern University. Her research interests include human–computer interaction, information design, and online learning.

Since 1998, she has served as Editor-in-Chief of *The Internet and Higher Education*, a refereed international journal published by Elsevier (www.elsevier.com/locate/iheduc).

Chan Du is Assistant Professor of Accounting & Finance at UMass Dartmouth.

Charles D. Dziuban is Director of the Research Initiative for Teaching Effectiveness at the University of Central Florida where he has been evaluating the impact of blended learning for the past two decades.

Bruce A. Fall is an Associate Education Specialist in the Biology Department at the University of Minnesota.

Catherine Gardner is Associate Professor of Philosophy/Women's & Gender Studies and Director of the Office of Faculty Development at UMass Dartmouth.

Andrew S. Gibbons is the Chair of the Instructional Psychology & Technology department at Brigham Young University.

Amy P. Ginsberg is Associate Dean of the School of Education at Long Island University, Brooklyn.

Charles R. Graham is the Associate Dean of the David O. McKay School of Education at Brigham Young University and a faculty member in the Instructional Psychology & Technology department.

Kyle Hammond is a software developer at Snowmint Creative Solutions LLC.

Lindsey Harness is a Learning Technology Consultant at the University of Wisconsin–Milwaukee.

Joel L. Hartman is Vice Provost for Information Technologies and Resources at the University of Central Florida in Orlando. As the university's CIO, he has overall responsibility for library, computing, networking, telecommunications, media services, and distributed learning activities. He was recipient of the 2008 EDUCAUSE Leadership Award and the 2011 Sloan Consortium Mayadas Leadership Award.

Curtis R. Henrie is a doctoral student researcher in Instructional Psychology & Technology at Brigham Young University.

Michael B. Horn is co-founder and Education Executive Director of Innosight Institute, a think tank devoted to applying the theories of disruptive innovation to the social sector. He is the co-author of the best-selling book *Disrupting Class: How Disruptive Innovation Will Change the Way the World Learns.*

Anne-Marie Hoxie is the Executive Director of the Office of Research and Data in the Division of Talent, Labor, and Innovation at the New York City Department of Education.

Isa Jahnke is Professor of ICT, media and learning (ICTML) at the Department of Applied Educational Science at Umea University in Sweden. She is leader of the research group Digital Didactical Designs; one of her projects is about the use of iPads in teaching and collaborative learning: https://iml.edusci.umu.se/ictml/

Tanya M. Joosten is Director of the Learning Technology Center at the University of Wisconsin–Milwaukee.

Andrea Lamont-Mills, Senior Lecturer in the Department of Psychology at the University of Southern Queensland, has a research focus on the discourse of drug taking in sport, and more recently in labor issues around workload in higher education.

Allana LeBlanc is a Student in the Faculty of Teaching and Learning at Mount Royal University in Calgary, Alberta, Canada.

Paige L. McDonald is an Assistant Professor of Clinical Research and Leadership at The George Washington University.

George L. Mehaffy serves as the Vice President for Academic Leadership and Change at the American Association of State Colleges and Universities (AASCU) in Washington, D.C. His division is responsible for developing and managing programs for member institutions in areas such as leadership development, undergraduate education, technology, international education, and teacher education.

Patsy D. Moskal is Associate Director of the Research Initiative for Teaching Effectiveness at the University of Central Florida.

Irene Naested is a Professor in the Faculty of Teaching and Learning at Mount Royal University in Calgary, Alberta, Canada.

Jodi Nickel is an Associate Professor in the Faculty of Teaching and Learning at Mount Royal University in Calgary, Alberta, Canada.

Anders Norberg is Education Strategist for the multi-institutional Campus Skellefteå in Northern Sweden, and a Ph.D. student at Applied Educational Science, Umeå University. His research interest is in educational logistics and access.

Kevin O'Connor is an Assistant Professor in the Faculty of Teaching and Learning at Mount Royal University in Calgary, Alberta, Canada.

Neal Olitsky is Assistant Professor of Economics at UMass Dartmouth.

Caitlin O'Neil is a fulltime lecturer in English at UMass Dartmouth.

Richard W. Peifer is an Instructor in the Biology Department at the University of Minnesota.

Anthony G. Picciano is a Professor and Executive Director of the Ph.D. Program in Urban Education at the City University of New York Graduate Center.

Jeannette E. Riley is Academic Director of Online Education and Professor English/Women's & Gender Studies at UMass Dartmouth.

Yoni Ryan is currently Professor of Higher Education at the Australian Catholic University, with major research interests in educational and staff development, online, distance and flexible educational environments and new technologies and the characteristics of "borderless education."

Jodi R. Sandfort is an Associate Professor of Public Affairs and Chair of the Leadership & Management Area at the Humphrey School of Public Affairs at the University of Minnesota.

Rogene Schnell is an Instructional Designer in the College of Biological Sciences at the University of Minnesota.

Janet L. Schottel is a Professor in the Department of Biochemistry, Molecular Biology & Biophysics at the University of Minnesota.

Amon B. Seagull is Associate Dean of Academic Affairs and Associate Professor in the Graduate School of Computer and Information Sciences at Nova Southeastern University.

Stefan Sikora is an Associate Professor in the Faculty of Teaching and Learning at Mount Royal University in Calgary, Alberta, Canada.

Karen Skibba, Ph.D., is an Instructional Designer for the Educational Innovation Program Development Initiative in the Division of Continuing Studies at the University of Wisconsin–Madison.

Heather Staker is a Senior Education Research Fellow at Innosight Institute. Staker graduated magna cum laude from Harvard College and received an MBA, with distinction, from Harvard Business School. She has experience as a consultant for McKinsey & Company and as a member of the California State Board of Education.

Gladys Sterenberg is an Associate Professor in the Faculty of Teaching and Learning at Mount Royal University in Calgary, Alberta, Canada.

Jennifer Stillman is a Research Analyst in the Office of Innovation at the New York City Department of Education.

Karen Swan is the James Stukel Distinguished Professor of Educational Leadership at the University of Illinois Springfield.

Kelvin Thompson serves as an Assistant Director for the University of Central Florida's (UCF) Center for Distributed Learning and a graduate faculty scholar within UCF's College of Education.

Katherine M. Tyler is an Instructional Designer at the Joint Special Operations University at MacDill AFB, Fl.

Belinda Tynan is Pro Vice-Chancellor (Learning, Teaching and Quality) at the University of Southern Queensland. She conducts research in the areas of quality, standards, staff development, and technology in higher education, and has taught in higher education in Asia as well as Australia and New Zealand.

Norman Vaughan is a Professor in the Faculty of Teaching and Learning at Mount Royal University in Calgary, Alberta, Canada.

Janelle DeCarrico Voegele is Assistant Director of Teaching and Learning in the Center for Academic Excellence at Portland State University.

J. D. Walker is a Research Fellow for Academic Technology Support Services at the University of Minnesota.

Nicole L. Weber is a Learning Technology Consultant at the University of Wisconsin–Milwaukee.

Susan J. Wegmann is a Professor of Education and the Director of Program Development and Special Programs at the Baptist College of Florida and her research focuses on the development and sustainability of interactions and rapport in online platforms.

Jim Zimmer is the Dean of the Faculty of Teaching and Learning at Mount Royal University in Calgary, Alberta, Canada.

PREFACE

In 2011, Anthony G. Picciano and Charles D. Dziuban, the Editors of *Blended Learning: Research Perspectives* published in 2007, began thinking about a new edition of their book. By early 2012, they were convinced that the time was right and invited Charles Graham to be a co-editor of a new edition: *Blended Learning: Research Perspectives, Volume 2*.

We three quickly found significant interest in this book, especially among publishers. After a careful review lasting more than six months, we are happy to be working with Routledge (Taylor & Francis Group). In seeking contributors, we also found a plethora of research appropriate for our new edition. In fact, selecting the authors of the 21 chapters that comprise this book proved a most difficult task. In total, 60 individual researchers contributed material, many of whom worked with modest budgets in pursuing their passion for studying blended learning technology. A glance at the table of contents reveals a span of research issues related to teaching, learning, course and program evaluation, faculty development and attitudes. The authors represent a broad spectrum of professionals in the field of educational technology; they are senior and junior faculty, administrators, and graduate students from traditional public and private colleges and universities, as well as international institutions, and K–12 schools. The high quality of their work is what has made editing this book a pleasure. Readers might also want to pay attention to the variety of research methods used to study blended learning. Survey research, quasi-experiments, case studies, participatory action research, qualitative approaches, phenomenography, and mixed-methods, among other research techniques, are represented in these pages. They provide excellent models for anyone interested in undertaking research in online or blended learning environments.

ACKNOWLEDGMENTS

The editors owe a debt of gratitude to many people who facilitated this project. First of all we appreciate the leadership and staff of the Sloan Consortium, both past and present, for underwriting the production of the first volume and supporting our work on the updated version. Mary Niemiec of the University of Nebraska and Tanya Joosten of the University of Wisconsin, Milwaukee chaired the Sloan-C blended workshop planning committee over the years bringing our community together into one of theory, research, and practice. They created the environment in which this work was able to take place. Alex Masulis of Taylor and Francis and his staff provided invaluable design, editorial, and production support for *Blended Learning: Research Perspectives, Volume 2*. Without them this book would still be in the planning stages. Alex, especially, provided the impetus to persevere though the hard times. Specifically, we are most grateful to Patsy Moskal, Associate Director, and Lauren Kramer, Jessica Thompson, and Genny DeCantis, Research Assistants at the Research Initiative for Teaching Effectiveness of the University of Central Florida, for the untold hours of editorial work on this book. There is no real way we can properly thank them for their efforts on our behalf. Lastly and most importantly, however, to the authors of the outstanding chapters found herein. This is not our book—it is a celebration of their outstanding research in the blended learning environment. Heartfelt thanks to you all.

Tony, Chuck, and Charles

1

INTRODUCTION TO *BLENDED LEARNING*: RESEARCH PERSPECTIVES, VOLUME 2

Anthony G. Picciano

In November 2002, a small group of colleagues attending the Annual Sloan-C Conference on Online Learning in Orlando, Florida had a discussion about what was then a new phenomenon: college faculty were mixing and matching face-to-face and online learning techniques and materials in their courses. This group of colleagues represented institutions such as the University of Illinois, the University of Central Florida, University of Maryland University College, the University of Wisconsin–Milwaukee, and the City University of New York. As the discussion went on, a consensus emerged; they were witnessing a new approach to teaching and learning that was different from either of its basic components. Face-to-face instruction had been around for centuries and fully online instruction had blossomed in the 1990s with the development and ubiquity of the Internet. They observed that there appeared to be no single pattern or model for blending these approaches. Some faculty taught basically a face-to-face course with a small portion of online activities. Others taught essentially online courses with a face-to-face component. In developing online components, various technologies such as interactive and non-interactive media, asynchronous discussion boards and blogs, as well as synchronous conferencing were being utilized to meet specific pedagogical goals and objectives. There were also distinctions in the development and scheduling of face-to-face components, some meeting once a week, others every other week, and still others once a month. This discussion resulted in the idea that a group of knowledgeable individuals from around the country be assembled to discuss "blended learning" and its implications for education. Funded by the Alfred P. Sloan Foundation, an invitation only workshop was held in April 2003 at the University of Illinois–Chicago. About 30 individuals met for 2 days and, while many ideas were floated and discussion at times was unwieldy, this group concluded that blended learning was important, needed further investigation, and would likely have significant pedagogical, administrative, and institutional ramifications. A community of professionals was born. Since 2003, this community, under the auspices of the Sloan Consortium, has held an annual workshop, which in 2012 attracted 665 participants.

In 2006, a dozen scholars who had attended previous workshops were invited to share their work in a book on research perspectives on blended learning. In 2007, *Blended Learning: Research Perspectives* was published. This book received a good deal of critical acclaim as the first book devoted entirely to research in blended learning. A. Frank Mayadas, Program Officer for the Alfred P. Sloan Foundation, was quoted as saying: "*Blended Learning: Research Perspectives* was the first major and long-overdue work of research on blended learning. ... A must read for anyone serious about understanding today's pedagogical practices" (Mayadas, 2007). Diane Oblinger, President of EDUCAUSE, commented: "if you are an administrator or faculty member who wants to do blended learning well, this [*Blended Learning: Research Perspectives*] is an important resource that integrates theory, research and experience" (Oblinger, 2007).

By 2012, the authors of *Blended Learning: Research Perspectives* knew that it was time for a new edition. In the world of technology and digital communications, five years is a lifetime. Many changes had occurred and new models had evolved that demanded study and research. Facilities such as YouTube videos, podcasting, wikis, and mobile technologies had emerged that were adding to the instructional blend. Massive open online courses, or MOOCs, radically changed the scale of instruction at a number of colleges and universities. Blended learning had evolved from individual courses to entire academic programs. At the Sloan-C Blended Learning Workshop held in Milwaukee in April 2012, the authors once again reached out to presenters to determine if there was any interest in contributing to a second book. A meeting was held on the afternoon immediately following the conference to discuss ideas and possibilities. More than 30 people attended, signaling much more interest than could be accommodated in the book the authors had in mind. Nevertheless, names and ideas were collected and invitations were issued for abstracts. In addition to the meeting attendees, the authors contacted colleagues from around the world who were doing important research in blended learning. Again the response was much more than could be accommodated. And so began the careful work of selecting the best ideas and research on blended learning that now comprise this book.

Extent of Blended Learning

Allen and Seaman (2013), after tracking online enrollments in colleges for 10 years, estimated that there were approximately 6.7 million students or approximately one-third of the total higher education population enrolled in at least one fully online course in American colleges and universities in the 2011–2012 academic year. There are few and perhaps no reliable estimates of the number of students enrolled in blended courses. While it is generally believed that blended learning has reached well into the mainstream of American higher education, little data are available that document this reach. There are several reasons why so little is known about this phenomenon.

First, many faculty do not necessarily identify themselves as teaching blended learning courses when, in fact, they are. Many college faculty, along with those in other segments of the general population, have become immersed in online technology. Using Internet tools for instruction has become second nature. They use these tools as they would overhead projectors or blackboards. As the mystique of teaching online that was present in the mid to late 1990s disappears, the faculty no longer see themselves as doing something unique or special. This is particularly true in blended learning environments where only a portion of the class is conducted online. As Eliot Masie (2003), president of the Masie Center for Learning and Technology, has observed: the "e" in e-learning is disappearing and it is all just learning.

Second, colleges and universities are not necessarily keeping records on faculty who teach blended courses. The Sloan Consortium in collaboration with the Babson Survey Research Group conducts annual national surveys on online learning at American colleges. The findings from these surveys represent important data on student enrollments in fully online courses including the percentage and nature of colleges and universities offering these courses. While these surveys are frequently cited in studies and articles on online learning, they contain very little data on blended learning. Jeff Seaman, one of the authors of these studies, is concerned and a bit frustrated that these data are not being systematically collected at most colleges and universities. While faculty might be teaching blended courses, many administrators do not necessarily know who they are or what they actually are doing in these courses. The lack of mechanisms for incorporating information on blended courses in college databases creates a situation in which a large-scale study becomes difficult and vulnerable to misinformation.

A third issue relates to definition. There is no generally accepted definition of blended learning. There are many forms of blended learning but a generally accepted taxonomy does not exist. One school's "blended" is another school's "hybrid," or another school's "mixed-mode." The issue is not just one of labels, but the lack of agreement among scholars and practitioners on a broad versus a narrow definition. Without a clear definition, blended learning is perceived as some nebulous combination of online and face-to-face instruction. Without a place within administrative systems for identifying blended learning courses and without a widely accepted definition or taxonomy, collecting data on blended learning remains difficult.

Definitions, Models, and Frameworks

In discussions with the contributors to this book, it became obvious that finding a single definition, model, or framework for blending learning was impossible. The word "blended" implies a combination or mixture. When a picture is pasted above a paragraph, a presentation is created that may be more informative to the viewer or reader, but the picture and text each remain intact and can be individually discerned. On the other hand, when two cans of different colored paints are mixed, the new paint will look different from either of the original colors. In fact, if the new paint is mixed well, neither of the original colors will continue to exist. Similar situations exist in blended learning. For instance, in a course that meets for three weekly contact hours, two hours might be allocated for meeting in a traditional classroom while the equivalent of one weekly hour is conducted online. The two modalities for this course are carefully separated and although they may overlap, they can easily be differentiated. In other forms of blended courses and programs, the modalities are not so easily distinguishable. Consider an online program that offers three online courses in a semester that all students are required to take. At the same time, students do a collaborative 15-week project that overlaps the courses. The students are expected to maintain regular communication with one another through email, wikis, and group discussion boards. They also are required to meet face-to-face once a month on weekends where course materials from the online courses are further presented and discussed, and time is also devoted to group project work. Towards the end of the semester there are group project presentations. These activities begin to blur the modalities in a new mixture or blend where the individual parts are not as discernible as they once were. In this book, the authors have allowed the contributors to define/describe the blended instruction they are studying as they wish without confining them to a rigid definition, model, or framework. Chapter 2 of this book will further examine the issues associated with definitions, models, and frameworks.

Outline of the Book

This book is organized with an introductory chapter, six sections, and a conclusion, as follows:

- Introduction
- Section I: Blended Learning Models and Scale
- Section II: Evaluation
- Section III: Faculty Issues
- Section IV: Studying Non-Traditional Learners
- Section V: International Perspectives

- Section VI: Blended Learning in K–12 Environments
- Conclusion

Section I—Blended Learning Models and Scale

In Chapter 2, Charles R. Graham, Curtis R. Henrie, and Andrew S. Gibbons examine blended learning models and frameworks to assist the reader in understanding the complexity of the term "blended learning." They review a number of major published works on this topic and suggest that flexibility in definitions be the norm.

In Chapter 3, Patsy D. Moskal and Tom Cavanagh describe the expansion of blended learning to 20 institutions through the development and dissemination of a "Blended Learning Toolkit" based on the best practices successfully implemented at the University of Central Florida. This chapter details the challenges in conducting an evaluation of such a large-scale initiative.

William Bloemer and Karen Swan, in Chapter 4, describe the extent and consequences of *informal blending* at one institution, the University of Illinois Springfield (UIS), with the hope that these findings might suggest patterns that are being replicated nationally. Findings verify the dramatic increase in the numbers of traditional on-ground students taking online classes at UIS.

Section II—Evaluation

In Chapter 5, Susan J. Wegmann and Kelvin Thompson discuss the viability and applicability of gathering and analyzing discourse data in blended courses as a means of studying student engagement. Using a SCOPe framework (**S**elf, **C**ontent, **O**thers, and the **P**latform), they specifically examine ways to analyze the health and sustainability of interactions in blended learning environments.

Janelle DeCarrico Voegele examines the relationships among social, teaching, and cognitive presence, pedagogical design, and students' perspectives on blended learning effectiveness in Chapter 6. Data from 39 undergraduate courses were analyzed to identify indicators of presence in students' observations about learning.

In Chapter 7, Norman Vaughan and his colleagues at Mt. Royal University in Calgary, Canada, describe an action research study that evaluated the effectiveness of a blended Bachelor of Education Elementary Program at a Canadian university from student and faculty perspectives using the National Survey of Student Engagement (NSSE) framework. Data were collected via online surveys, focus groups, and the use of an editable *Google Doc*.

Laurie P. Dringus and Amon B. Seagull, in Chapter 8, share their experiences in implementing a 5-year plan of blended learning initiatives in programs in computer science and information systems. In describing their process and implementation strategies to increase academic dialogue and exchange, they share student and faculty survey data from assessments dating from 2008–2011.

In Chapter 9, D. Christopher Brooks and Jodi R. Sandfort examine the impact of online multi-media learning materials as a substitute for traditional text-based cases in the teaching of public affairs courses. They explore how and why choosing the appropriate research design, level of analysis, and instrumentation is critical, but difficult, in the early stages of a research project. They highlight the limitations and successes of two quasi-experimental blended learning pilot projects. They conclude that a willingness to evaluate the strengths and limitations of previous attempts and the ability to respond creatively with tighter controls, better designs, and measures can only improve our understanding of blended approaches to learning.

In Chapter 10, J. D. Walker and colleagues at the University of Minnesota and Snowmint Creative Solutions LLC investigate the use of online practice exams to enhance learning in three large enrollment, blended-format biology courses over two years. The results indicated that online practice exams significantly improved student learning and exam performance regardless of student demographic and aptitude differences.

Section III—Faculty Issues

Jeannette E. Riley, Catherine Gardner, and colleagues from the University of Massachusetts, Dartmouth, open this section with an examination of a blended course (re)design project. Chapter 11 documents the training program that developed faculty blended teaching skills and learning assessment strategies. It is followed by individual case studies that demonstrate how student learning outcomes were affected by the blended course (re)designs.

In Chapter 12, Tanya M. Joosten, Dylan Barth, and associates at the University of Wisconsin, Milwaukee (UWM), document the faculty development program that has prepared hundreds of instructors for redesigning their courses in the blended format. The purpose of their study was to examine the relationship between instructional development and training and the effectiveness of blended courses at UWM measured against five variables: student interactivity, learning, satisfaction, retention, and success.

Amy P. Ginsberg and Elizabeth Ciabocchi, in Chapter 13, report on a survey of the current state of faculty training for blended instruction in traditional higher education institutions. The survey focuses on faculty development design, structure, and implementation; the perceptions of the most and least successful elements of faculty development; and the philosophical under-pinnings of program design.

Karen Skibba, in Chapter 14, shares a qualitative study that examines the following two research questions:

1. How do faculty members describe the process and implications of moving back and forth between teaching multiple course delivery formats within a blended program?
2. How do faculty members perceive teaching adults in a blended program influences their overall teaching practices?

Findings indicate that faculty members who teach in a blended program believe it is important to provide a choice of course delivery formats for both learning and teaching. However, they also share challenges of teaching face-to-face, online, and hybrid course formats within a blended program.

Section IV—Non-Traditional Learners

In this section we have two chapters that look at blended learning research involving non-traditional learners. Chapter 15 by Paige McDonald identifies and describes three different patterns representative of variation in adult learners' experiences of blended learning in higher education: Supplementary Learning, Interdependent Learning, and Adaptable Learning. The study's findings have implications for course design, learner success, and faculty presence in blended courses and for future research in each of these areas.

In Chapter 16, Katherine M. Tyler and Kent C. Dolasky examine a program at the Joint Special Operations Forces Senior Enlisted Academy that prepares senior enlisted leaders from the special operations forces to think strategically. The Academy is a blended learning experience focused on advancing students' critical thinking skills through research, writing, and a real-world capstone exercise. After adopting the community of inquiry model, students achieved higher levels of critical thinking skills and adopted the affective intent required to perform as warrior diplomats. The development of a distance learning team and additional staffing resulted in an increase in discussion forum postings and resource awareness.

Section V—International Perspectives

Section V includes two chapters from colleagues who provide international perspectives on blended learning. Anders Norberg and Isa Jahnke, in Chapter 17, explore European perspectives and provide an overview of several different understandings of blended learning. One result of their investigation is a series of basic questions. For instance: Is "blend" a suitable tool for a deeper analysis of what is happening? Maybe the "blended" discourse is too superficial, in need of clarification and theory support. Perhaps the "blended" discourse works better in educational practices than in building pedagogical theories?

In Chapter 18, Yoni Ryan, Belinda Tynan, and Andrea Lamont-Mills report on a study funded by the Australian Learning and Teaching Council that explored staff perceptions of increased workload attendant on teaching with digital technologies, how staff used particular technologies to manage teaching hours, and the models used by institutions to allocate workload. Their results indicate that "e-teaching" has become routine in Australian universities, and that the tasks associated with e-teaching have increased teaching hours, with large gains for student flexibility at the cost of staff time.

Section VI—Blended Learning in K–12 Environments

While starting slowly, blended learning has taken off in recent years in K–12 education. This section includes two chapters that examine primary and secondary education. In Chapter 19, Heather Staker and Michael B. Horn from the Innosight Institute examine various models of blended learning and posit that four models of blended learning are the most prevalent in the K–12 sector: the Rotation, Flex, Self-Blend, and Enriched-Virtual models. Some blended-learning models are examples of sustaining innovations; they improve the performance of the established classroom model along the dimensions that society has historically valued. Other models offer a very different value proposition, and one that could be disruptive to the traditional classroom.

In Chapter 20, Anne-Marie Hoxie, Jennifer Stillman, and Kara Chesal, from the New York City Department of Education, report on iLearnNYC, a comprehensive blended learning program designed to personalize instruction and create new educational opportunities for students. The purpose of their study was the examination of the ways in which NYC secondary school teachers implement blended learning in their classrooms. They explore how choices about online content and time allocation between online and face-to-face learning are associated with teacher attitudes towards blended learning, and describe early evidence of student impacts.

Conclusion

The book concludes with Chapter 21: Blending it All Together by Charles Dziuban, Joel L. Hartman, and George L. Mehaffy. They examine some of the issues raised by the work of the authors in the preceding chapters and provide recommendations for further study.

References

Allen, I. E., & Seaman, J. (2013). *Changing course: Ten years of tracking online education in the United States*. Retrieved from http://sloanconsortium.org/publications/survey/changing_course_2012. Accessed January 10, 2013.

Masie, E. (2003). *The AMA handbook of E-learning,* Chapter 26 E-learning, the near future. Retrieved from www.amanet.org/books/catalog/0814407218_ch26.htm. Accessed December 30, 2012.

Mayadas, A. F. (2007). Back cover testimonial. In A. G. Picciano & D. Dziuban (Eds.), *Blended learning: Research perspectives.* Needham, MA: The Sloan Consortium.

Oblinger, D. (2007). Back cover testimonial. In A. G. Picciano & D. Dziuban (Eds.), *Blended learning: Research perspectives.* Needham, MA: The Sloan Consortium.

Blended Learning Models and Scale

2

DEVELOPING MODELS AND THEORY FOR BLENDED LEARNING RESEARCH

Charles R. Graham, Curtis R. Henrie, and Andrew S. Gibbons

> *He who loves practice without theory is like the sailor who boards ship without a rudder and compass and never knows where he may cast.*
> (Leonardo da Vinci, 1452–1519)

The Need for Blended Learning Models and Theory

Developing models and theory is essential to the knowledge creation process. Models and theory by their very nature attempt to establish a common language and focus for the activities that take place in a scholarly community (Dubin, 1976). Burkhardt and Schoenfeld (2003) claimed that a "reasonably stable theory base . . . allows for a clear focus on important issues and provides sound (though still limited) guidance for the design of improved solutions to important problems" (p. 6). Well-established scholarly domains have common terminology and widely accepted models and theories that guide inquiry and practice, while researchers in less mature domains struggle to define terms and establish relevant models.

Limited efforts have been made to understand the development and use of theory in the domain of blended learning research (Drysdale, Graham, Spring, & Halverson, 2013; Graham, 2013; Halverson, Graham, Spring, & Drysdale, 2012). Blended learning research, though relatively new, is related to both educational technology research and distance education research (the former often focuses on contexts where teacher and learner are co-located and the latter on contexts where teacher and learner are separated in space and time). For several decades, educational technology as a field has struggled to find its theoretical roots (McDougall & Jones, 2006; Roblyer, 2005; Roblyer &

Knezek, 2003). Most recently, a broad theoretical framework referred to as *technological pedagogical content knowledge* (TPACK) has gained some traction (Mishra & Koehler, 2006). Similarly, some researchers in distance education have lamented the lack of research focus on theory (Moore, 2004). However, several prominent theories, such as transactional distance (Moore, 2013), community of inquiry (Garrison, Anderson, & Archer, 2000), interaction equivalency (Simonson, Schlosser, & Hanson, 1999), etc. are now driving the research questions and conversations.

This chapter does not seek to create new theory, but rather to understand and document the nature of the blended learning models and theories that are currently being developed through research. This synthesis will identify the strengths and limitations of the models and theories being developed and integrated in the blended learning research domain. This understanding can guide us in the selection and development of future models and theories.

Model and Theory Development in Design Fields

The definition of *model* and *theory* has been a source of debate. Some scholars have noted the interchangeable use of the terms (Dubin, 1976; Kaplan, 1964; Sutton & Staw, 1995; Whetten, 1989), while others have argued for clearer distinctions (Dickmeyer, 1989; Kaplan, 1964; Merton, 1967). We acknowledge that many researchers may prefer to use the term *model* because of the privileged status that scientists associate with the term *theory*. This chapter will treat the terms *model* and *theory* as two ends of a continuum. Whetten (1989) made the case that good social science theory is built upon:

- the *what* (variables/factors);
- the *how* (relationship between variables/factors);
- the *why* (underlying rationale justifying the what and how); and
- the *who, where, when* (context in which the theory is applicable).

The literature seems to agree that good theory creates an argument that clearly addresses the *why* undergirding the relationships it presents (Kaplan, 1964; Sutton & Staw, 1995; Whetten, 1989). Perhaps a distinction between what we feel comfortable calling a *model* vs. a *theory* lies in the strength of its argument (the *why*) and evidence supporting the claims (relationship between the *what* and *how*). As research data accumulate and arguments become more robust, researchers are more willing to refer to a model as a theory.

Educational research includes two major types of theory: technological (or design) and scientific. In *Sciences of the Artificial*, Herbert Simon (1999) distinguished between design fields (e.g., engineering, business, education, architecture, etc.) and the sciences, contrasting their processes for creating knowledge. While both design and science fields focus on systems (often the same systems), they try to solve different problems and generate different kinds of theory (Klir, 1969). Gibbons (2013) clarified by saying that "scientific theory is analytic—used to construct an understanding of the forces that drive natural and human-made phenomenon" while design theory produces "a body of synthetic principles which can be used to design, to plan, to prescribe, to devise, to invent, to create, and to otherwise channel natural forces for accomplishment of human purposes" (Gibbons, 2013, Chapter 6). In brief, "in [science] they are trying to understand *how and why* things happen, and in [technology, design] they are trying to discover *how to influence* things to happen" (Gibbons, 2013, Chapter 6, emphasis added).

In the domain of education, both Gibbons (Gibbons & Rogers, 2009; Gibbons, 2013) and Reigeluth (1999) have written extensively about the distinctive role of "instructional design theory" in informing both education practice and research. Interest has surged in design-based research that emphasizes inquiry principles and processes consistent with the purposes of knowledge creation and theory building in design fields (Barab, 2006; Collins, 1992). Understanding the distinctions between scientific and design research is particularly important in education research domains because most of the design models and theories developed are poor matches for scientific theory but good matches for design theory (sometimes called *technological theory*; Gibbons, 2003).

Explore, Explain, Design

Gibbons and Bunderson (2005) developed a taxonomy placing discussion of research and theories in perspective for design-related fields like education. They identified three important knowledge-producing enterprises: *explore*, *explain*, and *design*.[1] These three categories can be distinguished in terms of the questions for which answers are sought (see Table 2.1).

TABLE 2.1 Descriptions of Three Types of Theory Used in Research

Research-enterprise	Model/theory description
Explore (scientific and technological)	• Answers "What exists?" • Defines • Categorizes
Explain (scientific)	• Answers "Why does this happen?" • Looks for causality and correlation • Works with variables and relationships between them
Design (technological)	• Answers "How do I achieve this outcome?" • Describes interventions for reaching targeted outcomes • Describes "operational principles" that make an intervention or design work

Gibbons and Bunderson (2005) noted that progress in each of the research areas contributes to further questions and research in the other areas. While *explain* (scientific) research is commonly considered as necessarily preceding design (technological) research, there are many counter examples. For example, the Wright brothers built the first wind tunnel for experimenting with wing designs to create knowledge that Bernoulli's principle could not possibly supply (Vincenti, 1990). Similarly, a plethora of natural remedies (medicines) were developed in ancient cultures before scientists could explain their results.

Explore

Explore research seeks to define and categorize, identifying "what is there and what are possible groupings and relationships among what is there" (Gibbons & Bunderson, 2005, p. 927). With this kind of "natural history" research, Charles Darwin documented the similarities and differences in finches and other kinds of wildlife on the Galapagos Islands before developing a scientifically testable theory. Such research identifies patterns that become the foundation for questions in scientific inquiry (*explain*) or the basis for developing artifacts and processes (*design*), even though the underlying causal mechanisms may not be fully understood.

Figure 2.1 represents two common kinds of *explore* models: (1) attempts to define and distinguish a domain; and (2) identification of dimensions that characterize types within a domain. Both models seek to identify factors that matter, emphasizing connections among the factors but not their influence

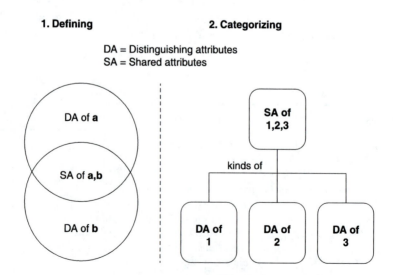

FIGURE 2.1   Visual Representation of Two Kinds of Explore Models

on each other. In the domain of blended learning (BL), *explore* models would: (1) try to distinguish BL from other closely related domains; and (2) try to characterize categories of blends within the domain.

Explain

Explain research is often labeled *scientific research*; it seeks to "explain why and explain how," specifically through "experimental inquiry into cause" (Gibbons & Bunderson, 2005, pp. 927, 929). *Explain* theory articulates generalizable relationships between two or more variables, typically establishing the nature of the relationships through correlational or experimental research (see a simplified representation in Figure 2.2). Its purpose is to explain the relationship, not to identify interventions that might be designed to affect one of the variables. Typical variables explained by blended learning research include constructs such as satisfaction, academic performance, social presence, and sense of community. The example in Figure 2.3 illustrates with variables from the Community of Inquiry (COI) framework (Garrison et al., 2000). *Explain* theory might posit a positive correlation between cognitive presence, social presence, teaching presence, and student performance, explaining how these factors interrelate but not dealing with what characteristics of the intervention impact any variation in the factors.

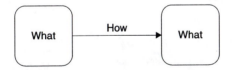

FIGURE 2.2   Simplified Visual Representation of the Nature of Explain Models

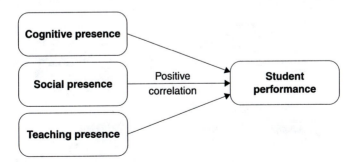

FIGURE 2.3   Simplified Visual Illustration of Explain Theory Using the Community of Inquiry Framework

Design

Design research describes intentional structuring of artifacts and intervention plans to increase the likelihood of particular outcomes (Gibbons & Bunderson, 2005). Design research differs from scientific research in that a target outcome is identified and interventions undergo experimentation and revision until that outcome is achieved.

Figure 2.4 is a simplified representation of *design* theory, which studies a combination of variables representing core attributes of an intervention that can be designed. Figure 2.5 demonstrates this theory using the practical inquiry model from the COI literature (Garrison & Vaughan, 2008). The model provides a specific process leading to the learning outcome of developing problem-solving abilities. This cyclical process begins with a triggering event, followed by exploration, integration, and resolution. Garrison and Vaughan

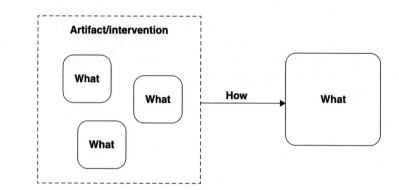

FIGURE 2.4   Simplified Visual Representation of Instructional Design Models

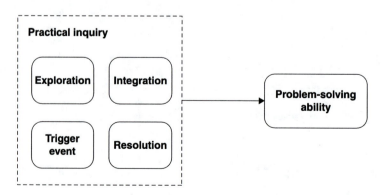

FIGURE 2.5   Simplified Visual Illustration of an Instructional Design Model Using the "Practical Inquiry Model"

outlined specific aspects of an intervention to create practical inquiry. For example, to create a triggering event they recommended a prereading assignment or activity on a specified topic or issue, followed by a self-assessment quiz, survey, or discussion forum to help learners discover what they know. Similar interventions are proposed for exploration, integration, and resolution (see Garrison & Vaughan, 2008, chapter 7). A design with the core attributes of practical inquiry could be tested by measuring how well it helps to achieve the desired learning outcomes. Previous *explain* research may have established the connection between practical inquiry and performance, and the purpose of the *design* research is to discover how to build an environment involving the integration of multiple variables that increases the chances that the desired outcomes will occur.

Design models and theory establish the core attributes of a specific design, what Gibbons (2013) referred to as the design's operational principles: what makes it work. Unlike experimental research, all variables do not need to be held constant in order to vary only one. The desired design outcome is typically understood, and one or more dimensions of the design are changed to impact the outcome. Reigeluth (1999) further elaborated that an important characteristic of instructional design theories is that they are design oriented (or goal oriented), in contrast to what most people consider to be scientific theories with deterministic cause/effect relationships. Instructional design theories specify effects resulting from flows of events in natural processes, which are almost always probabilistic (the cause increases the chances of the stated effect rather than always resulting in the stated effect).

Figures 2.6 to 2.8 represent three common patterns for *design* research (sometimes referred to as *design-based* research) in which the unit of analysis is the design. Figure 2.6 represents research focused on how an intervention (with a set of clearly identified core attributes) achieves a desired outcome. Figure 2.7 shows how one design might be compared with another design employing a different integration of variables. Figure 2.8 shows how one design might be changed over time and compared with previous design iterations.

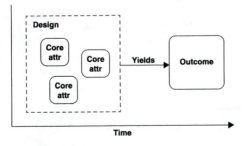

FIGURE 2.6   Visual Representation of Design Research that Measures the Outcome of a Particular Design

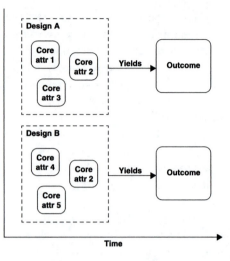

FIGURE 2.7   Visual Representation of Design Research that Compares Two Different Designs

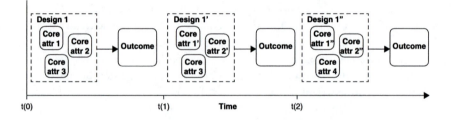

FIGURE 2.8   Visual Representation of Design Research that Compares Iterations of a Design Over Time

Explore, Explain, and *Design* in Blended Learning Research

In several previous articles, we have sought to understand what models and theoretical frameworks are driving the research in blended learning (Drysdale et al., 2013; Graham, 2013; Halverson et al., 2012). The outcomes of this previous work have primarily pointed to the need for a more robust description and analysis of model and theory development in the blended learning domain. This section uses the *explore, explain, design* framework to characterize the current state of blended learning model and theory development.

Explore *Models of Blended Learning*

Much of the early research in blended learning has been concerned with exploring and defining the phenomenon of blended learning. Picciano

(Chapter 1, this volume) described a historical perspective on this process within the Sloan Consortium. Many researchers have observed blended learning and created models attempting to show how blended learning is distinct from both distance education and traditional classroom learning. Exploring the boundaries of a domain as well as classifications within a domain is the core of *explore* research. The models that result from this research typically: (1) define what blended learning is and is not; and/or (2) provide categories of different kinds of blends.

Definitional Models

Early models began trying to define the contours of blended learning by answering the question "What is being blended?" in three competing ways (Graham, 2006, p. 4):

- Combining online and face-to-face instruction (Reay, 2001; Rooney, 2003; Sands, 2002; Ward & LaBranche, 2003; Young, 2002).
- Combining instructional modalities (or delivery media) (Bersin, 2003; Orey, 2002a, 2002b; Singh & Reed, 2001; Thomson, 2002).
- Combining instructional methods (Driscoll, 2002; Rossett, 2002).

Models adopting the first definition are the most prominent in the research, with the second definition maintaining some prominence in corporations, and the third definition rarely being used. Efforts to refine the first definition argued for reduced seat time or a certain percentage of online instruction as defining characteristics (see Graham, 2013 for a detailed analysis). For example, Picciano's (2009) definition required that "a portion (institutionally defined) of face-to-face time [be] replaced by online activity" (p. 10), while Allen and Seaman's (2007) definition identified four categories: (1) traditional as having 0% of content delivered online; (2) web facilitated as 1%–29% online; (3) blended as 30%–79% online; and (4) online as 80% or more online. Other definitions included quality descriptors such as "the *thoughtful integration* of classroom face-to-face learning experiences with online learning experiences" (Garrison & Kanuka, 2004, p. 96, emphasis added) or "courses that integrate online with traditional face-to-face class activities *in a planned, pedagogically valuable manner*" (Picciano, 2006, p. 97, emphasis added).

Model Categories

A second category of *explore* research models seeks to characterize categories of blended learning. Early work by Graham (2006) distinguished between blends at the activity, course, program, and institutional levels. Models began to emerge that identified different kinds of blended learning in terms of pedagogical rather than just physical characteristics: for example, physical and pedagogical dimensions identified by Sharpe, Benfield, Roberts, and Francis (2006). Additionally, Graham and Robison (2007) developed a model using scope, purpose, and the nature of pedagogical interventions to distinguish transforming, enhancing, and enabling blends found at a university. Other researchers developed more specific models distinguishing between types of blended learning based on both the physical and pedagogical structuring of the blended learning environment. Some of the most prominent models in the categories of higher education, K–12 education, and corporate training are outlined in Table 2.2.

Each model represents patterns that the researchers observed in practice. Descriptions are provided of features that distinguish the kinds of blends but do not prescribe design guidance for when and how the blends should be implemented or explain why specific models work under certain conditions.

Discussion of BL *Explore Models and Theories*

One pattern we noticed among *explore* models is that most focus on surface features (physical structuring) of BL systems as opposed to the pedagogical structuring. Early definitions focused on delivery media or physical environment (i.e., face-to-face vs. online). Models that have identified categories of blends have also focused heavily on surface structure. With few exceptions, the defining characteristics of the blends listed in Table 2.2 are not pedagogical, but focus on the *when*, *where*, and *who* of the instructional delivery. Some models (like the flipped classroom) may imply a particular kind of pedagogy (e.g., individual feedback, lecture, collaboration, etc.), but do not impose pedagogy or quality criteria. Staker and Horn (2012) explained, "[the models] set forth basic patterns that are emerging, but avoid setting tight parameters about how a model 'has to be'" (p. 1).

Explain *Theory for Blended Learning*

Explain theory articulates variables and relationships among variables (see the section "*Explain* research" in this chapter and Figure 2.2), seeking to understand these relationships, *not* to design an intervention that produces one of them. We reviewed dozens of studies, including the 50 most cited blended learning articles (Halverson et al., 2012), to try to understand how *explain* theory was being used in blended learning research. We found three basic patterns: (1) mention of theory; (2) application of theory; and (3) development of theory. Table 2.3 highlights examples of each.

TABLE 2.2 Examples of Categories of Blended Learning Models

A. Higher Education Twigg (2003)	B. K–12 Education Staker & Horn (2012)	C. Corporate Training Rossett & Frazee (2006)
A.1 Supplemental • Supplemental online materials • Online quizzes • Additional online activities • Flexibility of online activities for computer lab or home	**B.1 Rotation** • Rotation among learning modalities, at least one of which is online • *Station rotation*—rotations within a classroom • *Lab rotation*—rotations within locations on a school campus • *Flipped classroom*—rotation within a given course or subject including online remote (at home) • *Individual rotation*—individually tailored rotation schedule for a course or subject	**C.1 Anchor blend** • Introductory substantive face-to-face classroom experience • Subsequent independent online experiences **C.2 Bookend blend** • Introductory experience online or face-to-face • A substantive learning experience online or face-to-face • A conclusion that extends the learning into practice at work
A.2 Replacement • Reduction of in-class meeting time • Replacement of face-to-face class time with online activities • Flexibility of online activities for computer lab or home	**B.2 Flex** • Instruction primarily online in a classroom with customized face-to-face support when needed	**C.3 Field blend** • A range of instructional assets • Choice of when and where to use the assets as needed to meet work-related challenges • Availability of online instructional assets • A possible classroom experience as part of the mix
A.3 Emporium • Elimination of class meetings • Substitution of a learning resource center with online materials and on-demand personal assistance	**B.3 Self-blend** • Option of an entirely online course to supplement traditional courses	
A.4 Buffet • Several learning options from which students choose	**B.4 Enriched virtual** • School experience mostly online with some on-campus enrichment	

TABLE 2.3 Examples of *Explain* Research in the Blended Learning Literature

Use of explain theory	Examples
Mention of theory The research mentions a theoretical framing as part of a literature review or an argument for implementing or studying blended learning, but does not attempt to apply or confirm the theory.	Oliver & Trigwell (2005): Variation theory is offered as rationale for continued research and interest in blended learning. Variation theory states that learning occurs when variation is perceived. Authors hypothesize that blended learning has proved successful because of its ability to create and distinguish variation in what is to be learned. Mortera-Gutiérrez (2006): The author states that social presence theory, media richness theory, and media synchronicity theory have the potential to explain outcomes and phenomena of interest in blended learning.
Application of theory The research uses the variables and relationships proposed in the study to frame the collected and analyzed inquiry data as part of the inquiry, but does not seek to challenge or build on the theory.	Lynch & Dembo (2004): Previous research indicated that self-regulation was important to learner success in distance learning. The authors looked for correlations between student performance and motivation, internet self-efficacy, time management, study environment management, and learning assistance management to understand role of self-regulation in learner success in a blended learning environment. Ginns & Ellis (2007): The authors sought to better understand the correlational relationships between student perceptions of the online learning experience, student approaches to learning, and student grades in a blended learning environment. Previous research validated the relationship between student perceptions of learning experience, student approaches to learning, and the quality of the learning experience.
Development of theory The research proposes a new theory or seeks to challenge, change, or build on current theory.	Klein, Noe, & Wang (2006): The authors built on training motivation theory and the input-output process model of learning to examine correlations between motivation and learning outcomes, and correlations between learning goal orientation, perceived barriers/enablers, and delivery mode and motivation. So & Brush (2008): Research in distance education calls for closer attention to factors affecting psychological distance. To do so, the study examined correlational relationships among perceived levels of collaboration, social presence, and student satisfaction—variables synthesized from different theories that have been identified as important to understanding psychological distance.

Sometimes researchers would only briefly explain theoretical frameworks to provide background for the research or establish an argument for their blended approach. Another common use was in identifying variables to study, including:

- social, teaching, and cognitive presence from the Community of Inquiry (Akyol, Vaughan, & Garrison, 2011; Vaughan & Garrison, 2005);
- satisfaction, learning effectiveness, cost effectiveness, etc. from the Sloan-C Pillars (Lorenzo & Moore, 2002); and
- sense of community (Barnard-Brak & Shiu, 2010; Rovai & Jordan, 2004).

Often the implied research contribution was application of theory to a new context (blended learning) in order to show its utility in that setting. Rarely was the research intended to disconfirm or challenge a theory or the assumptions within a theory. In discussing what makes a theoretical contribution, Whetten (1989) stated that "applying an old model to a new setting and showing that it works as expected is not instructive by itself" (p. 493). He elaborated, "Theorists need to learn something new about the theory itself as a result of working with it under different conditions. That is, new applications should improve the tool, not merely reaffirm its utility" (Whetten, 1989, p. 493). In summary, while theoretical frameworks were often mentioned or even tested in *explain* research, studies that sought to develop specific aspects of a theory were uncommon.

Design *Models for Blended Learning*

Design models designate target outcomes and indicate core attributes of a design that affect or bring about those outcomes (see the section "*Design* research" in this chapter and Figure 2.4). The purpose of design models is to show how to manipulate an intervention to achieve a desired result. After reviewing the design research in blended learning, including the 50 most cited blended learning articles (Halverson et al., 2012), we identified three patterns: (1) model articulation; (2) model comparison; and (3) model iteration. Table 2.4 describes examples.

Much of the *design* research comprised comparison studies attempting to test the effectiveness of a blended course design or activity against a face-to-face or online counterpart. We noted a definite need for iterative *design* research, but few studies reported on iterations and subsequent model development. This type of research can lead to identification of core attributes that influence the desired outcomes of models, which can then be tested and better understood through *explain* research. Two limitations of many of the BL *design* studies were: (1) that core attributes of the interventions affecting student

TABLE 2.4 Examples of *Design* Research in the Blended Learning Literature

Use of design models/theory	Example(s)
Model articulation This research clearly articulates a blended learning (BL) model and the outcomes the model should achieve (see Figure 2.6).	Beatty (2013, in press) described the HyFlex model, which was developed to provide greater flexibility to students in class participation options and course selection. To achieve the desired flexibility, Beatty identified four core attributes the course design should include: alternative participation modes, equivalency in activities, reuse of learning objects or artifacts between modalities, and accessibility to technology and participation modes. Picciano (2009) developed the Blending with Purpose Multimodal Model. The outcome of the model is a design that can reach a variety of student and learning needs. The core attributes of the model are six pedagogical objectives for which to consider blending modalities: content, student social and emotional support, dialectic/questioning activities, reflection, collaboration, and synthesis/evaluation/assessment.
Model comparison This research compares a BL model to either a different type of BL or a non-BL model (see Figure 2.7).	Many studies compared course models distinguished by modality (blended, online, or face-to-face) on outcome measures of student performance or student satisfaction (Brown & Liedholm, 2002; Rivera, McAlister, & Rice, 2002; Tuckman, 2002; Utts, Sommer, Acredolo, Maher, & Matthews, 2003). Hoxie, Stillman, & Chesal (Chapter 20, this volume) compared Rotation and Flex blended learning models in middle and high schools in a New York City school district. The authors examined differences in teacher and student experiences, noting the impact of model type on teacher practice and on student motivation, satisfaction, and learning.
Model iteration This research articulates a BL model intended to achieve particular outcomes and systematically tested and improved over time (see Figure 2.8).	Power (2008) explained the Blended Online Learning model, developed over the course of several years as university faculty and designers worked together in developing online humanities courses. Over the course of iterations, the model progressed from a largely asynchronous distance education model to a blend of asynchronous and synchronous design and delivery.

performance or student satisfaction were neither well known nor clearly articulated; and (2) that identified differences in models typically focused on physical aspects of the course (e.g., online vs. face-to-face activities).

Articulation of Core Attributes

Commonly, qualitative case study research describes a particular design in great detail, which, although worthwhile, does not fill the *design* model role. *Design* models provide prescriptive guidance about what a design should be in order to increase the probability of achieving a desired outcome. For *design* research to be effective, researchers must clearly identify the core attributes that they postulate are making the design work along with the situational characteristics/ constraints that define the context in which the design functions. Without these details, other researchers cannot test and build on assumptions and hypotheses that are part of *design* models. Additionally, the models become less useful to practitioners who are looking for guidance as they make decisions about their own BL implementations.

Surface Features

A prominent feature of much of the *design* research to date has been a focus on surface features, or physical attributes (e.g., online, face-to-face), of the design without articulating clearly the core pedagogical attributes. This emphasis is one of the reasons that the meta-analysis commissioned by the U.S. Department of Education (Means, Toyama, Murphy, Bakia, & Jones, 2010) found statistically significant differences between blended, online, and traditional classrooms but was not able to identify factors leading to these findings. Such results are comparable to saying that generally "compact cars" get better gas mileage than "trucks," a claim that does not identify the core attributes that make compact cars more fuel efficient—the weight, shape, or engine size of the vehicle. Significant progress in BL research requires us to "look under the hood" and identify core pedagogical attributes of our BL systems and not maintain focus entirely on the physical attributes of the systems.

Design Layers

Gibbons and Rogers (2009) described a theory of design layers, which posits that instructional designs contain common elements or layers and that within each layer is a body of knowledge (and theory) applied to the layer's construction and operation. We consider this an important idea for the future of *design* research in the BL domain. While Gibbons and Rogers (2009) defined seven different design layers they considered important to instructional

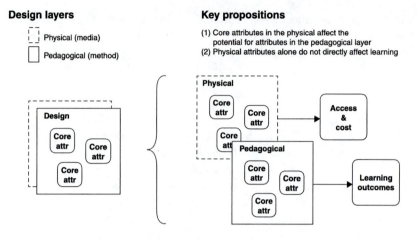

FIGURE 2.9   Visual Representation of Two Potential Design Layers

design, we simplify the concept to focus on just two: the *pedagogical layer* (what Gibbons calls the "strategy layer") and the *physical layer* (a merging of Gibbons' "representation layer" and others). The physical layer is the presentation or delivery of instruction, while the pedagogical layer is the strategy that enables learning to take place. We believe aspects of the physical layer can impact the availability and effectiveness of the pedagogical layer. Figure 2.9 illustrates the interplay between these two layers.

The prominent focus on the physical layer in BL *design* research and models can highlight differences in access and cost effectiveness, but tells little about the pedagogical attributes that actually influence learning outcomes and can lead to many of the problems inherent in media studies (Clark, 1983; Kozma, 1991). Greater attention needs to be given to identifying the core attributes in the pedagogical layer of the design that lead to the learning outcomes of interest as well as to understanding how attributes in different design layers complement each other and work together.

Conclusion

In this chapter we highlighted three distinct types of models/theory used in BL research: *explore, explain,* and *design.* We also identified some patterns suggesting ways to strengthen the models and theories being developed in the BL domain. First, many of the models and theories have not articulated clearly the core attributes, relationships, and rationale behind their selection and organization. In their critique of educational theories, Burkhardt and Choenfeld (2003, p. 10) commented,

Most of the theories that have been applied to education are quite broad. They lack what might be called "engineering power." To put it a different way, they lack the specificity that helps to guide design, to take good ideas and make sure that they work in practice.

Models and theories need to articulate more clearly and specifically the core building blocks of good theory in the social sciences identified by Whetten (1989) and recognize that they may exist within different layers of the design. (See the section "Model and Theory Development in Design Fields" in this chapter.)

Second, the heavy focus in existing models on physical or surface-level characteristics rather than pedagogical or psychological characteristics is impeding progress. Distance education research was able to make significant theoretical progress when it moved its focus beyond the physical layer to the psychological layer. Moore (2013) accomplished this by proposing that the essential research construct was not physical separation, but *transactional* (or psychological) distance between the instructor and the learner, which could be defined in terms of a relationship between dialog and structure and related to other psychological concepts such as autonomy. BL models and theories need to make the same transition. We believe that the concept of design layers is a powerful approach to this problem, as it allows BL models to specify the connection between physical and pedagogical layers of a design (see the section "Design Layers" in this chapter).

Third, our examination of research specific to BL identified a solid number of *explore* models, a very limited focus on *explain* models/theories, and an increasing number of *design* models (though many lacked appropriate specificity). We did not commonly find explicit development and improvement of the models/theories across multiple studies and/or between different researchers; more commonly, models were proposed or used only once. This may be because research in the blended learning domain is relatively new or because the limited specificity of the models does not enable meaningful replication across contexts. We believe that increased attention on theory development can help to focus the discourse happening in the BL research community as well as strengthen BL practice.

Finally, we challenge BL researchers to critically analyze their own models and theories to determine if they are clearly and sufficiently identifying the core building blocks of good theory identified by Whetten (1989). (See the section "Model and Theory Development in Design Fields" in this chapter.) We also encourage researchers to engage in more theory building, which includes systematically exploring, testing, and adjusting models and theory over time as well as seeking to develop models and theories that have wide appeal and applicability beyond a single classroom or institution.

Note

1 Because these words are used as specific terms labeling research, theory, and models, yet are verbs that describe related actions, the labeling use is italicized throughout the chapter, and the generic use is in roman type.

References

Akyol, Z., Vaughan, N., & Garrison, D. R. (2011). The impact of course duration on the development of a community of inquiry. *Interactive Learning Environments, 19*(3), 231–246. doi:10.1080/10494820902809147

Allen, I. E., & Seaman, J. (2007). *Online nation: Five years of growth in online learning.* Needham, MA: Sloan Consortium.

Barab, S. (2006). Design-based research: A methodological toolkit for the learning scientist. In R. K. Sawyer (Ed.), *The Cambridge handbook of the learning sciences* (pp. 153–169). New York, NY: Cambridge University Press.

Barnard-BraK, L., & Shiu, W. (2010). Classroom community scale in the blended learning environment: A psychometric review. *International Journal on E-Learning, 9*(3), 303–311.

Beatty, B. J. (2013, in press). Hybrid courses with flexible participation – the HyFlex course design. In L. Kyei-Blankson & E. Ntuli (Eds.) *Blended learning environments: Experiences in K-20 education.* Hershey, PA: IGI Global.

Bersin, J. (2003). *Blended learning: What works: An industry study of the business impact of blended learning.* Retrieved from www.bersin.com/Practice/Detail.aspx?docid=5870

Brown, B. W., & Liedholm, C. E. (2002). Can web courses replace the classroom in Principles of Microeconomics? *The American Economic Review, 92*(2), 444–448. doi:10.1257/000282802320191778

Burkhardt, H., & Schoenfeld, A. H. (2003). Improving educational research: Toward a more useful, more influential, and better-funded enterprise. *Educational Researcher, 32*(9), 3–14. doi:10.3102/0013189X032009003

Clark, R. E. (1983). Reconsidering research on learning from media. *Review of Educational Research, 53*(4), 445–459.

Collins, A. (1992). Towards a design science of education. In E. Scanlon and T. O'Shea (Eds.), *New directions in educational technology* (pp. 15–22). Berlin: Springer-Verlag.

Dickmeyer, N. (1989). Metaphor, model, and theory in education research. *Teachers College Record, 91*(2), 151–160.

Driscoll, M. (2002). Blended learning: Let's get beyond the hype. *E-learning, 3*, 54.

Drysdale, J. S., Graham, C. R., Spring, K. A., & Halverson, L. (2013). An analysis of research trends in dissertations and theses studying blended learning. *The Internet and Higher Education, 17*, 90–100. doi:10.1016/j.iheduc.2012.11.003

Dubin, R. (1976). Theory building in applied areas. In M. D. Dunnette (Ed.), *Handbook of industrial and organizational psychology* (pp. 17–39). Chicago, IL: Rand McNally College Publishing Company.

Garrison, D. R., Anderson, T., & Archer, W. (2000). Critical inquiry in a text-based environment: Computer conferencing in higher education. *Internet and Higher Education, 2*(2–3), 87–105.

Garrison, D. R., & Kanuka, H. (2004). Blended learning: Uncovering its transformative potential in higher education. *The Internet and Higher Education, 7*(2), 95–105. doi:10.1016/j.iheduc.2004.02.001

Garrison, D. R., & Vaughan, N. D. (2008). *Blended learning in higher education: Framework, principles, and guidelines.* San Francisco: Jossey-Bass.

Gibbons, A. S. (2003). The practice of instructional technology: Science and technology. *Educational technology, 43*(5), 11–16.

Gibbons, A. S. (2013, in press). *An architectural approach to instructional design.* New York, NY: Routledge.

Gibbons, A. S., & Bunderson, C. V. (2005). Explore, explain, design. In K. K. Leonard (Ed.), *Encyclopedia of Social Measurement* (pp. 927–938). New York, NY: Elsevier.

Gibbons, A. S., & Rogers, P. C. (2009). The architecture of instructional theory. In C. M. Reigeluth and A. Carr-Chellman (Eds.), *Instructional-design theories and models,* (Vol. III, pp. 305–326). Mahwah, NJ: Lawrence Erlbaum Associates.

Ginns, P., & Ellis, R. (2007). Quality in blended learning: Exploring the relationships between on-line and face-to-face teaching and learning. *The Internet and Higher Education, 10*(1), 53–64. doi:10.1016/j.iheduc.2006.10.003

Graham, C. R. (2006). Blended learning systems: Definition, current trends, and future directions. In C. J. Bonk & C. R. Graham (Eds.), *The handbook of blended learning: Global perspectives, local designs* (pp. 3–21). San Francisco, CA: Pfeiffer Publishing.

Graham, C. R. (2013). Emerging practice and research in blended learning. In M. G. Moore (Ed.), *Handbook of distance education* (3rd ed. pp. 333–350). New York, NY: Routledge.

Graham, C. R., & Robison, R. (2007). Realizing the transformational potential of blended learning: Comparing cases of transforming blends and enhancing blends in higher education. In A. G. Picciano & C. D. Dziuban (Eds.), *Blended learning: Research perspectives* (pp. 83–110). Needham, MA: The Sloan Consortium.

Halverson, L. R., Graham, C. R., Spring, K. J., & Drysdale, J. S. (2012). An analysis of high impact scholarship and publication trends in blended learning. *Distance Education, 33*(3), 381–413. doi:10.1080/01587919.2012.723166

Kaplan, A. (1964). *The conduct of inquiry: Methodology for behavioral science.* Philadelphia: Chandler Publishing Company.

Klein, H. J., Noe, R. A., & Wang, C. (2006). Motivation to learn and course outcomes: The impact of delivery mode, learning goal orientation, and perceived barriers and enablers. *Personnel Psychology, 59*(3), 665–702. doi:10.1111/j.1744-6570.2006.00050.x

Klir, G. J. (1969). *An approach to general systems theory.* New York, NY: Van Nostrand Reinhold Company.

Kozma, R. (1991). Learning with media. *Review of Educational Research, 61*(2), 179–211.

Lorenzo, G., & Moore, J. C. (2002). The Sloan Consortium report to the nation: Five pillars of quality online education. Retrieved from www.sloan-c.org/effective/pillarreport1.pdf

Lynch, R., & Dembo, M. (2004). Online learning in a blended learning context. *International Review of Research in Open and Distance Learning,* Retrieved from www.irrodl.org/index.php/irrodl/article/view/189/271

McDougall, A., & Jones, A. (2006). Theory and history, questions and methodology: Current and future issues in research into ICT in education. *Technology, Pedagogy and Education, 15*(3), 353–360. doi:10.1080/14759390600923915

Means, B., Toyama, Y., Murphy, R., Bakia, M., & Jones, K. (2010). *Evaluation of evidence-based practices in online learning: A meta-analysis and review of online learning studies.* Washington DC: U.S. Department of Education. Retrieved from www2.ed.gov/rschstat/eval/tech/evidence-based-practices/finalreport.pdf

Merton, R. K. (1967). *On theoretical sociology: Five essays, old and new.* New York, NY: Free Press.

Mishra, P., & Koehler, M. J. (2006). Technological pedagogical content knowledge: A framework for teacher knowledge. *Teachers College Record, 108*(6), 1017–1054.

Moore, M. G. (2004). Research worth publishing (editorial). *American Journal of Distance Education, 18*(3), 127–130.

Moore, M. G. (2013). The theory of transactional distance. In M. G. Moore (Ed.), *Handbook of distance education* (3rd ed., pp. 66–85). Mahwah, NJ: Lawrence Erlbaum Associates.

Mortera-Gutiérrez, F. (2006). Faculty best practices using blended learning in e-learning and face-to-face instruction. *E-learning, 5*(3), 313–337.

Oliver, M., & Trigwell, K. (2005). Can "blended learning" be redeemed? *E-Learning, 2*(1), 17–26. doi:10.2304/elea.2005.2.1.2

Orey, M. (2002a). *Definition of blended learning.* University of Georgia. Retrieved from www.arches.uga.edu/ mikeorey/blendedLearning

Orey, M. (2002b). *One year of online blended learning: Lessons learned.* Paper presented at the Annual Meeting of the Eastern Educational Research Association, Sarasota, FL.

Picciano, A. G. (2006). Blended learning: Implications for growth and access. *Journal of Asynchronous Learning Networks, 10*(3), 95–102.

Picciano, A. G. (2009). Blending with purpose: The multimodal model. *Journal of Asynchronous Learning Networks, 13*(1), 7–18.

Power, M. (2008). The emergence of a blended online learning environment. *MERLOT Journal of Online Learning and Teaching, 4*(4), 503–514.

Reay, J. (2001). Blended learning—a fusion for the future. *Knowledge Management Review, 4*(3), 6.

Reigeluth, C. M. (1999). *Instructional-design theories and models: A new paradigm of instructional theory* (Vol. 2). Mahwah, NJ: Lawrence Erlbaum.

Riffell, S., & Sibley, D. (2005). Using web-based instruction to improve large undergraduate biology courses: An evaluation of a hybrid course format. *Computers & Education, 44*(3), 217–235. doi:10.1016/j.compedu.2004.01.005

Rivera, J. C., McAlister, M. K., & Rice, M. L. (2002). A comparison of student outcomes & satisfaction between traditional & web based course offerings. *Online Journal of Distance Learning Administration, 5*(3). Retrieved from www.westga.edu/ distance/ojdla/fall53/rivera53.html

Roblyer, M. D. (2005). Educational technology research that makes a difference: Series introduction. *Contemporary Issues in Technology and Teacher Education, 5*(2), 192–201.

Roblyer, M. D., & Knezek, G. (2003). New millennium research for educational technology: A call for a national research agenda. *Journal of Research on Technology in Education, 36*(1), 60–71.

Rooney, J. E. (2003). Knowledge infusion: Blending learning opportunities to enhance educational programming and meetings. *Association Management, 55*(6), 26–32.

Rossett, A. (2002). *The ASTD e-learning handbook.* New York, NY: McGraw-Hill.

Rossett, A., & Frazee, R. V. (2006). *Blended learning opportunities.* American Management Association. Retrieved from www.grossmont.edu/don.dean/pkms_ddean/ET795A/WhitePaper_BlendLearn.pdf

Rovai, A. P., & Jordan, H. M. (2004). Blended learning and sense of community: A comparative analysis with traditional and fully online graduate courses. *International Review of Research in Open and Distance Learning, 5*(2). Retrieved from www.irrodl.org/index.php/irrodl/article/view/192/274

Sands, P. (2002). Inside outside, upside downside: Strategies for connecting online and face-to-face instruction in hybrid courses. *Teaching with Technology Today, 8*(6). Retrieved from www.uwsa.edu/ttt/articles/sands2.htm

Sharpe, R., Benfield, G., Roberts, G., & Francis, R. (2006). *The undergraduate experience of blended e-learning: A review of UK literature and practice.* York, UK: The Higher Education Academy. Retrieved from www.heacademy.ac.uk/resources/detail/Teachingandresearch/Undergraduate_Experience

Simon, H. A. (1999). *The sciences of the artificial* (3rd ed.). Cambridge, MA: MIT Press.

Simonson, M., Schlosser, C., & Hanson, D. (1999). Theory and distance education: A new discussion. *American Journal of Distance Education, 13*(1), 60–75.

Singh, H., & Reed, C. (2001). *A white paper: Achieving success with blended learning.* Centra Software. Retrieved from www.centra.com/download/whitepapers/blendedlearning.pdf

So, H., & Brush, T. (2008). Student perceptions of collaborative learning, social presence and satisfaction in a blended learning environment: Relationships and critical factors. *Computers & Education, 51*(1), 318–336. doi:10.1016/j.compedu.2007.05.009

Staker, H., & Horn, M. B. (2012). *Classifying K-12 blended learning.* Innosight Institute, Inc. Retrieved from www.innosightinstitute.org/innosight/wp-content/uploads/2012/05/Classifying-K-12-blended-learning2.pdf

Sutton, R., & Staw, B. M. (1995). What theory is not. *Administrative Science Quarterly, 40*(3), 371–384. doi: 10.2307/2393788

Thomson, I. (2002). Thomson job impact study: The next generation of corporate learning. Retrieved from www.netg.com/DemosAndDownloads/Downloads/JobImpact.pdf

Tuckman, B. (2002). Evaluating ADAPT: A hybrid instructional model combining web-based and classroom components. *Computers & Education, 39*(3), 261–269. doi:10.1016/S0360-1315(02)00045-3

Twigg, C. A. (2003). Improving learning and reducing costs: New models for online learning. *Educause Review, 38*(5), 28–38.

Utts, J., Sommer, B., Acredolo, C., Maher, M. W., & Matthews, H. (2003). A study comparing traditional and hybrid Internet-based instruction in introductory statistics classes. *Journal of Statistics Education, 11*(3). Retrieved from www.amstat.org/publications/jse/v11n3/utts.html

Vaughan, N., & Garrison, D. (2005). Creating cognitive presence in a blended faculty development community. *The Internet and Higher Education, 8*(1), 1–12. doi:10.1016/j.iheduc.2004.11.001

Vincenti, W. G. (1990). *What engineers know and how they know it: Analytical studies from aeronautical history.* Baltimore: Johns Hopkins University Press.

Ward, J., & LaBranche, G. A. (2003). Blended learning: The convergence of e-learning and meetings. *Franchising World, 35*(4), 22–23.

Whetten, D. A. (1989). What constitutes a theoretical contribution? *Academy of Management Review 14*(4), 490–495. doi:10.2307/258554

Young, J. R. (2002). "Hybrid" teaching seeks to end the divide between traditional and online instruction. *The Chronicle of Higher Education, 48*(28), A33–A34. Retrieved from http://eric.ed.gov/ERICWebPortal/recordDetail?accno=EJ645445

3

SCALING BLENDED LEARNING EVALUATION BEYOND THE UNIVERSITY

Patsy D. Moskal and Thomas B. Cavanagh

Imagine that you are one of the 58% of college students who fail to complete your bachelor's degree by age 26. Among low-income students, the bachelor's completion rate is just 26% (About Next Generation Learning, 2012). Perhaps you actually are in one of these groups. If so, you understand the unique challenges facing higher education today. The need to work, to care for families, to adhere to dictated schedules all compete for limited time and resources, forcing many students out of the educational pipeline, even if they have already accumulated a number of credits. Yet, educational access remains as important as ever for breaking the cycle of poverty (Bailey & Dynarski, 2011; Engle, Yeado, Brusi, & Cruz, 2012; Lee, Edwards, Menson, & Rawls, 2011; Schneider & Yin, 2012; Tavernise, 2012). "In 2008, the average wage for adults 25 and older with a four year degree was $60,954, compared to $33,618 for those with only a high school diploma and $24,686 for those with no high school diploma" (About Next Generation Learning, 2012). But how can higher education meet the public's need for educational access in such an environment of increasing work/life demands?

This is precisely the question at the center of the Next Generation Learning Challenges (NGLC) program, "a collaborative, multi-year initiative created to address the barriers to educational innovation and tap the potential of technology to dramatically improve college readiness and completion in the United States" (About Next Generation Learning, 2012). NGLC is led by EDUCAUSE in partnership with the League for Innovation in the Community College, the International Association for K–12 Online Learning (iNACOL), and the Council of Chief State School Officers (CCSSO), with funding provided by the Bill and Melinda Gates Foundation and the William and Flora Hewlett Foundation. The NGLC program consists of several "waves" of project funding, each with a slightly different focus.

In Wave 1 of the program, NGLC solicited proposals in four challenge areas designed to scale proven models to much wider student populations: Blended Learning, Open Educational Resources (OER), Learner Analytics, and Deeper Learning and Engagement. Only 29 Wave 1 projects were funded out of over 600 submissions. One of the Blended Learning projects was a collaboration between the University of Central Florida (UCF) and the American Association of State Colleges and Universities (AASCU) called "Expanding Blended Learning Through Tools and Campus Programs."

Project Background

Blended courses (also known as hybrid or mixed-mode courses), where a portion of the traditional face-to-face instruction is replaced by web-based online learning, have proven to be among the most popular choices for students at institutions where they are offered. At first glance, this popularity seems intuitive because blended courses allow students and faculty to take advantage of much of the flexibility and convenience of an online course while retaining the benefits of the face-to-face classroom experience.

Blended learning is conceptualized and implemented in various ways by different universities (Mayadas & Picciano, 2007; Norberg, Dziuban, & Moskal, 2011; Graham, 2006). Where blended courses have succeeded, they have most often done so when strategically aligned with an institution's mission and goals (Moskal, Dziuban, & Hartman, 2013; Graham, Woodfield, & Harrison, 2013). The development and delivery of blended courses can be used to address a variety of institutional, faculty, and student needs. For universities, blended courses can be part of a strategy to compensate for limited classroom space, as well as a way to think differently about encouraging faculty collaboration. For faculty, blended courses can be a method to infuse new engagement opportunities into established courses or, for some, provide a transitional opportunity between fully face-to-face and fully online instruction. For students, blended courses offer the conveniences of online learning combined with the social and instructional interactions that may not lend themselves to online delivery (e.g., lab sections or proctored assessments). If an institution's blended learning strategy can be designed to address the needs and dynamics of all three constituencies (institution, faculty, and student) simultaneously, then blended learning can become a powerful force for institutional transformation (Moskal et al., 2013).

The U.S. Department of Education, in a meta-analysis of online research, reported that students in online courses performed modestly better, on average, than those in face-to-face courses, with blended students performing the best (Means, Toyama, Murphy, Bakia, & Jones, 2010). Not only do students perform better in blended courses, but the electronic resources inherent in the modality offer other advantages as well. For example, student performance analytics (another NGLC focus area) can be used to study and better understand student

TABLE 3.1 UCF's Blended Learning Growth

Blended learning	2010–2011 academic year	Totals since 2002
Sections	777	5,808
Registrations	31,081	191,941
Student credit hours (SCH)	91,432	568,255

learning. Data analytics can also identify students who need early intervention, thus increasing retention (Dziuban, Moskal, Cavanagh, & Watts, 2012). The online tools available in blended courses can also significantly enhance student engagement, ensuring that all students participate in course discussions and benefit from collaborative learning.

Pioneering the modality since 1997, the University of Central Florida (UCF) has been an internationally recognized leader in blended learning. Since beginning this initiative, UCF blended course sections and course offerings have increased nearly 500% (Table 3.1).

Project Design

In order to achieve the NGLC stated goal of scale, UCF partnered with the American Association of State Colleges and Universities (AASCU) to disseminate UCF's successful blended initiative broadly across 20 AASCU member institutions (Table 3.2). AASCU consists of more than 420 public colleges and universities, representing six different Carnegie classifications and enrolling more than 3.8 million students (56% of the enrollment at all public four-year institutions). AASCU schools educate 55% of all minority students in public four-year institutions. A substantial portion of students at AASCU member institutions are the first in their families to attend college, and many are Pell grant recipients. Between 30% and 40% of all students admitted to AASCU member institutions require some form of remediation. AASCU also has strong ties to community colleges; half of all students who graduate from AASCU member institutions began their academic careers at community colleges (American Association of State Colleges and Universities, 2012).

The UCF/AASCU project expanded adoption of blended learning to 20 participating AASCU member institutions by developing and disseminating a "Blended Learning Toolkit" based upon the proven best practices that have been successfully implemented by the University of Central Florida. Included in this toolkit were strategies for blended course design and delivery, OER blended course models in Composition and Algebra, assessment and data collection protocols, and "train-the-trainer" materials and workshops. AASCU recruited the 20 collaborating institutions and leveraged their networks and conferences to work with these institutions on blended learning implementation, while at

TABLE 3.2 Participating AASCU Member Institutions (Individual and Statewide Systems)

Individual institutions	State coordinating institutions	State participating institutions
Columbia State University	**Missouri**	• Harris-Stowe State University
Fayetteville State University		• Lincoln University of Missouri
Grambling State University	Southeast Missouri State University	• Missouri Southern State University
Northwestern State University (LA)		• Missouri State University
Indiana University Kokomo		• University of Missouri-St. Louis
Texas A&M University-Corpus Christi	**Alabama**	• University of North Alabama
The College at Brockport, State University of New York	Troy University	• University of South Alabama
Thomas Edison State College	**Minnesota**	• St. Cloud State University
University of Maine at Fort Kent	Winona State University	

the same time making the toolkit and course models widely available to its entire 420 member institutions and systems.

Each of 20 partner institutions deployed one or more courses (either directly using the Composition and Algebra templates or building other high-need courses by using the strategies and resources contained in the Toolkit). These 20 institutions enroll over 250,000 students, including 33% low-income and 75% 25 years old or under, key demographics for the NGLC project.

The project connected the 20 participating AASCU institutions to a community of practice dedicated to curricular reinvention through technology. Faculty in these institutions worked with each other and with expert UCF faculty and staff to redesign the provided Composition and Algebra courses. UCF's team of faculty, assessment, and blended learning experts worked with their peers at the participating institutions to create a "bottom up" buy-in of blended learning, using the toolkit and model courses to jump start adoption and rigorous assessment to prove efficacy. At the same time, AASCU's unique position of influence among its network of members allowed the project team to help their participating institutional presidents and provosts understand the strategic value of blended learning, leveraging UCF's positive student learning outcomes and ROI as context.

The project consisted of the following elements:

- An open educational resource (OER) Blended Learning Toolkit containing:
  ○ Best practices, strategies, models, and course design principles.
  ○ Two OER prototype blended course templates in key core general education disciplines: Composition and Algebra.
  ○ Directions and suggestions for applying the toolkit resources to create original blended courses other than Composition and Algebra.
  ○ Train-the-trainer materials for development and delivery of the prototype open courses, as well as a 5-week massive open online course on general blended learning design and delivery.
  ○ Assessment and data collection protocols for all participating institutions, including survey instruments and standards.
  ○ Virtual and in-person workshops for participating institutions and others within the AASCU membership.
- Institutional support through a variety of existing AASCU meetings and conferences (such as separate semi-annual meetings for presidents and provosts; an annual leadership institute and academic leadership series webinars), which aligned AASCU's ongoing activities in technology and educational transformation with NGLC's goals.
- 217 new blended course sections (funded) across 20 project institutions nationwide.
- Targeted low-income students under age 26 (with the total population across the participating institutions being 187,500).

The Blended Learning Toolkit was made available via a public website (www.blendedlearningtoolkit.org) and covered by a Creative Commons licensing agreement (Attribution Non-Commercial Share-alike: BY NC SA). Included train-the-trainer materials provided faculty who delivered the blended courses specific instructions for effective deployment. Online webinars conducted by UCF staff and faculty supported the train-the-trainer materials through both the planning and delivery phases.

Also included in the package were protocols and a single entry point for ongoing data collection so that the project's wider impact and efficacy could be consistently evaluated over time. UCF has a long history of collecting and measuring data related to fully online and blended learning. The toolkit included survey instruments, collection protocols, definitions, etc., so that those institutions participating in the NGLC grant could collect their own data in a manner consistent with UCF's data reporting, allowing the team to assimilate project data from the field.

The Blended Learning Toolkit, along with its requisite components of best practices, prototype courses, training materials, and assessment guidelines, was distributed to the 20 participating AASCU institutions, with ongoing support from UCF experts. There were two categories of institutional participation: those included as individual institutions and those who were part of statewide consortia, whose activities were coordinated by a single lead institution.

Project Evaluation

With the grant spanning 20 campuses, evaluation posed logistical hurdles. Ideally, the goal of any evaluation is to provide a valid mechanism for collecting meaningful data, providing results to constituents to help them better determine impact for continual improvement. The NGLC evaluation had two goals. The first was to provide resources and guidance to the 20 campus sites so that they would be enabled to continue evaluating their blended learning initiatives after the grant had passed. The second was to conduct the grant evaluation and determine the successes and challenges of implementing the grant objectives.

Careful planning and coordination were necessary to deal with the logistics of requesting and obtaining student data from 20 different schools and thousands of dispersed students. GroupSpaces (www.groupspaces.com) provided a means to communicate with the various contacts at each campus. As participating faculty, administrators, or assessment personnel registered, they were asked to designate themselves as faculty—math, English, or other subject; primary point of contact for their campus; or assessment point of contact for the grant. In some cases, one person served in all three capacities and was the faculty member teaching the courses, as well as the assessment and primary point of contact. In other cases, the assessment person was a contact within the university's Institutional Research office and was savvy in data collection and format, and the primary contact may have been a high-level administrator. For evaluation purposes, the assessment point of contact served as the go-to person regarding any evaluation data required and this person dispersed evaluation information and requests to their campus faculty and/or institutional research staff.

Just as UCF's award-winning program (Center for Distributed Learning Awards, 2012) became the blended learning model for the grant, UCF's Distributed Learning Impact Evaluation became the model for how to evaluate this project. UCF has designed their campus evaluation to inform campus stakeholders with meaningful results. Over time, components of this model have been scaled from the classroom, to program, college, and institution. The NGLC grant provided an opportunity to determine which components could scale beyond the university to 20 remote sites and also provide the opportunity to identify issues related to the challenge of this large evaluation project. Because of the complexity of gathering data from many distributed sites, the design was simplified to encompass the data elements seen in Table 3.3.

TABLE 3.3 Evaluation Design for UCF/AASCU's NGLC Project

Target outcome	Index	Measure	How collected	Data analysis
Scale	Degree to which the model has been scaled and plans for continuation and expansion	Number of students, faculty, courses, and unique sections participating	Participants' institution data	Tabulation of each from course and student data provided by participating institutions
Success	Grade of A, B, C	Class roster of each blended class with all identification removed	Participants' institution data	Compute success proportion and variability overall and by low income
Withdrawal	Non-medical withdrawal	Same grade roster with withdrawals indicated	Participants' institution data	Compute withdrawal proportion and variability overall and by low income
Student Evaluation of Instruction (SEI)	Students' evaluation of their blended learning experience	UCF questionnaire developed and validated by UCF	UCF online	Tabulation and analysis of questionnaire response Content analysis of free responses
Faculty Evaluation of Instruction (FEI)	Faculty members' evaluation of their blended teaching experience	UCF questionnaire developed and validated	UCF online	Tabulation and analysis of questionnaire responses Content analysis of free responses

UCF's Institutional Review Board (IRB) analysis of the grant research found the project to be "exempt" from human subjects review. This approval for the project was provided to each of the 20 campus assessment contacts to assist them in gathering approval for participation on each of their campuses. UCF researchers provided assistance as needed throughout the IRB process, answering questions and providing input when required. A spreadsheet format was provided to each assessment contact to standardize the format of student data across the different participants. This institutional grade dataset included university/campus identifier, course prefix, number, section, teacher name, student age, gender, ethnicity, Pell status, and final course grade. The schools' student data were to be aggregated into the grant data file for analyses. Individual campuses were not identified in any analyses, and student identification was not provided in any dataset. The goal was to provide the campus contacts with the materials they needed to expedite and simplify their IRB process.

To ensure the evaluation was as straightforward as possible for participants, student and faculty surveys were developed and coded in Google Forms by UCF researchers. Faculty at each participating campus then received a request and reminders with the survey URL during the administration period near the end of the Fall and Spring semesters to encourage their students to participate. Using online surveys allowed UCF to maintain control over the survey data and also served to minimize the imposition on faculty. Faculty only had to advertise the survey within their blended courses. Data collected through Google Forms was maintained and analyzed by UCF. Requests to faculty to complete the faculty survey were made approximately 2 weeks after the student survey so as to minimize confusion. The UCF grant assessment coordinator was the point person for any questions faculty had regarding survey administration or problems they or their students posed.

Student grade data were de-identified and students' surveys were anonymous. Therefore, no comparisons could be made by grade and satisfaction. This was a conscious decision on the part of the UCF evaluation staff. Having anonymous student data ensured that UCF's IRB classified the research as "exempt" from human subjects review. This made the process significantly easier for those responsible for assessment at the 20 participating schools in terms of their obtaining IRB approval and handling student data. Even with this designation, several campuses required more information and were initially hesitant to release student data due to FERPA (Family Educational Right and Privacy Act) protection. These requests had to be handled individually by UCF's grant assessment coordinator, who provided the necessary details to meet individual campuses' requirements for human subjects review. Having student private identification would have greatly complicated this process, and would have hampered our ability to accomplish the evaluation in the aggressive 15-month grant time period. The result was losing a possible comparison between grades and satisfaction, but gaining quick access to the quality and quantity of data that we were able to obtain. In our experience, this was a necessary sacrifice.

Findings and Results

As the main focus of the grant was to scale blended learning beyond UCF, the number of course sections was a critical measure of the evaluation. Because the course identification was provided for student data, this allowed us to keep track of the number of unique course sections developed for each campus.

Course demographics allowed us to track the sections by discipline (English, math, other) and monitor enrollments for each. In addition, Pell status provided those details for low income students. One of the grant requirements was to provide summary data as needed to the external evaluators of the grant, SRI International. Overall enrollment figures, and number of unique sections, faculty and total course sections were computed and submitted each quarter in a provided spreadsheet.

Scaling Blended Learning

The primary directive for the grant was to investigate whether blended learning could be scaled to the 20 participating campuses. Table 3.4 illustrates the breakdown of each campus, indexed by students, faculty, and course metrics. Over all 20 campuses, 79 unique blended courses were developed by 131 faculty who delivered 217 sections to 5,798 students. Blended learning was embraced by some more than others, due in part to the rapid ramp-up time required to

TABLE 3.4   Scale of Blended Learning: Students, Faculty, Unique and Total Sections Delivered by Institution

Institution	Students	Faculty	Unique courses	Total sections
Columbus State University	93	5	4	5
Fayetteville State University	704	21	8	23
Grambling State University	361	6	4	11
Harris-Stowe State University	33	2	1	2
Indiana University Kokomo	76	2	2	2
Lincoln University Missouri	61	1	1	3
Missouri Southern State University	53	2	1	3
Missouri State University	108	5	1	5
Northwestern State University	49	4	2	4
Southeast Missouri State University	115	4	1	4
St. Cloud State University	1286	9	3	35
Texas A&M at Corpus Christi	230	9	6	20
The College at Brockport	203	6	5	8
Thomas Edison State College	15	3	4	4
Troy University	179	8	4	9
University of Maine, Ft. Kent	572	22	14	31
University of Missouri, Kansas City	39	2	2	2
University of Missouri, St. Louis	190	7	4	10
University of North Alabama	144	3	1	5
University of South Alabama	244	3	2	12
Winona State University	1043	7	9	19
TOTAL	**5798**	**131**	**79**	**217**

commit and participate in the grant and no doubt the varying milieu of the campuses. This may have been the motivation for slightly more than half of the total sections (121 out of 217) being delivered in the grant's second semester (Spring), as it provided those faculty with an extra semester to design and develop the course before delivery.

Students' Evaluation of Instruction

The student survey was administered in late Fall and Spring semesters, with faculty being sent reminders to advertise the survey to students. A follow-up reminder was sent to faculty approximately 2 weeks later asking them to nudge their students once more to participate. A total of 1,349 students returned completed surveys. Computing response rates becomes problematic because of the remote nature of relying on faculty to announce the survey and the assumptions that all faculty did so and all students were able to access the survey successfully. However, given that there were 5,798 students in participating courses, the response rate for 1,349 of those completing a survey is a respectable 23%. Sixty percent of the respondents indicated that they took a blended math course, 34% English, and 11% other. Seventy percent of the students indicated that this was their first blended learning course.

Table 3.5 indicates students' satisfaction with blended learning, with 60% responding they were very satisfied or somewhat satisfied with the course. Twenty-five percent indicated they were neither satisfied nor dissatisfied, while only 16% expressed dissatisfaction with the new modality.

Table 3.6 illustrates the top five reasons students indicated they liked the blended modality. Not surprisingly, the top attraction for those who responded to this open-ended question was the flexibility and convenience the blended format offers with 43% of students mentioning that as the feature they most liked about their blended course. Other top responses included the instructor (16%), the use of technology in instruction (15%), the ease of getting help (10%), and the ability to review materials whenever they wanted (9%).

While technology aspects were mentioned as being components students liked most, technology issues also topped the features liked least with 17% of

TABLE 3.5 Students' Satisfaction with Their Blended Course (n=1,315)

	Percent
Very dissatisfied	7
Somewhat dissatisfied	9
Neither dissatisfied nor satisfied	25
Somewhat satisfied	31
Very satisfied	29

TABLE 3.6 Top Five Things Students Like Most About Blended Learning (n=736)

	Percent
Time saving/convenient/flexible	43
Instructor (or other class characteristics)	16
Use of technology in learning (e.g., easier to get feedback, features of online assignments)	15
Easy methods of/and getting help	10
Able to review content/access material whenever	9

TABLE 3.7 Top Five Things Students Like Least About Blended Learning (n=807)

	Percent
Technology issues	17
Instructor/other class characteristics	17
Time-consuming/intensive	13
Less teaching time by instructor/less actual class time	13
Procrastination/time-management issues	9

TABLE 3.8 Students' Likelihood of Enrolling in a Future Blended Course (n=1,313)

	Percent
Definitely not	11
Probably not	9
Not sure	22
Probably	24
Definitely	34

respondents mentioning them. The instructor also appeared on both the most/least liked lists with 17% reacting negatively to the faculty teaching the course. Students felt the course was time consuming (13%) and some missed the face-to-face instruction, which was reduced in the blended modality (13%). Finally, students lamented their own procrastination and time-management issues as being one of the top factors they disliked about blended learning (9%).

Not surprisingly, students' satisfaction with blended learning was further iterated in their willingness to take another fully online course. Table 3.8 illustrates that more than half (58%) of students indicated they would probably or definitely take another blended learning course. Still, 20% of the respondents were negative, indicating they would probably or definitely not enroll in a blended course if they had a choice in the future. Twenty-two percent were unsure.

Faculty Evaluation of Instruction

Participating faculty were also asked to complete a survey indicating their perceptions of their experience teaching in the blended learning format. Seventy-three faculty completed the survey. Given that 131 faculty participated in the grant, and assuming all were notified regarding the survey itself, the response rate was a respectable 56%. Forty percent of the teachers responding indicated they were teaching a blended math course, 39% English, and 21% other disciplines.

Faculty were very positive regarding their experience teaching in the blended format with 74% indicating they would definitely or probably teach this modality in the future if given a choice. Only 7% of those responding were negative and definitely or probably would not teach in the blended format again if they had a choice. Nineteen percent of respondents were not sure if they would teach in this format in the future (Table 3.9).

When asked what they perceived as positive about teaching blended courses (Table 3.10), 42% of faculty who responded to this open-ended question indicated that they liked that it merged the best of both worlds, allowing for more materials available online and also helping their students access the course with anytime, anyplace instruction. Twenty-one percent of faculty mentioned that they felt they could give more time or individualized attention to their students and also that they had better interaction with their students in the blended

TABLE 3.9 Faculty Preference to Teach a Future Blended Course (n=73)

	Percent
Definitely not	1
Probably not	6
Not sure	19
Probably	21
Definitely	53

TABLE 3.10 Top Five Positive Aspects of Teaching a Blended Course (n=62)

	Percent
Best of both worlds/convenient/broader range of materials	42
Individualized/more attention to students	21
More and better interaction with students	21
Increases student independence	13
More face-to-face class time for specifics	8

format. Faculty felt that students were forced to become more independent (13%) and that they were able to spend more of the face-to-face class time on specific content (8%).

Faculty also indicated what they viewed as challenges to teaching online (Table 3.11). Twenty-eight percent felt that it was not a good experience for students who lacked the necessary discipline or who needed significantly more face-to-face attention. They also saw that students who were deficient in computer skills had challenges that made learning course material more difficult (25%). Issues related to the technology cut into face-to-face time (18%). Some felt more disconnected (16%) as they faced the challenge of a changing role in teaching in the blended format. Others (16%) viewed the online assignments as less important.

Student Success and Course Completion

Grade data for students were used to determine the percentage of students who enrolled, completed, and mastered the material in their blended course. Completion included all students who did not withdraw from the course after the add/drop period. We chose to use our definition of success (Dziuban et al., 2012) to represent mastery of the course material. This included any student who made an A, B, or C in the course. Table 3.12 shows the percentage of students who completed blended courses and those who succeeded in the courses by non-low income and low-income.

TABLE 3.11 Top Five Negative Aspects of Teaching a Blended Course (n=44)

	Percent
Doesn't work for students lacking discipline/ needing more individual attention	28
Problems for students not computer savvy	25
Issues cut into face-to-face class time	18
Lessened importance of online assignments	16
Feel disconnected	16

TABLE 3.12 Student Percent Completion and Success Rates by Income Level

	Enrollment	Completion	Success
Low income	2,669	93	61
Non low income	3,107	93	67
TOTAL	5,798	93	64

Completion rates were 93% for both low income and non-low income students. However, success rates (A, B, or C) were slightly lower for low income students (61%) than students who were not low-income (67%). These data will be provided to grant participants to give them a baseline for future research as their blended learning initiatives develop over time.

Grant Evaluation Outcomes

While the evaluation plan included a variety of measures such as student withdrawal, success, and perception, the primary determinants of success are the outcomes included in the original project proposal. These outcomes, as well as their final results, are summarized in Table 3.13. Overall, given the condensed time frame and hurdles involved with working with 20 geographically dispersed campuses, the primary objectives of the grant were successfully achieved.

Impact Beyond the Core Grant Activities

It is worth noting that the reach of the Blended Learning Toolkit and especially the general faculty development MOOC (http://blended.online.ucf.edu/blendkit-course/) far exceeded the team's expectations as described in the grant proposal. In fact, the project team has received anecdotal feedback from a

TABLE 3.13 Summary of Proposed Outcomes and Results

Outcome	Result
1. *Build blended learning infrastructure* 1a. Identify participating institutions and communicate requirements 1b. Develop Blended Learning Toolkit 1c. Package Composition and Algebra prototype courses 1d. Conduct train-the-trainer sessions	Outcome 1 and all sub-outcomes were completed on time as proposed
2. *Increased access to education via blended learning for low-income, under 26 students* 2a. Disseminate toolkit materials and prototype courses to participating institutions 2b. Implement courses across AASCU network 2c. Assess project success	Outcome 2 and all sub-outcomes were completed on time as proposed 217 new blended sections 5,798 total students impacted 2,587 low-income students
3. *Increased student success and retention*	Data were collected to support outcome 3 for a longer-term analysis

number of both partner and non-partner participants about their use of the materials, which leads the team to suspect that a far greater number of participants are using the materials without notifying the developers.

For example, Columbus State Community College has used the Blended Learning Toolkit as the foundation for its blended learning initiative. Tom Erney, the Columbus State Community College Dean of Distance Learning, commented, "I found the toolkit to be a comprehensive resource for any institution interested in exploring blended learning." Other institutions such as the University of Georgia and the SUNY Learning Network have leveraged the Blended Learning Toolkit materials to support their own initiatives. In addition, the Blended Learning Toolkit has been used by those in the K–12 arena to support their development. According to Amy Gross from OnlineEdgeK12. com, "I didn't expect to find materials as thorough, clear, and practical as yours. And I certainly didn't expect them to be available to me at no cost."

We continue to get feedback and queries from campuses who participated, and many who were not part of the grant, but have heard about the Blended Learning Toolkit through various presentations or publications and would like more information. We more than exceeded the scale we had expected to achieve. UCF conducted a second version of the general blended learning faculty development MOOC in Fall 2012 to help with the demand for more resources regarding blended learning.

Lessons Learned from Scaling the Evaluation

The scale of the evaluation provided us with several issues and lessons learned on conducting research of this scope. Overall, we feel our grant was a success. As the primary goal was to achieve scale of blended learning across 20 campuses, we exceeded the expected sections produced, and far exceeded the scope of students and faculty we expected. As with any grant, the evaluation was only one of the objectives of the grant. Given the parameters of funding, time, and personnel, we quickly realized the following issues impacted our evaluation:

Relying on the Kindness of Strangers

Careful thought was given to managing the interaction with personnel in the trenches of the 20 campus sites. We conducted a face-to-face meeting at the beginning of a grant, held at an AASCU summer meeting. However, the limited budget did not include funding to pay for the campus representatives to attend and so, while many did, some could not due to time or budget constraints. Gathering institutional data, as well as survey responses, meant that we had to rely on others to gather information (in the case of student grade and course data), or at the very least advertise surveys. Relying on others who are remote always generates unknown effects into the equation.

Differing Contexts

From the beginning, we were aware of the differences of each of the 20 unique campuses. While they were recruited by AASCU in part because they were positive about moving to blended learning (as well as their institutional percentages of targeted low-income students) we had to assume that faculty who were engaged were of varying experience and enthusiasm with regard to the shortened time frame in which they were asked to convert or design a blended course, and participate in an outside grant. We heard anecdotally from some who were excited to have the opportunity, but we have to assume that some were also ambivalent about the process. Campus support for technology-enhanced learning varied, course content varied, faculty varied, and even grading practices varied. Twenty differing campuses provided twenty different contexts into the mix.

Local Buy-in Unknown

Each campus was recruited by AASCU as being interested in blended learning and being incentivized with a small budget to convert courses. However, within the year-long grant, there were numerous changes that occurred as is the nature of higher education. Faculty left, the planned course sections changed, courses did not achieve enough enrollment to be offered, grant contacts left, and even several provosts changed. Much happens in a year in the life of a university. Multiply that effect by 20 and we have to assume that some of those factors may conceivably have influenced the grant.

Minimal Budget and Time

Contextually, we know the count of students, courses, and faculty, but we don't know the depth of change faculty experienced due to the training. It is possible that some dramatically changed their courses, while others may have minimally incorporated blended learning. Yet, the money and time limits of the grant did not allow for site visits or interviews, which may have provided valuable information as to exactly what transformations may have taken place, and given more insight as to how the differing contexts may have influenced the experiences of each of the participants.

No Measure of Learning Outcomes or Comparison

While grades were used to measure success and completion, they are not necessarily a measure of learning. Certainly, grades lose reliability across varying faculty, disciplines, departments, and even campuses in the case of this grant. Collapsing the grades into success rates helps to mute this phenomenon, but they are at best an easy-to-measure substitute for gauging true learning. There was also no funding or time to compare the blended courses with their face-to-face counterparts to determine whether improvement was made. Anecdotally, some of the participating schools indicated they were monitoring this comparison independent of the grant. UCF offered to help design these studies, if needed.

Key to the success of such a large-scale evaluation in a condensed time was the collaboration between UCF and AASCU, who recruited the schools in a very short time period and provided a mechanism to periodically meet with participants from the various campuses at their organized events. We were also aware of having to rely on staff at other universities and tried to be respectful of their time and experience with research. A conscious effort was made to ensure that any contact with participants was as easy and painless as possible. Automated surveys, spreadsheet templates, and a research design that was exempt from human subjects (IRB) review were critical to the evaluation success.

While we were pleased with the achievement of scale, we were disappointed to find that the success rates did not match UCF's success rates in blended courses. UCF's experience with blended learning has created a culture where success rates typically exceed those in face-to-face courses. We attribute this success to the institutional commitment that allowed for transformation to occur on our campus (Moskal et al., 2013). Such transformation takes time and continual improvement to succeed and is far beyond the scope of a limited grant. However, we are hopeful that this grant allowed some campuses to investigate blended learning at their institutions and seed an innovation that will take root and eventually flourish. Upon further reflection, it would be unrealistic to expect any of the partner institutions to achieve the same student success results as UCF, who has been growing and supporting blended learning on its own campus since 1997. With the experience gained through this project, as well as continuing access to the resources housed in the Blended Learning Toolkit, perhaps not only will the 20 grant partners, but also the many others who participated in a non-funded capacity, be able to effectively design and evaluate blended learning on their individual campuses on an ongoing basis, eventually both meeting and even exceeding UCF's historical results.

References

About Next Generation Learning (2012). Retrieved from http://nextgenlearning.org/the-program

American Association of State Colleges and Universities (2012). Retrieved from http://www.aascu.org

Bailey, M., & Dynarski, S. (2011). *Gains and gaps: Changing inequality in US college entry and completion.* (Working paper 17633). Cambridge, MA: National Bureau of Economic Research. Retrieved from www.nber.org/papers/w17633

Center for Distributed Learning Awards (2012). Retrieved from http://cdl.ucf.edu/home/awards-page/

Dziuban, C., Moskal, P., Cavanagh, T., & Watts, A. (2012). Analytics that inform the university: Using data you already have. *Journal of Asynchronous Learning Networks*, *16*(3), 21–38.

Engle, J., Yeado, J., Brusi, R., & Cruz, J. L. (2012). Replenishing opportunity in America; The 2012 midterm report of public higher education systems in the access to success initiative. *The Education Trust*, 1–23.

Graham, C. R. (2006). Blended learning systems: Definitions, current trends, and future directions. In Bonk, C. & Graham, C. (Eds.), *The handbook of blended learning: Global perspectives, local designs* (pp. 3–21). San Francisco: Pfeiffer.

Graham, C. R., Woodfield, W., & Harrison, J. B. (2013). A framework for institutional adoption and implementation of blended learning in higher education. *Internet and Higher Education*. doi:10.1016/j.iheduc.2012.09.003

Lee, J. R., Edwards, K., Menson, R., & Rawls, A. (2011). *The college completion agenda: 2011 progress report*. New York, NY: College Board Advocacy & Policy Center. Retrieved from http://advocacy.collegeboard.org/publications

Mayadas, F. A., & Picciano, A. G. (2007). Blended learning and localness: The means and the ends. *Journal of Asynchronous Learning Networks*, *11*(1), 3–7.

Means, B., Toyama, Y., Murphy, R., Bakia, M., & Jones, K. (2010). *Evaluation of evidence-based practices in online learning: A meta-analysis and review of online learning studies*. Washington, DC: U.S. Department of Education, Office of Planning, Evaluation, and Policy Development.

Moskal, P., Dziuban, C., & Hartman, J. (2013). Blended learning: A dangerous idea? *Internet and Higher Education*, *18*, 15–23.

Norberg, A., Dziuban, C., & Moskal, P. (2011). A time-based blended learning model. *On the Horizon*, *19*(3), 207–216.

Schneider, M., & Yin, M. L. (2012). *Completion matters: The high cost of low community college graduation rates*. Washington, DC: American Enterprise Institute for Public Policy Research. Retrieved from www.aei.org/outlook/education/higher-education/community-colleges/completion-matters-the-high-cost-of-community-college-graduation-rates/

Tavernise, S. (2012). Education gap grows between rich and poor, studies say. *The New York Times*. Retrieved from www.nytimes.com/2012/02/10/education/education-gap-grows-between-rich-and-poor-studies-show.html

4

INVESTIGATING INFORMAL BLENDING AT THE UNIVERSITY OF ILLINOIS SPRINGFIELD

William Bloemer and Karen Swan

According to Allen and Seaman's latest (2011) report, over 6.1 million or 31% of all higher education students took at least one online course during the Fall 2010 term. Data such as these have been used for several years as evidence of the growing importance of online learning, but they also point to another growing but somewhat invisible phenomenon: students mixing on-ground and online courses to complete post-secondary programs. This latter phenomenon, which we will call "*informal blending*," is largely unexplored. The purpose of this chapter is to describe the extent and consequences of informal blending at one institution, the University of Illinois Springfield, with the hope that these findings might suggest patterns in such data that are being replicated nationally.

Background

The University of Illinois Springfield (UIS) was founded in 1970 as Sangamon State University (SSU), an upper division and graduate commuter institution. SSU became UIS when it joined the University of Illinois system in 1995. UIS offered its first online courses in 1998 and the first fully online degree programs followed shortly thereafter. With the help of substantial funding from the Sloan Foundation, more than 10 programs were made available completely online in the next several years. By 2001, UIS had also begun to admit first-year students into the Capital Scholars program, a residential program for traditional-aged college students (native freshmen).

Today, UIS offers 23 undergraduate degree programs with 25 available minors, 20 master's degree programs and one doctoral degree. Just over 5,000 students are enrolled in these programs, with about 40% of the students enrolled in graduate programs. The Capital Scholars program has also been expanded, increasing the traditional age full-time residential population on campus. However, the upper division and graduate population (now a mix of online, commuting, and residential students) still comprise most institutional enrollments. Online programs have grown consistently for more than a decade and made up about 30% of the Fall 2012 headcount. While a formal definition of online students by majors (i.e., those students formally enrolled in online programs) has been adopted for purposes of e-tuition (see below), at UIS online programs are not the same thing as online classes. Indeed, many programs that cannot be taken completely online offer a considerable number of online classes, and the informal blending of on-ground and online courses by "on-ground" students as they assemble courses for their traditional degrees is an increasingly common event.

Online Courses at the University of Illinois Springfield

The University of Illinois Springfield (UIS) charges differential "e-tuition" to students enrolled in its fully online programs. While e-tuition is somewhat higher than in-state tuition, it does not include any out-of-state tuition differential. Online majors are also not charged most on-campus fees. Admission into UIS online programs involves a formal application and selection process. It has consistently been the case that about 40% of the online majors come from outside the state of Illinois. Only about 15% of in-state online majors reside in Sangamon County for which the institution was originally named, as the major population centers in Illinois are beyond commuting distance from UIS. Moreover, many online students, regardless of their location, have family and/ or work responsibilities that make traditional college attendance impossible. Thus, only about 10% of the students enrolled in online programs might have been expected to commute to UIS if the online enrollment option were not available. These students, like the original Sangamon State commuting students, tend to be mid-career adults with an average age near 35 at both the graduate and undergraduate level.

Online courses and programs have always been fully integrated into the existing campus departments, not housed in a separate administrative structure. Despite the obvious difference in delivery format, the degree requirements, and course requirements, staffing patterns and academic governance structure for online offerings are the same as they are for traditional, on-campus offerings. The development of online courses and programs at UIS is also firmly rooted in Sloan-C's five pillars of quality: learning effectiveness, institutional commitment, access, faculty satisfaction, and student satisfaction (Moore, 2002), making them high quality offerings. Although on-ground students must pay a small online course fee for online courses they take, many are opting to take some of their classes online. This chapter explores this phenomenon.

Blending On-Ground and Online Courses

There is a considerable literature including several books (e.g., Bonk & Graham, 2006; Garrison & Vaughan, 2008; Picciano & Dziuban, 2007) on the blending of face-to-face elements within courses, notwithstanding its quite recent emergence as an important means of instructional delivery. In spite of a perhaps longer history of blending on-ground and online courses within established programs,[1] there is little research beyond case studies of blending learning at the program level. To our knowledge, there has been no research on "informal blending" of traditional students' on-ground and online courses to satisfy course requirements, which is the subject of this chapter.

Graham and Robison (2007) distinguished three kinds of blended learning at the course level. *Enabling blends*, they argued, are blended learning formats whose purpose is to increase access to higher education or to make learning more convenient. Shea (2007) has opined that access is the problem to which blended learning is the solution. *Enhancing blends*, according to Graham and Robison, increase active learning. There is some evidence that suggests blended formats may support enhanced learning (Dziuban, Hartman, Moskal, Sorg, & Truman, 2004). Finally, Graham and Robison maintain that blended courses can be *transformative blends*, in which pedagogy is really altered and learning is improved. Garrison and Kanuka (2004) argue for just such a role for blended learning.

Although there is little research to confirm it, formal programs that blend on-ground and online courses would seem to fall into the category of *enhancing blends*, in that they tend to place courses that are primarily conceptual online, while offering courses that focus on skills in traditional face-to-face mode, thus taking advantage of the pedagogical affordances of each mode (Parker & Gemino, 2001). On the other hand, informal blending should probably be considered an *enabling blend* because traditional students must be choosing to take some courses online to improve their access to courses or degrees, at least at the present time. The research reported in this chapter, accordingly, used institutional data to explore issues of access among students informally blending on-ground and online courses at the University of Illinois Springfield. It asked the following research questions:

1. What is the extent of "informal blending" at the University of Illinois Springfield and how has it changed since 2005 when such data were first reported?
2. What are some of the consequences of informally blending on-ground and online courses at the University of Illinois Springfield that can be inferred from institutional data?

Methodology

Data analytics is the science of examining institutional datasets to extract useful information. It differs from experimental research in that it generally explores existing data from an entire population and is most often exploratory in nature (although confirmatory data analyses are often used to test existing hypotheses).

In 2004, the University of Illinois partnered with the Banner system to launch a comprehensive Enterprise Data system, spanning the large multi-campus system. While legacy information is not always easy to come by, information about student enrollment patterns since then are available through a common data warehouse (www.ds.uillinois.edu). These data were used in the analyses reported in this chapter. In most cases, that meant census snapshots taken on the tenth day of semesters and at the end of the terms.

Exploratory analyses and descriptive statistics were employed to answer the research questions. Data concerning all UIS students, both undergraduate and graduate, were used to distinguish among and compare students taking only on-ground courses, students taking only online courses, and students informally blending on-ground and online courses. In addition, the records of the subgroup comprising native UIS undergraduates were examined in greater detail.

Results

Informal Blending at the University of Illinois Springfield

Research question 1 asked about the extent of "informal blending," the practice in which traditional students mix online and on-ground courses to progress toward traditional degrees, at the University of Illinois Springfield. Our data show that more and more students at UIS are informally blending on-ground and online courses.

To begin with, online credit hour generation has increased steadily over the years. The pattern of that growth is shown in Figure 4.1. Note that the growth in online credits has mostly been great enough to offset the Fall to Spring decline that normally occurs in traditional course credits, with the 2008 break in the trend coinciding with a restructuring of general education requirements that produced a temporary shortage of online general education courses.

Although much of the growth in online credit hours is attributable to the growth in the number and size of online programs at UIS, not all of the online credit hours are taken by students enrolled in fully online programs. The increasing popularity of online courses among the on-campus student population is also a factor.

To explore this informal blending phenomenon, it is useful to classify students by their enrollment patterns rather than by their formal program

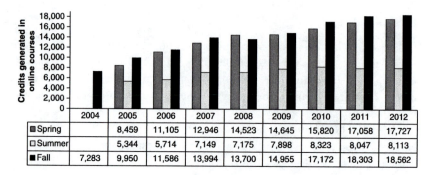

FIGURE 4.1   Growth in Online Credit Hours from Fall 2004 Through Fall 2012

classification. We distinguish three such patterns: students who took only online credits—*online only*; students who took only on-ground credits—*on-ground only*; and students who mixed on-ground and online credits during a single academic year. Students who are enrolled in online programs very rarely take on-ground courses because they then have to pay on-ground tuition and fees, rather than e-tuition. Those few cases in which credits were mixed in this manner were excluded from this study, so *mixed* credits in this context refers to just those instances in which on-ground students took both on-ground and online credits during one academic year, what we are calling *informal blending*.

Figures 4.2.1 through 4.2.3 show how enrollment patterns have changed at UIS. Figure 4.2.1 shows the percentages of credits generated by students with the three differing enrollment patterns for the 2004/05 academic year, the first year for which we have complete data. In the 2004/05 academic year, the majority of credits (56%) were taken by students taking only on-ground courses. Twenty-four percent of the credits came from students informally blending on-ground and online courses, while just 20% of the credits were taken by students taking only online courses, as online programs were in their early stages of development. The number of students taking courses only online was slightly larger than the number of online program majors, indicating that some "on-campus" students were taking only online courses that year.

Four years later, in the 2008/09 academic year, growth in both informal blending and students taking courses solely online resulted in the percentage of credits generated being evenly spread among enrollment patterns (Figure 4.2.2). In that year, 34% of the credits generated came from students taking only on-ground courses, 35% of the credits generated came from students taking only online courses, and 31% of the credits generated came from informal blending.

By the 2011–2012 academic year, the last full year for which data are available, the percentage of credits generated from students taking only online

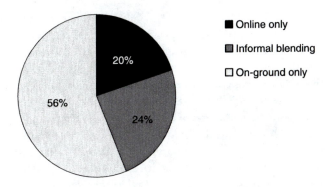

FIGURE 4.2.1 Percentage of Credits Generated from Students Taking Only Online, Only On-ground, or Both Online and On-ground Courses in the 2004/05 Academic Year

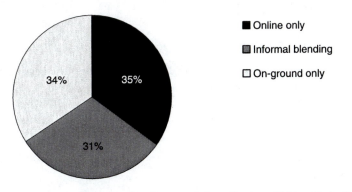

FIGURE 4.2.2 Percentage of Credits Generated from Students Taking Only Online, Only On-ground, or Both Online and On-ground Courses in the 2008/09 Academic Year

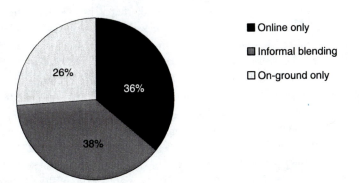

FIGURE 4.2.3 Percentage of Credits Generated from Students Taking Only Online, Only On-ground, or Both Online and On-ground Courses in the 2011/12 Academic Year

courses remained about the same at 36%, while the percentage of credits generated through informal blending had grown to 38%, and credits generated from students taking courses solely on-ground had shrunk to 24% (Figure 4.2.3).

The data indicate that enrollment patterns have changed quite radically at UIS, with credits generated from traditional (on-ground only) students today accounting for less than half the percentage of total credits they generated in 2004/05, and only about a quarter of the total credits generated in the 2011/2012 academic year. Although the decrease in credits from on-ground only students has been taken up by increased numbers of credits from both online only and informal blending students, the fact that there was little change in the percentage of credits from online only students, but a considerable increase in the percentage of credits generated through informal blending over the past three years, would seem to indicate that informal blending is being increasingly adopted by on-ground students. Indeed, it may be that informal blending is becoming the new normal, at least at UIS.

Consequences of Informal Blending at UIS

In any case, the fact that informal blending is accounting for increasing percentages of all credits taken at UIS must have consequences for the institution and for the students who are informally blending their courses. Research Question 2 asks about those consequences. In the sections that follow, we explore some of them.

Enrollment Management

An obvious consequence of the growth in informal blending is the problem it can cause for enrollment management and course scheduling. Adding online degree programs to a previously commuting/residential campus presents a significant enrollment management issue, in that it brings the obligation to provide online students with an adequate array of courses to complete their degrees in a timely manner. When a significant number of on-ground students also want to take online courses, the demand for online courses can quickly overwhelm the number of online courses offered.

One indication of this problem can be derived from demand reports, which compare the number of students who attempt to register for a course to the number that successfully enroll. Though not a perfect measure, the difference does give some indication of unmet need at the course level. Online courses consistently lead the list of courses with the greatest unmet need at UIS.

Another indication of unmet need can be found by examining the rate at which courses fill up. For that purpose, the cumulative number of course registrations can be plotted over time. Measured in terms of percent of final enrollment, the filling of online courses can be compared with that of on-ground courses on equal terms. From the institutional data, it appears that online courses do fill more rapidly than on-ground courses, but the effect is muted by the fact that many courses are restricted by major to limited groups of students. Using courses that are open to students from all majors removes that complication. Figure 4.3 shows the registration patterns for a typical fall semester (Fall 2007) for upper division general education courses, which are open to and required of majors in all baccalaureate programs. It shows time on the x axis in days before census (0), which occurs on the tenth day of classes. The difference in enrollment patterns between online and on-ground courses is pronounced. Only the fact that about half the seats in online courses are reserved for online majors prevents them from filling up shortly after registration begins in April or about 150 days before census. A factor contributing to the final bump in online enrollment is the addition of online sections in over-subscribed courses in response to demand.

In addition to the course registrations presented in Figure 4.3, it is informative to explore adds and drops of online courses before census for the same Fall semester and on the same scale. Figure 4.4 shows course registrations, course drops, and net enrollment (the difference between the two) as a function of time up to the census date. What is interesting here is that there is a pronounced increase not only in the number of adds, but also in the number of drops, during the first week of classes.

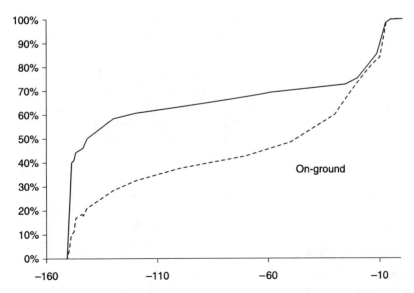

FIGURE 4.3 Relative Registration Patterns for Online and On-ground Upper Division General Education Courses

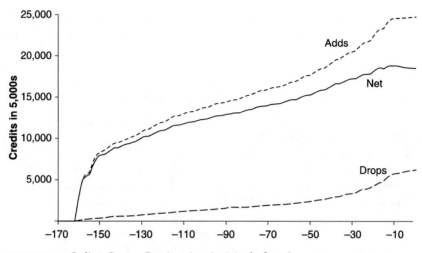

FIGURE 4.4 Online Course Registration Activity before Census

Looking at the student-level data, it becomes clear that the addition of sections of the most popular online courses does not always produce net new enrollments. Many students seem to drop one course so that they can add the one they really wanted in the first place. Indeed, there are even secondary waves of drop/adds as students fill the seats released by that process.

After the first week of classes, students must get the explicit approval of the instructor to enter a course, so the rate of new registrations slows down. Students are able, however, to drop courses. Beginning the second week of courses, the number of drops exceeds the number of new registrations and the net enrollment begins to decline. Anecdotal evidence suggests that some hoarding of online courses is occurring, as one might expect with a scarce resource. Students will register for more online courses than they intend to take in order to preserve their options, dropping one or two after they have had the chance to check things out. The resultant "churn" during the first two weeks of classes is surprising. A sort of "musical chairs" placement pattern cannot be a good thing at many levels.

Characteristics of Students Who "Informally Blend" Classes

There are several differences in the behaviors of students who informally blend online and on-ground courses when they are compared with the behaviors of students who exhibit the other two enrollment patterns—fully on-ground and fully online—which would seem to have consequences, or at least implications, for both the students themselves and the institutions they attend (UIS). These include average course load, course persistence rates, and commuting distances.

Average Course Loads

A casual calculation of the average course loads taken by students in the three enrollment pattern groups reveals that students who informally blend courses generally take higher course loads than either students taking only on-ground or only online courses. However, an accurate comparison requires a more careful look. Students who fall into the mixed category must be taking at least two courses by definition, while there are a significant number of students in both the completely online and completely on-ground categories taking only one course. Thus, the low course loads among students who could not possibly be informally blending is artificially lowering the average course loads in these two groups. For that reason, load comparisons need to include only those students who are taking at least two courses.

Table 4.1 shows the average course loads for students taking two or more courses per semester broken out by academic level and enrollment patterns. The average load for students informally blending courses is higher than that for the on-ground only students, providing evidence that some traditional students are taking online courses to pick up additional courses. This effect is most pronounced at the graduate level, where the average course load is more than one credit hour higher for the mixed students. The lower values for the average course loads among online only students simply reflects the fact that the majority of these students are online majors who are usually not full-time students.

The data on undergraduate course loads in Table 4.1 deserve further exploration as they combine information from two very different populations—native and transfer students—into single averages. Native freshmen at UIS are admitted into the Capital Scholars program. They are traditionally aged full-time students, living almost exclusively on campus. While some transfer students live on campus, the majority do not, and they tend to be older and are more likely to be attending UIS part-time.

Table 4.2 compares the average course loads between native and transfer students taking two or more courses by enrollment patterns. It also shows the percentages of each population in the different enrollment categories. Online

TABLE 4.1 Average Course Load in Credit Hours per Semester by Enrollment Patterns and Academic Level for Students Taking Two or More Courses per Semester, Fall 2005 through Spring 2012

	Undergraduate	Graduate
On-ground only	12.8	10.0
Informal blending	13.1	11.1
Online only	9.9	8.7

TABLE 4.2 Comparison of Average Course Loads in Credit Hours per Semester by Enrollment Patterns Between Native and Transfer Students Taking Two or More Courses per Semester, Fall 2005 through Spring 2012

	Native students		Transfer students	
	Average credit hours	Percent of total	Average credit hours	Percent of total
On-ground only	14.6	74.7	11.8	56.0
Informal blending	14.9	24.2	12.6	36.8
Online only	11.5	1.1	9.8	7.2

majors have been removed from both informal blending populations because few online majors blend on-ground courses into their course loads. Thus, while the percentages of students in the online category patterns may seem small, indeed they are small in the native student population, it is important to note that these are on-ground students (as classified by their majors) taking only online courses.

In fact, most native students (74.7%) at UIS take only on-ground courses, and as they are typically enrolled full-time, there is only a slight increase in average course loads resulting from informal blending. In comparison, the data for the transfer students are more like those of graduate students (Table 4.1). Although over half of the transfer students (56%) at UIS only take on-ground courses, transfer students who informally blend their classes have a greater average course load. These data suggest that informal blending is a strategy transfer students use to increase their average course loads by almost a full credit each semester, and so lower their time to degree.

Commuting Distances

Whether or not the inclusion of online courses allows students to commute greater distances to campus for their degrees is also a question that deserves investigation. What might seem to be a simple analysis is complicated by data quality issues in this case. The fundamental problem is that the address information available is self-reported by students. There is great variability, accordingly, in its quality and currency. Typos and shuffled address fields plague the street level data, so city level data were used for student addresses. Local address information is not always promptly recorded, so tenth day and end of term census snapshots are not reliable sources. Students who report a local or on-campus address at any point in the semester were considered to be living on campus throughout the semester. Commonly available databases were used to estimate commuting distances from students' cities to the UIS campus, which is located about six miles south and slightly east of Springfield, IL. Even with the exclusion of out-of-state addresses, shortcomings in the address data produce apparent commutes that are quite unlikely because of their excessive distance. The longer the apparent commute, the more likely it is that the student has a local address that has not been recorded. So, if the analysis is restricted to addresses within 20 miles of campus, the likelihood of such errors is small. Table 4.3 shows that the average commute for the students informally blending is slightly greater than the average commute for the on-ground online students. Table 4.3 also shows the results of increasing the apparent commuting distances included in the analysis. Though it is not possible to tell exactly where the line should be drawn to exclude the erroneously classified commuters, it is clear that the students informally blending are commuting from larger distances, no matter where that line is drawn.

The average commute for online only students is, of course, an oxymoron, as those students don't really commute to campus. As expected, the average distance from campus for these students was much greater than that for commuting students. This finding suggests that informal blending makes attending college possible for some students who might not have been able to attend UIS when all courses were offered in a traditional format.

Course Withdrawal Rates

Course persistence rate can be defined as the percentage of students enrolled at census who were still enrolled in a course at the end of the semester. Although persistence in online courses is slightly lower than persistence in on-ground courses at UIS, persistence rates are very high, well over 90%, for both.

TABLE 4.3 Average Distance from Campus by Enrollment Pattern for Non-residential Students

Maximum distance from UIS	Enrollment patterns		
	On-ground only	Informal blending	Online only
20	7.33	8.12	8.98
40	12.64	13.65	17.81
60	14.30	15.53	22.59
80	17.92	21.72	43.35
100	19.09	24.36	53.29
120	19.40	24.65	56.81
140	19.62	24.93	58.73
160	20.13	25.34	66.92
180	21.50	26.44	80.51
200	23.27	28.43	95.87
in IL, >200	23.83	29.30	105.49

Persistence rates are so high, in fact, that they tend to obscure differences related to enrollment patterns. Thus it can be more useful to explore differences in withdrawal rates, the percentages of students who withdraw from courses after census, among students with differing enrollment patterns.

Figure 4.5 compares course withdrawal rates between three groups of students: online majors taking online courses; on-ground majors taking on-ground courses; and on-ground majors taking online courses. As previously mentioned, it is highly unusual for online majors to take on-ground courses. Figure 4.5 shows that the withdrawal rates are, as might be expected, higher for students taking online courses than they are for students taking on-ground courses. If there is any surprise here, it is that on-ground majors have higher withdrawal rates from online courses than do their classmates who are online majors. This finding indicates that informal blending may place students at greater risk for withdrawing from a course than either online only or on-ground only enrollment patters. While this is a simple descriptive presentation, this factor has been tested in predictive models, which include many other factors, and remains a variable with significant effect size (Bloemer & Swan, August, 2012).

There are several possible explanations for informal blending placing students at greater risk for withdrawal from courses. To begin with, not all on-ground majors who opt for online courses may do so for good reasons. Misperceptions about online courses and misunderstandings of their difficulty abound. It also is probably the case that on-ground majors are, on occasion, forced into online courses, actually or effectively, and that some of these students may have trouble adjusting to the online format. Indeed, it is often the

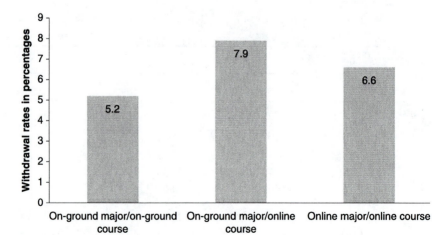

FIGURE 4.5 Comparison of Course Withdrawal Rates by Student Major and Course Delivery Mode

case that when online and on-ground sections of the same course are offered in a given semester, the on-ground section will struggle for enrollment, while the online section accumulates a waiting list. In some such instances, an on-ground section is converted to an online format near the start of classes, greatly frustrating those students who not only prefer, but who perhaps are better suited to, more traditional delivery modes. The frustration is more than a matter of speculation, it is something that some students voice with passion.

The fact is that many of the smaller programs at UIS have benefitted greatly from the infusion of a relatively large number of online majors who bring substantially greater resources including more available faculty to these programs. The availability of more faculty means more extensive and diverse course offerings, but unfortunately, students have no way of knowing that the course they would prefer to take on campus could not have existed at all without the online program. Cancellation of the low enrollment courses is inevitable, whether or not a corresponding online section is added. Managing enrollment options in such situations is important for purposes of retention as well as student satisfaction. Preserving sufficient seats for online majors who have no other enrollment options while providing preferred delivery options to on-ground students is one of the major complications of adding substantial online offerings to a residential campus in an integrated way.

Online Courses and the Native Student Population

The Capital Scholars students (residential, full-time, traditionally aged undergraduates who began at UIS as freshmen) were certainly not the intended audience for UIS online courses, and would presumably be the population least affected by them. At the surface level, this is true. Freshmen in the Capital Scholars program rarely take online courses. Capital Scholars' enrollment in online courses gradually increases, however, through their sophomore and junior years until informal blending among students in this population is comparable to that of the transfer student population by the time they are seniors. Indeed, a closer look at a 3-year sample of graduates of the Capital Scholars program reveals some interesting findings with regard to access, degree completion, and time to degree, even among this most traditional population.

About 10% of the Capital Scholars graduates actually finished early, completing their degrees in less than the full 4 years. Enrollment in summer online courses was clearly a contributing factor for these students, as shown in Figure 4.6. About 25% of the Capital Scholars graduates completed more than 8 credit hours (two courses) online during summer semesters while enrolled at UIS. Slightly more than 18 percent of those students graduated early. Among the 75% of the students who took less than 8 credit hours online during summer semesters, only 7.4% graduated early.

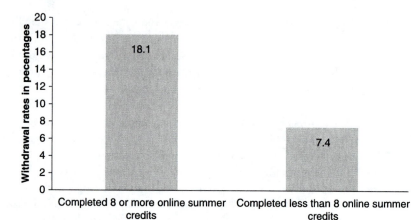

FIGURE 4.6 Percentage of Capital Scholars Who Graduated Early Among Students Who Took Eight or More Online Credits vs. Students Who Didn't

Indeed, except for individualized studies, the prospects for accumulating credits during summer terms on campus are limited for the Capital Scholars as residence halls are closed for the summer, and residential students return home, which is in most cases quite far away. Moreover, the majority of summer courses offered at UIS (about 75%) have been offered only online for some time. Accumulating online credits thus becomes the only realistic option for the Capital Scholars in the summer months. Indeed, the data suggest that about one fourth of them will take at least a couple of courses that way while at UIS and that doing so will increase the likelihood that they will graduate early by a factor of about 2.5.

The number of Capital Scholars graduates is small enough that examination of individual cases is possible. Such a review reveals patterns of access and retention made possible through informal blending. Although the Capital Scholars program is primarily residential, it is not exclusively so. There are some students who complete the program without ever having had a residential campus address. These students often come from the small towns surrounding Springfield, thus it seems likely that cost was a factor in their decision to live at home. These commuting Capital Scholars tend to take many more online courses than average for their population during regular fall and spring semesters, which would reduce commuting costs while giving them greater access to courses.

There are also some native students who evidently have left campus at some point during their studies. Some of these students appear to have returned home for a semester or longer, for reasons unknown to the student information system, before returning to finish their studies. These students, who ultimately graduate, commonly continue to accumulate credits online while they are at home, although often on a part-time basis. There are similarly students who complete the final courses for their degree online after a largely residential experience. Address information indicates that they have returned home or in some cases have left the state in their last term. It is clear in the records of these individual students, that online courses can be an important part of even a residential program such as the Capital Scholars in providing access to regional students who seek to minimize costs for room and board, and in increasing graduation rates among students who must leave the local area at some point during their studies.

Conclusions and Discussion

The informal blending of on-ground and online courses by students at the University of Illinois Springfield has dramatically increased over the 8 years for which data are available. In the 2004/05 academic year, students informally blending on-ground and online courses represented 24% of the credits generated at the University of Illinois Springfield, while credits generated from students taking solely on-ground courses accounted for 56% of the credits. By the 2011/12 academic year, students informally blending courses accounted for 38% of the total credits taken while students taking only on-ground courses accounted for only 26% of the credits taken. The data show that the number of credits generated by students taking only on-ground classes has shrunk to less than half of what it was 8 years ago, and that this enrollment pattern accounts for the fewest number of credits generated today. The number of students informally blending on-ground and online courses, on the other hand, continues to grow and today accounts for the greatest number of credits generated. Future research should follow this trend and qualitatively investigate why students are making such choices, both at UIS and nationally.

Our sense is that informal blending will continue to grow in importance at UIS and that it most likely will continue to grow nationally, whether or not students' home institutions offer online courses, as students search out the courses they need to accelerate and/or complete their programs (Bahr, 2009; Bloemer & Swan, 2012; McCormick, 2003). Thus, it only makes sense to explore the implications it holds both for students and for institutions.

Informal blending, at least at UIS, seems to be of the enabling type. Our data suggest that on-ground students take online classes to enhance their progression to degree in two ways. First, informally blending on-ground and online courses enables students to take higher course loads and so progress more quickly to degree. We found that students who informally blended courses generally had higher course loads than students who took only on-ground courses. We also found that Capital Scholars who took eight or more credits online during summer semesters were two and a half times more likely to graduate early. Second, residential data suggest that informal blending enables students to stay enrolled when they move away from campus for whatever reason and to maintain traditional enrollment levels when they commute from some distance. These findings clearly deserve further investigation.

However, informal blending does seem to have its downside for students. Our data show that on-ground students who enroll in online courses are more likely to withdraw from these courses than either fully online students or fully on-ground students. These results should be investigated further, both to understand why these students are dropping out of online courses, and to explore strategies for ameliorating such problems.

Informal blending seems to similarly be both a benefit and a challenge for institutions. As noted above, informal blending increases retention and reduces UIS students' time to degree by allowing students to take higher course loads and to stay enrolled through breaks in their residencies. It also extends our local reach by enabling students to attend full time from greater distances. At the same time, informal blending presents us with problems including the greater risk for withdrawal among on-ground students taking online courses, and enrollment management challenges. In particular, the demand for online courses created by informal blending, and the resultant "churning" during the first 2 weeks of classes as students drop and add courses, create major scheduling problems. Future research should examine possible solutions to this problem.

For the present, there do seem to be several things institutions can do to better manage informal blending. The first, of course, is to recognize its existence. Once recognized, the potential of informally blending classes can be put to better use in recruitment and marketing. The recognition of informal blending can also inform smarter scheduling as long as such scheduling is firmly grounded in the local culture and mission. Finally, particular institutional attention should be paid to students who blend courses. It is important to make sure they are oriented to online classes, and that they understand the affordances and constraints of both online and on-ground delivery so that they can make better choices.

The findings reported in this chapter are obviously limited to the University of Illinois Springfield. We believe that informal blending is probably occurring at institutions across the country but research is needed to test that assumption. A more important limitation comes from the use of institutional data, which constrains analyses to detailing what is happening. Explanations of why informal blending is growing, and, perhaps more importantly, how its benefits can be maximized and its challenges ameliorated is a matter of speculation. Qualitative studies that explore the whys and hows of informal blending are thus clearly needed.

Note

1 For example: Waldorf University, www.waldorf.edu/Online/Home; Rocky Mountain College of Art and Design www.rmcad.edu/hybrid-program; Michigan State

University, http://edutech.msu.edu/programs/doctoral/; Virginia Commonwealth University School of Nursing, http://www.nursing.vcu.edu/education/phd/index. html.

References

Allen, I. A., & Seaman, J. (2011). *Going the distance: Online education in the United States, 2011.* Newton, MA: Babson Survey Research Group.

Bahr, P. R. (2009). College hopping: Exploring the occurrence. Frequency, and consequences of lateral transfer. *Community College Review, 36*(4), 271–298.

Bloemer, W., & Swan, K. (August, 2012). Predicting student retention and success in online courses. Presentation given at the Conference on Distance Teaching and Learning, Madison, WI.

Bonk, C. J., & Graham, C. R. (2006). *The handbook of blended learning: Global perspectives, local designs.* Hoboken, NJ: John Wiley & Sons, Inc.

Dziuban, C., Hartman, J., Moskal, P., Sorg, S., & Truman, B. (2004). Three ALN modalities: An institutional perspective. In J. Bourne & J. C. Moore (Eds.), *Elements of quality online education: Into the mainstream.* Needham, MA: Sloan-C, 127–148.

Garrison, D. R., & Kanuka, H. (2004). Blended learning: Uncovering its transformative potential in higher education. *The Internet and Higher Education, 7*(2), 95–105.

Garrison, D. R., & Vaughan, N. D. (2008). *Blended learning in higher education: Framework, principles, and guidelines.* San Francisco: Jossey-Bass.

Graham, C., & Robison, R. (2007). Realizing the transformational potential of blended learning. In A. G. Picciano & C. D. Dziuban (Eds.) *Blended learning: Research perspectives.* Needham, MA: Sloan-C, 83–110.

McCormick, A. C. (2003). Swirling and double-dipping: New patterns of student attendance and their implications for higher education. *New Directions for Higher Education, 121,* 13–24.

Moore, J. (2002). *Elements of quality: The Sloan-C Framework.* Needham, MA: The Sloan Consortium.

Parker, D., & Gemino, A. (2001). Inside online learning: Comparing conceptual and technique learning performance in place-based and ALN formats. *Journal of Asynchronous Learning Networks, 5*(2), 64–74.

Picciano, A. G., & Dziuban, C. D. (Eds.) (2007). *Blended learning: Research perspectives.* Needham, MA: Sloan-C, 83–110.

Shea, P. (2007). Towards a conceptual framework for learning in blended environments. In A. G. Picciano & C. D. Dziuban (Eds.) *Blended learning: Research perspectives.* Needham, MA: Sloan-C, 19–36.

SECTION II
Evaluation

5

SCOPE-ING OUT INTERACTIONS IN BLENDED ENVIRONMENTS

Susan J. Wegmann and Kelvin Thompson

Introduction

Student engagement is an important aspect of the teaching–learning craft (Chen, Gonyea, & Kuh, 2008; Dewey, 1933; Gasiewski, Eagan, Garcia, Hurtado, & Chang, 2012; Gee, 1986; Hall, 2010). By *student engagement* we mean the passion and excellence of participation in classroom activities, as seen in such things as students' abilities to contribute to synchronous (i.e., face-to-face) and asynchronous (i.e., online) discussions with a willingness to build on one another's contributions. Instructors support or constrain discussions, by providing rubrics and evaluations. Instructors also measure student engagement by their participation in course work, as well as course discourse (Engle & Conant, 2002; Herrenkohl, & Guerra, 1998). Discourse analysis, which analyzes "language-in-use," or the language of the classroom, measures the level of students' engagement.

Statement of the Problem

In fully online classes, students may lack opportunities to interact, collaborate, and receive feedback and social support, which may lead to less engagement in the course (Tuckman, 2007). In fully face-to-face classes, students may find it difficult to gain the floor during a discussion or to raise questions, challenge the majority thinking, or initiate a new topic of discussion (Cazden, 1988). The blended environment (one in which students participate and receive instruction both online and face-to-face) offers the best of both worlds: rich opportunities for learning in a convenient online setting as well as face-to-face interactions with peers and instructors (Dziuban,

Hartman, & Moskal, 2004; Garrison & Vaughan, 2008). While the potential for ideal learning exists, a daunting concern remains: how do instructors monitor and enhance students' engagement in both settings, while sustaining a viable blended course?

This chapter will not be an exhaustive study of all possible ways to analyze the health and sustainability of interactions in the blended environment. It will, however, offer a synthesis of pertinent literature around the topic in order to inform blended instructors about ways to enhance interactions in their courses. This chapter will propose techniques to collect and analyze data from blended courses and will offer suggestions to improve teaching efficacy by improving interactions. We will also submit a framework to analyze interactions as an additional tool to aid in the analysis and conduct of engaging classroom activities both online and face-to-face. Throughout this chapter, we will refer to SCOPe as one framework for collecting and analyzing interaction data in a blended course. We will also offer rubrics, checklists, and data analysis techniques based on SCOPe interactions.

Literature Review

Importance of Interaction in the Teaching/Learning Act

Research has shown that social discourse and peer or instructor interactions can enhance learning. In other words, students will learn better when given opportunities to participate in social interactions (Garrison & Innes-Cleveland, 2005; Vygotsky, 1978; Wells, 1999). Distance educators have defined four types of interactions: (1) learner-teacher; (2) learner-content; (3) learner-learner; and (4) learner-interface (Hillman, Willis, & Gunawardena, 1994). Building on this, Thompson and Wegmann (2012a) posit that in blended courses, students interact with their own thinking (i.e., Self), the information in the course (i.e., Content), their peers (i.e., Others), and the way that the content is delivered (i.e., Platform). We developed the acronym SCOPe (Self, Content, Others, and the Platform) as one way to organize these types of interactions into measurable, observable parts. This chapter will describe ways to conduct a SCOPe analysis in subsequent pages.

Not all researchers agree that "more" interaction is necessarily "better" (Garrison & Innes-Cleveland, 2005), but most agree that deeper levels of interactions in face-to-face and online courses encourage a more optimum state of engagement and participation (Haythornthwaite, Kazmer, Robbins, & Shoemaker, 2000; Hull & Saxon, 2009; Imm & Stylianou, 2012; Juwah, 2009; Pena-Shaff, Altman, Stephenson, 2005; Picciano, 2002; Wagner, 2005).

Face-to-Face Interactions

Researchers have long agreed that face-to-face classroom discourse can reveal information about student engagement (Cazden, 1988; Dillon, 1994; Gee, 1986; Hawkes, 2010; Herrenkohl & Guerra, 1998; Mehan, 1979; Wilkinson, 1982). Using language to learn by interacting is a widely agreed upon notion among theorists and researchers (i.e., Dewey, 1933; Vygotsky, 1978). Interactions are measured by discourse analysis, which can make some of these dialogic processes visible by analyzing the language-in-use of classrooms.

Mehan (1979), Cazden (1988), and Wells (1993), among other researchers, conducted extensive analysis of face-to-face classrooms to reveal a prevailing IRE, or Initiate, Respond, and Evaluate, pattern. Teachers typically initiated questions or comments, students responded within a bounded parameter, and teachers evaluated students' responses. They found that the IRE pattern narrowed teachers' and students' possible ways of interacting, since they were limited to only three distinct moves, or functions and ways to use their language. More recently, researchers report that face-to-face classroom interactions continue to replicate this IRE pattern (Hall, 2010; Hawkes, 2010; Imm & Stylianou, 2012; Waring, 2009).

Measuring Face-to-Face Classroom Interactions

Discourse analysis techniques interpret oral speech by suggesting codes and moves, or meanings, behind what speakers might be doing with their language. This process offers suggestions for "What is going on here?" which is the primary research question asked by Stake (1985) and other qualitative research experts. Discourse analysis provides a picture of the kinds of things participants are using their language for, which allows instructors to make critical decisions about how to proceed in order to further students' learning.

For our purposes, this chapter will analyze the "content" of language-in-use, similar to Gee's notions of themes or issues (2003), and the content of language being used. Discourse analysis techniques can take on numerous forms (see Figure 5.1), but most follow the same basic pattern (Gee, 1986, 2003).

Figure 5.1 portrays the most typical way to conduct oral discourse analysis. After completing step 9, the answer to the specific research question should begin to crystalize and the researcher can begin to make sense of the discussion at hand. It is important to note, however, that discourse analysis of oral speech is, at best, a guess at underlying meanings (Cazden, 1988; Gee, 2003; Stake, 1985). However, identifying the moves of a particular dialogic chain (Bakhtin, 1986) can help the researcher infer what is going on (Stake, 1985). See Appendix B for an example of a transcript analyzed in this fashion, using the moves from Appendix A.

1. Clearly define the research question and the population of students to be studied.
2. Audio-record a targeted class's oral discussion.
3. Transcribe student text into two-columned chart (4≤for first column, 2≤for second column) with students' words of the left column and the right column blank.
4. Code student text fragments using "moves," or how students are using their language (you may use the moves listed in Appendix A and Figure 5.4 to add to or modify for your own purposes). After a list of moves is created, they may be collapsed together or divided into several different categories.
5. Repeat with additional rater(s), if possible. Check for inter-rater reliability.
6. Tabulate the kinds of moves that students used, keeping in mind the specific research question.
7. Revisit/remember the research question.
8. Make note of patterns among and between students. The quantity, quality, and types of moves that are used the most frequently are analyzed according to the research question.
9. Compare results of the analysis with the research question.

FIGURE 5.1   Process to Conduct Discourse Analysis with Face-to-Face Discussions

Online Interactions

Similar to face-to-face classrooms, online classrooms and student successes are enhanced by strong student engagement and participation (Anderson, 2003; Arbaugh & Benbunan-Fich, 2007; Juwah, 2009; Jain, Jain, & Cochenour, 2009; Shovein, Huston, Fox, & Damazo, 2005; Tutty & Klein, 2008). Wagner (2005) posits that the degree of interactivity will positively affect the perceived quality of a learning experience. In fact, interactions are such an important part of online courses that researchers have suggested that they need to be an intentional part of the instructional design (Ng, Cheung, & Hew, 2012; Smith, 2005; Wegmann & McCauley, 2007; Zhang, Perris, & Yeung, 2005). Added to this, instructors need to provide "multiple means of communication to support the need to engage in work and social interaction, both publicly and privately" (Haythornthwaite, Kazmer, Robbins, & Shoemaker, 2000, p. 3).

Interactions in online settings vary according to the platform, purpose, and instructor emphases. In fact, Chen, Gonyea, and Kuh (2008) posit that "the online environment provides students more opportunities to be involved in active learning as individuals, but limits students' ability to collaborate with each other" ("Results," para. 4). To counter this limitation, instructors can design opportunities for interaction. We offer here a continuum of student engagement that clarifies possible influences on one's design of learning activities and, thus, student interaction. The following Interaction Continuum (see Figure 5.2) is modified from Wilson (1996) and Barr and Tagg (1995, cited in Hartman, Dziuban, & Brophy-Ellison, 2007):

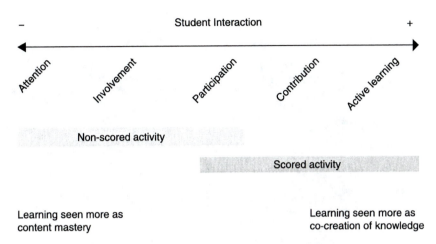

FIGURE 5.2   Interaction Continuum: A Range of Student Engagement

Some online courses offer very little opportunity for students to interact with one another, preferring instead a heavy interaction with content. Learning is mastery of the content, with evidence of test scores and assignment completion. These kinds of courses would appear to the left on the Interaction Continuum in Figure 5.2. On the other hand, some instructors value student-to-student interaction as part of the learning process and co-creation of knowledge. These types of courses tend to emphasize discussion board entries and interactions with peers, instructors, and the public and they would appear nearer to the right of the Interaction Continuum in Figure 5.2. Also appearing to the right of the continuum is a Connected Stance (Wegmann & McCauley, 2007, 2010), or the nexus of a high level of engagement and a high level of participation (see Figure 5.3).

Wegmann and McCauley (2007, 2010) found that online interactions enhanced content engagement, when the instructor organized graded interactions to encourage students to engage in deep thinking, even though Knowlton (2005) argued that grading students' discussion posts would impede students from freely reflecting on others' contributions. (See Appendix A for a list of the moves found in Wegmann & McCauley's 2007, 2010 studies with explanations.)

The moves in Figure 5.4 revealed what students were doing with their language on discussion posts and blogs, which was much more than simply giving information. Higher performing students (according to grade point averages at the end of the courses) were found to engage in a Connected Stance more often than lower performing students (Wegmann & McCauley, 2007). Also, instructor intervention and facilitation was found to prompt more students to assume a Connected Stance. A higher performer in a subsequent study

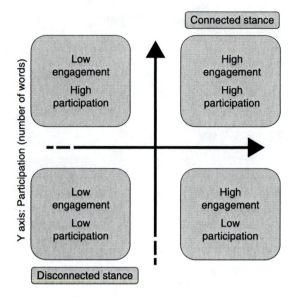

FIGURE 5.3   Connected Stance Quadrant

1. Introducing a new topic
2. Sharing opinion/sharing beliefs
3. Connecting to other readings
4. Connecting to own experiences
5. Connecting to their own classrooms
6. Connecting to their own thinking
7. Building rapport
8. Suggesting organizational theme
9. Revealing their own struggles
10. Responding to a peer's question
11. Giving information
12. Giving advice
13. Connecting to a previous thought
14. Questioning (or wondering)
15. Giving an example
16. Sharing a 'Grand idea'
17. Challenging a peer
18. Connecting to course content
19. Using humor

FIGURE 5.4   Nineteen Moves Found in an Online Asynchronous Discourse Analysis

(Thompson & Wegmann, 2011) had higher levels of participation and engagement on her blog; whereas a lower performer had lower levels of participation and engagement. A Connected Stance was visible among the higher performers in this project.

Most researchers agree that participant engagement and social presence are crucial aspects of effective online interactions (Hull & Saxon, 2009; Nippard & Murphy, 2007; Picciano, 2002; Pawan, Paulus, Yalcin, & Chang, 2003). Social presence is the extent to which learners feel a close proximity to instructors, peers, and content in an online setting (Moore, 1991; Short, Williams, & Christie, 1976; Russo & Benson, 2005; Stein, Wanstreet, Calvin, Overtoom, & Wheaton, 2005). In fact, Pena-Shaff et al. (2005) found that students who interacted more in online classes tended to feel a greater amount of satisfaction and even engage more deeply in course content. They found that students participating in consistent online discussions with the same people built a considerable amount of social presence through their discussions. To reach the goal of deeper learning, social presence plays a supporting role, aided by course design and facilitation (i.e., teaching presence) In fact students' reflective discourse leads most directly to learning (Garrison & Innes-Cleveland, 2005). Therefore, rich, engaging online interactions appearing in courses on either end of the Interaction Continuum can show that students are using language for multiple purposes and that they feel a measure of social presence, which, taken together, will increase their sense of engagement and learning.

Measuring Online Asynchronous Interactions

Knowing where courses fall on the Interaction Continuum is an important first step. However, discourse analysis techniques can act as a basis for analyzing online discussion boards, which will inform instructors about how to take the next step and modify course structures. Shea (2007) posits that "such analysis allows us to understand underlying processes and meanings inherent in online communication and to adjust the design of instruction based on findings" (p. 27)

In 2010, Weltzer-Ward conducted an exhaustive literature review of content analysis patterns for online asynchronous discussions. She found that researchers used 56 different coding schemes in the 136 research papers she analyzed. However, the context of each research study was different, making Weltzer-Ward's attempt to provide consistency across studies a difficult task. Even though researchers use numerous coding schemes, the general method of discourse analysis using online discussion boards is similar. Researchers collect students' words, assign moves, and then analyze them for content. Figure 5.5 details this process.

Figure 5.5 appears in a linear form, but this process is recursive, including revisiting the research question multiple times in order to stay focused during analysis.

1. Clearly define the research question and the population of students to be studied.
2. Compile written discussion posts from all students.
3. Paste text into two columned chart (4" for first column, 2" for second column) with students' words on the left column and the right column blank.
4. Code student text fragments using "moves," or how students are using their language (You may use the moves listed in Appendix A and add to or modify for your own purposes).
5. Repeat with additional rater(s), if possible. Check for inter-rater reliability.
6. Tabulate the kinds of moves that students used, keeping in mind the specific research question.
7. Revisit/remember the research question.
8. Make note of patterns among and between students.
9. Compare results of the analysis with the research question.

FIGURE 5.5   Process to Conduct Discourse Analysis on Asynchronous Discussion Board Posts

Composite Data Analysis of Online Interactions

Four past discourse analysis studies using the Connected Stance methodology (Wegmann & McCauley, 2007, 2010; Thompson & Wegmann, 2011, 2012b) have each resulted in the plotting of three purposively sampled students on a quadrant graph such as that shown in Figure 5.6. The quadrants are bounded by the intersections of the highest sampled word count, highest sampled move count, and the midpoints of these two ranges. While specific discourse samples vary in word/move count depending upon course context, the relative boundaries of the quadrants remain fixed.

Compositing the graph plots of each study's sampled students illustrates the relationship between student performance and student engagement/ interaction. This is shown in Figure 5.7 on p. 82. For instance, higher performing students appear consistently in the upper right ("Connected Stance") quadrant. However, one might suggest that such classifications are arbitrary. To address this concern, a simple hypothesis test was conducted on the composited data from these four studies.

The null hypothesis was stated as: *Higher student performance is unrelated to higher student participation and higher student engagement (as operationalized in word count and variety of moves in discourse contributions).*

Given the small numbers of students, classifications were pooled to arrive at one nominal variable with two values: "Connected Stance" and "non-Connected Stance." An exact binomial test, appropriate for non-parametric hypothesis testing with dichotomously classified data, was conducted. The resulting p value (0.003173828, $p < .05$) indicates the probability of obtaining the results plotted in the composited graph if the null hypothesis is true. Thus,

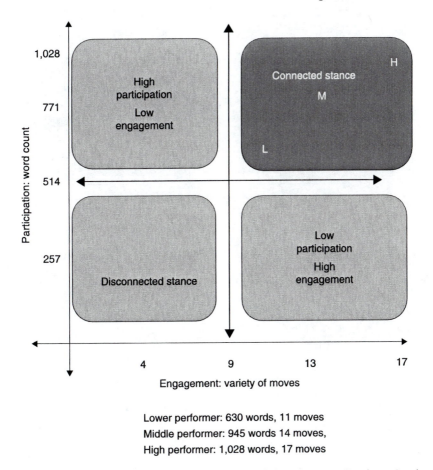

Lower performer: 630 words, 11 moves
Middle performer: 945 words 14 moves,
High performer: 1,028 words, 17 moves

FIGURE 5.6 Example Plotting of Purposively Sampled Students on Quadrant Graph

the null hypothesis is rejected. The evidence suggests that higher student performance is related to higher levels of student participation and engagement.

Collecting and Analyzing Data from Interactions in Blended Courses

Analyzing face-to-face and online interactions involve different, but related actions. Both ask the researcher to consider what the student was doing with their language-in-use, both give students credit for their own creation of knowledge, and both assume that students use language as a learning tool. However, analyzing synchronous face-to-face interactions requires that researchers convert oral speech into transcripts in order to analyze. This labor-intensive process is often the reason why researchers choose to conduct other

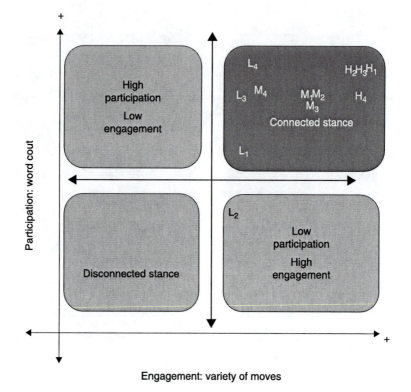

FIGURE 5.7 Composited Data Graph from Four Connected Stance Studies

types of interaction analyses when investigating oral language. Online interaction analysis often relies on discussion boards for capturing language, but they do not represent synchronous language interactions. With the advent of blended learning settings, a new kind of interaction analysis problem is emerging; one in which researchers analyze language-in-use in both face-to-face and online platforms as a cohesive whole.

"There are many forms of blended learning but a generally accepted taxonomy does not exist" (Picciano, 2009, p. 8). However, Garrison and Vaughan (2008) propose that face-to-face and online learning are "made better by the presence of the other" (p. 5), and that blended learning is composed of the best of what we know about both kinds of teaching. In other words, they assert that blended learning is not simply a combination of face-to-face plus online activities. Rather, they agree with Bonk, Kim, and Zeng (2006) and invite instructors to reflect on best practices in both, in order to create a new kind of structure for learning. For purposes of this literature review, we define blended learning as a combination of online and face-to-face course structure in which learners integrate, synthesize, and enlarge their knowledge base by interacting with content, self, others, and the platform with substantive content/ interaction offered both face-to-face and online.

In blended settings, students reported a higher level of satisfaction and inter-action (Dziuban et al., 2004; Waddoups & Howell, 2002; US Department of Education, 2009; Wingard, 2004), and more critical thinking (De George-Walker & Keeffe, 2010; Guiller, Durndell & Ross, 2007; Zhao, Lei, Yan, Lai, & Tan, 2005). Numerous researchers found benefits of both online and face-to-face discussions, suggesting that a blended approach may be the best option (Graham & Robison, 2007; Luppicini, 2007; Starenko, Vignare, & Humbert, 2007). However, some say that blended learning practice may have outpaced blended learning research (Jones, 2006). So, if interaction and engagement are important parts of face-to-face and online courses, what about detecting and analyzing interaction and engagement in a blended course? How might instruc-tors measure interactions while keeping up with the demands of the course?

Framework for Analysis of Blended Learning Interactions

Discourse analysis techniques, such as the ones described above, offer a way to measure the depth of interactions in face-to-face and online environments. When these environments are blended, discourse analysis techniques may still be used. However, these kinds of techniques are often time-consuming and unwieldy to use. Most blended learning instructors are interested in the levels of interaction in their courses, but may be unwilling to spend the time to analyze them fully. Interactions in blended learning courses may take the form of face-to-face-only interactions, online-only interactions, or some combina-tion of interactions in both the face-to-face and online sub-modalities.

SCOPe Level 1 Expedited Analysis

Researchers have set forth descriptions of online interaction patterns (Garrison & Vaughan, 2008), re-visions of Bloom's (1975) taxonomy for online teaching and learning (Anderson & Krathwohl, 2001), graphic depictions of maps of online learning (Howell-Richardson & Mellar, 1996; Hara, Bonk, & Angeli, 2000), and other schemes for understanding online and face-to-face language-in-use (i.e., Gee, 2003; Hillman et al., 1994; Jain et al., 2009; Knowlton, 2005; Lee & Dashew, 2011; Pawan et al., 2003). However, few have provided a systematic way to analyze discourse among students in blended courses.

To facilitate interaction analysis in blended courses, we suggest using SCOPe's two-level approach (Thompson & Wegmann, 2012a). The SCOPe acronym stands for interactions with Self, Content, Others, and the online Platform. If instructors are willing to spend the time to collect, transcribe, and deeply analyze face-to-face and online interactions, this falls into what we term

SCOPe Phase 2, which employs more traditional discourse analysis of interaction events. However, some instructors will benefit from a brief analysis of interactions, so we recommend SCOPe Phase 1 Expedited Analysis.

Instead of analyzing each communication event with full-fledged discourse analysis techniques, language usage is divided into four categories, or "meta moves," based on the acronym SCOPe:

- Self-referencing
- Content-referencing
- Other-referencing
- Platform-referencing

Table 5.1 shows the meta-moves with descriptions and examples of each.

Using these four meta-moves to analyze interactions in face-to-face and online segments of a blended course can provide valuable information to instructors, thereby determining if students are engaged in optimum interactions for that particular subject area. Instructors can find out which kinds of interactions students use the most.

TABLE 5.1 Phase I: Examples and Descriptions of Interactions with SCOPe (Self, Content, Others, Platform) in Face-to-Face and Online Discussions

Topic or meta-moves	Description	Examples
Interacting with **Self**	Sharing an opinion or belief, reflecting on their own thinking, revealing their own struggles, questioning or wondering, providing a personal example, connecting to their own experiences, connecting to their own classrooms, sharing a grand idea	"I am looking forward to creating more of a participant atmosphere where literacy is concerned and not only guiding the students toward information and higher-thinking, but also having them guide each other."
		"If a student cannot find something about which to say, 'I've always wondered about that!' or 'So that's what that is!' or 'I'm not so sure that is true,' then has the teacher really taught that student the deepest meaning of science?"
		"I can vividly remember lacking this kind of direction in the majority of my own middle and high school classes."

Interacting with **Content**	Connecting to course content, initiating a new topic to consider, providing information to support, leading up to and drawing a conclusion, challenging the course content, giving information, connecting to other readings	"I know that we are talking about reading in science, but I find myself trying to motivate my students to read in order to be successful in math." "Getting students actively involved in discussion helps them to better understand and retain the material. This method allows the student to use and expand their LERs." "I think there has to be a middle ground, one that you can go to that is sometimes more efficient, and sometimes you need to step outside your norms and inconvenience yourself."
Interacting with **Others**	Responding to a peer's questions, giving advice, challenging peer, using humor to present or make a point	"I can definitely see what you're talking about. If a teacher can create a true aesthetic stance for students toward academia, that is a true accomplishment." "While I like your idea of a common ground, I'm not quite sure if that is always attainable. Students come from so many different backgrounds and different understandings of topics that finding a common ground might be difficult." "I say to myself, 'I know these ideas are how things should be.' But I find myself saying, '*sigh. . . this is harder than I thought it would be!' I am having a hard time separating my feelings for certain of my 'knucklehead' students. :)"

(Continued)

TABLE 5.1 (*Continued*)

Topic or meta-moves	Description	Examples
Interacting with the **Platform**	Starting out or finishing up a topic, introducing the topic or explaining what was going to come next, finishing up the topic and wrapping it up; connecting to a previous thought, contributing to the discussion (i.e., gaining the floor in a face-to-face discussion), expressing usage of the learner management system (positive or negative)	"I can definitely see what you're talking about. If a teacher can create a true aesthetic stance for students toward academia, that is a true accomplishment." "This week in class we were supposed to read chapter 12 from the book and reflect on how Rosenblatt's Transaction Theory is seen in our own classrooms."

Since the placement of interactions and discourse vary in blended courses (i.e., online, face-to-face, or both), the "starting point" for capture/analysis may vary. However, we recommend that to begin, instructors can evaluate an online discussion board about a third of the way through the course, using the *SCOPe Phase I Checklist of Optimal Online Interaction on Asynchronous Discussion Boards.* (Please see Appendix C for the Checklist and directions.) This checklist expands the four meta-moves into indicators that will provide baseline information about one asynchronous online discussion board. The results of this checklist can be summarized into a statement or two about each meta-move and the relative health of interactions appearing on the discussion board.

"Promoting, facilitating, and integrating online and face-to-face interactions are essential to blended learning" (Shea, 2007). Shea reasons that face-to-face and online interactions need to be blended together, in that they should be an ongoing conversation rather than a discrete dialogic chain (Bakhtin, 1986). Similarly, Dziuban, Hartman, and Moskal (2007) make the case that online comments should be noted in face-to-face discussions and vice versa. The *Phase I Face-to-Face Checklist of SCOPe interactions – During Discussion* (please see Appendix D) includes the item, "Relates comments to online discussion board," which acknowledges this integration of virtual and physical interactions.

Since human interactions occur between and among individuals, the next step of SCOPe analysis is to focus on individuals' interactions. After three or four face-to-face and online class discussions, we recommend choosing a higher, middle, and lower performer in the course. This decision may be based on grades, participation in the course, or other measures. (We recommend that you identify, and then make anonymous the data you collect on these three students. Do not reveal your choices to the class, so as to not constrain their participation in the discussion.) The *Phase I Face-to-Face Checklist of SCOPe interactions – During Discussion* (Appendix D) coupled with the *Phase I Face-to-Face Classroom Discussion Checklist – After Discussion* (Appendix E) will help quantify and qualify the kinds of interactions that occur in the brick and mortar setting. At about the same point in the semester, complete the *Checklist of SCOPe Interactions for Three Students on one Online Post* (Appendix F), using the same higher, middle, and lower performer. The results of these checklists can be summarized and compared in order to analyze more deeply how students are interacting in both face-to-face and online settings. As an option, we have also provided directions on Appendix F for creating and plotting a graph, on which a Connected Stance (Wegmann & McCauley, 2007) can be measured for online discussion posts.

For this expedited analysis, worksheet tallies are used rather than the in-depth classroom discourse analyses, which were described earlier in this chapter. We found that SCOPe Phase 1 was easier to use in online and face-to-face discourse analysis. These checklists will provide a wealth of information about the interactions that occur in blended settings. If researchers encounter major issues with the interactions, or data that do not seem to "make sense," then a more expansive discourse analysis, or Phase II SCOPe Analysis, should be conducted.

Intensifying Meaningful Interactions in Teaching/Learning: Implications for Best Practices Targeting Interactions

After analysis of blended classrooms, instructors can evaluate and modify their practices. They can support meaningful interactions by providing certain kinds of structures and organizational schemes, which may enhance interactions. Making these structures and schemes visible is often a difficult task. Recommendations for enhancing and intensifying meaningful interactions in blended courses appear in Appendix G.

Future Studies

We are convinced that discovering and analyzing the interactions of a blended course can reveal whether students are learning at an optimum level. One area that warrants future exploration is flipped classrooms (Baker, 2000) or inverted classrooms (Lage & Platt, 2000). In these classrooms online videos, tutorials, or content-focused websites present the content. Then students attend face-to-face classrooms for laboratory experiments and small group or one-on-one sessions with the instructor. A compelling future study might be to analyze the interactions that occur during the face-to-face sessions of a flipped classroom. What do they reveal about student learning? How can instructors enhance this discourse? Another future study might target public arenas that support or constrain a Connected Stance. Blogs, wikis, glogs, and other online places where students respond publicly to course work might change the kinds of language that they use (Thompson & Wegmann, 2011). Will the public nature of these spaces strengthen, constrain, or transform interactions? How can instructors support healthy and encouraging kinds of interactions, when students' language is subject to public viewing?

Conclusions

Dziuban et al. (2007) asked, "What are the empowering constructs of blended learning?" To that we answer that one of them must be meaningful opportunities for interactions with self, content, others, as well as the platform. Language-in-use is a difficult thing to measure and is often ignored unless instructors purposefully set out to analyze these kinds of inter-actions. Even though complete discourse analysis can offer much in-depth information about the kinds of interactions that occur, it often includes a large amount of effort to capture and analyze oral and online language. Saving time and effort, a systematic analysis like SCOPe puts forth a mechanism for blended classroom instructors to collect and examine interactions. Ideally, instructors can use the results of SCOPe analyses to modify the structure and emphases of their courses, in order to intensify and support profound interactions.

References

Anderson, T. (2003). Modes of interaction in distance education: Recent developments and research questions. In D. M. Moore (Ed.), *Handbook of distance education* (pp. 129–144). Mahwah, NJ: Erlbaum.

Anderson, L., & Krathwohl, D. (2001). *A taxonomy for learning, teaching and assessing: A revision of Bloom's Taxonomy of educational objectives.* New York: Longman.

Arbaugh, J. G., & Benbunan-Fich, R. (2007). The importance of participant interaction in online environments. *Decision Support Systems, 43*(3), 853–865.

Baker, J. W. (2000). *The "classroom flip": Using web course management tools to become the guide by the side.* Paper presented at the 11th International Conference on College Teaching and Learning, Jacksonville, FL.

Bakhtin, M. (1986). The problem of speech genres. In M. Bakhtin (Ed.), *Speech genres and other late essays* (pp. 60–102). Austin, TX: University of Texas Press.

Bloom, B. (1975). Language development. In F. D. Horowitz (Ed.), *Review of child development research* (pp. 245–303). Chicago: University of Chicago Press.

Bonk, C.J., Kim, K., & Zeng, T. (2006). Future directions of blended learning in higher education and workplace learning settings. In C.J. Bonk & C.R. Graham (Eds.), *Handbook of blended learning: Global perspectives, local designs* (pp. 550–567). San Francisco: Pfeiffer.

Cazden, C. (1988) *Classroom discourse.* Portsmouth, NH: Heinemann.

Chen, P., Gonyea, R., & Kuh, G. (2008). Learning at a distance: Engaged or not? *Innovate, 4*(3). Retrieved July 31, 2012, from www.innovateonline.info/pdf/vol4_issue3/Learning_at_a_Distance-__Engaged_or_Not_.pdf

De George-Walker, L., & Keeffe, M. (2010). Self-determined blended learning: A case study of blended learning design. *Higher Education Research and Development, 29*(1), 1–13.

Dewey, J. (1933). *How we think: A restatement of the relation of reflective thinking to the educative process.* Boston: Heath.

Dillon, M. (1994). *Using discussion in classrooms.* Philadelphia: Open University Press.

Dziuban, C., Hartman, J., & Moskal, P. D. (2004, March, 30). Blended learning. *ECAR Research Bulletin, 7.* Retrieved from www.educause.edu/ecar/

Dziuban, C., Hartman, J., & Moskal, P. (2007). Everything I need to know about blended learning I learned from books. In A. Picciano & C. Dziuban (Eds.), *Blended learning* (pp. 265–286). Needham, MA: Sloan-C.

Engle, R. A., & Conant, F. R. (2002). Guiding principles for fostering productive disciplinary engagement: Explaining an emergent argument in a community of learners classroom. *Cognition and Instruction, 20*(4), 399–483.

Garrison, D. R., & Innes-Cleveland, M. (2005). Facilitating cognitive presence in online learning: Interaction is not enough. *American Journal of Distance Education, 19*(3), 133–148.

Garrison, D. R., & Vaughan, N. D. (2008). *Blended learning in higher education: Framework, principles, and guidelines.* San Francisco: Jossey-Bass.

Gasiewski, J. A., Eagan, M., Garcia, G. A., Hurtado, S., & Chang, M. J. (2012). From gatekeeping to engagement: A multicontextual, mixed method study of student academic engagement in introductory STEM courses. *Research in Higher Education, 53*(2), 229–261.

Gee, J. (1986). Units in the production of narrative discourse. *Discourse Processes, 9*(4), 391–422.

Gee, J. (2003). *An introduction to discourse analysis: Theory and method* (4th ed.). London: Routledge.

Graham, C. R., & Robison, R. (2007). Realizing the transformational potential of blended learning. In A. Picciano & C. Dziuban (Eds.), *Blended learning* (pp. 83–110). Needham, MA: Sloan-C.

Guiller, J., Durndell, A., & Ross, A. (2007). Peer interaction and critical thinking: Face-to-face or online discussion? *Learning and Instruction, 18,* 187–200.

Hall, J. (2010). Interaction as method and result of language learning. *Language Teaching, 43*(2), 202–215.

Hara, N., Bonk C. J., & Angeli, C. J. (2000). Content analysis of online discussion in an applied educational psychology course. *Instructional Science, 28*(20), 115–152.

Hartman, J., Dziuban, C., & Brophy-Ellison, J. (2007). Faculty 2.0. *EDUCAUSE Review, 42*(5), 62–76.

Hawkes, R. (2010). Talking to learn and learning to talk: Teacher and learner talk in the secondary foreign languages classroom. *International Journal of Learning and Change, 4*(3), 217–236.

Haythornthwaite, C., Kazmer, M. M., Robbins, J., & Shoemaker, S. (2000). Community development among distance learners: Temporal and technological dimensions. *Journal of Computer-Mediated Communication, 6*(1). Retrieved from www. ascusc.org/jcmc/vol6/issue1/haythornth waite.html

Herrenkohl, L. R., & Guerra, M. R. (1998). Participant structures, scientific discourse, and student engagement in fourth grade. *Cognition and Instruction, 16*, 431–473.

Hillman, D. C., Willis, D. J., & Gunawardena, C. N. (1994). Learner-interface interaction in distance education: An extension of contemporary models and strategies for practitioners. *The American Journal of Distance Education, 8*(2), 30–42.

Howell-Richardson, C. & Mellar, H. (1996). A methodology for the analysis of patterns of participation within computer mediated communication courses. *Instructional Science, 24*, 47–69.

Hull, D., & Saxon, T. (2009, April 1). Negotiation of meaning and co-construction of knowledge: An experimental analysis of asynchronous online instruction. *Computers & Education, 52*(3), 624–639.

Imm, K., & Stylianou, D. A. (2012). Talking mathematically: An analysis of discourse communities. *Journal of Mathematical Behavior, 31*(1), 130–148.

Jain, P., Jain, S., & Cochenour, J. (2009). Interactivity in an online class: An interdisciplinary analysis. Proceedings from AACE 2009: *World Conference on Educational Multimedia, Hypermedia and Telecommunications.* Chesapeake, VA.

Jones, N. (2006). E-college Wales: A case study of blended learning. In C. J. Bonk & C. R. Graham (Eds.), *Handbook of blended learning: Global perspectives, local designs* (pp. 182–193). San Francisco: Pfeiffer.

Juwah, C. (2009). *Interactions in online education: Implications for theory and practice.* New York: Routledge.

Knowlton, D. S. (2005). A taxonomy of learning through asynchronous discussion. *Journal of Interactive Learning Research, 16*(2), 155–177.

Lage, M. J., & Platt, G. J. (2000). The internet and the inverted classroom. *Journal of Economic Education, 31*, 11.

Lee, R., & Dashew, B. (2011). Designed learner interactions in blended course delivery. *Journal of Asynchronous Learning Networks, 15*(1), 68–76.

Luppicini, R. (2007). Review of computer mediated communication research for education. *Instructional Science, 35*, 141–185.

Mehan, H. (1979). *Learning lessons.* Cambridge, MA: Harvard University Press.

Moore, M. G. (1991). Distance education theory. *The American Journal of Distance Education, 5*(3), 1–6.

Ng, C. L., Cheung, W. S., & Hew, K. F. (2012). Interaction in asynchronous discussion forums: Peer facilitation techniques. *Journal of Computer Assisted Learning, 28*(3), 280–294.

Nippard, E., & Murphy, E. (2007). Social presence in the web-based synchronous secondary classroom. *Canadian Journal of Learning and Technology, 33*(1). Retrieved from: http://cjlt.csj.ualberta.ca/index.php/cjlt/article/view/24/22

Pawan, F., Paulus, F. M., Yalcin, S., & Chang C.-F. (2003). Online learning: Patterns of engagement and interaction among in-service teachers. *Language Learning & Technology, 7*(3). 119–140.

Pena-Shaff, J., Altman, W., & Stephenson, H. (2005). Asynchronous online discussions as a tool for learning: Students' attitudes, expectations, and perceptions. *Journal of Interactive Learning Research*, *16*(4), 409–430.

Picciano, A. G. (2002). Beyond student perceptions: Issues of interaction, presence and performance in an online course. *Journal of Asynchronous Learning Networks*, *6*(1), 21–40.

Picciano, A. G. (2009). Blending with purpose: The multimodal model. *Journal of Asynchronous Learning Networks*, *13*(1), 7–18.

Russo, T., & Benson, S. (2005). Learning with invisible others: Perceptions of online presence and their relationship to cognitive and affective learning. *Educational Technology & Society*, *8*(1), 54–62.

Shea, P. (2007). Towards a conceptual framework for learning. In A. Picciano & C. Dziuban (Eds.), *Blended learning* (pp. 161–178). Needham, MA: Sloan-C.

Shovein, J., Huston, C., Fox, S., & Damazo, B. (2005, November–December). *Challenging traditional teaching and learning paradigms: Online learning and emancipatory teaching*. Retrieved from http://findarticles.com/p/articles/mi_hb3317/is_6_26/ai_n29227982/pg_3/?tag=content;col1

Short, J., Williams, E., & Christie, C. (1976). *The social psychology of telecommunications*. London: John Wiley & Sons.

Smith, R. (2005). Working with difference in online collaborative groups. *Adult Education Quarterly*, *55*(3), 182–199.

Stake, R. E. (1985). Case study. In J. Nisbet (Ed.) *World yearbook of education, 1985: Research, policy, and practice* (pp. 277–301). London: Kogan Page.

Starenko, M., Vignare, K., & Humbert, J. (2007). Enhancing student interaction and sustaining faculty instructional innovations through blended learning. In A. Picciano & C. Dziuban (Eds.), *Blended learning* (pp. 161–178). Needham, MA: Sloan-C.

Stein, D. S., Wanstreet, C. E., Calvin, J., Overtoom, C., & Wheaton, J. E. (2005). Bridging the transactional distance gap in online learning environments. *The American Journal of Distance Education*, *19*(2), 105.

Thompson, K., & Wegmann, S. (2011, November 9). Is student blogging a suitable alternative to online discussions? A connected stance applied. Presentation at Sloan-C ALN Conference, Orlando, FL. Retrieved from http://ofcoursesonline.com/?p=130

Thompson, K., & Wegmann, S. (2012a, April 23). Perfecting interaction in blended courses through discourse analysis. Presentation at Sloan-C Blended Learning Conference and Workshop, Milwaukee, WI. Retrieved from http://ofcoursesonline.com/?p=182

Thompson, K., & Wegmann, S. (2012b, October 10). A comparison of interaction patterns in student blogging: Instructor-chosen vs. student-chosen topics. Presentation at Sloan-C ALN Conference, Orlando, FL. Retrieved from http://ofcoursesonline.com/?p=269

Tuckman, B. W. (2007). The effect of motivational scaffolding on procrastinators' distance learning outcomes. *Computers & Education*, *49*(2), 414–422.

Tutty, J., & Klein, J. (2008). Computer-mediated instruction: A comparison of online and face-to-face collaboration. *Educational Technology Research and Development*, *56*(2), 101–124.

US Department of Education (2009). Evaluation of evidence-based practices in online learning: A meta-analysis and review of online learning studies. Retrieved from: www2.ed.gov/about/offices/list/opepd/ppss/reports.html

Vygotsky, L. S. (1978). *Mind in society: The development of higher psychological processes.* Cambridge, MA: Harvard University Press.

Waddoups, G. L., & Howell, S. L. (2002). Bringing online learning to campus: The hybridization of teaching and learning at Brigham Young University. *International Review of Research in Open and Distance Learning, 2*(2).

Wagner, E. (2005). Interaction strategies and experience design: Guidelines for technology-mediated learning. In P. Kommers & G. Richards (Eds.), Proceedings from AACE 2009: *World Conference on Educational Multimedia, Hypermedia and Telecommunications.* Chesapeake, VA.

Waring, H. Z. (2009). Moving out of IRF (Initiation–Response–Feedback): A single case analysis. *Language Learning, 59*(4), 796–824. Retrieved from: www.tc.columbia.edu/faculty/tesolal/Waring%20(2009).pdf

Wegmann, S., & McCauley, J. (2007) Can you hear us now? Stances toward interaction and rapport. In Y. Inoue (Ed.), *Online education for lifelong learning.* Hershey, PA: Information Science Publishing.

Wegmann, S., & McCauley, J. (2010, November 5). Investigating asynchronous online communication: A connected stance revealed. Proceedings from Sloan Consortium Annual Conference. Orlando, FL.

Wells, G. (1999). *Dialogic inquiry towards a sociocultural practice and theory of education.* Cambridge, MA: Cambridge University Press.

Wells, G. (1993). Reevaluating the IRF sequence: A proposal for the articulation of theories of activity and discourse for the analysis of teaching and learning in the classroom. *Linguistics and Education, 5*, 1–37.

Weltzer-Ward, L. (2010). Content analysis coding schemes for online asynchronous discussion. *Campus-wide Information Systems, 28*(1), 56–74.

Wilkinson, L. C. (1982) Introduction: A sociolinguistic approach to communicating in the classroom. In L. C. Wilkinson (Ed.), *Communicating in the classroom* (pp. 3–12). New York: Academic Press.

Wilson, B. (1996). Introduction: What is a constructivist learning environment? In B. Wilson (Ed.), *Constructivist learning environments: Case studies in instructional design.* Englewood Cliffs, NJ: Educational Technology Publications.

Wingard, R. G. (2004). Classroom teaching changes in web-enhances courses: A multi-institutional study. *Educause Quarterly, 27*(1). Retrieved from: http://net.educause.edu/ir/library/pdf/eqm0414.pdf

Zhang, W., Perris, K., & Yeung, L. (2005). Online tutorial support in open and distance learning: students' perceptions. *British Journal of Educational Technology, 36*(5), 789–804.

Zhao, Y., Lei, J., Yan, B., Lai, C., & Tan, H. (2005). What makes the difference? A practical analysis of research on the effectiveness of distance education. *Teachers College Record, 107*(8), 1836–1884.

Appendices

Available at http://bit.ly/ch5_appendices

6

STUDENT PERSPECTIVES ON BLENDED LEARNING THROUGH THE LENS OF SOCIAL, TEACHING, AND COGNITIVE PRESENCE

Janelle DeCarrico Voegele

In the first edition of *Blended Learning: Research Perspectives*, Vignare (2007) noted that research on the nature of learning in blended settings was difficult to find and ambiguous. Scholarship on blending learning has progressed toward more comprehensive understanding of effective blended course design practices (e.g., Greener, 2008; Napier, Dekhane, & Smith, 2011), but very little investigation has focused on how these practices foster learning from students' perspectives. In response, researchers have increasingly advocated holistic approaches that seek to understand how various components of blended settings are integrated, and the implications for student learning (Bluic, Goodyear, & Ellis, 2007).

This exploratory study focused on understanding the role of social, teaching, and cognitive presence in students' perspectives on blended learning effectiveness. The concept of presence has emerged as a promising avenue for understanding how blended environments can support communities of inquiry (Garrison & Vaughan, 2008). However, most of this research has been conducted in fully online, rather than blended, settings. How is presence connected to students' learning experiences across classroom and distributed learning formats? Implications for pedagogy emerging from the role of presence in students' learning experiences potentially form a foundation for further investigation into blended learning outcomes, as well as provide direction for leadership efforts toward systemic postsecondary educational change.

Community of Inquiry (CoI) Framework

Garrison, Anderson, and Archer (2000) introduced the community of inquiry model (CoI) to explore and better understand engaged online learning experiences. More recently, researchers have begun to adapt the model to investigate blended learning settings (Garrison & Vaughan, 2008; So & Brush, 2008). Grounded conceptually in the work of John Dewey (1938) and in learning theories aligned with social constructivism, the CoI conceptualizes teaching and learning in terms of three overlapping components: social presence, teaching presence, and cognitive presence. Social presence is defined as "the ability of participants in a community of inquiry to project themselves socially and emotionally, as 'real' people (i.e., their full personality), through the medium of communication being used" (Garrison et al., 2000, p. 94). Teaching presence is "the design, facilitation and direction of cognitive and social processes for the purpose of realizing personally meaningful and educationally worthwhile learning outcomes" (Anderson, Rourke, Garrison, & Archer, 2001, p. 5). Cognitive presence refers to "an environment that enables learners to construct and confirm meaning through sustained reflection and discourse in a critical community of inquiry" (Garrison, Anderson & Archer, 2001, p. 11).

The three presence elements are further defined by categories and indicators, originally developed to guide the coding of online transcripts (Garrison, 2007). Social presence is defined by open communication, group cohesion, and affective/interpersonal expression. The components of teaching presence are instructional design and organization, facilitating discourse, and direct instruction. Cognitive presence is conceived as a practical inquiry cycle consisting of triggering, exploration, integration, and resolution. While numerous studies have provided validation of the CoI framework (Diaz, Swan, Ice, & Kupczynski, 2010; Garrison, Cleveland-Innes, & Fung, 2010), more research on the relationship between the framework elements and learning outcomes is needed (Akyol & Garrison, 2011), as well as research in blended settings. Thus the following questions guided the present study:

- R1: What indicators of social, teaching, and cognitive presence emerge from students' perceptions of blended learning?
- R2: How does social, teaching, and cognitive presence help or impede learning in blended courses, from students' perspectives?
- R3: What pedagogical practices are associated with indicators of social, teaching, and cognitive presence in students' perceptions of learning?

The following section outlines the procedure used to better understand the role of social, teaching, and cognitive presence in students' perspectives on blended learning.

Method

Midquarter assessment data were collected in 74 blended courses at a large public urban university between Fall 2010 and Fall 2011 using a small group instructional diagnostic (SGID), a modified focus group technique (Angelo &

TABLE 6.1 Indicators of Social, Teaching, and Cognitive Presence by Category

Presence categories	What is helping	What could be changed
Social presence (n=428)		
Open communication	171	93
Group cohesion	45	51
Affective/interpersonal	31	37
Teaching presence (n=673)		
Design/organization	76	203
Facilitation of disclosure	89	87
Direct instruction	98	120
Cognitive presence (n=198)		
Triggering	17	16
Exploration	76	37
Integration	25	11
Resolution	11	4

Cross, 1993; McGowan & Osguthorpe, 2010). Student focus groups responded to questions about their learning experiences in blended courses, including what was helping them to learn, what could be changed to improve learning, and specific suggestions for implementing changes. A sample of 39 undergraduate courses representing 16 disciplines was selected for the present study, containing responses from 471 student focus groups totaling 1,886 students. The analysis proceeded as follows.

First, to isolate indicators of social, teaching, and cognitive presence in students' perspectives on learning, a coding framework adapted from Garrison and Vaughan (2008) and Diaz et al. (2010) was used to conduct a secondary analysis of the existing assessment data. Presence "indicators" were individual statements from focus group data that were coded to presence categories and subcategories. This analysis resulted in a total of 1,299 indicators of presence as summarized in Table 6.1. The resulting data set of presence indicators was then used to investigate research questions 2 and 3: a thematic analysis conducted within and across courses using a constant comparison design. Finally, a meta-analysis of primary cross-course themes associated with presence, student learning and pedagogical practices revealed commonalities in students' experiences with organizational and design aspects of courses. These commonalities resulted in four pedagogical course groupings that will be the primary focus of this chapter.

Findings

This section briefly summarizes selected results from coding and thematic analysis. These results formed the foundation for a cross-course meta-analysis of pedagogical themes, presented in the following section.

Indicators of Presence

A total of 1,299 indicators of social, teaching, and cognitive presence were coded from 2,057 statements, or 63% of students' statements about learning. Table 6.1 summarizes the number and indicators of presence identified by category.

The relatively large numbers of suggested changes in the category of "design/ organization" included multiple observations about integration of course components, both within and across course formats. Indicators of cognitive presence were less common overall, and were primarily in the exploration category. However, courses characterized by high levels of perceived integration and inquiry were an exception to this pattern, to be explained below.

Primary Themes Connected to Social, Teaching, and Cognitive Presence

The next step in the research process was a thematic analysis of presence indicators guided by the second and third research questions. Two of the primary themes that emerged across courses are briefly summarized below: interaction with peers and perceptions of blending connected to integration.

Interaction with Peers

The second research question focused on aspects of presence connected to students' perceptions of what was helping and hindering learning. Thematic analysis revealed not only the importance of peer interaction, but also the dynamic interaction between presence categories. For example, students connected comfortable self-expression in class and online (social presence) with an environment that motivated them to explore and sustain critical reflection (cognitive presence), as in the following observation:

> During class time, where we deliberately have to prepare for quality critical discussion in groups [helps us to learn]. This helped us to get more comfortable with opposing views on [*course topic*], and a better online environment, where groups express themselves openly.

"More interaction" and "meaningful interaction" were common requests to improve learning, particularly when a disparity between course formats was noted, as in the following:

> Class time should have more student interaction to complement how we interact online, instead of just PowerPoints. We get to be involved online but in here we're just muted.

Perceptions of Blending: Integration

The third research question focused on pedagogical practices associated with presence. Although several themes emerged related to blended pedagogy, students' perceptions of blending connected to presence most frequently emphasized the pedagogical *integration* between face-to-face and online learning. Students mentioned aspects of course design and organization that connected classroom and online learning such that social connections between peers and instructors were strengthened, and perceptions of worthwhile learning were increased. For example:

> Strategic connection of online work and discussion back into the class increases our ability to integrate the class concepts and also deepens connections to other students. Important in a school where you really don't get to know others in classes that well.

Conversely, students' observations also revealed a perceived lack of integration between course formats. For example, classroom and online pedagogical practices related to directed facilitation and encouraging discourse were sometimes observed as disconnected:

> We don't know if professor reads what goes on online, since points get made that were discussed online ad nauseam like it was the first time we heard of them.

Overlapping Meta-Themes: Integration and Inquiry

A meta-analysis of primary thematic findings that emerged from the second and third research questions revealed two central pedagogical patterns across courses: the degree to which transmission or inquiry approaches were perceived as central to course structure, and the degree to which learning experiences were perceived as integrated or nonintegrated within and between course formats. A transmission approach refers to learning as acquired via delivery of predetermined content, while inquiry approaches are those in which instructor–learner and learner–learner interactions are perceived as central to creating meaningful interpretations of course material. Courses categorized as integrated were those in which interaction and learning activities were perceived as consistently and continually connected within and between course formats. Nonintegrated courses were those in which learning activities were perceived as primarily disassociated within and/or between course formats.

When combined, these dimensions result in a categorization of blended course orientations in four general groupings, illustrated in Table 6.2:

TABLE 6.2 Pedagogical Course Groups Characterized by Overlapping Dimensions of Integration and Inquiry

	Nonintegrated	*Integrated*
Transmission	(n=8)	(n=14)
	Peer interaction and learning activities perceived as primarily disassociated within and between course formats	Peer interaction and learning activities perceived as consistently connected within and between course formats
	Learning as acquired via transmission	Learning as acquired via transmission
	Peer interaction primarily for knowledge acquisition	Peer interaction primarily for knowledge acquisition
Inquiry	(n=11)	(n=6)
	Inquiry and learning activities perceived as primarily disassociated within and/or between course formats	Inquiry and learning activities perceived as consistently connected within and between course formats
	Learning perceived as constructed via peer–peer and peer–instructor interaction	Learning perceived as constructed via peer–peer and peer–instructor interaction
	Inquiry inconsistently observed as central to process of learning	Inquiry consistently observed as central to process of learning

Nonintegrated/Transmission

In the eight courses primarily reflecting nonintegrated/transmission, students commonly equated teaching presence with classroom activity. Likewise, the classroom was perceived as the format most conducive to personal contact with instructors, with limited opportunities for peer interaction and collaboration. Overall, limited cognitive presence indicators of triggering and exploration were found, and more peer interaction was often mentioned as a change that would improve learning.

Discourse activities connected to learning were generally perceived as disassociated across formats. Social presence was primarily connected to classroom discourse. Although online individual student activity might follow from a course lecture (such as viewing an online lecture, taking a quiz, comprehension module, or applied activity), the process and outcomes of these activities were not perceived to impact future class meetings. In some cases, students perceived no connection between classroom and online activities.

Nonintegrated/Inquiry

In the 11 courses categorized as nonintegrated/inquiry, students perceived inquiry as important to constructing meaningful interpretations of course material, but perceptions of the value of the inquiry process varied most widely across courses in this group. The variation stemmed from the following observations:

(a) inquiry activities that were not, from students' perspectives, meaningfully assessed;
(b) inquiry that did not contribute to other activities or assignments;
(c) inquiry in one, but not both, course formats; and
(d) inquiry processes in both formats perceived as disassociated.

Students often requested more interaction in the format perceived as missing peer inquiry, more class time for personal contact and instructor perspective, more involvement from professors in online inquiry, more classroom preparation for online collaboration, and more incorporation of the results of online inquiry into the classroom agenda. Although some students enjoyed participating in peer discussions online, in other courses, online discussions became "something just to check off," perceived as irrelevant or lacking direction. The perceived disconnect between perspectives generated by peer inquiry and other dimensions of course experience were observed as barriers to cohesion, motivation, and progression past the exploration stage.

Integrated/Transmission

The 14 courses categorized as integrated/transmission were consistently perceived as highly integrated within and across course formats, but peer inquiry was not perceived as central to course design. Teaching presence indicators in the categories of "course organization" and "direct instruction" were connected to both classroom and online contexts. For example, students often observed that class time was deliberately devoted to preparing them for online activities, as well as instructor-directed debriefing of previous online activities. Teaching presence was frequently equated with instructors' awareness of students' challenges and questions that arose when completing online tutorials and modules, and a willingness to use that knowledge to modify upcoming classroom formats, activities, and lectures. Thus classroom and online learning experiences were often observed to build on one another, continually directed by instructors' interpretations of progress and challenges in both formats.

Integrated/Inquiry

In the six courses categorized as integrated/inquiry, inquiry was perceived as central to the process of learning, and purposefully integrated within and between course formats. Students in these classes followed the general pattern of preferring class time for questions and clarification, but indicators of teaching presence reflecting facilitation of discourse in both formats were more consistently mentioned in this group, even when instructors were no more likely to "be online" from students' perspectives than instructors in the other course categories. This finding may be associated with the number of observed pedagogical actions reinforcing the development of community, including the strategic integration of classroom and online inquiry.

Students often indicated that they were involved in the identification of connections between formats, and the implications for course modification. In addition to integrating cognitive work face-to-face and online, students mentioned facilitated activities that promoted cohesion and effective intergroup communication, as in the following example:

> In this class we are learning how to pull off an extensive group project working together in real time and online. Professor has been very helpful providing timely guidance on how to do this, in class and online.

Social presence indicators of group cohesion and affective/interpersonal dimensions were significantly higher for the integrated/inquiry course group: 46% of all group cohesion and affective indicators observed as helping learning were found in this small group of courses. Finally, although cognitive presence indicators of integration and resolution were least commonly found in courses overall, courses in the integrated/inquiry group were more likely to contain indicators of all four components of the practical inquiry cycle, including 32% of total integration and resolution indicators observed as helpful to learning.

Discussion and Future Directions

Although previous scholarship has explored both integration of blended course elements and the development of communities of inquiry, students' observations of learning in this study connected to social, teaching, and cognitive presence highlighted the role of inquiry *in relation to* strategic, purposeful integration of complex course elements. The results suggest pedagogical dimensions of blended learning design that warrant further study.

First, more investigation of effective pedagogical practices for well-integrated course models and their relationship to student learning is needed. Caulfield (2011) observed that integrating various components of blended courses is one of the most difficult challenges for instructors. The present study highlights how students perceived integration, inquiry, and presence connected to their experiences of learning. Students desired "voice" in the classroom to balance what they perceived as the positive impact of online presence, something many groups reported as a unique and novel aspect of blended courses. Students wanted to further articulate and build upon what had transpired prior to class meetings, they valued the extension of their online insights with input from their instructors, and they valued the opportunity to enhance their classroom interaction with integrated, relevant work online. They equated the integration between classroom and online discourse with perceptions of community, collaborative inquiry, and deeper levels of learning. Conversely, these findings also suggest that perceptions of presence, community, and learning are not necessarily enhanced by the opportunity to meet face-to-face. For example, perceptions of social, teaching, and cognitive presence often became problematic for students when efforts to establish interpersonal rapport online were not perceived as meaningfully connected to classroom activities.

Second, research on blended courses reflecting an integrated/inquiry approach could focus on pedagogical practices associated with high levels of sustained, critical inquiry. Brown, Smith, and Henderson (2007) noted that "[d]esigning and facilitating effective collaborative communities of practice is itself an area that merits attention" (p. 158). Students in integrated/inquiry courses acknowledged instructors' strategic preparation of students for inquiry, observed the time necessary to establish cohesion and community in both course formats, and connected those efforts to more effective outcomes from inquiry processes. A related avenue for future scholarship is the relationship between integration, inquiry, and the development of cognitive presence in collaborative, constructivist learning environments, including the assessment of specific learning outcomes (e.g., Akyol & Garrison, 2011).

Finally, future research could focus on instructors' pedagogical philosophies and roles in relation to blended learning design and instruction. Recently explored in the CoI literature (Akyol, Ice, Garrison & Mitchell, 2010) as well as in blended scholarship more broadly (e.g., Comas-Quinn, 2011; Kaleta, Skibba & Joosten, 2007), there is still much to learn about the relationship between instructors' pedagogical assumptions and blended course organization. For example, it is reasonable to suggest that inquiry will be deeply and meaningfully integrated into planned learning experiences only to the extent that it is assumed to be central to the process of learning. How do blended settings impact instructors' assumptions about learning? What encourages instructors to revisit assumptions about learning in light of blended teaching experiences, particularly those instructors who do not have the advantage of participating in regular discussions on blended pedagogies? Further study of instructors' identities as educators in blended settings is needed to understand the pedagogical and institutional transformative potential of blended learning.

Researchers and practitioners have consistently acknowledged the complexities in thoughtful, integrated campus and technology-mediated learning opportunities, and scholarship on blended settings should continue to focus on the interrelationship between blended practices and significant learning experiences. Comprehensive knowledge of how blended settings can promote the assumed goal of higher education—learner-centered, empowering education that prepares students to be engaged, informed, lifelong learners and citizens—can provide a counter-balance to the inevitable pressures and unspoken norms of efficiency and fiscal exigency facing campuses today. Higher education has much to gain if, in the process of addressing the increasing pressures it faces in the twenty-first century, more widespread understanding of deep and transformative learning might emerge as a result.

References

Akyol, Z., Ice, P., Garrison, D. R., & Mitchell, R. (2010). The relationship between course socio-epistemological orientations and student perceptions of community of inquiry. *Internet and Higher Education, 13,* 66–68.

Akyol, Z. & Garrison, D. R. (2011). Understanding cognitive presence in an online and blended community of inquiry: Assessing outcomes and processes for deep approaches to learning. *British Journal of Educational Technology, 42*(2), 233–250. doi: 10.1111/j.14678535.2009.01029.x

Anderson, R., Rourke, L., Garrison, D. R., & Archer, S. (2001). Assessing teaching presence in a computer conferencing context. *Journal of Asynchronous Learning Networks, 5*(2), 1–17.

Angelo, T. A. & Cross, K. P. (1993). *Classroom assessment techniques: A handbook for college teachers.* San Francisco: Jossey-Bass.

Bluic, A. M., Goodyear, P., & Ellis, R. A. (2007). Research focus and methodological issues in studies into students' experiences of blended learning in higher education. *Internet and Higher Education, 10,* 231–244.

Brown, G., Smith, T., & Henderson, T. (2007). Student perceptions of assessment efficacy in online and blended learning classes. In A. G. Picciano and C. D. Dziuban (Eds.), *Blended learning: Research perspectives* (111–143). Needham, MA: Sloan Consortium.

Caulfield, J. (2011). *How to design and teach a hybrid course: Achieving student centered learning through blended classroom, online and experiential activities.* Sterling, VA: Stylus.

Comas-Quinn, A. (2011). Learning to teach online or learning to become an online teacher: An exploration of teachers' experiences in a blended learning course. *ReCALL, 23*(03), 218–232. doi: 10.1017/S0958344011000152.

Dewey, J. (1938). *Experience and education.* New York: Collier Books.

Diaz, S. R., Swan, K., Ice, P., & Kupczynski, L. (2010). Student ratings of the importance of survey items, multiplicative factor analysis, and the validity of the community of inquiry survey. *Internet and Higher Education, 13,* 22–30.

Garrison, D. R. (2007). Online community of inquiry review: Social, cognitive and teaching presence issues. *Journal of Asynchronous Learning Networks, 11*(1), 61–72.

Garrison, D. R., Anderson, T., & Archer, W. (2000). Critical inquiry in a text-based environment: Computer conferencing in higher education. *Internet and Higher Education, 2* (2–3), 87–105.

Garrison, D. R., Anderson, T., & Archer, W. (2001). Critical thinking, cognitive presence and computer conferencing in distance education. *American Journal of Distance Education, 15*(1), 7–23.

Garrison, D. R., Cleveland-Innes, M., & Fung, T.S. (2010). Exploring causal relationships among teaching, cognitive and social presence: Student perceptions of the community of inquiry framework. *Internet and Higher Education, 13,* 31–36.

Garrison, D. R. & Vaughan, N. D. (2008). *Blended learning in higher education: Frameworks, principles and guidelines.* San Francisco: Jossey-Bass.

Greener, S. L. (2008). Self-aware and self-directed: Student conceptions of blended learning. *Merlot Journal of Online Learning and Teaching, 4*(2), 243–253.

Kaleta, R., Skibba, K., & Joosten, T. (2007). Discovering, designing and delivering hybrid courses. In A. G. Picciano and C. D. Dziuban (Eds.), *Blended learning: Research perspectives* (111–143). Needham, MA: Sloan Consortium.

McGowan, W. R. & Osguthorpe, R.T. (2010). Student and faculty perceptions of effects of midcourse evaluation. In J. E. Miller and J. E. Groccia, (Eds.), *To Improve the Academy: Resources for Faculty, Instructional and Organizational Development, 29,* 160–172.

Napier, N. P., Dekhane, S., & Smith, S. (2011). Transitioning to blended learning: Understanding student and faculty perceptions. *Journal of Asynchronous Learning Networks, 15* (1), 20–32.

So, H. J. & Brush, T. A. (2008). The content analysis of social presence and collaborative learning behaviors in a computer-mediated learning environment. In C. K. Looi, D. Jonassen, and M. Ikeda (Eds.), *The 13th annual conference on computers in education* (pp. 413–419). Amsterdam: IOS Press.

Vignare, K. (2007). Review of literature on blended learning: Using ALN to change the classroom – will it work? In A. G. Picciano and C. D. Dziuban (Eds.), *Blended learning: Research perspectives.* Needham, MA: Sloan Consortium.

7

TO BE OR NOT TO BE

Student and Faculty Perceptions of Engagement in a Blended Bachelor of Education Program

Norman Vaughan, Allana LeBlanc, Jim Zimmer, Irene Naested, Jodi Nickel, Stefan Sikora, Gladys Sterenberg, and Kevin O'Connor

Introduction

The idea of blending different learning experiences has been in existence since humans started thinking about teaching (Williams, 2003). The recent infusion of web-based technologies into the learning and teaching process brings this term into current consideration (Allen & Seaman, 2010; Clark, 2003). These technologies have created new opportunities for students to interact with their peers, teachers, and content.

Blended learning is often defined as the combination of face-to-face and online learning (Sharpe, Benfield, Roberts, & Francis, 2006; Williams, 2002). Ron Bleed, the former Vice Chancellor of Information Technologies at Maricopa College, argues that this is not a sufficient definition for blended learning as it simply implies "bolting" technology onto a traditional course, using technology as an add-on to teach a difficult concept, or adding supplemental information. He suggests that blended learning should be viewed as an opportunity to redesign how courses are developed, scheduled, and delivered through a combination of physical and virtual instruction: "bricks and clicks" (Bleed, 2001). Joining the best features of in-class teaching with the best features of online learning that promote active, self-directed learning opportunities with added flexibility should be the goal of this redesigned approach (Garnham & Kaleta, 2002; Littlejohn & Pegler, 2007; Norberg, Dziuban, & Moskal, 2011). Garrison and Vaughan (2008) echo this sentiment when they state that "blended learning is the organic integration of thoughtfully selected and complementary face-to-face and online approaches and technologies" (p. 148). A survey of e-learning activity by Arabasz, Boggs, and Baker (2003) found that 80% of all higher education institutions and 93% of doctoral institutions offer hybrid or blended learning courses.

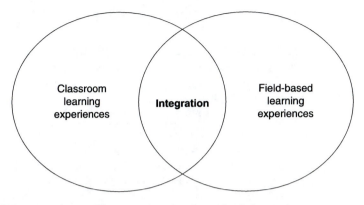

FIGURE 7.1   Bachelor of Education Approach to Blended Learning

Most of the recent definitions for blended courses indicate that this approach to learning offers potential for improving how we deal with content, social interaction, reflection, higher order thinking and problem solving, collaborative learning, and more authentic assessment in higher education potentially leading to a greater sense of student engagement (Graham, 2006; Mayadas & Picciano, 2007; Norberg et al., 2011). Moskal, Dziuban, and Hartman (2013) further suggest that "blended learning has become an evolving, responsive, and dynamic process that in many respects is organic, defying all attempts at universal definition" (p. 4). In this research study, the authors define blended learning as the intentional integration of classroom and field-based learning experiences through the use of digital technologies (Figure 7.1).

Study Context

Mount Royal University is a 4-year undergraduate institution located in Calgary, Alberta, Canada (www.mtroyal.ca/). In Fall 2011, the university launched a new Bachelor of Education (B.Ed.) program: a 4-year direct entry B.Ed. degree with an emphasis on connecting theory with practice through early, consistent, and on-going field experiences (www.mtroyal.ca/bed/). In the first 2 years of the program, students have a core education course each semester that meets once a week with a 20- or 30-hour field-placement. In the third and fourth years of the program, the students have extended field place-ments connected to program of studies courses and a capstone experience designed to integrate theory (of the coursework) and practice (of the field experiences) (Table 7.1).

TABLE 7.1 Bachelor of Education Field-Based Learning Experiences

	Volunteer field placements
Year one	Fall semester—30 hours
	Winter semester—30 hours
Year two	Fall semester—20 hours
	Winter semester—20 hours
	Practicum placements
Year three	5-week practicum combined with four program of studies courses
Year four	9-week practicum combined with four program of studies courses and a capstone experience course

To facilitate opportunities for communication and reflection between the classroom and field-based learning experiences, the institution has adopted the use of *Google Applications* (http://google.mtroyal.ca/): *Gmail* for communication; *Google Docs* (http://tinyurl.com/bedjournal) for reflective journaling; and *Google Sites* (http://tinyurl.com/bedportfolio) to construct a learning portfolio throughout the program.

This action research study evaluates the effectiveness of the integration between the classroom and field-based learning experiences in this B.Ed. program from a student and faculty perspective, using the National Survey of Student Engagement (NSSE) framework (2011).

Theoretical Framework

The concept of student engagement has been discussed extensively in the educational research literature (Kuh et al., 2005). In 1912, the first president of our institution emphasized the importance of "enabling the young mind to catch the gleam" through a higher education experience that would engage them as citizens (Baker, 2011, p. iv) and, more recently, Littky and Grabelle (2004) have advocated a curriculum redesign that stresses relevance, rigor, and relationships (3Rs of engagement). This redesign would enable students to meaningfully engage in sustained learning experiences that may lead to a state of optimal flow, which Csíkszentmihályi (1990) defines as "the mental state of operation in which the person is fully immersed in what he or she is doing by a feeling of energized focus, full involvement, and success in the process of the activity" (p. 9).

In 1998, the National Survey of Student Engagement (NSSE) was developed as a "lens to probe the quality of the student learning experience at American colleges and universities" (NSSE, 2011, p. 3). The NSSE defines student engagement as the amount of time and effort that students put into their classroom studies that lead to experiences and outcomes that constitute student success, and the ways the institution allocates resources and organizes learning opportunities and services to induce students to participate in and benefit from such activities.

These conceptions of student engagement in higher education are grounded in several decades of prior research, and particularly in four key antecedents: Pace's (1980) "quality of effort" concept, Astin's (1984) theory of student involvement, Chickering and Gamson's (1999) principles of good practice in undergraduate education, and Pascarella and Terenzini's (2005) causal model of learning and cognitive development. Based on this research and a meta-analysis of the literature related to student engagement, the NSSE has identified five clusters of effective educational practice. These benchmarks are (NSSE, 2011):

- Student interactions with faculty members.
- Active and collaborative learning.
- Level of academic challenge.
- Enriching educational experiences.
- Supportive campus environment.

These five clusters of effective educational practice have been used to guide this action research study.

Methods of Investigation

A participatory action research (PAR) approach directs this study. Gilmore, Krantz, and Ramirez (1986) define such a framework as:

> Action research . . . aims to contribute both to the practical concerns of people in an immediate problematic situation and to further the goals of social science simultaneously. Thus, there is a dual commitment in action research to study a system and concurrently to collaborate with members of the system in changing it in what is together regarded as a desirable direction. Accomplishing this twin goal requires the active collaboration of researcher and client, and thus it stresses the importance of co-learning as a primary aspect of the research process.
>
> (p. 161)

In addition, Stringer (1999) indicates that PAR is a reflective process of progressive problem solving led by individuals working with others in teams or as a part of a "community of practice" to improve how they address issues and solve problems. This research approach should result in some practical outcome related to the lives or work of the participants, which in this study is effective integration of classroom and field-based learning experiences in the Mount Royal University B.Ed. program, using a mixture of quantitative (i.e., survey) and qualitative (i.e., focus group) research methods.

Data Collection

An undergraduate student research assistant (USRA) collected data for the study. The USRA invited all students enrolled in the first year of the B.Ed. program to be part of this research project and a total of 77 students participated (86% response rate). In addition, she invited all of the faculty members who taught first year courses in this pre-service teacher education program to participate in this action research study (n=5, 83% response rate). The project received institutional ethics approval.

The data collection process began with an online survey during the first week of classes in September 2011, collecting base-line data about students' initial perceptions regarding their engagement in the B.Ed. program and their rationale for becoming a teacher. The investigators obtained survey questions from the Beginning College Survey of Student Engagement (BCSSE, 2011) and used the *SurveyMonkey* (www.surveymonkey.net) application to administer the survey online.

In March 2012, the investigators asked students to complete another online survey that focused on their perceptions of engagement after completing the first year of the B.Ed. program. The investigators based the questions for this survey on the National Survey of Student Engagement (NSSE, 2011) and, once again, used *SurveyMonkey* to facilitate the online process. During this time, the investigators asked faculty members to complete a similar online survey that used questions from the Faculty Survey of Student Engagement (FSSE, 2011).

At the end of March 2012, the USRA and the principal investigator for this study collated the survey results and posted them to an editable *Google Document* (http://tinyurl.com/bedfirstyearstudy). During the first two weeks of April 2012, students and faculty, who had participated in the online surveys, were invited to add comments and recommendations to this *Google Doc*. In addition, the investigators conducted a student focus group to discuss the survey results (n=24) and held a departmental retreat with the USRA to begin making plans to implement the recommendations generated from this action research study (n=8).

Data Analysis

The authors used a constant comparative approach to identify patterns, themes, and categories of analysis that "emerge out of the data rather than being imposed on them prior to data collection and analysis" (Patton, 1990, p. 390). Descriptive statistics (e.g., frequencies, means, and standard deviations) were calculated for the online survey items using *MS Excel*. Comments and recommendations from the student and faculty focus group sessions were added directly to the *Google Document*. The authors compared the results from the BCSSE and NSSE student surveys and focus group to identify "disappointment gaps" between students' beginning and end of first-year perceptions of engagement. Similarly, the authors compared the NSSE and FSSE survey and focus group results to highlight "misunderstanding gaps" between students' and faculty perceptions of engagement at the end of the first year of the B.Ed. program (Mancuso Desmarais, Parkinson, & Pettigrew, 2010).

Findings and Recommendations

The authors report a summary of the results for this action research study for each of the five NSSE benchmarks:

1. Student Interactions with Faculty Members

Students learn firsthand how experts think about and solve problems by interacting with faculty members inside and outside of the classroom because their teachers have become role models, mentors, and guides for continuous, lifelong learning (Chickering & Gamson, 1999). One of the student participants commented that "I believe the Bachelor of Education teachers are very knowledgeable and really enjoy what they are teaching. When they love what they are teaching it keeps me engaged and really interested in what I am learning" (Student Focus Group Participant 15). Light (2001) echoes the sentiment and indicates that a close working relationship with at least one faculty member is the single most important factor in student success.

The online survey results suggest that students and faculty perceive that email is the principal form of communication outside of the classroom and that that they receive prompt feedback on academic performance (Table 7.2). Faculty involved in this study recommended that email response protocols should be established with the students and the mentor teachers in the field placements to ensure timely responses, but also to manage expectations and workload.

Conversely, only 25% of the students often or very often discuss ideas with faculty members outside of the classroom and only 11% report that they frequently work with faculty members on activities other than coursework. This appears to be a university-wide trend, as demonstrated by a NSSE benchmark comparison with other Canadian institutions (Mount Royal Office of Institutional Analysis and Planning, 2011, Table 7.3).

TABLE 7.2 Student Interactions with Faculty Members

Question	Student response Sept 2011 Often/very often	Student response March 2012 Often/very often	Faculty response March 2012 Often/very often
Used e-mail to communicate with an instructor		92%	100%
Received prompt feedback from faculty on your academic performance (written or oral)	71%	78%	75%
Discussed grades or assignments with an instructor	59%	49%	25%
Talked about career plans with a faculty member or advisor		38%	25%
Discussed ideas from your readings or classes with faculty members outside of class	29%	25%	25%
Worked on a research project with a faculty member outside of course or program requirements	11%	24% (plan to do in the future)	
Worked with faculty members on activities other than coursework (committees, orientation, student life activities, etc.)	19%	11%	0%

The study participants provided several recommendations for increasing the opportunities for education students to communicate and work with faculty members, outside of the classroom, on activities other than coursework. Students suggested that faculty and field placement mentors use web-based synchronous conferencing tools (e.g., Skype) to establish "virtual" office hours. Many of the students reside a great distance from campus and their field placements and they indicated that the use of these conferencing tools would allow them to have "real-time" conversations from their homes.

Students recommended that faculty be more pro-active in helping students become members of department, faculty, and institutional committees (http://tinyurl.com/studentcommittee) and a student representative should be present at all department meetings and functions. An administrative staff member initiated weekly brown-bag lunch student sessions with faculty members based on specific topics and issues (http://tinyurl.com/wedbrownbag), which the students found helpful.

TABLE 7.3 Student–Faculty Interaction Items Compared with Other Canadian and NSSE Institutions

Student–faculty interaction items		Mount Royal compared with . . .		
		Canada	Canadian high satisfaction universities	NSSE 2011
Received prompt written or oral feedback from faculty on your academic performance	FY	↑	↑	↑
	SR	↑	↑	↑
Discussed grades or assignments with an instructor	FY	↑	↑	⇓
	SR	↑	↑	⇓
Talked about career plans with a faculty member or advisor	FY	↑	↑	⇓
	SR	↑	↑	↔
Discussed ideas from your readings or classes with faculty outside of class	FY	↑	↑	↑
	SR	↑	↑	↑
Worked with faculty members on activities other than coursework	FY	⇓	⇓	⇓
	SR	↑	⇓	⇓
Worked on a research project with a faculty member outside of course or program requirements	FY	↑	↑	⇓
	SR	⇓	↔	⇓

Legend
↑ = above Canadian and NSSE institutional averages
⇓ = below Canadian and NSSE institutional averages
FY = first year
SR = senior year

2. Active and Collaborative Learning

Students learn more when they are intensely involved in their education and are asked to think about and apply what they are learning in different settings (Chickering & Ehrmann, 1996). Collaborating with others in solving problems or mastering difficult material prepares students to deal with unscripted problems that they might encounter both during and after university. A student in the focus group reinforced the need for collaboration by stating that "the education classes were more interactive than others. I found it to be very helpful in my learning and it made it easy to relate to our own lives and teaching in the future" (Student Focus Group Participant 8).

The online survey results demonstrate how students believe that they made more class presentations and worked with their peers on projects during class time more frequently than they initially perceived at the beginning of the academic year (Table 7.4). The students emphasized how important it was for faculty to dedicate classroom space and resources for project work because finding

TABLE 7.4 Active and Collaborative Learning

Question	Student response Sept 2011 Often/very often	Student response March 2012 Often/very often	Faculty response March 2012 Often/very often
Make a class presentation	46%	72%	50%
Work with other students on projects DURING class	68%	70%	50%
Ask questions in class or contribute to class discussions	66%	64%	100%
Discuss ideas from your readings or classes with others outside of class (students, family members, co-workers, etc.)	46%	60%	50%
Work with classmates OUTSIDE of class to prepare class assignments	30%	57%	50%
Participate in a community-based project as part of a regular course	34%	53%	75%
Tutor or teach other students (paid or voluntary)	23%	22%	25%

time outside of class was an on-going challenge due to conflicting course schedules plus work and family responsibilities. They also stressed the importance of *Google* applications for collaborative work between class sessions; for example, *Google Docs* could be used to create shared group papers and presentations.

All student and faculty responses to the NSSE questions related to the active and collaborative learning benchmark were very positive except tutoring or teaching other students even though the education students spent 60 hours in K to 12 school field placements during their first year of the program. A comparison of this NSSE benchmark with other institutions suggests that this is a university-wide issue (Table 7.5).

Based on these findings, a learning activity has been designed for the first foundational education course to introduce students experientially to the concept of peer tutoring and the supervisor of the university's peer tutoring program has been invited to facilitate an in-class workshop on peer tutoring. The students will then be required to conduct a peer-tutoring activity in their field-based experience through conversations with their K to 12 mentor teachers and provide a reflective journal entry about the process. Hopefully, this activity will encourage the education students to become more actively involved in the university's peer tutoring (http://tinyurl.com/mrupeertutor)

TABLE 7.5 Active and Collaborative Learning Items Compared with Other Canadian and NSSE Institutions

Active and collaborative learning items		Mount Royal compared with . . .		
		Canada	Canadian high satisfaction universities	NSSE 2011
Asked questions in class or contributed to class discussion	FY	↑	↑	↑
	SR	↑	↑	↑
Made a class presentation	FY	↑	↑	↑
	SR	↑	↑	↑
Worked with other students on projects **during class**	FY	↑	↑	↑
	SR	↑	↑	↑
Worked with classmates **outside of class** to prepare class assignments	FY	↑	↑	↑
	SR	↑	↑	↑
Discussed ideas from readings or classes with others outside of class (students, family members, co-workers, etc.)	FY	↑	↑	↑
	SR	↑	↑	↑
Participated in a community-based project as part of a regular course project	FY	↑	↑	⇓
	SR	↑	↑	↑
Tutored or taught other students (paid or voluntary)	FY	⇓	⇓	⇓
	SR	⇓	⇓	⇓

and student technician and resource tutor programs (www.mtroyal.ca/start/), which provide paid employment opportunities.

In addition, a draft of the university's new strategic plan recommends enhancing peer-to-peer programs and services, including peer tutoring (Mount Royal University, 2012a), and to support this recommendation a new additional staff member has recently been hired for the peer-tutoring program.

3. Level of Academic Challenge

Challenging intellectual and creative work is central to student learning and collegiate quality. Universities promote high levels of student achievement by setting high expectations for student performance (Graham, Cagiltay, Lim, Craner, & Duffy, 2001). During the first year of the program, education students take four foundational general education courses. The following table illustrates how these courses have contributed to students' ability to think critically and analytically (Table 7.6). Once again, the student participants commented on how the use of *Google's* social media applications facilitated opportunities to work effectively with their peers and field placement mentors to acquire relevant knowledge and skills for their future teaching practice.

TABLE 7.6 Level of Academic Challenge

How has your first year experience at MRU contributed to your knowledge, skills, and personal development in the following areas?	Initial student response Sept 2011 prepared/very prepared	Student response March 2012 quite a bit/very much	Faculty response March 2012 quite a bit/very much
Thinking critically and analytically	45%	92%	50%
Working effectively with others	86%	85%	100%
Acquiring job or work-related knowledge and skills		84%	100%
Acquiring a broad general education		83%	100%
Learning effectively on your own	75%	81%	100%
Writing clearly and effectively	51%	80%	75%
Speaking clearly and effectively	54%	67%	50%
Using computing and information technology	45%	65%	75%
Analyzing math or quantitative problems	22%	34%	25%

Bornfreund (2012) observes concern about whether pre-service education students are adequately prepared to teach math and science concepts to elementary children. The online survey results indicate that after the first year of the program, only one-third of the students think that they are prepared to analyze math or quantitative problems. University data also suggest that students spend less time on studying and academic work than at other institutions (Table 7.7).

We have begun to implement strategies to help our education students develop their numerical and scientific literacy based on these findings. For example, students in their first year will be encouraged to take a foundational general education course that focuses on scientific and mathematical literacy for the modern world. A new educational elective course entitled *An Introduction to Visual Arts and Mathematics* will be introduced in the Fall 2012 semester and a minor in math and science is currently being developed for the program. Two new faculty members, who specialize in math and science education, have also been recently hired.

4. Enriching Educational Experiences

Educational research has demonstrated that complementary learning opportunities inside and outside of the classroom augment the academic program (Kuh, 2008). Experiencing diversity teaches students valuable things about

TABLE 7.7 Level of Academic Challenge Items Compared with Other Canadian and NSSE Institutions

Level of academic challenge items		Mount Royal Compared with . . .		
		Canada	Canadian high satisfaction universities	NSSE 2011
Coursework emphasizes: **Analysis** of the basic elements of an idea, experience, or theory	FY	↑	↑	↑
	SR	↑	↑	↑
Coursework emphasizes: **Making judgments** about the value of information, arguments, or methods	FY	↑	↑	↑
	SR	↑	⇓	↑
Coursework emphasizes: **Applying** theories or concepts to practical problems or new situations	FY	↑	↑	↑
	SR	↑	↑	↑
Number of written papers or reports of **20 pages or more**	FY	⇓	↑	↑
	SR	⇓	⇓	↑
Number of written papers or reports **between 5 and 19 pages**	FY	↑	↑	↑
	SR	⇓	⇓	↑
Worked harder than you thought you could to meet an instructor's standards or expectations	FY	↑	↑	↑
	SR	↑	↑	⇓
Coursework emphasizes: **Synthesis** and organization of ideas, information, or experiences into new, more complex, interpretations and relationships	FY	↑	↑	⇓
	SR	↑	↑	↑
Number of written papers or reports **fewer than 5 pages**	FY	↑	↑	⇓
	SR	⇓	⇓	⇓
Spent significant amounts of time studying and on academic work	FY	⇓	⇓	⇓
	SR	⇓	⇓	⇓
Number of assigned textbooks, books. or book-length packs of course readings	FY	⇓	⇓	⇓
	SR	⇓	⇓	⇓
Hours spent preparing for class (studying, etc.)	FY	⇓	⇓	⇓
	SR	⇓	⇓	⇓

themselves and other cultures. Used appropriately, technology facilitates learning and promotes collaboration between peers and instructors. Internships, community service, and senior capstone courses provide students with opportunities to synthesize, integrate, and apply their knowledge. Such experiences make learning more meaningful and, ultimately, more useful because what students know becomes a part of who they are.

Student focus group participants commented that the field placements and school tours were the highlight of their first year experience.

> I really enjoyed the volunteer school experience. It reassured me that I was going into the right career. I also enjoyed the school tours as they helped me gain a better understanding of what the education system is heading towards, and what programs are out there to assist struggling students.
>
> (Student Focus Group Participant 2)

They also indicated how important the *Google Doc* journal and *Google Site* portfolio were for "integrating my Mount Royal class and volunteer placement experiences and establishing a philosophy of education that I truly believe in" (Student Focus Group Participant 9).

Students also indicated, however, that time constraints were a major challenge to participation in these types of "out-of-class" activities. Table 7.8 demonstrates that 75% of the students work more than 10 hours a week (more working hours than homework hours) and almost 20% spend at least this amount of time commuting to the university each week.

A similar trend exists at the university level, potentially resulting in lower student participation in co-curricular activities than at other Canadian institutions (Table 7.9).

TABLE 7.8 Enriching Educational Experiences

During this academic year, about how many hours did you spend in a typical 7-day week doing each of the following?	*Student response Sept 2011 More than 10 hours*	*Student response March 2012 More than 10 hours*	*Faculty response March 2012 More than 10 hours*
Working for pay on or off campus	68%	75%	100%
Preparing for class (studying, reading, writing, doing homework or lab work, analyzing data, rehearsing, and other academic activities)	60%	56%	50%
Relaxing and socializing (watching TV, partying, etc.)	33%	41%	100%
Commuting to class (driving, bus, walking, etc.)		19%	0%
Participating in co-curricular activities (organizations, campus publications, student government, fraternity or sorority, intercollegiate or intramural sports, etc.)	13%	12%	25%
Providing care for dependents living with you (children, spouse, parents)		9%	0%

TABLE 7.9 Level of Enriching Educational Experience Items Compared with Other Canadian and NSSE Institutions

Enriching educational experience items		Mount Royal Compared with . . .		
		Canada	Canadian high satisfaction universities	NSSE 2011
Used an electronic medium to discuss or complete an assignment	FY	↑	↑	↑
	SR	↑	↑	↑
Had serious conversations with students of different race or ethnicity	FY	↑	↑	↑
	SR	↑	↑	↑
Did a practicum, internship, field experience, co-op experience, or clinical assignment	FY	↑	↑	↑
	SR	↑	↑	↑
Had serious conversations with students of different religious beliefs, political opinions, or personal values	FY	↑	⇓	↑
	SR	↑	↔	↑
Participated in a learning community or some other formal program where groups of students take two or more classes together	FY	↑	↑	⇓
	SR	↑	↑	↑
Participated in an independent study or self-designed major	FY	↑	↑	↔
	SR	⇓	⇓	⇓
Encouraged contact among students from different economic, social, racial, or ethnic backgrounds	FY	↑	↑	⇓
	SR	↑	↑	↑
Participated in community service or volunteer work	FY	↑	↑	⇓
	SR	⇓	⇓	⇓
Culminating senior experience (senior project or thesis, comprehensive exam, etc.)	FY	⇓	⇓	⇓
	SR	↑	↑	⇓
Completed foreign language course work	FY	⇓	⇓	⇓
	SR	⇓	↔	⇓
Studied abroad	FY	⇓	⇓	⇓
	SR	⇓	↔	⇓
Participated in co-curricular activities (organizations, campus publications, etc.)	FY	⇓	⇓	⇓
	SR	⇓	⇓	⇓

At the program level, these findings suggest that faculty and staff need to work closely with the Education Undergraduate Society (EUS) to provide meaningful academic and social activities to help foster a vibrant student community. In the focus group, a student advised other students "to get as involved as they can with the school. The EUS meetings and workshops really do contribute to your overall understanding as a teacher, so try to soak in as much knowledge as possible" (Student Focus Group Participant 11). The EUS, therefore, created a blog (http://mrueus.blogspot.ca/) and established a Twitter feed (@MRU_EUS) to increase communication about education student events.

The new institutional strategic plan recommends establishing a co-curricular transcript record to recognize student participation in enriching educational experiences (Mount Royal University, 2012a).

5. Supportive Campus Environment

Students perform better and are more satisfied at universities that are committed to their success and cultivate positive working and social relations among different groups on campus (Chickering & Gamson, 1987). This NSSE benchmark asks students to rate the quality of their relationships with their peers, faculty members, and administrative personnel and offices. Tables 7.10 and 7.11 illustrate that students perceive reasonably high quality relationships with their peers and faculty members, but not as much with administrative personnel and offices.

The high quality of relationships with peers and faculty members can be attributed to the priority that the university places on smaller than average class sizes and teaching excellence (Mount Royal University, 2012b). Regarding administrative personnel and offices, the students in the focus group stated that they have very positive relationships with the staff in the education program but "as this is a new program I understand that it is all not mapped out yet and at times my questions were not as clearly answered as I would have liked" (Student Focus Group Participant 7). The University is currently developing a curriculum map for this new B.Ed. program with student input (http://tinyurl. com/bedcurrmap) to address this issue.

In addition, the university acknowledges "that support staffing levels in academic departments and faculties have not kept pace with recent growth in

TABLE 7.10 Supportive Campus Environment

Quality: Your relationships with:	Student response March 2012 (6 and 7 out of a 7-point scale)
Other students	61%
	Friendly, supportive, sense of belonging
Faculty members	50%
	Available, helpful, sympathetic
Administrative personnel and offices	25%
	Helpful, considerate, flexible

TABLE 7.11 Level of Supportive Campus Environment Items Compared with Other Canadian and NSSE Institutions

Supportive Campus Environment Items		Mount Royal compared with . . .		
		Canada	Canadian high satisfaction universities	NSSE 2011
Quality of relationships with other **students**	FY	↑	↑	↑
	SR	↑	↔	↑
Quality of relationships with **faculty members**	FY	↑	↑	↑
	SR	↑	↑	↑
Quality of relationships with **administrative personnel and offices**	FY	⇓	⇓	⇓
	SR	↑	↑	↔
Campus environment provides the support needed to succeed academically	FY	↑	↑	↑
	SR	↑	↑	↑
Campus environment helps to cope with non-academic responsibilities (work, family, etc.)	FY	↑	↑	↑
	SR	↑	↑	⇓
Campus environment provides the support needed to thrive socially	FY	↑	⇓	⇓
	SR	↑	⇓	⇓

size and complexity" and thus we are "investigating ways to make procedures and practices more efficient" (Mount Royal University, 2012b, p. 15). Recently, the institution has implemented a web-based application entitled *mruGradU8* (www.mtroyal.ca/mruGradU8/), which allows students to track their program progress by reviewing their academic history and identifying course requirements that they still need to complete to graduate.

Conclusion

Over the past decade, there has been an increased focus on student engagement in higher education because of rising tuition costs and concerns about student success and retention rates (Kuh et al., 2005). This action research study has demonstrated how departmental and institutional NSSE benchmark data can be evaluated in partnership with students, faculty, and administration to design and plan the intentional integration of classroom and field-based learning experiences in a blended Bachelor of Education program. As the African proverb suggests, "it takes a village to raise a child," to which Saint-Jacques (2013) adds "that a shift toward a 'we-learning' conceptualization of education" will benefit us all (p. 34).

References

Allen, I. E. & Seaman, J. (2010). *Class differences: Online education in the United States, 2010*, Babson Survey Research Group, The Sloan Consortium. Available online at: http://sloanconsortium.org/publications/survey/class_differences

Arabasz, P., Boggs, R., & Baker, M. B. (2003). Highlights of e-learning support practices. *Educause Center for Applied Research Bulletin, 9*. Retrieved from: http://net. educause.edu/ir/library/pdf/ERB0309.pdf

Astin, A. (1984, July). Student involvement: A developmental theory for higher education. *Journal of College Student Personnel*, 297–308.

Baker, D. N. (2011). *Catch the gleam: Mount Royal from college to university, 1910–2009*. Calgary, AB: University of Calgary Press.

Beginning College Survey of Student Engagement. (BCSSE, 2011). *Administering BCSSE*. Retrieved from: http://bcsse.iub.edu/_/?cid=16

Bleed, R. (2001). A hybrid campus for a new millennium. *Educause Review, 36*(1), 16–24.

Bornfreund, L. (2012, May 3). Preparing teachers for the early grades. *Educational Leadership Magazine*. Retrieved from: www.newamerica.net/publications/articles/2012/preparing_teachers_for_the_early_grades_67138

Chickering, A. W. & Ehrmann, S. E. (1996, October). Implementing the seven principles: Technology as lever. *American Association of Higher Education*, 3–6.

Chickering. A.W. & Gamson, Z. F. (1999). Development and adaptations of the seven principles for good practice in undergraduate education. *New Directions for Teaching & Learning, 80*, 75–82.

Chickering, A.W. & Gamson, Z.F. (1987) Seven principles for good practice in undergraduate Education. *American Association of Higher Education Bulletin, 39*(7), 3–7.

Clark, D. (2003). Blend it like Beckham. *Epic Group PLC*. Retrieved from: www.epic.co.uk/content/resources/white_papers/blended.htm

Csikszentmihalyi, M. (1990). *Flow: The psychology of optimal experience*. New York: Harper and Row.

Faculty Survey of Student of Engagement (FSSE, 2011). *Administering FSSE*. Retrieved from: http://fsse.iub.edu/_/?cid=14

Garnham, C. & Kaleta, R. (2002). Introduction to hybrid courses. *Teaching with Technology Today, 8*(6). Retrieved from www.uwsa.edu/ttt/articles/garnham.htm

Garrison, D. R. & Vaughan, N. D. (2008). *Blended learning in higher education*. San Francisco: Jossey-Bass.

Gilmore, T., Krantz, J., & Ramirez, R. (1986). Action based modes of inquiry and the host–researcher relationship. *Consultation, 5*(3), 160–176.

Graham, C. R. (2006). Blended learning systems: Definitions, current trends, and future directions. In Bonk, C. & Graham, C. (Eds.), *The handbook of blended learning: Global perspectives, local designs* (pp. 3–21). San Francisco: Pfeiffer.

Graham, C., Cagiltay, K., Lim, B., Craner, J., & Duffy, T. (2001). Seven principles of effective teaching: A practical lens for evaluating online courses. *The Technology Source* (March): A Publication of The Michigan Virtual University.

Kuh, G.D. (2008). *High impact educational practices: What they are, who has access to them, and why they matter*. Washington DC: Association of American Colleges and Universities.

Kuh, G. D., Kinzie, J., Schuh, J. H., Whitt, E. J., & Associates (2005). *Student success in college: Creating conditions that matter*. San Francisco: Jossey-Bass.

Light, R. J. (2001). *Making the most of college: Students speak their minds.* Boston: Harvard University Press.

Littky, D. & Grabelle, S. (2004). *The big picture: Education is everyone's business.* Alexandria, VA: Association for Supervision and Curriculum Development.

Littlejohn, A. & Pegler, C. (2007). *Preparing for blended e-learning: Understanding blended and online learning (Connecting with e-learning).* London: Routledge.

Mancuso, M., Desmarais, S., Parkinson, K., & Pettigrew, B. (2010). *Disappointment, misunderstanding and expectations: A gap analysis of NSSE, BCSSE and FSSE.* Toronto: Higher Education Quality Council of Ontario.

Mayadas, F. A. & Picciano, A. G. (2007). Blended learning and localness: The means and the end. *Journal of Asynchronous Learning Networks, 11*(1), 3–7.

Moskal, P., Dziuban, C., & Hartman, J. (2013). Blended learning: A dangerous idea? *Internet and Higher Education,18,* 15–23.

Mount Royal University. (2012a). *The new rules for undergraduate education: A strategic plan for Mount Royal University 2012–2017.* Unpublished draft.

Mount Royal University. (2012b). *Inspiring learning: Academic plan 2012–2017.* Retrieved from: www.mtroyal.ca/wcm/groups/public/documents/pdf/academic_plan.pdf

Mount Royal Office of Institutional Analysis and Planning. (2011). *2011 Mount Royal benchmark comparisons.* Retrieved from: www.mtroyal.ca/documents/2011_MRU_NSSE.pdf

National Survey of Student Engagement (2011). *Fostering student engagement campus wide-annual report 2011.* Bloomington, IN: Center for Postsecondary Research.

Norberg, A., Dziuban, C. D., & Moskal, P. D. (2011). A time-based blended learning model. *On the Horizon, 19*(3), 207–216.

Pace, C. (1980). Measuring the quality of student effort. *Current Issues in Higher Education, 2,* 10–16.

Pascarella, E. & Terenzini. P. (2005). *How college affects students: A third decade of research* (2nd ed.). San Francisco: Jossey-Bass.

Patton, M. Q. (1990). *Qualitative evaluation and research methods* (2nd ed.). Newbury Park, CA: Sage Publications.

Saint-Jacques, A. (2013). Effective teaching practices to foster vibrant communities of inquiry in synchronous online learning. In Z. Akyol & D. Garrison (Eds.), *Educational communities of inquiry: theoretical framework, research and practice* (pp. 84–108). Hershey, PA: Information Science.

Sharpe, R., Benfield, G., Roberts, G., & Francis, R. (2006). *The undergraduate experience of blended e-learning: A review of UK literature and practice.* London: Higher Education Academy.

Stringer, E. T. (1999). *Action research* (2nd ed.). Thousand Oaks, CA: Sage Publications.

Williams, J. (2003). Blending into the background. *E-Learning Age Magazine, 1.*

Williams, C. (2002). Learning on-line: A review of recent literature in a rapidly expanding field. *Journal of Further and Higher Education, 26*(3), 263–272.

8

A FIVE-YEAR STUDY OF SUSTAINING BLENDED LEARNING INITIATIVES TO ENHANCE ACADEMIC ENGAGEMENT IN COMPUTER AND INFORMATION SCIENCES CAMPUS COURSES

Laurie P. Dringus and Amon B. Seagull

Introduction

In early 2007, the faculty and administration of the Graduate School of Computer and Information Sciences (GSCIS) at Nova Southeastern University discussed the need to adopt blended learning initiatives to extend support for our campus-based master's students. The graduate school is committed to the university's core belief that engagement is substantially tied to student learning and that the academic environment exists beyond the physical classroom and its class schedule. With this belief, we recognized the need to further engage students in the educational process by exploring various technology mechanisms for access and exchange to be used outside of the campus class. At the same time, blended learning was recognized as a relatively new instructional modality (Picciano, 2011), as few academic institutions, in general, had fully adopted blended learning or initiated blended learning in traditional class offerings. However, GSCIS has a long history of online learning and blended learning since 1983 (Dringus & Scigliano, 2000). GSCIS had pioneered its unique doctoral programs (in information science and other areas) using part-distance (computer-based) and part-campus (several cluster weekend meetings on site per year) as the instructional modality. In parallel, GSCIS has also offered various fully online master's degree programs since 1986.

In 2007, the campus-based master's programs, offered for local students who preferred campus-based instruction to online instruction, were still not formally blended. Access to peers outside class meetings was limited particularly for this group. After several months of pre-planning, by 2008 our instructors deployed the first phase of blended learning initiatives. Our blended learning project is currently in its fifth year of progress.

Context: Enhancing Student Engagement through Dialogue and Exchange

The GSCIS Blended Learning (BL) project, named "Blended Learning: Enhancing Student Engagement in Campus-Based Courses with Online Discussion Activities," is part of Nova Southeastern University's Quality Enhancement Plan (QEP). (The Southern Association of Colleges and Schools (SACS) requires higher educational institutions to implement a QEP of the institutions' creation as part of the accreditation review process.) NSU's QEP is a university-wide effort that centers on the theme of enhancing student engagement, involving all academic units of the institution; each unit is required to focus on a specific strategy. As an academic unit, our GSCIS QEP project developed under the strategy, *NSU QEP Enhancing Student Academic Engagement Strategy II. Academic Dialogue and Exchange*. In applying this strategy, the GSCIS BL project involves the deployment of faculty initiatives using online delivery systems in campus courses that include, for example, using discussion boards to facilitate communication in group projects; lecture recaps and extensions; student resource sharing; and online Q&A.

In this chapter, the authors share experiences and data in highlighting a 5-year implementation plan of blended learning initiatives included in campus course offerings in computer science and information systems. In describing our process and implementation strategies to increase academic dialogue and exchange, we also share student and faculty survey data from assessment periods dating from 2008–2011. We share reflections on our process in regard to the success and sustainability of the blended learning experience, and share what we perceive at this point in the project to have been the most significant challenges and lessons learned.

Related Literature

At the inception of the GSCIS BL project, research was forming on blended learning models and effective practices. Research evolved that, for example, defined blended learning (Picciano, 2011), provided perspectives on blended learning (Vaughan, 2007), and reported data from institutions that had fully or partially developed online and blended learning programs (Dziuban, Moskal, & Hartman, 2005; Picciano & Dziuban, 2007). As we explain the evolution of our project, in many respects, the research works we cite reflect many challenges that we faced and continue to face in developing sustained blended learning. We relate research literature on faculty issues and faculty initiatives in the scope of describing our project, specifically in the following contexts: recognizing a logistical need for adopting blended learning, conceptualizing and planning for blended learning, and preparing sustainable blended learning initiatives.

Recognizing a Logistical Need for Adopting Blended Learning

Shea (2007) raised an interesting question regarding the reason(s) for implementing blended learning: to what problem and to what purpose is blended learning a solution? Like Kenney and Newcombe (2011), we adopted blended learning to "increase student participation, engagement, and interactivity" (p. 45) in our campus courses. We recognized a logistical problem in that GSCIS campus-based master's students are working adults attending evening classes who have limited ability to visit the campus to meet regularly with faculty and engage with other students outside conventional class time. Shea (2007) stated there is a need to recognize "the pre-conditions and activities likely to result in high levels of learning and high levels of student and faculty satisfaction, and ultimately increased access and more efficient deployment of existing physical resources" (p. 20).

The discussion about the problem of limited student visits to campus led also to discussions about the benefits and sustainability of blended learning. In this regard, blended learning serves to fill a broader logistical need for improving service quality for campus-based students that can lead to a number of positive gains. Some positive gains noted in the literature include, for example, increased convenience and access to the course and to the course instructor (Shea, 2007), increased connectivity with faculty and other students (Vignare, 2007), increased student engagement and active participation (Vaughan, 2010), and an increased sense of classroom community (Woods, Badzinski, & Baker, 2007). Garrison and Vaughan (2008) indicated that classrooms are becoming more like open learning spaces and that "blended learning is about flattening the hierarchical control of the classroom with increased interaction and engagement" (p. 147).

Contextualizing and Planning for Blended Learning

Picciano (2011) described blended learning in the context of two key elements: (1) a valuable and pedagogically planned integration of online and face-to-face class activities that is (2) driven by an institutionally defined portion of face-to-face time that is replaced by online activity (p. 4). Additionally, in looking at patterns of online and blended course delivery methods across higher education programs in the United States, Allen, Seaman, and Garrett (2007) found there was "a great deal of diversity among course delivery methods used by instructors" (p. 5) and a course or program that blends online and face-to-face delivery 30–79% of the time is said to be "blended." Picciano (2007) noted that there are various ways to contextualize blended learning. Also, there may be notable overlaps of online and blended modalities, given the variance of the instructional situation and technologies employed in the educational environment, to the extent that "the definition of blended learning becomes very fluid" (p. 8).

For example, the ubiquitous integration of social media in the educational environment makes it more challenging to differentiate blended from online or from traditional class interaction.

Blended learning is not a mere "bolting together of disparate technologies with any clear vision of the result" (Garrison & Vaughan, 2008, p. 148). Moreover, Dziuban, Moskal, and Futch (2007) contextualized blended learning as "a mental model that is evolving" (p. 197). Dziuban, Hartman, and Moskal (2007) noted that institutions need to have their own vision for blended learning, including a "well-defined mental model" for program development that "fits the institution's needs" in determining successful blended learning initiatives (p. 267). They indicated that having a clear vision for the blended learning initiative is better than merely following a prescribed label or definition that does not scale well to how an institution or academic program conceptualizes blended learning.

At the onset of project planning, we did not set out to define blended learning nor to set new policy about class seat time or how online activities combined with campus course activities would be balanced. The objective was to integrate engaging student-to-instructor and/or student-to-student activities, using selected online communication tools (and other online learning technologies that were soon to follow) to increase student dialogue and exchange. Garrison and Vaughan (2008) and Vignare (2007) reported that students' value improved communication and interaction with their peers and their instructors, and frequent interaction produces higher student course satisfaction ratings (Cao, Griffin, & Xue, 2009). We anticipated that students would perceive the online activities as increasing their access to faculty and to other students outside the campus class. We also predicted that students would anticipate their potential for learning course content would increase significantly; in turn, this would lead also to increased levels of student satisfaction ratings of courses. Dziuban et al. (2005) indicated from their large dataset of over 200,000 student surveys, compiled over 7 years at the University of Central Florida, that blended learning initiatives resulted in high levels of student satisfaction at UCF. Though our findings will show data of a much smaller scale due to modest enrollments in our campus-based master's programs, our findings indicate similarly that there are high levels of student satisfaction and increased perceived levels of student engagement with blended learning initiatives.

Without a set definition of blended learning or prescribed initiatives, we allowed our initiatives to grow "organically." Garrison and Vaughan (2008) indicated, "Blended learning is the organic integration of thoughtfully selected and complementary face-to-face and online approaches and technologies" (p. 148). Faculty members did not want to be stifled by using one kind of technology or prescribed initiatives to implement in their campus courses. Instructors wanted autonomous control over their choice of online activity implementation (Vignare, 2007) and to define their own ways to enhance the engagement of students.

We discovered over time that our project has advanced successfully without imparting a strict definition of blended learning or by following prescribed benchmarks for student engagement (such as National Study of Student Engagement, NSSE, 2007). However, we believe our initiatives are identifiable in recognizing broader NSSE-like quality and satisfaction benchmarks of student engagement identified by Vaughan (2010, p. 61), such as supportive campus environment, enriched educational experiences, increased student interactions with faculty members, and benchmarks identified by Dziuban et al. (2007, p. 199), such as cooperative involvement, iterative feedback, and engagement. Dziuban et al. indicated that the confluence of these components "forms a workable theoretical base for the pedagogy of blended learning" (p. 199). In retrospect, we discovered in characterizing the scope of blended learning that "fluidity" is advantageous; that it has led to the organic growth of successful blended learning strategies in accord with recognizing our instructors' unique teaching practices and instructional preferences.

Preparing Sustainable Blended Learning Initiatives

As the GSCIS BL project was tied to NSU's *QEP Enhancing Student Engagement* initiative (as part of SACS accreditation and institutional-level self-evaluation) and discussion on the benefits of blended learning ensued, faculty began exploring creative initiatives deemed appropriate on the course level. This exploration process led to relegating choice of technology, strategy, and quality control to the instructors. Vignare (2007) indicated that faculty satisfaction is tied to how instructors perceive they have quality control over a course regardless of whether the course is blended, online, or campus-based. As our project developed and initiatives were tested by instructors in their campus courses, and student survey data revealed a positive response to those initiatives (data will be described in detail in the findings section), there was also an increased satisfaction level expressed by instructors who felt that their choice of blended learning initiatives had impacted students positively.

Fundamental to employing blended strategies of their choice, instructors must be prepared through receiving ample technological and pedagogical support (Garrison & Vaughan, 2008). Vaughan (2007) reported many faculty members need professional development support in that course redesign often requires faculty to acquire new technology skills and learn new teaching strategies to apply to new technologies. Kaleta, Skibba, and Joosten (2007) reported that several of their instructors desired to develop innovative interactive online activities to provide students options or choices for learning course content, but this effort required a certain level of preparedness and professional development support to effect.

In GSCIS, some faculty members seek such training or advice from university technology support personnel to enhance pedagogical and engagement aspects in using technology tools. Some faculty members with expertise in instructional systems design and/or in designing online courses advise or mentor other faculty members and adjuncts on effective use of technology tools for enhancing academic and student engagement in online and blended modalities. Similarly, students may attend online information sessions before starting the master's program; this includes an orientation to technologies being used in the school. Dziuban et al. (2007) noted that there is a taxonomy of expertise in blended learning that takes time for faculty and students to develop, and not all faculty or students share the same expertise level or experience with technology integration in the teaching and learning space. In addition, they stated that fluency takes time to develop, as instructors may be initially learning new ways to integrate technology and students are learning how to use the technology in the context of the learning activity. With cumulative experience, eventually there is an "effortless flow" and a "self-sustaining energy" to doing blended learning to the point where "many instructors no longer think in terms of blended learning courses" (Dziuban et al., 2007, p. 198).

Student satisfaction is linked to how students feel they are prepared to use the technologies employed in online and blended courses (Vignare, 2007). Kaleta et al.(2007) reported faculty concerns about students' lack of technological proficiency and that technological proficiency is not to be assumed, even of younger students. Students require technical support from the institution, including orientation and technology training, access to technology support, and online library access (Vignare, 2007, p. 49). Students also want to know how much time they will spend in class and how much time they need to spend online when taking a blended course (Kerres & DeWitt, 2004). Therefore, the flexibility and preparation involved in blended learning includes understanding "redesign" aspects of blended course delivery and the boundaries and affordances that are tied to sustained success of blended initiatives.

Method

We present data of a 5-year implementation plan of blended learning initiatives in campus course offerings in computer science and information systems. Our data focus on student responses to end-of-term surveys that relate to the specific initiatives in campus courses students have taken each semester. We also report faculty reflections on their own blended initiatives. Our reporting covers data from academic years 2008–2011. (Partial data for academic year 2012, in progress, are not included.)

Overarching Research Question/Goals

Our overarching research question is framed in the context of our ongoing project goals on evaluating the effectiveness of blended learning initiatives in campus course offerings:

- Goal 1: Students will demonstrate enhanced academic engagement in their dialogue and exchange by perceiving increased satisfaction with online interactivity included in campus-based courses.
- Goal 2: Students will demonstrate enhanced learning as a result of dialogue and exchange afforded by the initiative.

The effectiveness of blended learning is measured through the two goals. Measures of (1) student satisfaction, (2) student assessment of learning, and (3) instructor assessment of learning were included with the review of each initiative. The objective of our assessment is to gain perspectives of students and each faculty member with the particular type of engagement activity initiative in each course, and to gain a school-wide perspective on the myriad activities undertaken in the school. Participation data were also culled from the learning management system (mainly WebCT), however, for brevity purposes, we report this data minimally in this chapter.

Participants

Our data stem from a total of 1032 duplicated student headcounts derived from a total of 4 academic years; student headcounts were distinguished in each academic semester and each year from Fall 2008 through Spring 2011. In the population of (duplicated) students, over 75% were male. Their ages ranged from 20 to 60, with a median of 30 years. (Almost 85% of the students were under 40 years old.)

Instructors involved in our project consisted of 11 full-time faculty and 5 adjunct instructors who taught campus courses spanning academic terms from 2008–2011.

Data Collection and Data Sources

Student Survey

Student satisfaction is measured through an end of term survey. Each term, we ask each instructor teaching a campus course to identify before the term begins the online activity or activities that will be used in the course to increase student–faculty and/or student–student interaction. For example, a specific question is posed to a faculty member who regularly initiated group assignments online: *For your operating systems course, do you plan to utilize discussion boards for student communication supporting group assignments, as you have done in the past?*

We then incorporate particular survey items into a 5-point Likert-scale end of term survey that measures the impact/utility of exactly what the instructor aimed to do online. Instructors are given summaries of the student responses to evaluate what initiatives students perceive are effective or need improvement in the course. The following is an example template for student survey items:

- *I am satisfied with use of [online tool(s) specified] to provide additional interaction in the course. (Goal 1)*
- *[Some online tool] helped me understand the course material better. (Goal 2)*

Faculty Survey

Enhanced learning is measured through the instructor's assessment through a faculty survey. The faculty survey is quantitative (4-point Likert-scale) and open-ended, requesting instructors to provide ratings and to provide their comments or reflections about the instructor's perceived efficacy or satisfaction with integrating the selected online tool(s) into their courses to enhance student engagement and interaction during non-class hours. The following are example questions prompting comments by each faculty member with respect to their particular online activity they had integrated into their campus course:

- *To what extent did the online environment [the online tool specified] enhance student understanding in your course? What comments do you have regarding the implementation?*
- *Can you also indicate to whether you thought the initiative contributed (0) not at all, (1) minimally, (2) somewhat, or (3) a great deal to student understanding?*

Activity Data from the Learning Management System

In addition to the surveys, we also have taken quantified measures from the Learning Management System (LMS), where applicable, to examine activity (e.g., number of posts in a discussion forum, other), as a proxy for satisfaction and level of student engagement. However, we have found that participation frequency data is limited for our assessments. (In the Discussion and Conclusions section, we address the need for more meaningful participation tracking activity measures.)

Data Considerations

Many studies have reported data on several similar measures we use in our study related to student satisfaction, faculty satisfaction, and/or perceptions about experiences with blended learning courses or initiatives (Dziuban & Moskal, 2011; Dziuban et al., 2007; Kenney & Newcombe, 2011; Vaughan, 2010; Woods et al., 2007). Often an end-of-course survey has been employed in these studies as well as faculty interviews or surveys about faculty members' perceptions of student engagement. Participation data were reported from tracking statistics from the online tools (Kenney & Newcombe, 2011; Woods et al., 2007).

Our data are limited to satisfaction levels and perceived enhanced learning culled from the surveys. Dziuban and Moskal (2011) indicated that course evaluations may play a standard part of assessment, but for students, the class is "an increasingly complex network of interactions" (p. 240); such interactions are difficult to understand through summative evaluation. In addition, we have not evaluated the effectiveness of the initiatives against other potential variables or interactions that may influence student satisfaction and perceived enhanced learning, including class size, group composition, course content, expectations, student performance or grades, or time availability, among others.

Data Analysis

Data were aggregated in the form of the number of student responses (i.e., "responding") to the 5-point Likert survey (strongly disagree, disagree, agree, strongly agree, N/A). The data include all participating campus-based class sections over all semesters of each academic year, from project Year 1 (2008), Year 2 (2009), Year 3 (2010), through Year 4 (2011). We compared previous year to current year data; we aimed for year-to-year improvement as reflected from our surveys and LMS participation data.

Findings

Summary of Student Survey Data

Each year we provide NSU administration with a summary report of our QEP project. We report the stage of implementation, a brief summary of assessment data, and challenges we noted with the project during that academic year.

TABLE 8.1 GSCIS QEP Assessment Data from Student Surveys: Year 1–Year 4

	Goal 1						Goal 2						
	Students reporting satisfaction (%)						Students reporting enhanced learning (%)						
Year	Responding	SD	D	A	SA	N/A	[S]A	Responding	SD	D	A	SA	N/A	[S]A
2008	183/287	0	7	84	79	13	89.1	183/287	1	10	78	78	16	85.2
2009	142/292	5	9	53	52	23	73.9	139/292	5	13	51	45	25	69.1
2010	158/235	1	2	70	61	24	82.9	158/235	1	10	59	44	44	65.2
2011	131/218	1	2	51	58	19	83.2	131/218	0	4	56	35	36	69.5

Note: Scale: SD=strongly disagree; D=disagree; A=agree; SA=strongly agree; N/A = no opinion/not applicable; [S]A=proportion of "agrees"

Table 8.1 presents the general assessment data on reflecting on the two goals from Year 1 (2008) through Year 4 (2011). In each year, the vast majority of students report increased satisfaction and learning, with a larger proportion of students agreeing with increased satisfaction than with increased learning. That difference, however, is only significant in years 2010 and 2011. We suspect that this may be attributed to our migration from the WebCT to BlackBoard Learn in 2010.

Summary of Faculty Survey Data

We ask faculty members to rate and comment if their unique online initiatives in their campus-based master's courses had perceivably enhanced student learning. Below, under "QEP Initiatives Summary," we share averaged ratings of faculty members' perceived contribution of the initiative and excerpts of insightful comments by faculty culled from open-ended questions from the faculty surveys from 2009–2011.

QEP Initiatives Summary

Various creative forms of online discussions were implemented to enhance student interactivity outside of the campus class, including using discussion boards to facilitate communication in group projects; synchronous lectures; forums for key concepts, questions, and problems; asynchronous discussions; lecture recaps; student resource sharing; and online Q&A. We report a summary of instructors' blended learning initiatives together with student survey response data. The eight initiatives below were deployed by 12 instructors in 50 course sections that represent 19 different catalog courses from January 2009 through April 2011.

In the listing of initiatives below, we summarize the quantitative measures from the student survey assessments for satisfaction and learning. As seen in the tables, students are very positive across the board about the initiatives deployed in the courses. Because there is little variance in this measure, we sort the initiatives in the listing by the average rating given by instructors of the initiative's effectiveness.

Using Discussion Boards to Facilitate Communication Among Group Members

Two instructors who were using group projects in their courses (n=107 enrolled students in three catalog courses over eight course sections) found that the threaded discussion boards provided a good mechanism for the group members to interact. For each course section, the instructor rated the contribution of the interaction toward learning at 3 out of 3. The student responses, as shown in Table 8.2, were similarly positive for this initiative.

TABLE 8.2 Using Discussion Boards to Facilitate Communication Among Group Members

Goal 1						Goal 2					
Students reporting satisfaction						Students reporting enhanced learning					
Responding	SD	D	A	SA	N/A	Responding	SD	D	A	SA	N/A
60/107	2	1	27	25	5	60/107	0	4	28	18	10

The number of student broadcasts in these courses was quite large, averaging 24 per student in each course. That volume is unique to this initiative.

Excerpts from Faculty Comments

I believe the integration of course content and discussion within the assignment encouraged a deeper thought process. This ultimately resulted in a better artifact in the form of a design and implementation.

Since a great portion of this communication led to the creation of documents of significant size, I think the implementation worked as well as it could given the inherent limitations of a discussion forum. If we had a document/source-code version control system built into the discussion forum then I think the entire collaborative process would have been more rewarding.

Distribution of News, Articles of Interest

One instructor in 11 course sections (n=141 enrolled students in two catalog courses) used this technique. The average rating from this instructor of the impact on learning is 2.8 out of 3 across those 11 sections. Table 8.3 presents the students' survey responses for this initiative.

TABLE 8.3 Distribution of News, Articles of Interest

Goal 1						Goal 2					
Students reporting satisfaction						Students reporting enhanced earning					
Responding	SD	D	A	SA	N/A	Responding	SD	D	A	SA	N/A
53/141	1	1	11	37	3	53/141	1	1	19	25	7

Excerpts from Faculty Comments

> *I did a better job [this term] filtering articles that closely related to the topics being covered at that time. By providing this information on a regular basis to my students, they were able to learn about what is going on in the IS [information systems] world.*

> *Messages created trigger points to discuss (in class) items relevant to lecture material.*

Synchronous Lecture

One instructor (n=43 enrolled students in four course sections, two catalog courses) used Wimba Classroom to supplement on-campus lectures. (In one instance, the instructor also used online discussion forums in a "2-part" QEP deployment.) The instructor rated the initiative's contribution to learning at 2.8 out of 3 for the three responses filed. Table 8.4 presents the students' survey responses for this initiative.

Excerpts from Faculty Comments

> *As to using online [synchronous lectures] for on-campus classes, I have tried many different formats, and none seem to appeal to the students. They feel that they attend class on campus, and don't want to do any additional online work, other than assignments.*

> *I feel that Wimba has helped many of the students. Although I don't know how many review the archived presentations, I have had students say they appreciated my interaction. I will probably continue with Wimba.*

Forums for Key Concepts, Questions, and Problems

One instructor (n=104 enrolled students in eight course sections and three catalog courses) used the online discussion boards to essentially deploy a combination of instructor Q&A, lecture extension, and online discussions for problem solving.

TABLE 8.4 Synchronous Lectures

| Goal 1 | | | | | | Goal 2 | | | | | |
| Students reporting satisfaction | | | | | | Students reporting enhanced learning | | | | | |
Responding	SD	D	A	SA	N/A	Responding	SD	D	A	SA	N/A
21/43	0	0	8	9	4	21/43	0	2	8	5	6

TABLE 8.5 Forums for Key Concepts, Questions, and Problems

Goal 1 Students reporting satisfaction						Goal 2 Students reporting enhanced learning					
Responding	SD	D	A	SA	N/A	Responding	SD	D	A	SA	N/A
77/104	1	2	35	30	9	76/104	2	9	28	23	14

The instructor rated the effectiveness of this initiative on average 1.5 out of 3, over the eight sections. Table 8.5 presents the students' survey responses for this initiative.

Excerpts from Faculty Comments

> There wasn't much discussion (this was a small class of seven students). The discussions were mostly limited to trivial implementation issues. . . . Again, the lack of contributions from online discussions is largely because the students weren't too interested and I couldn't get them to engage in any meaningful discussions.

Online Discussions

Five instructors in nine course sections (n=116 enrolled students; six catalog courses) used the discussion forums to engage students in asynchronous discussions around a topic. On average, they rated the effectiveness of this initiative at 1.4 out of 3. Table 8.6 presents the students' survey responses for this initiative.

Excerpts from Faculty Comments

> [I] tried to create discussion sections for topics of interest—with an introductory message or question. These did not generate as much traffic as was hoped for.

> Students, who were confused about assignments (e.g., they hadn't been in class, or perhaps dosed through an explanation), posted questions to the discussion and received replies from other students (or occasionally the instructor). This forum worked well.

TABLE 8.6 Online Discussions

Goal 1 Students reporting satisfaction						Goal 2 Students reporting enhanced learning					
Responding	SD	D	A	SA	N/A	Responding	SD	D	A	SA	N/A
81/116	1	4	40	21	15	81/116	0	8	31	16	26

It seems the on-campus students prefer face-to-face or one-to-one communication. They would rather write me emails or drop by my office to ask questions.

Post Lecture Recaps

Two instructors in seven course sections (n=71 enrolled students in five different catalog courses) utilized the discussion board area to post summaries after each on-campus meeting, and invite feedback. In some cases, the discussion forum allowed for anonymous posts. The two instructors gave an average effectiveness rating of 1.3 out of 3 across those seven sections. Table 8.7 presents the students' survey responses for this initiative.

Excerpts from Faculty Comments

I have seen low response rates on this for almost all my past on-campus courses. I think they are mainly due to the nature of the courses (face-to-face interactions are better ways for communicating technical problems) and the low enrollment for on-campus courses. I am not confident to continue with this for the following terms based on my observation. Maybe Blackboard will provide a better tool to motivate students' engagement.

I have received only sporadic comments on these recaps, but students have told me that they take security in knowing that, should they miss class, they will have the recap to consult. As it is a simple exercise, I will likely continue to follow this practice in the future.

Share Resources

One faculty member in one course section (n=16 enrolled students) created an area where students could share resources they had located through their course activities. The instructor rated the contribution of this initiative toward learning at 1 out of 3 (minimal). Table 8.8 shows the students' survey responses for this initiative.

TABLE 8.7 Post Lecture Recaps

Goal 1 Students reporting satisfaction						Goal 2 Students reporting enhanced learning					
Responding	*SD*	*D*	*A*	*SA*	*N/A*	*Responding*	*SD*	*D*	*A*	*SA*	*N/A*
44/71	1	0	18	14	11	44/71	1	1	16	10	16

TABLE 8.8 Share Resources

Goal 1 Students reporting satisfaction						Goal 2 Students reporting enhanced learning					
Responding	SD	D	A	SA	N/A	Responding	SD	D	A	SA	N/A
12/16	0	0	6	4	2	12/16	0	0	6	3	3

Excerpts from Faculty Comments

> *The intention is good, however. I have attempted to incorporate applied discussions in the assignments, where students have to discuss analytical questions in addition to the questions that require them to solve a problem.*

Create an online Q&A session for students to get questions answered outside of class

Two instructors tried this initiative in two different catalog courses (n=20 enrolled students). The one instructor response filed rated the initiative's contribution to learning at 0, no impact. Table 8.9 presents the students' survey responses for this initiative.

Excerpts from Faculty Comments

> *As usual, on campus students prefer to ask questions in the classroom or come to my office before the class.*

Discussion and Conclusions

We reflect on the issue of the sustainability of blended learning, given that there is evidence from our data which suggests that within 5 years implementation of some form of blended learning practice is mainstreamed in our campus courses, with further evidence that the vast majority of students report that they value

TABLE 8.9 Create an Online Q&A Session for Students to Get Questions Answered Outside of Class

Goal 1 Students reporting satisfaction						Goal 2 Students reporting enhanced learning					
Responding	SD	D	A	SA	N/A	Responding	SD	D	A	SA	N/A
14/20	0	0	7	3	4	14/20	0	0	7	3	4

having blended learning activities in their courses. From our view, blended learning practice is sustainable, and, when mainstreamed, becomes nearly an invisible entity among those who practice it. Dziuban and Moskal (2011) recognized this in the context that technological innovations are naturally creating an "unbundled environment" and that most "traditional courses are undergoing some form of enhancement" (p. 236) through the use of technology in the course. The data we have collected suggest that some on-campus students value the online medium, and others want even more technological innovation.

While students have indicated a positive response toward the integration of online tools and activities in enhancing their class experience, faculty have discussed that there are constraints likely to persist that will also impact the significance and/or the interpretation of the outcomes. Some constraints identified by the faculty include the course being taught, students' and faculty preferences, and expectations of an on-campus course, class size, and the "extra" work on faculty and students in balancing class seat time. In addressing the constraint about "extra work," for example, we recognize the problems with "the course and a half syndrome" described by Kaleta et al. (2007). Without adjustments to class seat time or how instructors "pack on" additional course content or online activities to the existing course, instructors and students complain about "overloaded courses." The syndrome of doing too much, and applying different delivery modes, requires consideration of new policy about class time and developing guidelines on balancing online activities with campus activities (Graham & Allen, 2009; Picciano, 2009, 2011).

On the surface, it may appear that sustainability is an indicator that the life of the project requires only a periodic assessment. However, one should not discount that to sustain positive efforts there is a need for ongoing evaluation of the effectiveness of this modality to refine effective practices. There is a need also to advance analytics to support "getting the right data and getting the data right" in defining meaningful measures for online and blended learning (Dringus, 2012, p. 98). This relates to data that are measurable and transparent from the online environment to show critical aspects of student engagement, learning, and persistence. For example, we learned that much of the student participation data from the LMS were frequency-oriented; merely a broad measure was taken of the number of student broadcasts ("accesses or hits" as per Woods et al., 2007) to serve as a proxy for increased student interaction. As learning analytics filters its way into LMS reporting tools, direct measures for analyzing meaningful levels of student activity and performance will be necessary to track and support student progress.

As our project developed, our faculty used discussion forums, but they also adopted other forms of interaction strategies that present diverse perceptions and practices, which result in enhanced information richness of course content

(Graham & Robison, 2007), including small online groups, discussions used to promote critical thinking on course content, and problem-based exercises, among many other strategies. Surely, our prototype efforts involve "value added" constructs, such as those identified by Norberg, Dziuban, and Moskal (2011, p. 209) in terms of improving enhancement, presence, and access, in that "blending becomes a mix of place versus non-place events." However, to sustain effective blended learning efforts, it is important to deemphasize a focus on "tool centric" categories of engagement and reemphasize "course centric" categories of engagement so that faculty can find "the right blend" (Graham & Allen, 2009) and focus more on the instructional and/or pedagogical gains of what blended practices they are doing in their courses.

In achieving these milestones, we note that improvements to our process are needed to discover deeper contexts in how blended learning improves the instructional and learning experience. Looking ahead, some general questions about blended learning may help reflect on deeper contexts: What are the effective practices for achieving quality online discussions for blended courses? What is the effective balance of online and class discussions in enhancing learning course content? How successful is blended learning in improving a sense of community in the class or in feeling that one is part of the larger institutional community? How can learning analytics inform instructors of students' learning in the blended course? Picciano (2009) duly noted that in higher education, "it is accepted that colleges and universities need to do more to engage students" (p. 8). With ubiquitous technology use on the rise and in empowering and engaging students from beyond campus walls, it seems to matter less if a course is online, blended, or face-to-face. Perhaps Norberg et al.'s (2011, p. 214) prediction will hold true that "in the future we will be able to discontinue conversations about space, blending, and perhaps even time." Until then, our initiatives will persist to clearly extend student engagement in ways that are dynamically supportive of an academic environment that exists beyond the physical classroom and its class schedule.

References

Allen, I. E., Seaman, J., & Garrett, R. (2007, March). *Blending in: The extent and promise of blended education in the United States.* Needham, MA: Sloan-C.

Cao, Q., Griffin, T., & Xue, B. (2009). The importance of synchronous interaction for student satisfaction with course web sites. *Journal of Information Systems Education, 20*(3), 331–338.

Dringus, L. P. (2012). Learning analytics considered harmful. *Journal of Asynchronous Learning Networks, 16*(3), 87–100.

Dringus, L. P., & Scigliano, J. A. (2000). From early to current developments in online learning at Nova Southeastern University: Reflections on historical milestones. *The Internet and Higher Education, 3,* 23–40.

Dziuban, C., & Moskal, P. (2011). A course is a course is a course: Factor invariance in student evaluation of online, blended and face-to-face learning environments. *The Internet and Higher Education, 14*(4), 236–241.

Dziuban, C., Hartman, J., & Moskal, P. (2007). Everything I need to know about blended learning I learned from books. In A. G. Picciano & C. D. Dziuban (Eds.), *Blended learning research perspectives* (pp. 265–286). Needham, MA: Sloan-C.

Dziuban, C., Moskal, P., & Futch, P. (2007). Reactive behavior, ambivalence, and the generations: Emerging patterns in student evaluation of blended learning. In A. G. Picciano & C. D. Dziuban (Eds.), *Blended learning research perspectives* (pp. 179–202). Needham, MA: Sloan-C.

Dziuban, C., Moskal, P., & Hartman, J. (2005). Higher education, blended learning, and the generations: Knowledge is power–no more. In J. Bourne & J. C. Moore (Eds.), *Elements of quality online education: Engaging communities* (pp. 85–100). Needham, MA: Sloan-C.

Garrison, D. R., & Vaughan, N. D. (2008). *Blended learning in higher education. Framework, principles, and guidelines.* San Francisco: John Wiley.

Graham, C. R., & Allen, S. (2009). Designing blended learning environments. *Encyclopedia of Distance Learning, 2*, 1–9.

Graham, C. R., & Robison, R. (2007). Realizing the transformational potential of blended learning. In A. G. Picciano & C. D. Dziuban (Eds.), *Blended learning research perspectives* (pp. 83–110). Needham, MA: Sloan-C.

Kaleta, R., Skibba, K., & Joosten, T. (2007). Discovering, designing, and delivering hybrid courses. In A. G. Picciano & C. D. Dziuban (Eds.), *Blended learning research perspectives* (pp. 111–144). Needham, MA: Sloan-C.

Kenney, J., & Newcombe, E. (2011). Adopting a blended learning approach: Challenges encountered and lessons learned in an action research study. *Journal of Asynchronous Learning Networks, 15*(1), 41–57.

Kerres, M., & DeWitt, C. (2004). A didactical framework for the design of blended learning arrangements. *Journal of Educational Media, 28*(2–3), 101–113.

Norberg, A., Dziuban, C. D., & Moskal, P. D. (2011). A time-based blended learning model. *On the Horizon, 19*(3), 207–216.

Picciano, A. G. (2007). Introduction. In A. G. Picciano & C. D. Dziuban (Eds.), *Blended learning research perspectives* (pp. 5–18). Needham, MA: Sloan-C.

Picciano, A. G. (2009). Blending with purpose: the multimodal model. *Journal of Asynchronous Learning Networks, 13*(1), 7–18.

Picciano, A. G. (2011, February). Introduction to the special issue on transitioning to blended learning. *Journal of Asynchronous Learning Networks, 15*(1), 3–7.

Picciano, A. G. & Dziuban, C. D. (Eds.) (2007). *Blended learning research perspectives.* Needham, MA: Sloan-C.

Shea, P. (2007). Towards a conceptual framework for learning in blended environments. In A. G. Picciano & C. D. Dziuban (Eds.), *Blended learning research perspectives* (pp. 19–36). Needham, MA: Sloan-C.

Vaughan, N. (2007). Perspectives on blended learning in higher education. *International Journal on E-Learning, 6*(1), 81–94.

Vaughan, N. (2010). A blended community of inquiry approach: Linking student engagement and course redesign. *The Internet and Higher Education, 13*(1–2), 60–65.

Vignare, K. (2007). Review of literature on blended learning. In A. G. Picciano & C. D. Dziuban (Eds.), *Blended learning research perspectives* (pp. 37–64). Needham, MA: Sloan-C.

Woods, R., Badzinski, D. M., & Baker, J. D. (2007). Student perceptions of blended learning in a traditional undergraduate environment. In A. G. Picciano & C. D. Dziuban (Eds.), *Blended learning research perspectives* (pp. 203–229). Needham, MA: Sloan-C.

9

TRIAL AND ERROR

Iteratively Improving Research on Blended Learning

D. Christopher Brooks and Jodi R. Sandfort

As scholars interested in technology enhanced learning, we think it is essential to bring our empirical skills to help us assess and improve teaching innovations. In this chapter, we share our experience developing and studying portable learning objects used in teaching professionals about public policy and management. Specifically, we describe our development of a new generation of learning materials to refresh written teaching cases, a signature pedagogy in public affairs education (Rosenbloom, 1995; Shulman, 2005). Our research examines the impact of using new, multimedia, teaching cases rather than traditional, written, cases in public and nonprofit management courses. This chapter recounts our conceptualization of the research, our multiple rounds of research with a rigorous design, and results. We illustrate how using appropriate research designs, identifying the proper levels of analysis, and specifying dependent and independent variables often are iterative in blended learning studies.

Teaching and Learning in Public Affairs

The field of public affairs encompasses professional schools of public policy, public administration, and nonprofit management (Lynn, 1996) as well as courses focusing on these topics in undergraduate programs in sociology, political science, and social work. In public affairs classrooms, students develop both the analytical abilities to investigate problems and the social skills to navigate nuanced social and political settings to develop or implement solutions. A number of pedagogies support this multi-faceted learning: problem-based learning, interactive lecturing, discussion-based teaching, problem-based exercises, and case studies. In contrast to instruction that focuses on the mastery of an academic field, this pedagogical approach often is shaped by inquiry-guided learning (Lee, 2004).

Within this field, there is a long tradition of using teaching cases to deepen classroom learning (Gibson, 2008; Gilmore and Schall, 1996; Rosenbloom, 1995; Yeung, 2007). Teaching cases often tell a story of a difficult problem, providing written accounts of context-rich settings that enable students to actively grapple with specific organizational settings, complex field relationships, and the ambiguity inherent in public problem solving. Students read the case before class and teachers ask a series of questions about underlying dynamics of the case to stimulate new ideas and connect to other course concepts. These case studies can also provide context for additional course assignments. For example, in the research applications described below, students wrote one-page management memos analyzing a case situation with recommendations about strategic actions to leaders described in the case.

The increasingly low cost of multimedia content and sharing power of the Internet allows for the enhancement of this traditional pedagogical tool. We began our research by exploring a prototype of that idea focused on creating a decision-forcing teaching case with new media. The particular case assembled multimedia assets—video, audio, hyper-links to live web-sites, PDFs—in a story-line in which students needed to assume the perspective of a nonprofit leader and decide how to best develop a program to combat predatory lending targeting low-income people. After the initial prototype, the e-case was streamlined and rebuilt as part of the Hubert portfolio, a growing collection of multimedia public affairs learning objects. The repository also includes other portable learning objects, including video briefs and curated cases that can be incorporated in face-to-face, blended, or fully on-line courses (see: www.hubertproject.org). The portability of these materials points to their potential significance for public affairs education and why we conduct research on their impact on student learning.

Initial Research Deployment

When initially exploring the e-case prototype, we employed a quasi-experimental design comparing the relative impact of exposure to the multimedia case with a paper-based case in four undergraduate and four graduate sections of two management courses (N = 183). We gathered data after students experienced both cases through a theoretically grounded survey instrument that captured key demographic variables and measured five constructs based on Fink's (2003) typology of significant learning experiences: 1) foundational, content recall; 2) application of knowledge and integration of creative and practical problem solving; 3) human dimension of learning about oneself and others; 4) increased interests and new opinions; and 5) learning to learn through inquiry.

For our initial analysis, we tested the null hypotheses that there is no significant difference in responses between students after exposure to written cases and multimedia cases for each construct with simple comparison of means. Failing to reject the null hypotheses would mean that there are no significant differences between our comparison groups; rejecting the null hypotheses would mean that there are significant differences observed. From these tests, we have three possible sets of findings: 1) paper and multimedia cases have the same effect on student learning, 2) paper cases have a greater impact than do multimedia ones on student learning, and 3) multimedia cases have a greater impact than do paper cases on student learning. Our test results were mixed (see Table 9.1). For the foundational knowledge questions, we rejected the null hypothesis for three of the four items, with exposure to the multimedia case producing the significantly larger results. For the application and integration questions, exposure to the paper case was more significant than the multimedia case for half of the items, with no difference observed for the other half. The results for the human dimension tests were evenly distributed across all three possible outcomes. No significant difference was found between the two case formats in 20% of the increased interest items; the remaining 80% was distributed evenly between paper and multimedia having the larger impact. We failed to reject the null hypothesis of no difference for any of the questions in the learning how to learn category.

We have a number of potential explanations for these initial mixed results. First, the multimedia case itself was a prototype in which navigation challenges and content overload could have created easily more barriers to learning than the traditional cases presented in familiar written format. Additionally, there were other confounding factors including treatment sequencing, instructor experience, and course levels. While we explored the possibility that demographic variation might be responsible for the disruption of a clear pattern of results, the analysis of sex, age, ethnicity, professional experience, and

TABLE 9.1 Categorical Distribution of Results of Difference of Means Tests for Pilot Project by Question Family

	Paper > multimedia	Paper = multimedia	Paper > multimedia
Foundational knowledge	0.0%	25.0%	75.0%
Application and integration	50.0%	50.0%	0.0%
Human dimensions	33.3%	33.3%	33.3%
Increased interest	40.0%	20.0%	40.0%
Learning how to learn	0.0%	100.0%	0.0%
AVERAGE	26.1%	39.1%	34.8%

familiarity with using cases studies revealed no systematic patterns. These results did suggest to us, however, that we needed to improve the multimedia case and explore a new research design to control for potential confounding factors.

Modification of Research Design

We rebuilt the prototype multimedia case, streamlining it by presenting content around learning objectives to reduce cognitive overload and to improve visual appeal and navigability. We also reconsidered how to test rigorously our central research question regarding the impact of case modality on student learning. We again employed a quasi-experimental design in three sections of a management course (N = 60) using the same instrumentation. This time, however, we used a new research design to correct for the confounding factors identified in the previous trial: students in one section received a written version of the same case content; students in another section received a blended content (written for part A and multimedia for parts B and C); and students in the third section only experienced the multimedia case. This approach afforded the opportunity for us to isolate more carefully the impact of the media, since the content was consistent across the treatment.

Using a comparison of means, we again tested the null hypotheses that there are no significant differences in item responses based on case format. We failed to reject the null for 97.2% of the items; we rejected the null hypothesis for only one item (from the learning how to learn construct) in favor of the superiority of the multimedia case (see Table 9.2). We again made comparisons across the aforementioned demographic categories, none of which revealed any systematic patterns in the data. While these results suggest that the multimedia case at least "does no harm" compared to written cases, the results defy our expectations that the digital or blended case treatments should enhance student learning across the five theoretical constructs representing student learning in our instrument.

TABLE 9.2 Categorical Distribution of Results of Difference of Means Tests for Second Phase of Project by Question Family

	Paper > *multimedia*	*Paper =* *multimedia*	*Paper <* *multimedia*
Foundational knowledge	0.0%	100.0%	0.0%
Application and integration	0.0%	100.0%	0.0%
Human dimensions	0.0%	100.0%	0.0%
Increased interest	0.0%	100.0%	0.0%
Learning how to learn	0.0%	75.0%	25.0%
AVERAGE	0.0%	97.2%	2.8%

Unlike the first trial where implementation challenges of a prototype could likely explain some of the non-findings, our second design controlled some of the confounding factors. We initially considered whether or not our null outcomes resulted not from the intervention, but from our conceptualization of the desired results. While our constructs were well grounded in Fink's (2003) model of significant learning experience and the model was based on course-level interventions, our assumption that we could use a general idea of course-level learning outcomes to measure precisely the effects of using one learning object now seemed misguided. We asked students to report their learning experiences from a fairly modest intervention, yet the reflective nature of many items may have induced students to consider other or prior aspects of learning experiences in the courses, thereby introducing additional, confounding pieces of information that clouded their responses. Moreover, self-reports about learning tend to be questionable when compared to more evidentiary proxies for learning (e.g., grades). Finally, the instrumentation we developed simply may be operating at a level of analysis that is insensitive to the impact of the learning object (e.g., case) treatment on student learning. Because of these factors, we focused again on ways to specify outcomes germane to our research question and intent.

Reconceptualizing our Model

We realized that other data sources and specification of outcomes might yield more accurate understanding of the differences between how traditional cases and multimedia influence student learning. First, we had student grade information that might overcome many of the limitations of the survey data. Second, by sequencing the cases and written memoranda assignments systematically, we were able to isolate the impact of the multimedia case treatments: three memo assignments were given in all sections, the second of which included our focal case. Thus, in each section using the multimedia case, the first memo served as the baseline, the second as the treatment, and the third as a posttest; the section using only the paper case was our control. Third, we obtained official demographic and aptitude data from the University's Office of Institutional Research that we matched to student identification numbers. This afforded the opportunity to control for a number of additional factors ignored previously.

We examined grades on the interim assignments connected to the learning objects and tested for differences between men and women, international and domestic students, traditional and non-traditional students, and ethnic divisions. None of these tests revealed a consistent pattern in differences between the various sections in which students used the multimedia case treatment and written paper case control. However, pooled comparisons of all the sections using multimedia cases (e.g., full multimedia case *and* blended content) versus

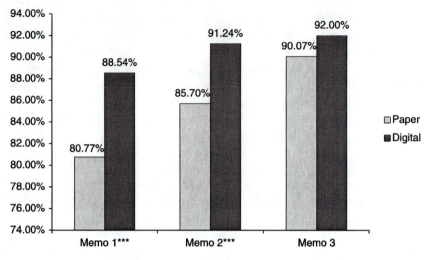

FIGURE 9.1 Differences of Means Tests of Student Grades, Paper vs. Digital, ★★★p < .001

paper cases revealed three interesting patterns (see Figure 9.1): 1) students receiving the paper controls saw their average memo grades improve steadily in each iteration; 2) students receiving the multimedia digital treatments saw their average memo grades improve substantially between Memo 1 and Memo 2 before a plateau between Memo 2 and Memo 3; and 3) the significant, but absolute, differences between multimedia and paper students' average grades decreased from 7.77% for Memo 1 to 5.54% for Memo 2 and, finally, to a statistically insignificant difference of 1.93% for Memo 3. These results suggested to us that students were learning how to do the memos better with repeated attempts, but that there may be differences in how they are learning to do the memos depending on the particular form of the learning object.

Since our data included measures of *a priori* aptitude (Verbal GRE scores) and sequential grade data (Memo 1 followed by Memo 2 followed by Memo 3), we employed a structural equation model (SEM) to better understand this process. We hypothesized that a student's memo grade would be predicted significantly by a student's aptitude *and* any memo grades that precede it. The grades for Memo 1 would be partially determined by Verbal GRE scores; the grades for Memo 2 would be influenced by Verbal GRE scores *and* grades for Memo 1; Memo 3 grades would be predicted by Verbal GRE scores *and* the grades for Memos 1 and 2. The first model uses data from the course section where students only experienced the written case (see Table 9.3). In that section, students' Verbal GRE scores predict significantly all three of their memo grades at approximately the same levels (b = 0.023, b = 0.019, and b = 0.025, respectively). For the second memo, however, the grade for the

TABLE 9.3 Structural Equation Model of Verbal GRE Scores and Prior Memo Grades as Predictors of Memo Grades

Structural Model	Variables	Model 1: Paper	Model 2: Multimedia
Memo 1	Verbal GRE	0.023*	0.010
		(0.010)	(0.012)
	Constant	69.535***	82.775***
		(5.617)	(6.707)
Memo 2	Verbal GRE	0.019*	0.021***
		(0.009)	(0.006)
	Memo 1	0.562***	0.259***
		(0.154)	(0.074)
	Constant	31.572**	56.298***
		(11.538)	(7.029)
Memo 3	Verbal GRE	0.025***	−0.003
		(0.006)	(0.006)
	Memo 1	0.052	0.236**
		(0.122)	(0.081)
	Memo 2	0.097	0.615***
		(0.129)	(0.142)
	Constant	64.973***	16.613
		(8.380)	(10.526)
Variance	Error Memo 1	35.801	45.714
		(10.335)	(9.430)
	Error Memo 2	20.454	11.839
		(5.905)	(2.442)
	Error Memo 3	8.224	11.226
		(2.374)	(2.316)
Log likelihood		−355.409	−680.639
N		24	47

Note: Cell entries are regression coefficients with standard errors (in parentheses).
*$p < .05$; **$p < .01$; ***$p < .001$

first memo predicts considerably better than Verbal GRE scores; holding all other factors constant, for every one point increase in the grade for Memo 1, students earn a corresponding increase of 0.562 points on the grade for Memo 2 ($p < .001$). This suggests that while Verbal GRE scores remain a good predictor of performance, the effect of what students learned from their experience and feedback on Memo 1 is about 30 times greater than the impact of their measured aptitude. However, the grades earned on the first two memos do not have a statistically significant impact on the grade students receive on the third memo. Instead, only Verbal GRE scores remain a significant, but consistently weak, predictor of student grades while the student experience of writing case memos fail to inform students' subsequent efforts.

A different pattern emerges when we use the same SEM to examine data from sections in which students experience the multimedia case treatment. In these sections, students' aptitude does not predict significantly their grades for the first baseline memo. This initial disruption may be attributed to any one of the aforementioned confounding factors, but there is no clear pattern in the data that explains why students in the sections receiving the digital treatments outperformed their paper-case peers on Memo 1. On Memo 2, we obtain a similar result to that of the paper-based case analysis: both students' Verbal GRE scores and Memo 1 grades predict significantly their grades on the second memo, although the effect of the first memo is less than half of its counterpart in the first model. The similarities, however, stop there. Both the first *and* second memos predict significantly student grades for Memo 3, while the impact of student aptitude is reduced both in magnitude and significance. Thus, compared with the model results for the students reading the written case, exposure to multimedia case appears not only to have an enduring, positive impact on student learning as measured by memo grades, but also a disruptive one that allows students to transcend their abilities and outperform our expectations.

Certainly, our attempts to model the relationships between student aptitude and performance with written teaching cases and multimedia cases are anything but definitive. While our evidence suggests that something about using multimedia cases changes the manner in which students learn, we cannot say anything about whether or not those changes are for the better, how they happen, or why they happen without better measures and more rigorous research designs. They do allow, however, these types of questions to come into clearer focus for our ongoing research.

Implications for Blended Learning Research

This account also suggests some implications for other scholars committed to using research to shape ongoing development of blended learning. It highlights that conducting research on the consequences of blended learning treatments is difficult, especially when under the field conditions of live courses where the ability to control for confounding factors is limited. While some researchers may initially realize appropriate research designs, proper levels of analysis, and effective instrumentation to capture variables of interest, it is more likely that research teams will confront numerous obstacles. We should follow the lead of instructors, instructional designers, and learning object creators who know that knowledge about blending learning is gleaned iteratively and cumulatively. As researchers, we must be able to begin, implement quickly, evaluate, and adjust. We must be willing to consider the strengths and limitations of previous attempts and respond creatively with tighter controls, better designs, and more precise measures. Such persistence improves our understanding of the impact of blended approaches on student learning and helps assure that further iterations of tools are informed by scientific inquiry.

References

Fink, L. D. (2003). *Creating significant learning experiences*. San Francisco: Jossey Bass.

Gibson, P. A. (2008). Evaluative criteria to create and assess case studies for use in ethical decision-making analysis. *Journal of Public Affairs Education, 14*(3), 297–309.

Gilmore, T. N., & Schall, E. (1996). Staying alive to learning: Integrating enactments with case teaching to develop leaders. *Journal of Policy Analysis and Management, 15*(3), 444–456.

Lee, V. S. (Ed.). (2004). *Teaching and learning through inquiry: A guidebook for institutions and instructors*. Sterling, VA: Stylus Publishing.

Lynn, L. E. (1996). *Public management as art, science, and profession*. Chatham, NJ: Chatham House.

Rosenbloom, D. H. (1995). The use of case studies in public administrative education in the USA. *Journal of Management History, 1*(1), 33–46.

Shulman, L. S. (2005). Signature pedagogies in the professions. *Daedalus, 134*(3), 52–60.

Yeung, R. (2007). The inter-university case program: Challenging orthodoxy, training public servants, creating knowledge. *Journal of Public Affairs Education, 13*(3/4), 549–564.

10

PRACTICE MAKES PERFECT?

Assessing the Effectiveness of Online Practice Exams in Blended Learning Biology Classes

J. D. Walker, D. Christopher Brooks, Kyle Hammond, Bruce A. Fall, Richard W. Peifer, Rogene Schnell, and Janet L. Schottel

Introduction

In recent years, budgetary shortfalls have increased class sizes throughout the US educational system (Dressen, 2004), resulting in teaching and learning challenges in large-format college classes (Carbone, 1999; Cuseo, 2007; Wulff, Nyquist, & Abbott, 1987), including lack of student engagement with course material, minimal opportunities for students to construct their own under-standings of course concepts, and difficulty in providing student feedback. Active learning techniques can foster a more engaged learning environment in a class with over 200 students (Walker, Cotner, Baepler, & Decker, 2008), but doing so is difficult and can be intimidating for all but the most experienced instructors. A blended-learning format, however, which includes online materials, resources, and activities, can provide pedagogically constructive opportunities otherwise hard to achieve: student–student interaction, active engagement, multimedia curricular enhancements, and feedback on individual student knowledge and performance.

Educational theory and basic research indicate that practice exams are a potentially useful pedagogical tool because they provide feedback on student performance. Feedback gives students an opportunity for processing, which encourages encoding and storage in long-term memory (Ausubel, 1968) and can lead to longer retention of knowledge (Semb & Ellis, 1994). Students need to understand what they know and what they do not know to focus their studies, and feedback is crucial in creating this understanding (Bransford, Brown, & Cocking, 2000; Chickering & Gamson, 1987; Fink, 2003). Prompt, constructive feedback has been shown in numerous studies to be effective in improving student performance (Bangert-Drowns, Kulik,

Kulik, & Morgan, 1991; Fink, 2003; Higgins, Hartley, & Skelton, 2002; Wiggins, 1997).

Empirical research on the use of practice exams or quizzes does not yield a clear verdict about whether such exams improve student performance, however. A number of studies have yielded results favoring the use of formative quizzes and exams. Johnson and Kiviniemi (2009) found that compulsory reading quizzes improved students' exam and overall course performance. DeSouza and Fleming (2003) compared online quizzes with paper quizzes and found a performance advantage for the online format, possibly because online quizzes remove spatial and temporal constraints. Hadsell (2009) studied quiz timing and concluded that completing quizzes shortly after relevant material is presented in class improves exam performance. Similar findings were reported by Dobson (2008), Brar, Laube, and Bett. (2007), Grimstad and Grabe (2004), Maki, Maki, Patterson, and Wittaker (2000), and Olson and McDonald (2004). In contrast, many investigations have produced null results. For instance, Azorlosa and Renner (2006), Wilder, Flood, and Stromsnes (2001), and Haberyan (2003) gave in-class quizzes, but produced no evidence of improved exam performance. Palmer and Devitt (2008) reached similar conclusions, as did Brothen and Wambach (2001), and Peat and Franklin (2003).

The current study investigates the impact of online practice exams on student learning in large, blended-format biology courses. Our hypothesis states that providing online practice exams for students in large classes would address some of the shortcomings of such classes, in particular that large lecture environments reduce the frequency of assessment and thus provide fewer opportunities for feedback (Carbone & Greenberg, 1998).

The research questions explored in this study are:

1. Does the use of online practice exams improve student performance in introductory biology courses?
2. Do other variables, such as demographic characteristics of students and scholastic aptitude, moderate the effects of online practice exams on performance?

Methods

Design

This study used a posttest-only, non-equivalent groups design involving three instructors who taught two sections each of an introductory biology course at the University of Minnesota in the 2008 and 2009 Spring semesters. The instructors kept as many factors as possible constant between the two sections, using the same syllabus, curriculum, in-class learning activities, assessments, and reading materials. The only difference between the two versions of the course was the move, in 2009, to a blended format that included a series of three online practice exams.

The introduction of practice exams constitutes the main treatment variable in this study. The practice exams were delivered online through the Blackboard-Vista course management system to provide students with feedback on their understanding of course concepts in preparation for the three for-credit exams in the course. Each online practice exam consisted of 40 multiple-choice questions, which covered topics relevant to the for-credit exams. The practice exam questions were different from the questions used in the for-credit exams, but were of similar format and were designed to be at least as challenging at the cognitive level as the for-credit questions. Students were given 75 minutes to complete the practice exam to simulate the time allowed for the for-credit exam.

Faculty posted the practice exams on the course website approximately 5 days before the for-credit exam, where they were available to students up to the time of the in-class for-credit exam. When taking the practice exam, students were presented with the questions one at a time and could return to questions and change their answers. When finished, students submitted their practice exam and received their (non-credit) score. They could also print out the practice exam questions with the correct answers for further review. Students were allowed to take each practice exam only once.

Participants

The total number of student participants in this study was 1,525 across all six sections. Most of the participants were in the early stages of their academic careers. The sample was heavily Caucasian (76.6%), which is consistent with the student population at the University of Minnesota. The sample included students from a wide variety of academic majors.

In this quasi-experimental design, students were not randomly assigned to groups, so steps to establish the equivalence of the comparison groups were taken at the outset of the study.

Faculty obtained demographic data for participating students from the University's Office of Institutional Research that included sex, academic level, ethnicity, ACT score, GPA, and age. Faculty used parametric statistical tests to compare the group of students who took a practice exam with the group of students who did not on these demographic dimensions. These tests yielded only one significant difference between the two groups, namely that students who took a practice exam were 0.61 years younger than students who did not ($t = 4.079$, $p < .001$). The age variable, therefore, was included as a predictor in the data analysis to control for any effects it might have on the outcome variables despite its relatively tight distribution.

Data

Data for each of the practice exams were downloaded from the Blackboard-Vista system, and a dichotomous variable, which represented whether each student had taken each practice exam or not, was used as the independent variable of interest. The vast majority of Spring 2009 students took each of the practice exams (80.5%, 81.3%, 78.4% for practice exams 1, 2, and 3, respectively), and Spring 2009 students who did not take a practice exam, were grouped with Spring 2008 students for the main analysis.

The outcome variables of interest were student scores on each of three for-credit exams (Table 10.1). Because the content of the for-credit exams varied slightly between the Spring 2008 and Spring 2009 sections of each class, a percentage score was calculated for each student using only the exam questions that were common to the two semesters, and this percentage score was used as the dependent variable. The percentage of common questions varied by exam and by instructor, from a low of 62% to a high of 100%, and, in all but two cases, was above 90%. Faculty used preliminary independent sample t-tests to compare the common question exam scores of practice exam takers with the scores of students who did not take the practice exams. All of these comparisons were highly statistically significant, indicating the need for further analysis.

Faculty obtained and included data on two measures of general student aptitude, composite ACT score, and cumulative GPA in the analysis because of their likely association with exam performance (ACT, 1998; ACT, 2007). Several demographic variables, namely age, sex, academic level, and ethnicity, were also included in the analysis as predictors because some research has shown a relationship between these variables and the use of, or attitudes toward, educational technology (Smith, Salaway, & Borreson Caruso, 2009; Walker & Jorn, 2009).

TABLE 10.1 Summary Exam Statistics

Variable	Overall mean score	Standard deviation	N	Mean score, practice exam takers	Mean Score, no practice exam	t-statistic
Exam 1	66.86	18.36	1519	69.47	64.50	−5.341***
Exam 2	69.66	18.43	1468	72.70	66.67	−6.353***
Exam 3	69.65	16.54	1397	72.11	67.17	−5.643***

Note: Exam scores are percentages of total possible points using questions that were common between the two semesters; ***$p < .001$

Results and Discussion

Model Outcomes

Data for the participating instructors were aggregated and three multivariate ordinary least squares (OLS) regression models were constructed and used to predict students' performance on the three for-credit exams. The predictor variables of interest were whether or not students had taken the practice exam corresponding to each for-credit exam. Each of the models was highly significant in predicting the grades on each of the for-credit exams as described by the F test (Table 10.2). Moreover, the models account for a considerable amount of the variation in the dependent variables with adjusted r^2 coefficients all near 0.50.

The first practice exam variable was not statistically significant (t = 1.495, p = .135), indicating that students who took the first practice exam achieved scores on the corresponding for-credit exam that were statistically equal to the scores of students who did not take that practice exam. However, the second practice exam variable was statistically significant (t = 3.452, p < .01, beta = 4.326), as was the third practice exam variable (t = 4.616, p < .001, beta = 5.742), indicating that students who took these practice exams achieved significantly higher scores on the corresponding for-credit exams than students who did not take the practice exams.

Three of the other predictor variables were statistically significant in all three models: ACT, GPA, and sex. The age variable was statistically significant only in the third model, which was a predictor of student scores on the third for-credit exam. Finally, the dichotomous dummy variable that encoded the Hispanic level of the ethnicity data was statistically significant only in the first and second models.

The data in this study show that taking an online practice exam can improve student scores on a corresponding for-credit test. The effect of taking online practice exams became larger over the course of the semester, reaching statistical significance at Exam 2 and peaking with Exam 3, the final exam. On average, students who took practice exam 2 scored about 4.3 percentage points higher on Exam 2 than students who did not take the practice exam, and students who took practice exam 3 scored on average about 5.7 percentage points higher on Exam 3 than students who did not. These effects can be considered of moderate size, given that they represent approximately ¼ to ⅓ of a standard deviation in student scores on the two for-credit exams.

The results of this study are important because when practice exams are delivered in an online environment and students have complete freedom as to whether to take the practice exams or not, it is entirely possible that the high-performing, motivated students will choose to take the practice exams, rather than the group of students who are in more need of academic assistance. Since this study controlled for factors that research and theory indicate may affect test scores such as students' academic aptitude, the results show that the benefit of practice exams is not simply an artifact of student self-selection.

TABLE 10.2   OLS Regression of Practice Exam on Grades by Exam

	Model 1: Exam 1	Model 2: Exam 2	Model 3: Exam 3
Practice exam 1	1.128 (0.754)		
Practice exam 2		4.326★★ (1.253)	
Practice exam 3			5.742★★★ (1.244)
ACT	1.300★★★(0.109)	1.165★★★(0.113)	1.258★★★(0.103)
GPA	16.520★★★(0.717)	17.890★★★(0.757)	16.017★★★(0.713)
Age	0.475(0.313)	0.415(0.326)	0.962★★(0.298)
Sex	6.492★★★(0.754)	2.838★★★(0.774)	5.443★★★(0.702)
Hispanic	−5.866★(2.476)	−5.241★(2.589)	−0.428(2.573)
Constant	−31.809(7.553)	−26.488(7.837)	−37.163(7.180)
N	1285	1245	1188
Adjusted R^2	0.509	0.493	0.522
F Test	96.081★★★	81.616★★★	82.010★★★

Note: Cell entries are unstandardized OLS coefficients with standard errors in parentheses;
★$p < .05$, ★★$p < .01$, ★★★$p < .001$

Practice Exam 1

An important question is why practice exam 1 did not have a statistically significant effect on student performance on the corresponding for-credit exam, while the later practice exams did have such an effect (Table 10.2). The proportion of students who took each practice exam was approximately the same, and an inspection of the demographic breakdown of the students who took each practice exam did not reveal any large or striking differences. One hypothesis is that the null results for practice exam 1 have to do with students' sense of urgency or need. After the first for-credit exam, students may have realized the need for more thorough exam preparation and hence concentrated harder on practice exams 2 and 3 than they did on the first practice exam.

Secondary Analyses

Time on Task

An analysis of time on task for each practice exam, which was tracked by the Blackboard-Vista system, revealed that students took substantially longer with practice exams 2 (a mean of 38.5 minutes, about ⅝ of a standard deviation greater than practice exam 1) and 3 (31.5 minutes, about ¼ of a standard deviation greater than practice exam 1) than they did with practice exam 1 (27.5 minutes). Even though there was no significant correlation between time on task for any of the practice exams and score on the corresponding for-credit exam, time on task may serve as a proxy for effort because student scores on the first for-credit exam may have caused them to take better advantage of the aids. Spending more time on the practice exams most likely reveals that the effort, concentration, or intensity of engagement with the practice exams makes the difference, not the duration of use.

Aptitude

To investigate whether practice exams help students of different aptitude differentially, aptitude–practice exam interaction effects were coded for each practice exam and for each of two measures of aptitude, GPA and ACT score. These variables were added to the three predictive models, but none was statistically significant, indicating that the practice exams help students at all levels of the aptitude spectrum equally.

Sex

Data analysis showed a significant effect along sex lines, with men outperforming women by 2.8 to 6.5 percentage points even after controlling for aptitude in the form of ACT scores and students' GPAs (Table 10.2). It was, therefore, important to ask whether men benefited more from the practice exams than women did, thus boosting the mean score for men in this study. To test this possibility, interaction effects were coded for sex and each of the practice exams. However, when these variables were added to the three models, none was significant, leading to the conclusion that the practice exams benefit both sexes equally.

Conclusions

The results of this study indicated that the use of online practice exams significantly improved student learning in blended-learning biology courses, as reflected in enhanced student performance on final exams. All students benefited significantly from taking the practice exams regardless of sex or aptitude. Regarding these positive results, future studies may investigate the use of more frequent practice exams given at shorter intervals during the semester to help students evaluate their understanding of a more focused set of biology concepts prior to a major in-class exam. Also, giving students an opportunity to take the practice exams more than once may increase their confidence in mastering the material and decrease anxiety that may be associated with taking an exam that is given in a standardized format.

References

ACT (1998). *Prediction Research Summary Tables*. Iowa City, IA: ACT.

ACT (2007). *The ACT Technical Manual*. Iowa City, IA: ACT.

Ausubel, D.P. (1968). *Educational psychology: A cognitive view*. New York, NY: Holt, Reinhart and Winston.

Azorlosa, J. L., & Renner, C. H. (2006). The effect of announced quizzes on exam performance. *Journal of Instructional Psychology, 33*, 278–283.

Bangert-Drowns, R. L., Kulik, C. C., Kulik, J. A., & Morgan, M. (1991). The instructional effect of feedback in test-like events. *Review of Educational Research, 67*, 601–607.

Bransford, J., Brown, A.L., & Cocking, R.R., (Eds.) (2000). *How people learn: Brain, mind, experience, and school*. Washington, DC: National Academy Press.

Brar, M., Laube, D., & Bett, G. (2007). Effect of quantitative feedback on student performance on the National Board Medical Examination in an obstetrics and gynecology workshop. *American Journal of Obstetrics and Gynecology, 197*, 530.e1–530.e5.

Brothen, T., & Wambach, C. (2001). Effective student use of computerized quizzes. *Teaching of Psychology, 28*, 292–294.

Carbone, E. (1999). Students behaving badly in large classes. *New Directions for Teaching and Learning, 77*, 35–43.

Carbone, E., & Greenberg, J. (1998). Teaching large classes: Unpacking the problem and responding creatively. In M. Kaplan (Ed.), *To Improve the Academy*, No. 17 (pp. 311–326), Stillwater, OK: New Forums Press and The Professional and Organizational Development Network in Higher Education.

Chickering, A., & Gamson, Z. (1987). Seven principles for good practice in undergraduate education. *AAHE Bulletin, March*, 3–7.

Cuseo, J. (2007). The empirical case against large class size: Adverse effects on the teaching, learning, and retention of first-year students. *Journal of Faculty Development, 21*, 5–22.

DeSouza, E., & Fleming, M. (2003). A comparison of in-class quizzes vs. online quizzes on student exam performance. *Journal of Computing Higher Education, 14*, 121–134.

Dobson, J. (2008). The use of formative online quizzes to enhance class preparation and scores on summative exams. *Advances in Physiology Education, 32*, 297–302.

Dressen, R. (2004). Investing in our future: Seeking a fair, understandable, and accountable 21st century education finance system for Minnesota. School Funding Task Force. Retrieved from http://education.state.mn.us/mdeprod/groups/Finance/documents/Report/004128.pdf

Fink, D. (2003). *Creating significant learning experiences: An integrated approach to designing college courses*. San Francisco: Jossey-Bass.

Grimstad, K., & Grabe, M. (2004). Are online study questions beneficial? *Teaching of Psychology, 31*, 143–146.

Haberyan, K. (2003). Do weekly quizzes improve student performance on general biology exams? *The American Biology Teacher, 65*, 110–114.

Hadsell, L. (2009). The effect of quiz timing on exam performance. *Journal of Education for Business, 84*, 135–141.

Higgins, R., Hartley, P., & Skelton, A. (2002). The conscientious consumer: Reconsidering the role of assessment feedback in student learning. *Studies in Higher Education, 27*, 53–64.

Johnson, B., & Kiviniemi, M. (2009). The effect of online chapter quizzes on exam performance in an undergraduate social psychology course. *Teaching of Psychology, 36*, 33–37.

Maki, R.H., Maki, W.S., Patterson, M., & Wittaker, D. (2000). Evaluation of Web-based introductory psychology course: I. Learning and satisfaction in online versus lecture courses. *Behavior Research Methods, Instruments & Computers, 32*, 230–239.

Olson, B., & McDonald, J. (2004). Influence of online formative assessment upon student learning in biomedical science courses. *Journal of Dental Education, 68*, 656–659.

Palmer, E.J., & Devitt, P.G. (2008). Limitations of student-driven formative assessment in a clinical clerkship. A randomized controlled trial. *BMC Medical Education, 8*. Retrieved from www.biomedcentral.com/1472-6920/8/29

Peat, M., & Franklin, S. (2003). Has student learning been improved by the use of online and offline assessment opportunities? *Australasian Journal of Educational Technology, 19*, 87–99.

Semb, G.B., & Ellis, J.A. (1994). Knowledge taught in school: What is remembered? *Review of Educational Research, 64*, 253–286.

Smith, S., Salaway, G., & Borreson Caruso, J. (2009). *The ECAR study of undergraduate students and information technology, 2009.* EDUCAUSE Center for Applied Research, Boulder, CO. Retrieved from www.educause.edu/ecar

Walker, J. D., & Jorn, L. (2009). 21st century students: Technology survey, University of Minnesota. Retrieved from www.oit.umn.edu/evaluation-research/technology-surveys/

Walker, J. D., Cotner, S. H., Baepler, P., & Decker, M. (2008). A delicate balance: Integrating active learning into a large lecture course. *CBE-Life Sciences Education, 7*, 361–367.

Wiggins, G. (1997). Feedback: How learning occurs. *AAHE Bulletin, 50*, 7–8.

Wilder, D. A., Flood, W. A., & Stromsnes, W. (2001). The use of random extra credit quizzes to increase student attendance. *Journal of Instructional Psychology, 28*, 117–120.

Wulff, D. H., Nyquist, J. D., & Abbott, R. D. (1987). Students' perceptions of large classes. In M. Weimer (Ed.), Teaching large classes well. *New Directions for Teaching and Learning, 32*, 17–30, San Francisco: Jossey-Bass.

SECTION III
Faculty Issues

11

IMPLEMENTATION OF BLENDED LEARNING FOR THE IMPROVEMENT OF STUDENT LEARNING

Jeannette E. Riley, Catherine Gardner, Sarah Cosgrove, Neal Olitsky, Caitlin O'Neil, and Chan Du

In 2009, UMass Dartmouth received a grant from the Davis Educational Foundation for a project entitled "Implementation of Blended Learning for the Improvement of Student Learning,"[1] which we refer to as "IBIS." IBIS grew out of our recognition that online learning offers higher education an ideal site for innovative pedagogy and the growth of faculty skill sets designed to increase student learning. For example, as the recent U.S. Department of Education report, "Evaluation of Evidence-Based Practices in Online Learning: A Meta-Analysis and Review of Online Learning Studies" (2009), documents, a review of research literature from 1996 to 2008 demonstrates that, "on average, students in online learning conditions performed better than those receiving face-to-face instruction" (p. ix). In addition, the study demonstrates that "Instruction combining online and face-to-face elements had a larger advantage relative to purely face-to-face instruction than did purely online instruction" (p. xv).

Within this context and within the university's mission, our project developed to put these student outcomes into practice by joining together the resources and expertise of the campus Office of Faculty Development with the Instructional Development Team (ID Team), a team devoted to integrating instructional technologies into the learning experience, to aid faculty in developing courses that blend face-to-face interactions with online learning activities that create a culture of assessment and reflection focused on facilitating and improving student learning. As such, the IBIS program is a multi-pronged approach that involves blended learning techniques to engage faculty in the development of effective teaching materials and to assist faculty in developing effective tools and methods to incorporate a culture of assessment and scholarly teaching into their curricula.

Blended Learning: "Finding the Mix"[2]

At the foundation of the IBIS program is a faculty development program that not only develops faculty knowledge and skills in blended teaching strategies and course design, but also develops faculty understanding of assessment practices and implements a peer-mentor program designed to foster collaboration and ongoing quality review of the courses before they start and after they end, along with how they unfold during the semester. Our philosophy is that only through such a thorough-going process of both faculty training and quality assessment can deep and transformative student learning be produced. Simply adding the bells and whistles of current technology to already existing classes—an add and stir model—will not achieve any student outcomes of value.

To engage faculty in developing blended learning courses, we first require that they complete a workshop entitled "Blended Learning: Finding the Mix." This workshop is blended with both online and face-to-face components. Training begins with a kickoff meeting where participants meet one another and share why they would like to design a blended course and what course they will be blending. The session also engages faculty in activities that ask them to rethink who their students are and their teaching practices. This session is followed by a 2-week, fully online training via our campus learning management system. The training is facilitated by the campus Instructional Development Team and the grant project directors (Riley/Gardner).

The online training is at the heart of the faculty development process. There, faculty begin with an introductory module designed to introduce them to the various definitions of blended learning and the challenges in creating an effective blended learning environment. What we stress to faculty is that no matter how we define blended, the key to a successful blended learning experience for students is the thoughtful integration of the face-to-face and online course sessions so that all aspects of the course work in tandem. In the research bulletin "Blended Learning" (2004) for *Educause*, Charles D. Dziuban, Joel L. Hartman, and Patsy D. Moskal offer this view of blended learning that we impart throughout the workshop:

> It is our position that blended learning should be viewed as a pedagogical approach that combines the effectiveness and socialization opportunities of the classroom with the technologically enhanced active learning possibilities of the online environment, rather than a ratio of delivery modalities. In other words, blended learning should be approached not merely as a temporal construct, but rather as a fundamental redesign of the instructional model with the following characteristics:
>
> • a shift from lecture- to student-centered instruction in which students become active and interactive learners (this shift should apply to the entire course, including the face-to-face contact sessions);

- increases in interaction between student–instructor, student–student, student–content, and student–outside resources; and
- integrated formative and summative assessment mechanisms for students and instructor.

(Dziuban, Hartman, & Moskal, 2004, p. 3)

Faculty discover that this act of redesign takes time to plan out, as well as critical reflection about their teaching practices. To assist faculty, we provide resources such as access to the Educause webinar *Best Practices for Designing Successful Blended Courses*, links to case studies at Simmons College, blended design examples on our own campus, and design-mapping tools. Once they have reviewed these materials, and conversed with colleagues about their plans, each faculty member is required to create a blended course (re)design plan that is then peer reviewed by the faculty cohort, the Instructional Development Team, and the Director of Faculty Development.

One of the most important activities that faculty engage in is a discussion of their course learning objectives in a module devoted to assessing student learning. As they begin to design their blended course, we continually ask them: "How do you find the best mix of face-to-face and online activities?" What we want them to learn is what Jennifer Hofmann suggests in "Why blended learning hasn't (yet) fulfilled its promises" (2006). It is important to not look at the overall subject of your course for the answer. Instead, faculty need to learn to "look at each individual learning objective," a process that in turn will provide them with "the flexibility to determine the best way to deliver each component" (Hofmann, 2006, p. 32). Through this focus on student learning objectives, we guide faculty to developing alignment between their student learning objectives and course assignments, whether they are completed in class or online.

Additionally, the assessment module asks faculty to analyze their actual course design. Faculty, in our experience, tend to lack experience analyzing their course design for effectiveness. This type of analysis is imperative for a blended course design as the integration of face-to-face and online instructional activities needs to not only help students reach the course learning objectives, but to also understand how these different learning environments are working in tandem to get them there. Faculty learn that assessment of a course can occur on many levels. As the workshop teaches them, a faculty member could focus on assessing the use of a LMS tool that s/he introduced to a course. The assessment process would investigate if the desired learning outcome was accomplished through the use of the tool.

Alternatively, assessment could be focused solely on a faculty member's course design. In what ways does a site design impact student learning? Assessment could also be focused on the course learning outcomes as a whole if a certain assignment is designed to demonstrate student accomplishment of those outcomes, such as a major final project. Ultimately, our goal is to teach the faculty to continually ask themselves key questions: How well does your course make connections between learning objectives, course activities, and selection of site tools to accomplish the assignments? How well do face-to-face and out of class time learning activities complement each other?

As the faculty complete the training course, they are also matched up with a peer mentor. The mentoring process is designed to encourage a culture of collaborative exchange and open discussion about teaching practices on campus. There are four guiding points for the mentoring program:

1. Peer-to-peer mentoring is equal and the mentor will not necessarily have more knowledge or experience than the mentee.
2. Focus is on student learning not instructor evaluation.
3. It is the responsibility of both parties to start and maintain the interaction.
4. Both the mentor and mentee will do a final report documenting their experience.

Through this program, faculty receive feedback on their course design and assessment plans as they share expertise and experiences across disciplines. The peer mentor collaboration takes place throughout the semester that the blended course runs, with the peer mentor observing the face-to-face classroom two times, as well as observing the activities taking place via the online course site. The peer mentor also completes the "Blended Course Quality Rubric," which was created by faculty and approved for use on campus by the Faculty Senate. This rubric provides guidelines for assessing the effectiveness of the "blend" itself and is a tool for providing further feedback to the faculty member on his/her course design and the actual execution of the course.

Case Studies: Blending in Action

As the project reaches its third year, faculty have engaged in a number of different approaches to the blended classroom. Some faculty have focused on discussion forums based on readings and short online activities that are incorporated into the blended course and designed to replace some face-to-face class discussions. Others have moved peer review activities online so that classroom time can be spent more on discussion of concepts and readings. Several faculty have experimented with having students complete before-class online activities after viewing posted PowerPoint slides and textbook readings in preparation for face-to-face class with the goal of increasing student participation and actual application of concepts in the face-to-face setting.

The following case studies represent the range of blends developed. Neal Olitsky and Sarah Cosgrove, both economics faculty, researched the use of online homework, online discussion work, and team wiki projects to assess how well students attained a specific student learning outcome vs. students who participated in a traditional face-to-face course setting with no online components. Chan Du, an accounting professor, investigated how a blended course design impacted and improved student performance and satisfaction. Finally, Caitlin O'Neil's blended course project sought to see if online course quizzes and support modules could increase student writing performance in an intermediate writing class.

Does Blended Coursework in Economics Affect Learning Outcomes?

Neal Olitsky and Sarah Cosgrove partnered to assess the effectiveness of blending on student learning of a particular student learning outcome (SLO) in their introductory economics courses. The target SLO, "compute and compare opportunity costs of different decision-makers to determine the most efficient specialization of production," is central to all of economic decision-making.

To maximize consistency across sections, both instructors used the same textbook, online homework management website, course management system, assignments, and exam. The instructors collected data from two blended sections and five face-to-face sections. For the target SLO, all students were required to complete: 1. a chapter reading from the textbook; 2. a pair-and-share practice problem set (face-to-face); and 3. an assignment from an online homework management website with interactive graphs, tables, and corresponding questions (online). The students in the blended sections had one fewer 75-minute face-to-face class during this unit. In its place, the students were required to read an article applying opportunity costs and complete follow-up discussion board questions online and complete a small group wiki project. The goals of the discussion board were to prompt students to engage with the material, to involve all students in the conversation, and to encourage students to engage with each other. The small group wiki project required students to develop their own example with computations and analysis and post it online for their classmates to review. The assessment outcomes of interest consisted of exam scores and online homework performance.

Once the assessment data were collected, each student's results were matched to his/her college transcript data and demographic information to control for both academic achievement and student's background. The transcript data reported each course in which a student enrolled and the grades they earned for each course. The demographic data provided information on the following characteristics: program of study, college major, cumulative credits earned, cumulative GPA, US citizenship status, first term enrolled at the university, SAT Math and Verbal scores, and race/ethnicity. The final sample consisted of 318 observations.

Two estimation strategies were used to assess the difference between learning in a blended environment and a face-to-face environment. First, a simple ordinary least squares (OLS) regression was estimated. Second, because previous research found a large selection bias when students chose to take a blended course (Coates, Humphreys, Kane, & Vachris, 2004), a propensity score matching (PSM) approach was employed to account for students choosing a blended class as opposed to being randomly assigned to a blended section. The results, with few exceptions, suggest no significant effect of blending on any of the outcomes considered. Significant differences in the raw means exist between the results from the blended and non-blended classes, but after controlling for individual academic and demographic characteristics, no significant differences in outcomes were found between the blended and non-blended sections. Both the OLS specification and the PSM specifications produce this result, suggesting no causal link between blended coursework and reduced learning.

The only outcome for which the effect of blending is consistently negative is the SLO-specific online homework assignment. Depending on the specification, the effect of blending on online homework scores ranges from a decrease of 4 points to a decrease of 1.3 points. This effect is considerably larger than the others; one possible reason for this result is that students in blended classes had other assignments besides the online homework to which they allocated their time. While students in the blended sections were less successful on the online homework, they learned the material using the wiki and discussion boards, so there was no overall loss of learning as measured by the exam scores. In addition, students in the face-to-face sections had one more class period *before* the online assignment was due. As a result, the negative effect of blending on this outcome may be an artifact of having less exposure to the material; this negative effect disappeared when students took the exam.

Although these results are not generalizable to the population of college students, they provide a number of implications for blended coursework. First, the results suggest that blended coursework in economics may provide a flexible alternative to traditional face-to-face classes without sacrificing student learning. This additional flexibility may increase access to education for students who are unable to take traditional courses. In addition, because less classroom space is needed, blended courses in economics may increase flexibility of course offerings for institutions with increasing space constraints.

Second, the results suggest that, like fully online courses, students are selecting non-randomly into, and out of, blended classes, and accounting for this selection is important when determining the effect of blended coursework. Although students did not know at the time of enrollment whether they were in the treatment group, other student characteristics, such as past economics courses affect the choice of course selection. Subsequent research on this topic should be careful to account for this type of selection when drawing conclusions about the effects of blended classes on student learning.

Using Online Quizzes to Enhance Comprehension of Key Concepts

In Intermediate Composition (ENL260), Caitlin O'Neil teaches the arts of exposition, persuasion, and argumentation in writing. It is a requirement for English majors with a writing concentration and liberal arts majors that expands upon the work they have done in their freshman English classes. Many of the students enrolled in this class are only familiar with the standard five-paragraph essay or a research paper. The class endeavors to broaden their ideas about what writing can do and to give them the opportunity to implement these new ideas in their own writing. In Fall 2011, O'Neil designed and implemented a blended learning section of the course to determine if supplementing face-to-face coursework with online activities improved student comprehension and application of core writing concepts. To address one of the class's primary student learning objectives (SLOs)—identifying the elements of successful persuasive arguments—O'Neil decided to implement online quizzes, reusable learning objects, and other online support processes to more deeply engage students in the learning process. O'Neil hoped to help students better grasp the building blocks of argument and reinforce basic argument concepts before they tackled the course's major essays.

Before the class work began on each content module, O'Neil asked students to take a brief pre-test self-assessment that gauged their knowledge of successful persuasive arguments. These assessments were short and quite basic; most students are not all that familiar with the elements and strategies of arguments at the outset of class. After in-class discussion and examination of sample arguments, she asked students to click through an online module that reviewed key concepts and then complete quizzes on the material they had read and discussed in class. Through seven content modules that provide lecture notes and additional materials on the course content, O'Neil provided for students the elements of persuasive writing, in which they employ voice, exploit the concepts of ethos, pathos, and logos, and consider their audience. O'Neil hoped that the online content and quizzes would reinforce these elements, which are necessary for students to develop persuasive essays.

As a control, O'Neil taught a face-to-face class that did not have access to the self-assessment or additional resource materials via a course site. Additionally, the face-to-face class completed the same quizzes with pen and paper. O'Neil then compared the quiz results from both the blended class and the face-to-face class and compared the two groups to see if the blended students fared better.

The overall average score on all the quizzes was slightly higher in the blended class, 59.19 vs. 57.98, or a difference of 1.21. On the individual quizzes, the blended class performed consistently better than the face-to-face class on five out of the seven tests. The average grade for the blended class was also higher than the face-to-face class, 79.4 vs. 73.6, which led O'Neil to believe that the quizzes did help the blended class students better absorb the concepts that they executed in their essays. These data suggest that the blended course format positively impacted student learning. The online quizzes (and the scaffolding around them—the self-assessments and review modules) allowed deeper engagement with the material and thus a deeper understanding of the concepts that was crucial for the students' subsequent execution of the class's main essay assignments.

Traditional vs. Blended Learning in an Introductory Principles of Accounting Course

It has been argued that blended learning allows faculty to integrate the best of the online learning environment with the best of the face-to-face learning environment (Graham, 2006), and that blended learning works better than purely online and purely face-to-face learning. However, experts have not reached a consensus on how to effectively integrate face-to-face and online learning in accounting education. For example, Dowling, Godfrey, and Gyles' (2003) blended model for an Accounting Information System course includes a combination of 3-hour face-to-face interactive practical work every 2 weeks and multimedia resources that contains PowerPoint slides with narration attached and the WebCT discussion board. On the other hand, Keller, Hassell, Webber, and Johnson's (2009) blended model for their Principles of Managerial Accounting course meets once per week in person for lectures and once per week via the web working as teams on problems outside of the classroom. The current case study provides additional evidence for the design of a blended financial accounting course to improve student performance and satisfaction.

Principles of Accounting I (ACT 211), taught by Chan Du, is an introductory financial accounting course and is required for all students and all degrees offered by the business school. In addition, a portion of students come from other colleges such as Arts & Sciences and Engineering. For a large portion of the students, this class will be the only accounting course that they take. Among these students, many tend to have negative attitudes towards accounting (Mladenovic, 2000).

Prior to Fall 2010, the course was delivered using a traditional teaching model that involved two 75-minute sections each week, supplemented by WebCT. Lecture slides were posted on WebCT for student convenience. Announcements were made though email and WebCT. Homework solutions were posted after returning the students' assignments. Student grades were updated each week on WebCT. The instructor collected the homework assignments and handed them back after grading them. The class meeting included lecture discussion and in-class exercises. In Fall 2010, the course was redesigned from web-enhanced learning to blended learning.

To go beyond replicating face-to-face methods, the blended course design in ACT 211 was not to just post materials online as web-enhanced learning.

Utilizing Bloom's Taxonomy, which classifies the education objective into the six categories of Knowledge, Comprehension, Application, Analysis, Synthesis, and Evaluation (Bloom, 1956), Du recognized that lower levels of Knowledge and Comprehension could best be learned by the students themselves before class and tested through short online quizzes (Shibley, 2009). As a result, Du's blended course design shifted many of the learning activities online. For example, online tools were designed so that students could learn by themselves and from each other before and after classes. Opportunities for students to learn before class included posting knowledge-based before-class quizzes online and required students to submit answers before face-to-face classes started. Opportunities for students to learn during class included in-class discussions and individual or group cases and exercises. Finally, opportunities for students to learn after class included: 1. asking students to post on a discussion board what was the most confusing part of the class and what they thought was the main point of the class; 2. after-class online individual homework and quizzes; and 3. online group real company analysis postings and comments.

The effect of the blended course design on student performance and satisfaction was examined by a comparison of the traditional and blended learning models in an introductory financial accounting course over the period 2009–2011. Both traditional and blended classes were taught by the same instructor using the same materials. Both classes used the same textbook, homework assignments, publisher's online quizzes, exams, and writing project. The additional blended assessment components included before-class quizzes, after-class online homework, after-class question and comment postings, and real company case and project postings.

The sample includes students who completed Principles of Accounting I from 2009–2011. In Fall 2009, 40 out of 51 students completed the course; in Spring 2010, 82 out of 88 students completed the course; in Fall 2010, 51 out of 52 students completed the course; and in Spring 2011, 46 out of 50 students completed the course. A student was classified as having completed the course if he/she had attempted the final examination (Dowling et al., 2003). The regression analysis on final exam grades (final course grade) showed that after controlling for gender, transfer status, math grade, prior GPA, academic affiliation, and academic level, switching from a traditional teaching model to a blended teaching model improved students' final performance through in-depth in-class activities. Additional t-tests that compared the course evaluations from traditional and blended learning models showed that students' satisfaction had also improved.

The Impact of Blended Learning

Each of the representative samples shows individual lessons that the principal investigators, Gardner and Riley, have learned from the IBIS project. Du's case study shows us that blended learning had a positive effect on student learning and student satisfaction. Du demonstrates this result through a comparison with a course that was taught face-to-face. Du's project also demonstrates the way that blended learning breaks down temporal–geographical barriers to learning. Learning is not just done in the classroom. It is done before, during, and after class. This is something that is valuable for students to understand and experience, and it is something that will continue in their other classes.

Olitsky and Cosgrove show that students in a blended learning class did not score as well on a targeted assignment, although it is possible that other factors, such as additional work, played into this result. Despite the results on the targeted assignment, there was no difference in overall grades between students in the blended course and the face-to-face course on the unit exam. This "no-result" is just as valuable as Du's positive result. As Olitsky and Cosgrove point out, there is a shift towards online and blended learning, something that is potentially beneficial for students who need flexibility in their schedules, and it is crucial to see that this shift does not have a detrimental effect on student learning.

O'Neil shows that online quizzes and the scaffolding (self-assessments and review modules) that surround them appear to lead to more in-depth learning. O'Neil's results are provocative. She is not making the simple statement that online quizzes lead to improved performance; rather it would appear that all the elements required to make online quizzes effective lead to improved performance. What she calls "scaffolding"—the integration of self-assessments and review modules—is integral to a more in-depth understanding of the material.

Overall, the IBIS project has demonstrated that blended learning has a slight positive impact on student learning, with learning defined in broad terms of retention of knowledge and evidenced through such things as grades on written assignments and exams. Equally importantly, the principal investigators, with their colleagues, have found that blended learning does not have a negative impact on student learning. This is a central finding, as more and more institutions of higher learning develop blended courses. It is particularly significant for our institution, as we have limited classroom space, and blended courses will allow us to maximize space without compromising instructional quality.

The most unexpected finding, however, was the impact on what we are calling "learning behaviors." These learning behaviors cover a wide range of characteristics from improved study skills, such as reading, to improved collaboration with other students, to a heightened confidence in and value placed on learning. The evidence for this was found in the reports by faculty, student focus groups, and student satisfaction surveys. Student focus groups and surveys revealed that students appreciate the more effective use of face-to-face class time when quizzes and other assignments were moved online, as well as the flexibility for learning that the blended classroom offers them. Further, students believe that online quizzes and resources outside of class time improved their reading retention and contributed to more effective face-to-face class discussions. Most importantly, students recognize that the blended classroom forces them to learn more independently—they have to take responsibility for their learning and time management more fully.

The causal relationship between a blended environment and developments in learning behaviors can be drawn out from a consideration of the type of learning that happens in a well-designed blended environment. Obviously, emphasis has to be placed here on the quality of the design of the environment, which is why the project is a joint faculty development project not simply an instructional technology project.

O'Neil and Du provide examples of courses that lead to developments in learning behaviors. O'Neil's course has a multi-level approach to her learning objective, which she calls the scaffolding. Simply giving the students the information to pass the quiz is not adequate pedagogically in the online component of a blended course; O'Neil needs to add review modules and self-assessments to prepare students properly. These review modules teach study skills by modeling what students need to do to prepare for a quiz. Self assessments show students the importance of testing their own knowledge while they learn to develop confidence in their increasing knowledge. Du's approach leads to student understanding that learning is not confined by the set hours of the course. These are valuable behaviors, among other behaviors, that will benefit the student in future courses.

As stated above, the impact on student learning behaviors was an unexpected finding. Our initial expectation was that we would find that blended learning had a positive impact or no impact on learning, with learning understood in terms of content knowledge. In our continuation of the project, we are now focusing more on teasing out the effect on learning behaviors. The cohort of Fall 2012 have been asked to consider this issue in the development of their individual projects. We have been allowed to carry over funding into Fall 2013, so that we can continue with pressing this question as well as our initial project question.

Whatever our final results, the current and future impact of blended learning on higher education should not be underestimated. The rising generation of students—"millennials"—are used to instant access to information and to connect with others at any time in any place. Pedagogies that were successful 20, even 10, years ago do not engage these students, and if these students are not engaged, then they will not learn.

Notes

1   The grant was received from the Davis Educational Foundation established by Stanton and Elisabeth Davis after Mr. Davis's retirement as chairman of Shaw's Supermarkets, Inc.

2   This term was coined by Eliot Maisie (2006) in "The Blended Learning Imperative." We find it to be a phrase that resonates with faculty as they learn to (re)design a blended course.

References

Bloom, B. (1956). Taxonomy of educational objectives *Handbook I: The cognitive domain*. New York: David McKay, Co. Inc.

Coates, D., Humphreys, B. R., Kane, J., & Vachris, M. A. (2004). No significant distance between face-to-face and online instruction: Evidence from principles of economics. *Economics of Education Review, 23*(3), 533–546.

Dowling, C., Godfrey, J. M., & Gyles, N. (2003). Do hybrid flexible delivery teaching methods improve accounting students' learning outcomes? *Accounting Education, 12*(4), 373–391.

Dziuban, C., Hartman, J., & Moskal, P. (2004). Blended learning [PDF]. *Educause Center for Applied Research Bulletin,* 2004(7). Retrieved from net.educause.edu/ir/library/pdf/ERB0407.pdf

Graham, C. R. (2006). Blended learning systems: Definition, current trends, and future directions. In C. J. Bonk & C. Graham (Eds.), *The handbook of blended learning: Global perspectives, local designs* (pp. 3–21). San Francisco: John J. Wiley and Sons.

Hofmann, J. (2006). Why blended learning hasn't (yet) fulfilled its promises: Answers to those questions that keep you up at night. In C. J. Bonk & C. Graham (Eds.), *The handbook of blended learning: Global perspectives, local designs* (pp. 27–40). San Francisco: John J. Wiley and Sons.

Keller, J. H., Hassell, J. M., Webber, S. A., & Johnson, J. N. (2009). A comparison of academic performance in traditional and hybrid sections of introductory managerial accounting. *Journal of Accounting Education, 27*(3), 147–154.

Maisie, E. (2006). The blended learning imperative. In C. J. Bonk & C. Graham (Eds.), *The handbook of blended learning: Global perspectives, local designs* (pp. 22–26). San Francisco: John J. Wiley and Sons.

Michaelsen, L. K., & Black, R. H. (1994). Building learning teams: The key to harnessing the power of small groups In higher education. In S. Kadel & J. Keehner (Eds.), *Collaborative learning: A sourcebook for higher education* (Vol. 2). State College, PA: National Center for Teaching, Learning and Assessment.

Mladenovic, R. (2000). An investigation into ways of challenging introductory accounting students' negative perceptions of accounting. *Accounting Education, 9*(2), 135–155.

Shibley, I. (Producer) (2009). 10 ways to improve blended learning course design. *Magna Publications Online Seminar.*

U.S. Department of Education Office of Planning, Evaluation, and Policy Development Policy and Program Studies Service (2010). Evaluation of evidence-based practices in online learning: A meta-analysis and review of online learning studies [PDF]. Retrieved from www.ed.gov/rschstat/eval/tech/evidence-based-practices/finalreport.pdf

12

THE IMPACT OF INSTRUCTIONAL DEVELOPMENT AND TRAINING FOR BLENDED TEACHING ON COURSE EFFECTIVENESS

Tanya M. Joosten, Dylan Barth, Lindsey Harness, and Nicole L. Weber

Blended learning is becoming a prominent mode of programming and delivery in education. It is swiftly emerging and transforming higher education to better meet the needs of our students, providing them with more effective learning experiences. This movement is leading to a renovation of the way courses are taught and programs support their students. Instructional and faculty development provide the core foundation to institutional programming in providing a framework for implementing blended learning pedagogy in the classroom. This student-centered, active learning pedagogy has the potential to alter the traditional classroom by enhancing course effectiveness through increased interactivity, leading to superior student outcomes.

Blended learning continues to grow, becoming increasingly popular on campuses. According to Allen, Seaman, and Garrett (2007), "Overall, 36 percent of schools offer at least one blended program" (p. 36). Also, blended learning growth is predicted to be greater than growth in online courses. A recent study reported that "Respondents . . . anticipated that the number of students taking online courses will grow by 22.8% and that those taking blended courses will grow even more over the next 2 years" (Picciano, Seaman, Shea, & Swan, 2012, p. 128). As the demand for blended learning opportunities increases, so does the need for development of instructors to teach and design blended courses. Instructional development is necessary since blended teaching requires a significant course transformation, including rethinking the course design, creating new learning activities, integrating online and face-to-face course components, and learning new teaching skills in order to successfully manage online interaction, incorporate new methods of assessment, and use tools in the learning management system.

Blended learning is our future. Many are predicting that blended learning is one of the most important modes of delivery in the future of education. As PEW Internet declared in their *Future of Higher Education* report, colleges are delving into blended learning and many experts believe that there will be further movement to blended classes (see Anderson, Boyles, & Rainie, July 27, 2012). Many grant funding agencies have identified the potential benefits and are supporting the move to blended learning in higher education. For example, the Sloan Consortium Localness initiative and the Gates Foundation's Next Generation Learning Challenges have and are supporting numerous universities' and colleges' ability to support blended learning opportunities. There is an increased commitment to blended learning efforts based on the benefits and potential identified.

The continued growth and gains in popularity lie in the opportunities offered by blended learning. Blended learning, which is sometimes called hybrid learning, is a combination of face-to-face and online learning activities. These courses "blend" the two mediums in order to be able to find the most effective method of teaching, which is dependent on the characteristics of the medium. As Aycock, Garnham, and Kaleta illustrate (March, 2002), "Hybrid courses are courses in which a significant portion of the learning activities have been moved online, and time traditionally spent in the classroom is reduced but not eliminated" (para. 1). More specifically, Picciano (2006) describes blended learning as:

1.   courses that integrate online with traditional face-to-face class activities in a planned, pedagogically valuable manner; and
2.   where a portion (institutionally defined) of face-to-face time is replaced by online activity.

(p. 97)

The benefits of the blended model lie in its pedagogical potential to provide flexibility in learning and to embrace the additional opportunities afforded by online and face-to-face environments for instructors to achieve student-centered learning.

With the growing popularity in blended programming in higher education, increasing support for blended learning by private foundations, and mounting need for instructional development, we will examine the relationship between instructional development and training and the effectiveness of blended courses.

Blended Learning Effectiveness

The growing interest in blended learning and an increasing number of blended learning initiatives undertaken on campuses are due, in part, to instructors' implementation of the blended model in order to take advantage of the pedagogical rewards in using two mediums, online and face-to-face (Godambe,

Picciano, Schroeder, & Schweber, 2004), which includes the opportunity to make student learning more active. For example, Kaleta, Skibba, and Joosten (2007) describe that "faculty decided to try the hybrid model because of the many teaching and learning benefits . . . including the ability to provide more 'active learning' and 'engage' students by using technology" (p. 136). Other often cited reasons for the increased interest in blended learning relate to opportunities for improving student learning and success (Dziuban, Hartman, & Moskal, 2004), increasing student satisfaction (Dziuban & Moskal, 2001), and increasing retention and access (Picciano, 2006). For instance, Picciano (2006) explains that "well-designed blended learning environments have the potential of increasing access to a higher education because they improve retention" (p. 100). Due to the potential of the blended model to improve student interactivity, learning, satisfaction, retention, and success, it is not surprising to see the increasing acceptance and adoption of blended learning.

As blended learning continues to gain prominence in higher education and as instructors proceed to redesign their courses for the blended format, institutions will increasingly depend on instructional development programs to prepare and support instructors through the redesign process. According to Dziuban et al. (2004), "Maximizing success in a blended learning initiative requires a planned and well-supported approach that includes a theory-based instructional model, high-quality faculty development, course development assistance, [and] learner support" (p. 3). More specifically, drawing upon the work of Bates (2000), Dziuban, Hartman, Moskal, and Robison (2007) suggest that redesigning courses for the online and blended formats often demands "fundamental re-thinking of objectives and instructional strategies" that "require a shift in personal theories of teaching and in instructional behaviors (new mental models)—becoming a 'coach' rather than a 'teacher'— especially in environments that emphasize active student learning" (p. 271). Programs centered on blended pedagogy can effectively assist instructors through this necessary pedagogical transformation, one that can lead to increased student learning, retention, and satisfaction. Not surprisingly, providing these instructional development programs in a blended format can help instructors see the potential for blended learning in their own classes (Hayslett, O'Sullivan, Schweizer, & Wrench, 2009), which empowers them to effectively transform those classes while providing the flexibility of support and training that the blended modality affords (Schaber, Wilcox, Whiteside, Marsh, & Brooks, 2010).

Instructional Development

The University of Wisconsin–Milwaukee (UWM) has been providing instructional development and blended learning opportunities to students for over a decade. Since 2001, UWM has developed eight blended degree programs.

In the Fall of 2012, UWM offered approximately 100 blended courses and enrolled 7,655 students (26%) in at least one blended course. The average age of a blended undergraduate student is 24, 23% are students of color, and 64% are from the Milwaukee metro area. UWM (2012) defines blended courses as,

> courses where 20% or more of the traditional face-to-face classroom time is replaced by online assignments and activities. Students spend less time in the classroom and more time working and interacting online, providing greater flexibility regarding when and where coursework can be completed.
>
> (para 1)

UWM continues to see growth, as the nation does, and continues to provide opportunities for students to best meet their needs.

UWM's Learning Technology Center offers a program for blended teaching providing instructional development earning an international reputation in the field. The program guides the pedagogical design to move more didactic activities online while keeping tasks that require a richer media due to equivocality and uncertainty in the face-to-face environment. This increases the capacity for mastery of content and of deeper learning outcomes. The reduction of seat time is on average between 40–60%. The model focuses on active learning providing students with an engaging, interactive experience with frequent, low-stakes assessment facilitating constant feedback on their learning. An emphasis is placed on rethinking existing assumptions about effective pedagogical practices—as new skills and teaching techniques are required during the redesign process—and on viewing the redesign experience as a protracted and recursive process. Instructor attendance in instructional development and training programs can increase their competence in blended teaching and learning where this competence can impact student outcomes (Castle & McGuire, 2010).

The program is delivered in a blended format with multiple face-to-face meetings and integrated online activities. The blended format allows instructors to experience blended learning and provides the facilitators the opportunity to model good pedagogical practices in the blended learning environment. The program includes presentations by experienced blended instructors, online and face-to-face discussions and group work, creation of course materials, and peer and facilitator feedback. As part of the program, participants begin to develop their blended courses, leaving with the draft of a syllabus, a redesign plan, a learning module, and an assessment plan (Aycock, Mangrich, Joosten, Russell, & Bergtrom, 2008). The model is currently shared through the faculty development program and is being used by hundreds of faculty, teaching academic staff, and teaching assistants across many disciplines, course levels, and course sizes, illustrating its ability to scale on UWM's campus and on other college campuses.

The program focuses on effective pedagogical practices that are rooted in current research on both the design and implementation aspects of blended course development. As mentioned, the program emphasizes active learning and learner- or student-centered pedagogy for blended formats. Bonwell and Eison (1991) identify active learning as a pedagogical practice where a greater emphasis is placed on developing student skills through engaging activities requiring high order thinking than on information transmission. Students receive more immediate feedback in order to increase their learning. The pedagogical benefits of active learning in higher education are well noted in the existing scholarship (Adler, 1982; Chickering & Gamson, 1987; Silberman, 1996). Therefore, the blended pedagogical model requires a transformation for some instructors that have traditionally used a teacher-centered approach to developing learning activities and an assessment plan illustrating an active learning pedagogy while taking on a facilitation role or "guide on the side" over the "sage on the stage" (Kaleta et al., 2007). Not only are instructors learning and implementing a new pedagogical model, they are learning and implementing new skills and strategies as teachers.

In addition to developing instructor competence and implementing an active learning model, the program highlights strategies to carefully utilize and integrate new learning environments (face-to-face and online). Instructors need to examine their learning objectives and determine which can be better accomplished online and which can be better accomplished face-to-face. As Precel, Eshet-Alkalai, and Alberton (2009) mention, leveraging the most effective learning environments to accomplish the stated learning objectives should be prioritized as well as designed in advance. Appropriate media choice (what goes online and what goes face-to-face) and integration strategies or "closing the loop" between these two environments are key practices in the program.

Designing and implementing such well-designed blended courses requires that instructors encourage interactivity. Enhancing student–student and student–instructor interactions through course design can positively affect student learning (Chickering & Gamson, 1987; Kuh & Hu, 2001). In particular, many researchers have continued to find that formal and informal student interactions with faculty enhance student learning and success (Astin, 1993; Carini, Kuh, & Klein, 2006; Kuh & Hu, 2001; Pascarella & Terenzini, 1991; Tinto, 2000) as well as student satisfaction (Sher, 2009; Starenko, Vignare, & Humbert, 2007). The program inspires the development of learning activities that facilitate interactions among students (group work and discussions) and between students and instructors (feedback, presence, and communication), which can have an impact on student outcomes.

In creating interactivity, it is particularly important to develop presence and provide feedback. Social presence is the degree to which a person is perceived to be real or a human being (Joosten, 2012; Russo, 2000). The program illustrates the importance of developing a connection with students and establishing presence due to the limited channels or cues available when communicating and interacting online. By establishing presence, interactions between instructors and students can be enhanced (Schubert-Irastorza & Fabry, 2009; Swan & Shih, 2005). Further, the program emphasizes the need to have frequent low-stakes feedback that is timely. Prompt feedback can impact student learning (Chickering & Gamson, 1987) and student satisfaction (Dennen, Darabi, & Smith, 2007). While instructor satisfaction with the program remains high, we will examine the impact of the program on course effectiveness.

Research Question

The purpose of this study was to understand the impact of instructional development and training on the effectiveness of blended courses, and to use this information to motivate instructors and institutions to improve blended teaching and learning. The study's overarching question asked, what is the relationship between instructional development and training and the effectiveness of blended courses? We identified five variables to measure effectiveness: student interactivity, learning, satisfaction, retention, and success.

There are three parts to this study. The first part of the study examines instructors' perspectives or self-reported data of their students' interactivity, learning, and satisfaction in their most recently taught blended course illustrated in their responses to a series of Likert-survey items, while the second part of the study examines their responses to a series of open-ended survey items exploring the same variables. The third part of the study examines course level data from 2008–2012 to examine retention and students' success. Two groups were examined, courses where the instructors participated in development and training and courses where the instructors did not.

Methods

Participants

Participants were solicited from an email list of instructors of records for blended courses. Participants (N=29) consisted of 10 males (35%) and 18 females (62%) and one unreported. The ages of participants representing all included age categories with the average age in the 40–49 years age range. A range of roles were represented in the sample with participants representing two professors (7%), nine associate professors (31%), two assistant professors (7%), nine academic staff (31%), two lecturers (10%), and one teaching assistant (3%). An array of schools and colleges were represented with most participants reporting Letters & Science (31%), Health Sciences (17%), Education (14%), and Art (10%).

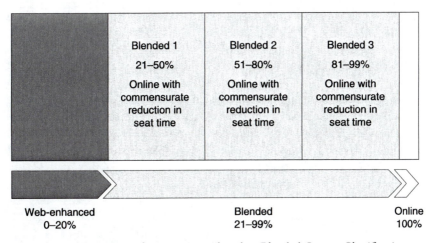

Blended 1	Blended 2	Blended 3
21–50%	51–80%	81–99%
Online with commensurate reduction in seat time	Online with commensurate reduction in seat time	Online with commensurate reduction in seat time

Web-enhanced
0–20%

Blended
21–99%

Online
100%

FIGURE 12.1   University of Wisconsin–Milwaukee Blended Course Classification

For parts one and two of the study, participants completed a 76-item web-based survey on their perceptions of their blended course and their instructional development in blended course design and teaching. Participants reported the percentage of seat time replaced by online activities for the courses that were part of the study. Based on the classification system of blended courses (see Figure 12.1), 69% of the courses reported were level 1 or 21% to 50% of seat time replaced, 28% of the courses reported were level 2 or 51% to 80%, and 3% of the courses reported were level 3 or 81% to 99% of seat time replaced. The sample represents a diversity of demographic groups, roles, and disciplines, and courses taught by the instructors represent all levels of blending.

Part three of the study includes course level data from blended courses delivered from Fall of 2008 to Summer of 2012 (N=476), which were noted in the data warehouse as blended courses.

Instrumentation

A survey (N=76) was administered to participants including 37 items on a 5-point Likert scale from Strongly Agree (1) to Strongly Disagree (5) and 23 open-ended items measuring the instructors' perceptions of student interactivity, student learning, student satisfaction, and course organization for parts one and two of the study.

Measures and Data Analysis

In part one of the study, independent measures included self-reported data from participants including:

1. attendance at the UWM Faculty Development Program for Blended Learning;
2. attendance at any blended and online teaching training;
3. number of additional UWM learning technology workshops attended.

Likert items were measured using various univariate analyses. A factor analysis was performed before the reliability tests to ensure that the measures were unique constructs. The measures did form separate constructs, although a few items that did not have a loading of greater than .5 on the proper construct were eliminated. Following the factor analysis, the reliability analysis was conducted with the remaining items for the measures.

Response Scales

Instructor surveys employed a series of scales. A complete set of scale items is available from the authors. Instructor scales measured the perception of student interactivity (alpha = .82), learning (=.83), and satisfaction (alpha = .89).

Open-ended Responses

In part two of the study, open-ended questions were analyzed using an inductive analytic process incorporating many of the procedures of the constant comparative method to conduct theoretical sampling (Patton, 2001). Researchers analyzed instructors' responses to the open-ended questions for key themes. Researchers compared data to further distill the themes.

Once key themes were identified, data were reexamined using matrices developed from the input variable ("attended instructional development"), making it possible to look at similarities and differences related to survey variables. Therefore, overall themes of faculty perceptions of student interactivity, learning, and satisfaction were derived and the themes were examined between those who participated in the instructional development and training and those who did not to identify the differences and similarities.

Quality control measures included peer reviews (Lincoln & Guba, 1985). Peer reviews took place as three researchers double-checked coding and verified the themes throughout the study.

Course Level Data

In a continuation of part one and part three of the study, student retention data and success data were examined. Part one of the study examined the retention and success data of the survey respondents. In part three of the study, course level data were examined.

Student Retention

The dependent measures were the number of persons failing to complete the course after the normal drop/add period passed. As a consequence, the transcript would indicate the dropped course. Drops can occur for many different reasons including medical conditions, military deployment, job relocation, and others.

Student Success

The dependent measure examines the number of students who earned a letter grade of C or better in the course and indicates successful completion of the course. Student success considers the grades awarded to students in the course. The grading scheme for each participant involved is identical.

Results

Interactivity, Learning, and Satisfaction

Part 1, Response Scales Between Group Differences

In examining the sample of instructors who completed the survey, a one-way between subjects ANOVA was conducted to compare the effect of instructional development and training on interactivity, learning, and satisfaction. The three levels of instructional development and training included no attendance, some attendance at training, and attendance at the UWM Faculty Development Program for Blended Learning. There was a significant effect of the independent variable (IV), instructors who attended the UWM program, on the dependent variable (DV), interactivity, at the $p < .05$ [$F (2, 27) = 4.918$, $p = .015$]. Post hoc comparisons using the Tukey HSD test indicated the mean score for those instructors that attended the program ($M = 9.21$, $SD = 2.26$) was significantly different from those who did not ($M = 6.82$, $SD = 2.18$). However, the other training condition ($M = 6.25$, $SD = 2.06$) did not significantly differ from the other conditions. In examining the impact on learning and on satisfaction, there was not a significant effect of the IV on the DV, learning, at the $p < .05$ [$F (2, 27)$ $=.409$, $p = .669$], nor on DV, satisfaction, at the $p < .05$ [$F (2, 27) = 1.189$, $p=.320$].

Results indicate perceptions of student interactivity were higher among instructors who attended the UWM Faculty Development Program for Blended Learning than those who did not. However, there were not significant results when examining the impact of instructional development and training on instructors' perceptions of student learning or student satisfaction.

Part 2, Open-ended Between Group Differences

Analysis of participants' responses to a series of open-ended questions regarding student interactivity, learning, and satisfaction illustrated differences and similarities between those who attended the UWM Faculty Development Program for Blended Learning and those who did not. The most notable similarity was the benefits of the flexibility afforded by the blended format, while the most noted difference was the efficacy of online learning.

The blended format creates an opportunity for students to engage with course material more at their own pace with a reduction in seat-time. Results suggest that particularly when comparing blended courses with those that are primarily face-to-face, faculty perceive the fluidity enabled by the blended format as valuable for ensuring learning-centered education. As one instructor explained, "Students could master some content at their own pace which removes some of the pressure from them in class meeting time." Since blended courses require students only to meet face-to-face a specific number of times during the semester, students have the freedom to engage with and comprehend the course material at their own pace.

The importance of flexibility within blended formats should not be underestimated. Given the busy schedules many of today's students experience, the blended format allows students the "convenience of accessing the material at times that suited their schedule" providing them a prime role in making the decision as to when and where they learn the best. Another instructor noted, "it also helped . . . part-time students keep up with work since they could better fit it around their schedules." The flexibility that blended learning provides is positive for all students, but particularly advantageous for non-traditional or part-time students as it makes completing course requirements easier to fit into schedules often including work and families.

The most notable difference between instructors who had attended the UWM program and those who had not was the perception of efficacy of online and media choice. Specifically, instructors reported different perceptions and practices in using the two environments, face-to-face and online. Those who participated in the UWM program reported specific focused effort on how to best use each environment. These instructors held a belief that both environments, face-to-face and online, can lead to community building and an increase in learning. Those who did not attend focused primarily on the face-to-face environment and indicated disbelief that students could build connections and community in the online environment.

Participants were asked how the blended format impacted student interactions in their class. Both groups (e.g., those who had participated in a blended faculty development program and those who had not) reported that the blended format increased student interactions in their course due to the use of resources such as online discussion boards, moving lectures online, and having activities in both components of the course. Individuals also reported from both groups that the blended format did not increase student interactions in their course. Instructors from both groups remarked that the online component of the blended format allowed students to be better prepared for their face-to-face component. While these groups had various similarities, there were also a few differences between groups regarding the importance of the face-to-face time.

The group that had not participated had more individuals report that they only used the online component in a minimal manner. One participant wrote, "[T]he online material was not used when the students were in class only after class." Another participant indicated that they could not "judge if it [blended] had an impact [on satisfaction] because the blended portion was minimal." Finally, an instructor reported that their "course had minimal focus on the online portion" and "the online portion was used for a project, however, because the students met regularly in-person the interaction online for the project was not robust." These participants did not fully integrate the components or loop them together in a fashion where they were holistically seen as one blended course where both components are given equal importance and status.

The current analysis suggests those instructors who did not attend the program lacked the knowledge of practices in integration and medium choice resulting in a dominant use and preference for face-to-face. Therefore, blended courses structured by instructors who did not effectively blend their course result in little influence on student outcomes.

Retention and Success

In examining all blended courses for 2008 to 2012, an independent-samples t-test was conducted to compare student success in those courses where the instructor attended the UWM Faculty Development Program for Blended Learning (IV level 1) and those courses where the instructor did not attend (IV level 2). There was not a significant difference in retention for IV level 1 (M = .94, SD = .07) and IV level 2 (M = .94, SD = .09) conditions; $t(475) = .541$, $p = .589$. However, there was a significant difference in student success for IV level 1 (M = 26.80, SD = 37.34) and IV level 2 (M = 20.38, SD = 24.79) conditions; $t(475) = 2.24$, $p = .015$.

Participants who attended the program had more effective blended courses since their students were more likely to complete the course and were more likely to earn a letter grade of C or better in the course. As students receive higher marks in these courses, findings illustrate that instructors who participate in blended instructional development are more likely to design and teach blended courses that have a positive impact on student success.

Recommendations

Enhance interactivity by incorporating community building activities, including networking opportunities, discussion activities, and group and team opportunities, while considering media choice (face-to-face and online) and integration strategies in the blended course design.

A number of recommendations for enhancing interactivity are derived from the findings of this study. First, provide face-to-face time for students to connect with each other, establish presence, and build learning community. Many of the surveyed instructors praised the blended format's ability to facilitate strong relationships between students and, in turn, improve not only discussion participation but also the substance of the conversations regarding course material. One instructor noted, "Having some in-class time early in the course helped students get to know each other in person before they were in discussions online. This helped them know who they were talking to and led to stronger, richer discussions." Another noted, "Students liked meeting their classmates after they had spent 5 weeks online with them. It felt almost like a 'reunion' of sorts. They felt they had gotten to know everyone online, talking, discussing, (and) sharing." Despite diverging opinions regarding when and through which medium students should interact face-to-face, participants agreed that encouraging familiarity between students online and face-to-face was imperative to enhancing discussions and increasing comprehension of the material.

Those that had not attended the program commented about their propensity for work in the face-to-face environment. One instructor indicated that dedicating a significant amount of face-to-face time at the beginning of the class was helpful: "The face-to-face classes were at the beginning and then the rest was online. Being able to meet the other students at the beginning helped with online discussions." This instructor indicates a belief in the necessity of face-to-face time in order to set the tone for the course and help students to get to know one another. Another instructor who had not taken the program noted the great amount of face-to-face time they dedicated early in the course in order to allow students to get to know one another better. The instructor believed this strategy helped students "know who they were talking to," leading to "stronger, richer discussions." According to these instructors, students needed the time to get to know one another in the face-to-face environment in order to make the online component effective.

The second recommendation that can be made from the current results is to incorporate class discussion activities in the face-to-face and online environments. Several instructors noted the advantages of using both the online and face-to-face environments. One participant remarked, "There were hands-on activities in the in-class component and online discussions in the online component so the students got to interact in both portions of the class. I feel that they bonded." Another instructor remarked, students "who did online work were also very active in face-to-face and did very well." Findings strongly suggest the amalgamation of face-to-face and online communication leads to a sense of familiarity between students and, resultantly, ensures more robust and effective application of course material than if the classes were primarily online or face-to-face.

A third recommendation is to include group activities (discussions or project teams) in the face-to-face and online environments. One instructor stated,

> I created groups that work both F2F [face-to-face]and in D2L. I found the groups formed far deeper relationships than when I taught this course only F2F. This surprised me and was the single most important reason I became a believer in on-line learning.

Another instructor stated, "Since we were in writing groups, they felt that the f2f provided them with the personal connection they need to write to each other as an audience. This community continued when we moved online." Group work provides an opportunity for students to interact, create a community and develop connections with each other, and improve their opportunities for higher order learning.

A further recommendation is to take advantage of delivering content in the online environment to enhance student learning by increasing the opportunities for students to prepare and reflect for class discussions, to apply their knowledge to achieve higher order learning, and to gain access and repetition for unique populations.

Additionally, several recommendations can be made for delivering content in the online environment. First, delivering content in the online environment allows students to interact with the content increasing the comprehension of content and preparing students for the active learning activities in the face-to-face. Several instructors noted the value of students receiving content and creating foundational knowledge online resulting in students coming to class prepared and ready to apply content. Therefore, instructors can use class time for more application of content. One instructor stated, "Online were lectures and discussion questions which allowed most f2f time to be used for application activities. These were done usually in small groups so that increased interaction as well." Another instructor stated that students were "able to use class time for group work, guest presentations, discussion versus content delivery." Face-to-face class time in a blended course is better served with rich and collaborative activities requiring immediate feedback or additional cues.

Online components for blended courses often are good spaces for didactic pedagogical tasks, such as delivering content. Face-to-face components provide a richer medium for small group activities, guest presentations, and further discussion around the content materials. Instead of being face-to-face-centric, instructors teaching blended learning should concern themselves with finding the right activity for the right medium. Media choice (face-to-face or online) should be determined based on the task requirements (Daft & Lengel, 1986), which can be considered instructor pedagogical need (Joosten, 2012), or what you are trying to accomplish in the classroom to increase student learning.

Not only does delivering content online increase preparation for and interactivity in the face-to-face portion of a blended class, the study's findings indicate that it can enhance student learning and performance. Delivering content online enables ample time for student reflection, enhances understanding of course material, and increases preparation, encouraging more effective application. Several of the instructors in this study identified increased student engagement with the material. For instance, one faculty member explained, "Online assignments allowed students time to reflect and demonstrate application of course content," while another stated, "It seems to have promoted more reflection (sic) and time to think about the different concepts brought up in class." The flexibility of the online portion not only decreased the pressure to apply content in a short about of time, as is often the case in face-to-face classes, but also led to more effective application of the material as students were given the opportunity to engage the material, comprehend it, and reflect upon it before discussing it with instructor and peers. Added time to engage and reflect on the material leads to an increase in comprehension of the concepts, analysis, and evaluation levels of thinking. One participant remarked that his/her students' test and quiz scores were noticeably improved in comparison with his/her "all face to face class."

Delivering content online has implications for providing access and an enhanced learning experience for particular student populations. One instructor reflected, "the blended format helped . . . non-native English speakers because they could replay the recorded slides and read my notes." The blended environment is text and media rich allowing students the benefit of re-reading or replaying as deemed necessary. The same instructor went on to remark, "nontraditional and visa students were very satisfied" with the blended course, but traditional students expressed that they "sometimes did feel a bit disconnected." As educational environments move forward with blended inquiry instructors must be aware of the differences in student population in regards to benefits of blended learning and preferences in learning formats.

Based upon the results, instructors who complete an instructional development and training program for blended teaching and learning will have a greater opportunity to increase student interactivity in their courses and better understand the implications of media choice, face-to-face and online, and integrating those two mediums. Further, this development can lead to an increase in student success.

The active learning pedagogical model shared through a program leads to greater interactivity and engagement. Implementing educational practices promoting communication and contact between students both online and offline will ensure participation from all students by building a sense of familiarity with each other and a learning community. The relationships created between students in blended courses will positively influence the frequency, duration, manner, and degree of effectiveness in which the students interact with each other and the course material resulting in a greater impact on student learning. By delivering content online, interactivity in the classroom is increased but also students receive an opportunity and flexibility in engaging with the course content, which can lead to opportunities for higher order learning by all students and provide access to learning opportunities for non-traditional students. The value of instructional development programming, including faculty development, for blended teaching and learning is necessary for the delivery of effective blended courses and ensuring quality in blended programming.

References

Adler, M. J. (1982). *The Paideia proposal: An education manifesto*. New York: Macmillan.

Allen, I. E., Seaman, J., & Garrett, R. (2007, March). Blending in: The extent and promise of blended education in the United States. Retrieved from http://sloanconsortium.org/publications/survey/pdf/Blending_In.pdf

Anderson, J., Boyles, J. A., & Rainie, L. (2012, July 27). The future of higher education. Retrieved from http://pewinternet.org/Reports/2012/Future-of-Higher-Education.aspx

Astin, A. (1993). *What matters in college? Four critical years revisited*. San Francisco: Jossey-Bass.

Aycock, A., Garnham, C., & Kaleta, R. (2002, March). Lessons learned from the hybrid course project. *Teaching with Technology Today, 8*(6). Retrieved from: www.uwsa.edu/ttt/articles/snds2.htm

Aycock, A., Mangrich, A., Joosten, T., Russell, M., & Bergtrom, G. (2008). *Faculty development for blended teaching and learning: A Sloan-C certificate program*. Needham, MA: Sloan Consortium.

Bonwell, C. C., & Eison, J. A. (1991). Active learning: Creating excitement in the classroom. ASHE-ERIC Higher Education Report No. 1. Washington, DC: The George Washington University.

Carini, R. M., Kuh, G. D., & Klein, S. P. (2006). Student engagement and student learning: Testing the linkages. *Research in Higher Education, 47*(1), 1–32.

Castle, S. R., & McGuire, C. J. (2010). An analysis of student self-assessment of online, blended, and face-to-face learning environments: Implications for sustainable education delivery. *International Education Studies, 3*(3), 36–40.

Chang, S. H., & Smith, R.A. (2008). Effectiveness of personal interaction in a learner-centered paradigm distance education class based on student satisfaction. *Journal of Research on Technology in Education, 40*(4), 407–426.

Chickering, A.W., & Gamson, Z. F. (1987). Seven principles for good practice. *AAHE Bulletin, 39*(7), 3–7.

Daft, R. L., & Lengel, R. H. (1986). Organizational information requirements, media richness and structural design. *Management Science, 32*(5), 554–571.

Dennen, V. P., Darabi, A. A., & Smith, L. J. (2007). Instructor–learner interaction in online courses: The relative perceived importance of particular instructor actions on performance and satisfaction. *Distance Education, 28*(1), 65–79.

Dziuban, C., & Moskal, P. (2001). Emerging research issues in distributed learning. Orlando, FL: Paper delivered at the 7th Sloan-C International Conference on Asynchronous Learning Networks.

Dziuban, C., Hartman, J., & Moskal, P. (March 2004). Blended Learning. *EDUCAUSE Center for Applied Research: Research Bulletin, 7*. Retrieved October 8, 2008, from http://net.educause.edu/ir/library/pdf/ERB0407.pdf

Dziuban, C., Hartman, J., Moskal, P. C., & Robison, R. (2007). Everything I need to know about blended learning I learned from books. In A. G. Picciano & C. D. Dziuban (Eds.), *Blended learning: Research perspectives* (pp. 265–286). Needham, MA: Sloan-Consortium.

Godambe, D., Picciano, A. G., Schroeder, R., & Schweber C. (2004). Faculty perspectives. Presentation at the 2004 Sloan-C Workshop on Blended Learning, Chicago, IL.

Hayslett, C., O'Sullivan, E., Schweizer, H., & Wrench, J. (2009). Using cognitive apprenticeship to provide faculty development in the use of blended learning. *Journal of the Research Center for Educational Technology, 5*(2), 92–117.

Joosten, T. (2012). *Social media for educators.* San Francisco, CA: Jossey Bass.

Kaleta, R., Skibba, K., & Joosten, T. (2007). Discovering, designing, and delivering hybrid courses. In A.G. Picciano & C.D. Dziuban (Eds.), *Blended learning: Research perspectives* (pp. 111–143). Needham, MA: Sloan Consortium.

Kuh, G. D., & Hu, S. (2001). Learning productivity at research universities. *Journal of Higher Education, 72,* 1–28.

Lee, R., & Dashew, B. (2011). Designed learner interactions in blended course delivery. *Journal of Asynchronous Learning Networks, 15*(1), 72–80.

Lincoln, Y. S., & Gula, E. G. (1985). *Naturalistic inquiry.* Beverly Hills, CA: Sage Publications, Inc.

Pascarella, E., & Terenzini, P. (1991). *How college affects students: Findings and insights from twenty years of research.* San Francisco: Jossey-Bass.

Patton, M. Q. (2001). *Qualitative research and evaluation methods* (3rd ed.). Thousand Oaks, CA: Sage Publications, Inc.

Picciano, A.G. (2006). Blended learning: Implications for growth and access. *Journal of Asynchronous Learning Networks, 10*(3). Retrieved from: http://sloanconsortium. org/jaln/v10n3/blended-learning-implications-growth-and-access

Picciano, A. G., Seaman, J., Shea, P., & Swan, K. (2012). Examining the extent and nature of online learning in American K–12 Education: The research initiatives of the Alfred P. Sloan Foundation. *Internet and Higher Education, 15*(2), 127–135.

Precel, K., Eshet-Alkalai, Y., & Alberton, Y. (2009). Pedagogical and design aspects of a blended learning course. *International Review of Research in Open and Distance Learning, 10*(2). Retrieved from: www.irrodl.org/index.php/irrodl/article/view/618/1221

Russo, T. (2000). Social presence: Teaching and learning with invisible others. Paper presented at Creating Effective Online Instruction, University of Kansas, Lawrence, KS.

Schaber, P., Wilcox, K. J., Whiteside, A., Marsh, L., & Brooks, D. C. (2010). Designing learning environments to foster affective learning: Comparison of classroom to blended learning. *International Journal for the Scholarship of Teaching and Learning, 4*(2). Retrieved from: http://eaglescholar.georgiasouthern.edu:8080/jspui/handle/10518/4132

Schubert-Irastorza, C., & Fabry, D. (2009). Improving student satisfaction with online faculty performance. *Journal of Research in Innovative Teaching, 4*(1), 168–178.

Shea, P., Pickett, A., & Pelz, W. (2003). A follow up investigation of "teacher presence" in the SUNY Learning Network. *Journal of Asynchronous Learning Networks, 7*(2), 61–80.

Sher, A. (2009). Assessing the relationship of student–instructor and student–student interaction to student learning and satisfaction in web-based online learning environment. *Journal of Interactive Online Learning, 8*(2), 102–120.

Silberman, M. (1996). *Active learning.* Boston: Allyn & Bacon.

Starenko, M., Vignare, K., & Humbert, J. (2007). Enhancing student interaction and sustaining faculty instructional innovations through blended learning. In A.G. Picciano & C. D. Dziuban (Eds.), *Blended learning: Research perspectives* (pp. 161–178). Needham, MA: Sloan Consortium.

Swan, K., & Shih, L. F. (2005). On the nature and development of social presence in online course discussions. *Journal of Asynchronous Learning Networks, 9*(3), 115–136.

Tinto, V. (2000). Linking learning and leaving. In J. M. Braxton (Ed.), *Reworking the departure puzzle* (pp. 81–24). Nashville, TN: Vanderbilt University Press.

University of Wisconsin—Milwaukee (2012). Schedule of Classes. Retrieved September 30, 2012 from: www4.uwm.edu/schedule/?a1=results&strm=2129&coursetype=HYBRID

13

GROWING YOUR OWN BLENDED FACULTY

A Review of Current Faculty Development Practices in Traditional, Not-for-Profit Higher Education Institutions

Amy P. Ginsberg and Elizabeth Ciabocchi

A recent study of over 2,500 institutions of higher education revealed that, in 65%, online learning is a critical part of their long-term strategy. This study also reported a 10% growth rate for online enrollments, which far outpaces the < 1% growth for the overall higher education student population. Indeed, 31% of all higher education students now take at least one course online (Allen & Seaman, 2011).

Similar to online education, blended instruction (involving a combination of face-to-face and online elements, with some replacement of face-to-face time by online work) is also on the rise, as indicated by the fact that approximately 79% of public higher education institutions in the US now offer blended courses (McGee & Reis, 2012). In addition, considerable resources have been developed over the past decade to support blended course design and delivery, which indicates that blended course offerings are a priority for U.S. higher education (McGee & Reis, 2012).

With the proliferation in online and blended education, it is logical and necessary to inquire about faculty development in this area. For online teaching, there is no single institutional training approach, but the vast majority of institutions (94%) do have some kind of training or mentoring, with internally run courses as the most common training approach, followed by informal mentoring. Other approaches include formal mentoring, certification programs, and externally run training courses. Institutions of various types were far more likely to use internally vs. externally run training courses (Allen & Seaman, 2011).

Despite the rapid proliferation of blended learning programs, and the undeniable reality that faculty development is critical to this effort, the research to date about faculty development specifically for blended instruction within traditional higher education institutions—where much of this growth is taking place—is scarce.

Literature Review

Structure and Implementation of Faculty Development Programs

Faculty teaching blended or online courses need to be well prepared with new skills, competencies, instructional objectives, and strategies that differ from those employed in face-to-face instruction (Dziuban, Hartman, & Moskal, 2007; Kaleta, Skibba, & Joosten, 2007; Moore & Kearsley, 2012; Ragan, 2011; Vaill & Testori, 2011). Organizational structure and campus support resources are also important factors that influence institutional models and scale of faculty development in blended instruction (Dziuban et al., 2007). Given the many variables that impact faculty development models, it is not surprising that institutional requirements for faculty development or certification in blended/online formats also vary widely. For example, on the one hand, Syracuse University School of Information Studies' distance education programs require all new faculty to complete a 6-day online asynchronous training course (Lorenzetti, 2011). On the other hand, some institutions have requirements that span weeks or months over a semester or academic year. Faculty training formats also vary and may include face-to-face, online, and/or blended formats. Institutional size, type (doctoral/research vs. 2-year college), and geographic distribution (single vs. multiple campuses) influence the organization of faculty development as either distributed or centralized (Diaz et al., 2009). Furthermore, the focus of faculty development (e.g., technology training or teaching/pedagogy) and availability of resources also influence which institutional unit is responsible for its delivery, e.g., information technology, the library, the academic officer or academic unit (Diaz et al., 2009).

Some institutions require faculty development for blended instruction and/or provide incentives for participation, while others do not. Such incentives vary greatly across institutions and may include course release time, financial compensation, contribution to the departmental faculty development fund, or access to free faculty development courses/programs. It has been argued that faculty perceptions regarding time, money, and pressure from others (e.g., peers and/or students) may motivate faculty to use instructional technologies. For example, an institution might encourage early adopters to use technology in their courses in order to build early successes and thereby impact the perceptions of their peers regarding distance education (Lorenzetti, 2011). Another way in which perceptions might be impacted is to authenticate faculty readiness to teach blended or online courses by awarding an institutionally granted certification, such as is done by Valencia College, which certifies faculty as "Digital Professors" upon completion of 20 hours of professional development in pedagogy and technology in online/hybrid teaching and learning. Similarly, the University of Illinois awards a Master Online Teacher Certificate upon successful completion of four core courses, one elective course, and an online teaching practicum.

The requirements for certification as a blended or online instructor may be multi-faceted, including elements other than training courses. The University of Wisconsin-Milwaukee awards faculty a certificate in online and blended teaching upon successful completion of its Faculty Development Program for Online and Blended Course Redesign; the development and instruction of an online or blended credit-bearing course; peer or technological staff course evaluation; a letter of reflection; joining a group listserv for faculty teaching blended and online courses; and allowing one's syllabus to be shared with other faculty. Some institutions also differentiate between the knowledge and skills required to teach blended courses and those required for teaching with technology in the classroom, and provide development and training accordingly.

Attributes of Successful Faculty Development Programs

A study at Babson College showed that factors deemed critical to success include creating and matching faculty development programs with the phases of curriculum innovation identified by the institution, and the development of incentives and delivery methods to encourage faculty participation (Fetters & Duby, 2011). Other factors cited in the literature include administrative support; program design rooted in best practices; effective teaching and learning environment, including mixed delivery formats and flexible scheduling; emphasis on improving teaching and learning effectiveness; financial support; technology resources, including online resources; regular program assessment for continuous improvement; and skilled facilitators (Diaz et. al., 2009; Eib & Miller, 2006; Reilly, Vandenhouten, Gallagher-Lepak, & Ralston-Berg, 2011).

Institutional Philosophy

A growing body of literature demonstrates that higher education institutions offer faculty development programs in blended instruction grounded in educational theory and best practices; there does not, however, appear to be a "one size fits all" philosophical approach to such programs. For example, notable community-based faculty development programs for blended teaching and learning have been developed at the University of Central Florida, University of Wisconsin–Milwaukee, and Miami University (Vaughan & Garrison, 2006). Similarly, faculty development programs at the University of Calgary and the University of Wisconsin–Green Bay are based on a faculty learning community model to reduce feelings of isolation and facilitate deeper learning among participants (Eib & Miller, 2006; Reilly et al., 2011).

At Penn State Harrisburg, a faculty development program grounded in adult and transformative learning theories was designed for faculty teaching in a blended format. The adult learning theory framework challenges participants to examine fundamental assumptions about teaching and learning, with the aim of changing face-to-face teaching practices through engagement in online learning and reflection (McQuiggan, 2011). Bay Path College used a similar framework for its faculty development program for those teaching online and blended courses (Vaill & Testori, 2011).

Babson College promotes curricular innovation in blended courses/ programs via faculty development activities tailored to faculty characteristics and dispositions, from risk-taking innovators and early adopters to technology laggards. The match between the faculty member's disposition toward technology and the curricular innovation phase for which he/she seeks development and guidance is a key characteristic of this approach (Fetters & Duby, 2011).

Research Focus

With these current practices in mind, this survey centered on three primary research questions:

1. How are faculty development programs for blended teaching and learning structured and implemented in these five areas: optional vs. required, mode of delivery, responsible office, incentives for participation, and demonstration of faculty member's readiness/proficiency to teach in a blended format?
2. Which elements of the faculty development program for blended teaching and learning have been most/least successful, and why?
3. What is the underlying philosophy that drives institutional decisions regarding the structure and delivery of faculty development in blended teaching and learning?

Method

Participants

This survey focused on traditional, not-for-profit higher education institutions in the US offering blended courses and programs. Representatives from approximately 500 institutions were identified via their membership in three professional organizations focusing on educational technology, and online and blended education.

Measures

The researchers created a 17-item survey with both quantitative and qualitative elements. Participants were asked to describe their institution's training of faculty for blended instruction with respect to whether the training is required, the type(s) of training provided, the mode(s) of delivery, the institutional offices responsible for the training, incentives, and the availability of an institutional certification. In addition, participants were asked for their perceptions of the most and least successful aspects of faculty development for blended instruction at their institutions, their understanding of the contributing factors, and how faculty development for blended instruction could be strengthened at their institutions. Finally, participants were asked about the relationship of faculty development for blended instruction to their institutions' strategic plan and the underlying institutional philosophy in this regard.

Procedures

The researchers distributed the survey electronically to approximately 500 higher education institutional representatives identified via website information and listservs of professional organizations that promote educational technology and blended/online education. Email messages to institutional representatives included a link to an online survey managed by CampusLabs, LLC.

Results

Of the 116 survey respondents—after eliminating those representing for-profit institutions or those without blended course offerings—responses from 109 individuals were utilized. Training for faculty who teach blended courses was required by 25% of the institutions, recommended by 51%, and not provided by 10%. Of the remaining 13% who indicated "other," the prevailing comment was that training was offered/available but not required or recommended.

Research Question #1: Structure and Implementation of Faculty Development Programs

The majority of respondents represented public institutions, which were far more likely to recommend—as opposed to require—faculty development for blended instruction (see Figures 13.1 and 13.2). Conversely, private institutions (n = 39) were more likely to require faculty development for blended instruction than public institutions, but also less likely to offer it. Most institutions, both public and private, offered blended courses primarily in face-to-face programs. Public institutions were also more likely than private institutions to offer online programs including blended courses.

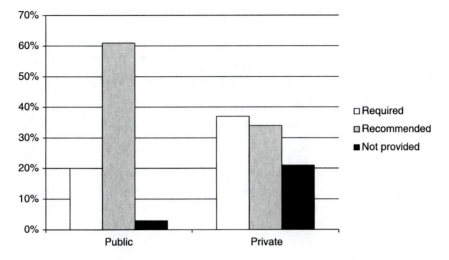

FIGURE 13.1   Public vs. Private Institutional Requirements for Faculty Development for Blended Course Instruction

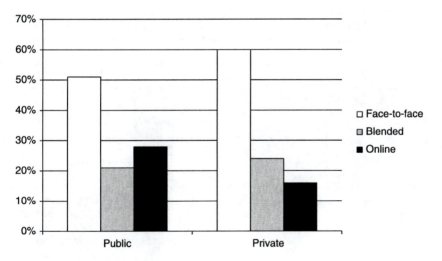

FIGURE 13.2   Public vs. Private Institutions by Type of Programs in Which Blended Courses are Offered

The most common types of faculty development for blended course instruction (see Figure 13.3) were internal training courses (69%), informal mentoring (67%), and formal mentoring (31%). Institutional certification programs, external training courses, and external certification programs were less common. As indicated in Figure 13.4, face-to-face instruction was the most common delivery mode (72%), followed by asynchronous online instruction

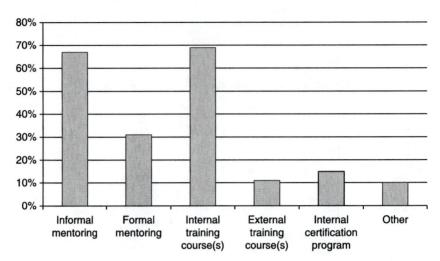

FIGURE 13.3 Types of Faculty Development for Blended Instruction

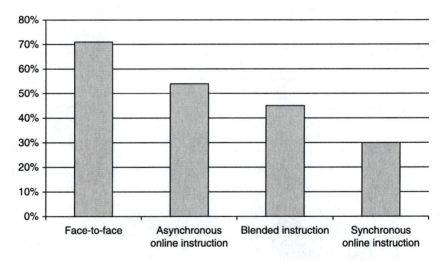

FIGURE 13.4 Delivery Modes of Faculty Development for Blended Instruction

(55%), blended instruction (45%), and synchronous online instruction (30%). The institutional offices most often responsible for faculty development were academic affairs (40%), distance education (26%), and information technology (26%). Other offices mentioned less frequently were academic departments/divisions, schools/colleges, teaching and learning centers, continuing education, instructional design offices, and the library.

Fifty-seven percent of respondents indicated that their institutions offer no incentives for participation in faculty development for blended instruction,

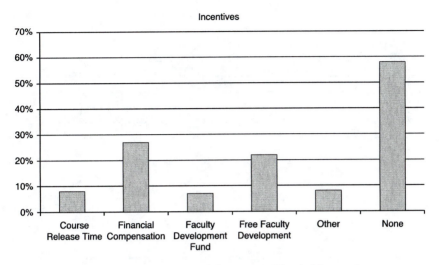

FIGURE 13.5   Incentives for Faculty Development in Blended Instruction

more than double the number of institutions (27%) that offered financial compensation for such participation (see Figure 13.5). Relatively few (8%) offered course release time, contribution to a department faculty development fund, or incentives at the discretion of an academic dean or department.

The vast majority of institutions (80%) did not offer an internal certification in blended course instruction, although 14% did so, and 6% reported that they did not know if their institutions offered an institutional certification. Of those offering an internal certification, nearly all required a faculty development course(s) and the development of a blended course. Less often required were peer or staff course evaluation, blended course instruction, an online teaching practicum, and participation in a blended faculty learning community.

Research Question #2: Most Successful Elements and Suggestions for Improvement

Respondents reported that the most successful elements of faculty development (see Figure 13.6) for blended course instruction at their institutions were the program design (48%), quality of instruction (47%), convenience of the delivery format (43%), and faculty involvement/buy-in (43%). Comments frequently referenced the importance of financial incentives and quality of the training to faculty buy-in and engagement, as well as institutional support to sustain faculty motivation and instructional quality. Some stated that institutional mandates are not well received by the faculty, and optional or recommended as opposed to required training contributed to success.

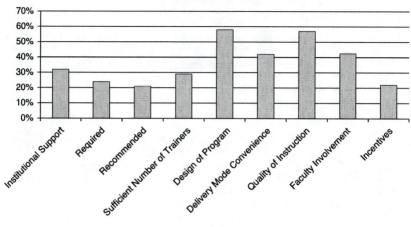

FIGURE 13.6   Most Successful Elements of Faculty Development Programs

Least successful elements of the faculty development program for blended instruction included incentives for faculty participation (28%), training is recommended but not required (24%), faculty involvement/buy-in (19%), and sufficient number of qualified training staff (19%). Respondents' comments indicated a prevailing sense that institutions offer insufficient incentives and support for faculty development in blended instruction. One respondent aptly summarized this problem, stating that "faculty-driven learning with little support or incentive cannot overcome the constraints of time and energy for most instructors to learn new skills." A number of respondents also commented on the difficulties caused by the absence of an institutional mandate for faculty development in blended instruction. For example, one respondent stated,

> If it is just recommended and not required, no one will take the time to come. It isn't that they don't care, or aren't interested. Their workload has become very heavy in the last few years and if it isn't required, most opt to not add anything more.

Given these issues, it follows that respondents reported (see Figure 13.7) that their institutional faculty development for blended instruction could be strengthened by providing incentives for faculty participation (48%), requiring the training (47%), and increasing the number of qualified training staff (43%). Respondents also suggested increased institutional support/funding (38%), improving the design of the faculty development program (29%), offering a more convenient delivery format (18%), and improving the quality of the instruction of the faculty development program (15%).

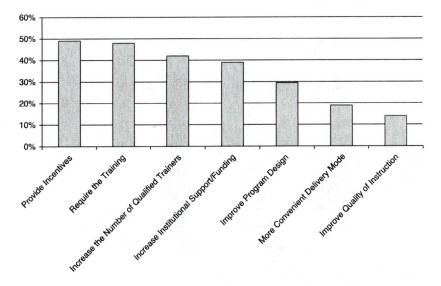

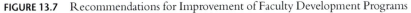

FIGURE 13.7 Recommendations for Improvement of Faculty Development Programs

Research Question #3: Institutional Philosophy and Strategic Plan

The highest percentage of respondents (38%) indicated that faculty development for blended course instruction was important to the institution's strategic
plan, followed by 30% who indicated that it was tangential. A smaller number
indicated that it was either vital to the institution's strategic plan (14%) or not
at all related (13%). Two respondents reported that they did not know the
answer to this question, and 17 did not respond to this question.

Faculty development for blended course instruction was vital or important
to the institution's strategic plan in 58% of public institutions vs. 42% of private
institutions. It was tangential or not at all related to the institution's strategic
plan in 48% of private institutions, as compared with 30% of public institutions
(see Figure 13.8). Not surprisingly, a significant relationship was found
between the faculty development requirement for instructors teaching blended
courses and the perception of its importance to the institution's strategic plan
($x_2 = 33.135$, $df = 15$, $p = .004$).

Researcher Bias and Limitations of Survey

The researchers are academic administrators at a large, multi-campus, private
university that is presently grappling with strategic planning and infrastructure
development to expand blended and online learning across the institution
(Calderon, Ginsberg, & Ciabocchi, 2012). The decision to examine the relationship of faculty development to institutions' strategic plans for blended

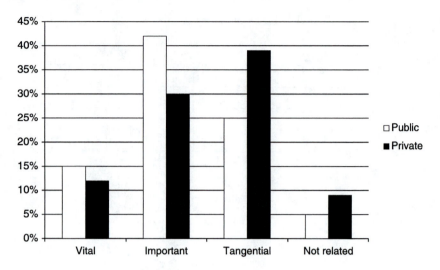

FIGURE 13.8 Importance of Faculty Development in Blended Instruction to Institutional Strategic Plan

learning and the philosophical underpinnings of their faculty development models was influenced by the researchers' respective roles in creating faculty development opportunities for blended learning, and the desire to gain insight into the priority assigned to blended instruction in similar institutions. Given its relatively small sample size and the convenience sampling strategy employed, the data presented in the survey should be viewed as preliminary and not generalized to all U.S. non-profit higher education institutions.

Discussion and Recommendations

The findings from this survey reveal current faculty development practices at traditional institutions of higher education engaged in blended teaching and learning. Noteworthy patterns in the quantitative findings are accompanied by illustrative and thought-provoking comments from respondents that suggest a number of areas for future investigation. The qualitative responses to items throughout the survey reveal a complex picture of the interrelationships among the factors involved in the structure, implementation, and success of faculty development for blended course instruction. For example, when blended courses are taught primarily in face-to-face programs, as is the case for the majority of institutions in this sample, how does this this affect institutional and individual perception of the need for training in blended course instruction? Several respondents noted that faculty development is required for online course instruction, but not for blended course instruction. In this sample, public institutions were more likely than private institutions to offer blended courses as part of online programs. When this is the case, is faculty development for blended course instruction more likely to be offered and utilized? And how is this related to the priority assigned to faculty development for blended course instruction and support?

Public institutions in this sample gave greater priority to faculty development for blended course instruction than did private institutions. Not only did a greater percentage of public institutions require or recommend the training, but they also were more likely than private institutions to prioritize faculty development for blended course instruction in strategic planning. Underlying factors that might be further explored may include the relationship of blended learning to institutional mission, resource allocation, and the priority and scope of previously established online programs at the institution.

The findings of the survey are consistent with the literature regarding the most common types of faculty development programs offered for online or blended instruction at the institutions under investigation, i.e., internally offered programs, informal mentoring, and formal mentoring, as well as the variability of institutional practices and faculty development models for blended instruction. More important, perhaps, is the finding that most institutions offered a variety of training opportunities and delivery formats, creating convenience and flexibility for faculty that were viewed as critical to their success.

Respondents' comments regarding successful elements in their faculty development programs for blended instruction, and their recommendations to strengthen their respective programs, may be instructive for similar institutions developing or expanding faculty development in this area:

1. Require training in blended course instruction.
2. Provide incentives for faculty participation.
3. Offer flexibility and convenience via multiple training opportunities and delivery formats (referenced above).
4. Allocate sufficient human, financial, and technical resources to support the faculty development program, including an ample number of qualified training staff.
5. Ensure that the faculty development program has a strong pedagogical design.

Each of these topics requires thorough investigation and consideration within the systems of a particular institution, whether public or private. For institutional decision-makers, they provide a starting point for discussions among administrators, faculty, and instructional designers to maximize the success of faculty development for blended course instruction. Fortunately, each of these recommendations is sufficiently broad to permit internal stakeholders—those who know it best—to figure out how to plan a faculty development system creatively that will result in institutional success.

References

Allen, I. E., & Seaman, J. (2011). Going the distance: Online education in the United States, 2011. Babson Survey Research Group and Quahog Research Group, LLC.

Calderon, O., Ginsberg, A., & Ciabocchi, L. (2012). Multidimensional assessment of blended learning: Maximizing program effectiveness based on faculty and student feedback. *Journal of Asynchronous Learning Networks, 16*(3), 23–37.

Diaz, V., Garrett, P. B., Kinley, E. R., Moore, J. F., Schwartz, C. M., & Kohrman, P. (2009). Faculty development for the 21st century. *EDUCAUSE Review, 44* (May/June), 46–55.

Dziuban, C., Hartman, J., & Moskal, P. (2007). Everything I need to know about blended learning I learned from books. In A. G. Picciano & C. D. Dziuban, (Eds.) *Blended learning research perspectives* (pp. 265–285). Needham, MA: Sloan-C.

Eib, B. J., & Miller, P. (2006). Faculty development as community building. *International Review of Research in Open and Distance Learning, 7*(2). Retrieved from: www.irrodl. org/index.php/irrodl/article/view/299/639

Fetters, M. L., & Duby, T. G. (2011). Faculty development: A stage model matched to blended learning maturation. *Journal of Asynchronous Learning Networks, 15*(1). Retrieved from: http://sloanconsortium.org/jaln/v15nl/faculty-development-stage-model-matched-blended-learning-maturation

Kaleta, R., Skibba, K., & Joosten, T. (2007). Discovering, designing, and delivering hybrid courses. In A. G. Picciano & C. D. Dziuban, (Eds.), *Blended learning research perspectives* (pp. 265–285). Needham, MA: Sloan-C.

Lorenzetti, J. P. (2011). Developing faculty competency in online pedagogy. In C. Hill (Ed.), *Faculty development in distance education: Issues, trends and tips* (pp. 8–9). Madison, WI: Magna Publications.

McGee, P., & Reis, A. (2012). Blended course design: A synthesis of best practices. *Journal of Asynchronous Learning Networks, 16*(4), 5–22.

McQuiggan, C.A. (2011). Faculty development for online teaching as a catalyst for change. *Journal of Asynchronous Learning Networks, 16*(2), 27–62.

Moore, M.G., & Kearsley, G. (2012). *Distance education: A systems view of online learning.* Belmont, CA: Wadsworth, Cengage Learning.

Ragan, L. (2011). Defining competencies for online teaching success. In C. Hill (Ed.), *Faculty development in distance education: Issues, trends and tips* (pp. 4–5). Madison, WI: Magna Publications.

Reilly, J. R., Vandenhouten, C., Gallagher-Lepak, S., & Ralston-Berg, P. (2011). Faculty development for e-learning: A multi-campus community of practice (COP) approach. *Journal of Asynchronous Learning Networks, 16*(2), 99–110

Vaill, A. L., & Testori, P. A. (2011). Orientation, mentoring and ongoing support: A three-tiered approach to online faculty development. *Journal of Asynchronous Learning Networks, 16*(2), 111–120.

Vaughan, N., & Garrison, D. R. (2006). How blended learning can support a faculty development community of inquiry. *Journal of Asynchronous Learning Networks, 10*(4). Retrieved from: http://sloanconsortium.org.jaln/v10n4/how-blended-learning-can-support-faculty-development-community-inquiry

Vignare, K. (2007). Review of literature blended learning: Using ALN to change the classroom—Will it work? In A. G. Picciano & C. D. Dziuban (Eds.), *Blended learning research perspectives* (pp. 37–63). Needham, MA: Sloan-C.

14

CHOICE DOES MATTER

Faculty Lessons Learned Teaching Adults in a Blended Program

Karen Skibba

Introduction

To increase access to the growing adult population, many colleges are offering blended programs that include courses that are face-to-face and fully and partially online. Partially online course delivery formats are described as hybrid (Kaleta & Garnham, 2001) or blended (Picciano, 2007). The Sloan-Consortium (Allen, Seaman, & Garrett, 2007) published a survey report that focused on blended learning and programs called "Blending In: The Extent of Promise of Blended Education in the United States." This national sample of 1,000 colleges and universities found that 36% of institutions offer at least one blended program. This report defined blended programs as the same as hybrid or blended courses, which is when between 30% and 79% of the course content is delivered online. To avoid confusion, this chapter will refer to courses as hybrid and programs as blended.

There are a number of ways to structure blended programs: Institutions mix online and face-to-face courses, offer all hybrid courses, or mix all three course delivery formats. Faculty members are expected to teach within these blended programs and move from teaching in the classroom to teaching on their computers. The Sloan-C survey of U.S. colleges and universities (Allen, Seaman, & Garrett, 2007) found that core faculty members teach online courses (64.7%) about as frequently as they teach face-to-face-courses (61.6%), and a large percentage of faculty members teach hybrid courses (67.4%).

When learning to teach adults in a blended program, faculty members face many challenges as they experiment with teaching more than one course delivery format, especially online and hybrid courses. Challenges include identifying effective learning strategies, preparing students for online learning, redesigning courses using technology, learning how to facilitate courses, handling technology issues, developing content, managing workload, providing student feedback, and assessing learning (Bogle, Cook, & Day, 2009; Dziuban, Hartman, Cavanagh, & Moskal, 2011; Moloney et al., 2007).

Adding to these challenges, many faculty members do not receive training on how to teach as a practice or keep up with trends that affect their teaching, including the growth of the number of adult students and the increased use of new course delivery formats (King & Lawler, 2003). This chapter investigates what faculty members have learned from the challenges and opportunities of teaching adult learners in blended programs.

Research Method and Participants

This chapter reports research based on selected findings and further analysis of a dissertation study on how faculty members learn to teach adult learners in a blended program (Skibba, 2011). Two research questions were investigated:

1. How do faculty members describe the process and implications of moving back and forth between teaching multiple course delivery formats within a blended program?
2. How do faculty members perceive teaching adults in a blended program influences their overall teaching practices?

A basic qualitative interpretive approach was employed. Data collection instruments were: in-depth interviews, a faculty background questionnaire with reflective questions, and a teacher learning audit. The data were analyzed using the constant comparative method (Patton, 2001). Methods used to assure quality and trustworthiness were triangulation, pilot tests, member checking, and peer review of data.

Ten faculty members from two blended adult degree programs participated in this study: Five participants taught in an undergraduate degree program and five taught in a graduate degree program. The undergraduate program has been in existence since 1972 and offers adult learners the opportunity to earn a degree that builds on credit granted for prior coursework and experience. Students select from concentrations in human services, teacher licensure, and business leadership. The graduate program, a master's degree in educational technology for practicing K–12 teachers and administrators, started in 1983. This program is offered year round following a cohort model with many courses offered nationwide to instruct in-service teachers.

Research Findings

Ross and Gage (2006) explained that participating in a blended program "means that a student is not a 'traditional student' or an 'online student' but has the freedom to choose from all types of courses to earn a degree" of which some courses are hybrid, face-to-face, and online (p. 156). The major theme that emerged from the interview data was the "importance of choice." This theme was analyzed through three lenses: (1) how adult students learn; (2) how to teach adult students; and (3) challenges of multiple course delivery formats.

How Adult Students Learn

Nontraditional students are enrolling in college at all ages, bringing with them very diverse life and work experiences, personalities, educational preparation, goals, expectations, and motivations for attending college. According to Kasworm, Polson, and Fishback (2002), because many adults are "place-bound and time-pressed," they are often attracted to adult degree programs that offer courses at convenient locations with flexible days and times (p. 48). Nontraditional students, especially women, must fit courses into busy lives that include work and family commitments, or they are not able to complete a degree. When this study was conducted, both the blended programs were undergoing changes to include more online or hybrid courses to accommodate the needs of adult students.

The undergraduate program originally offered face-to-face courses, added hybrid courses nine years ago, and added online courses four years ago. In the year that this research study was conducted, almost all face-to-face courses were eliminated. While the undergraduate degree program is keeping hybrid courses, administration is evaluating how many to offer, based on registrations. One undergraduate program faculty member explained that his is a self-sustaining program and "[we] are going to respond to adult students because that's our marketplace."

The adult graduate blended degree program also originally offered face-to-face courses, most of which were taught during weekends, and for 15 years offered many courses online. Now the graduate program has "a mandate to reduce our face-to-face component by 50% across the program," so they will have a "mix and match" approach offering face-to-face, online, and hybrid courses all in the same program.

Despite being offered all three options at both programs, adult students were "voting with their feet" and registering for more online courses. Most of the research participants voiced their concerns that some students will not be able to adapt to online learning and will not be successful. One faculty member said that some students prefer and are more successful taking face-to-face courses and even dislike online courses; however, this "was the only way to finish the program." Other adult students said they prefer to learn more from learner-centered and collaborative approaches used in online and hybrid courses (Cercone, 2008; Hiltz & Shea, 2005).

A research participant explained that adult learners register for online courses for convenience and flexibility, and some think online learning will be easier.

During the first semester it is like "throwing cold water on people" to help them realize that "online learning is *not* easy and it's *not* easier than doing it live." Therefore it was important to make students aware of the challenges of learning in online and hybrid courses and prepare them academically and technologically, including how to manage their time and expectations. Other modifications the faculty members needed to make for busy adult learners included providing more flexible due dates, clear guidelines, an organized course structure, and fast communication so that the students would not feel isolated and would know what was expected. The research participants noted that these are critical modifications to make in online or hybrid courses because more self-directed learning is required.

Despite adult students' demand for online courses, the research participants said they believe that adult students should have a choice of course delivery format. One faculty member explained that offering choices allows students to take courses in a way that fits their lifestyles and abilities. Another faculty member explained that offering choices helps students learn in new ways and be prepared for today's work world.

How to Teach Adult Students

After teaching in a blended program, the research participants said it was important to have a choice of how to teach. When the faculty members were exposed to multiple course delivery formats, they learned to choose the format that best achieved learning goals. One research participant explained, "Then the question is, how do you create sort of a goodness of fit so that the exercise you want to do live is something you can use online or vice versa?" Another said she preferred to demonstrate technology in person while others preferred to use online tutorials and web conferencing to show students how to learn new technologies. In addition, most of the faculty members explained that they prefer assignments to be turned in online and many prefer online discussions to face-to-face discussions. The research participants liked being able to choose the best course delivery format based on preference, comfort level, content, learning activities, and for variety. Ultimately, teaching in a blended program offered the most flexibility and success when teaching adults students.

The research participants learned how to take elements of all course delivery formats to create the best learning environment for their students. Because of this flexibility, they described teaching multiple course delivery formats in many ways. For example, "It's like being in an amusement park because there are so many different media and ideas and ways of doing things that it's really exciting." Another said:

> It's like being a chef. You pick the best ingredients from your face-to-face and your online experiences and then experiment to see if the flavors

really do work together, and if not, you may have to come up with some new things.

One research participant described teaching in a blended program like "going to a toy store" because she could try new technologies and "play with and rethink my pedagogy." The research participants discovered that teaching a variety of course delivery formats resulted in improving pedagogy in other course formats: "Having the online element made me rethink pedagogy and so that has made my teaching develop and evolve in a new way." One faculty member explained teaching multiple course delivery formats "forces you to look at the essence of your teaching." This finding is supported by a qualitative study that found that learning and using technology offered opportunities to reflect on practice and rethink and evaluate teaching and learning (King, 2002).

Also, while gaining insight into their own teaching, the research participants found that they learned more about their students' learning needs. One faculty member explained that teaching in different course delivery formats forced her to question her assumptions of how students learned. This study and the literature affirm that offering a blend of online and face-to-face courses and activities can improve student and faculty satisfaction, offer multiple ways and technologies to learn, and provide opportunities to improve learning outcomes (Picciano, 2009).

Even though the research participants are experienced adult educators who used participatory learning methods previously, they needed to transform their teaching by incorporating online activities that encouraged students to become even more engaged in their own learning. They incorporated constructivist methods, including providing flexibility with assignments, building on student experiences, providing relevant and experiential activities, and offering collaborative and interactive learning opportunities. In addition, the research participants learned to: improve course organization, provide more meaningful assessments, and utilize a variety of online resources and technologies. To reduce student isolation and lack of participation, the participants also found that it was important to build "camaraderie" and "cohesiveness" to create a "community of learners," which is a well-known challenge in online education (Brufee, 1999).

The research participants found that the more they experimented with and taught different course delivery formats, the more they learned new teaching and learning strategies that improved their overall teaching practice. One faculty member summarized, "I believe that blended and online education can be just as rich and powerful and transformative as live education—and sometimes more so. And I believe that we are just beginning to learn how to do this effectively and efficiently." By experimenting with various course delivery formats, faculty members can unleash a "playground of pedagogical possibilities" that can lead to learning new ways to enhance teaching and learning.

Challenges of Multiple Course Delivery Formats

Bonk, Kim, and Zeng (2006) noted, "Blended learning highlights the need for instructional skills in multiple teaching and learning environments" (p. 564). Yet faculty members are being required to offer a variety of course delivery formats in which they may have received no formal training. This is problematic since the instructor's ability to provide positive learning experiences is a major factor in adult retention and degree completion (Flint, 2005).

The research literature has mainly focused on how time consuming it is to design online (Seaman, 2009) or hybrid courses (Kaleta, Skibba, & Joosten, 2007). The participants in this study also observed how challenging and time consuming it was to keep up with the constant redesign and updating of content since they were required to teach the same course in two or three course delivery formats. One research participant observed that course creation continues to be "brutally time consuming." The faculty members explained that online learning "has to be excruciatingly well organized," otherwise, "students get lost."

In addition, a qualitative study by Kaleta, Skibba, and Joosten (2007) found that faculty members teaching hybrid courses succumbed to the "course and a half syndrome" because they "tended to overload both the online and face-to-face activities and needed to rethink the amount of work they assigned students and, consequently, themselves" (p. 127). Because of this, the participants in this study said the course format that caused the most difficulty was hybrid since they had to carefully plan and manage the activities and workload of both the face-to-face and online environments.

While workload and time commitment are common concerns of just teaching one course, especially online and hybrid, the challenges were multiplied when teaching more than one course delivery format at the same time. For example, one research participant described teaching multiple course delivery formats "like running a triathlon" because faculty members have to "shift gears" when teaching three different course delivery formats. "You have to be incredibly organized and careful with scheduling." Another described the scheduling "like being on a rollercoaster" because there are many times you need to go really fast and then slow down.

The research participants said they rely on the course management system to keep track of all of the student activities in various courses; however, there is still a lot to manage and sometimes "balls get dropped." All the faculty members said they were overwhelmed and overworked because teaching in a blended program requires expertise in organizing, designing, and teaching more than one course delivery format.

Most of the research participants liked the variety of teaching in a blended program; however, they expressed concern that it is "unreasonable" to expect faculty members to perform well teaching all three course delivery formats at the same time. "If you're good teaching in one mode, that doesn't necessarily mean you're going to be good in another or even want to be." The research participants were concerned that administrators or faculty members do not have an understanding that it takes special skills, preparation, and time to design and teach courses in different modes. This created concern for their students since faculty members who are not trained well to teach in these formats can "mess up" the learning experience for students. The same concern is supported by the literature, which found that the instructor's ability to provide quality learning experiences and facilitate learning is a critical factor in retention of adult learners and for online courses (Flint, 2005; Hiltz & Shea, 2005).

Conclusion and Research Directions

Despite the fact that adult learners are "voting with their feet" and registering for more online courses, the participants in this study made it clear that offering a choice of course delivery formats benefits both faculty members and adult learners. However, the challenges and benefits of choice of course delivery format may not always be clear to students or other faculty members who have not taught all three course delivery formats. Therefore, it would be helpful to clearly communicate both the opportunities and challenges of the various course formats to both students and faculty. Students should be made aware of the expectations and requirements when taking online and hybrid courses so that they are prepared. And faculty members should be made aware of what it takes to design and teach online and hybrid course formats so that they can create positive learning environments.

To meet market demands and increase revenues, many colleges promote the benefits of online learning; however, it is just as important to share the challenges that students will encounter *before* they register. Each course format has value in helping students learn since some students learn best face-to-face while others learn better online. The research participants felt that a mix of course delivery formats was most effective; therefore, administrators may want to consider the implications of eliminating face-to-face courses and clearly explain the benefits of learning in a blended program.

Since registrations dictate what type of courses are offered, educating students may increase demand for all course delivery formats, thus allowing faculty members to still have a choice of teaching the course delivery formats that they feel best achieve course learning objectives. As more adult learners continue to re-enter education and take more online courses, additional research would help to broaden our understanding of this growing population and how faculty members can meet their needs utilizing multiple course delivery formats.

Also, it would be beneficial for administrators to provide faculty members with the resources, training, and opportunities to teach different course formats so they can experiment with technology and discover for themselves the pedagogical benefits. However, the research participants noted that it is important to not overburden faculty members to teach all three course delivery formats at the same time. Therefore, it is important to evaluate each instructor's ability to teach various course delivery formats instead of just assigning them to teach online or hybrid without training or enough time and resources to develop quality courses. Future studies could research how structures such as appraisal and reward systems, tenure, stipends, time off, and faculty development opportunities can support faculty members to be successful teaching new course delivery formats.

Teaching in a blended program provides a laboratory to experiment with many pedagogical possibilities to teach, design courses and learning activities, and meet the needs of adult learners. While the faculty members in this study were excited about the possibilities of using multiple course formats, they were also concerned as to whether they would have time, would be supported by their institution, and would know how to use technology to enhance learning. Teaching in a blended program multiplied both the challenges and opportunities for education, student learning, and faculty success.

References

Allen, I. E., Seaman, J., & Garrett, R. (2007). *Blending in: The extent of promise of blended education in the United States.* Needham, MA: Sloan Consortium.

Bogle, L., Cook, V., & Day, S., K. (2009). Blended program development: Applying the Quality Matters and Community of Inquiry frameworks to ensure high quality design and implementation. *Journal of the Research Center for Educational Technology, 5*(2), 51–66.

Bonk, C. J., Kim, K. J., & Zeng, T. (2006). Future directions of blended learning in higher education and workplace learning settings. In C. Bonk & C. Graham (Eds.), *The handbook of blended learning: Global perspectives local designs* (pp. 550–567). San Francisco: Pfeiffer.

Brufee, K. A. (1999). *Collaborative learning: Higher education, interdependence, and the authority of knowledge* (2nd ed.). Baltimore: Johns Hopkins University Press.

Cercone, K. (2008). Characteristics of adult learners with implications for online learning design. *AACE Journal, 16*(2), 137–159.

Dziuban, C. D., Hartman, J. L., Cavanagh, T. B., & Moskal, P. D. (2011). Blended courses as drivers of institutional transformation. In A. Kitchenham (Ed.), *Blended learning across disciplines: Models for implementation* (pp. 17–37). Portland, OR: Book News, Inc.

Flint, T. A. (2005). *How well are we serving our adult learners? Investigating the impact of institutions on success and retention.* Chicago, IL: Council for Adult and Experiential Learning (CAEL).

Hiltz, S. R., & Shea, P. (2005). The student in the online classroom. In S. R. Hiltz & R. Goldman (Eds.), *Learning together online* (pp. 145–168). Mahwah, NJ: Erlbaum.

Kaleta, R., & Garnham, C. (2001). *UW System Hybrid Course Project – Overview, faculty development, student resources.* Paper presented at the 17th Annual Conference on Distance Teaching and Learning, University of Wisconsin–Madison.

Kaleta, R., Skibba, K., & Joosten, T. (2007). Discovering, designing and delivering hybrid courses. In A. G. Picciano & C. D. Dziuban (Eds.), *Blended learning: Research perspectives* (pp. 111–143). Needham, MA: The Sloan Consortium.

Kasworm, C. E., Polson, C. J., & Fishback, S. J. (2002). *Responding to adult learners in higher education.* Malabar, FL: Krieger.

King, K. (2002). Technology catalyzing change in how faculty teach and learn. *Journal of Continuing Higher Education, 50*(2), 26–37.

King, K., & Lawler, P. (2003). Trends and issues in the professional development of teachers of adults. In K. King & P. Lawler (Eds.), *New directions for adult and continuing education: New perspectives on designing and implementing professional development of teachers of adults* (Vol. 98, pp. 5–13). San Francisco: Jossey-Bass.

Moloney, J. F., Hickey, C. P., Bergin, A. L., Boccia, J., Polley, K., & Riley, J. E. (2007). Characteristics of successful local blended programs in the context of the Sloan-C Pillars. *Journal of Asynchronous Learning Networks, 11*(1), 29–47.

Patton, M. (2001). *Qualitative research and evaluation methods* (3rd ed.). Thousand Oaks, CA: Sage.

Picciano, A. G. (2007). Introduction. In A. G. Picciano & C. D. Dziuban (Eds.), *Blended learning: Research perspectives.* Needham, MA: The Sloan Consortium.

Picciano, A. G. (2009). Blending with purpose: The multimodal model. *Journal of the Research Center for Educational Technology, 5*(1), 4–14.

Ross, B., & Gage, K. (2006). Global perspectives on blended programs. In C. Bonk & C. Graham (Eds.), *The handbook of blended learning: Global perspectives, local designs* (pp. 155–168). San Francisco: Pfeiffer.

Seaman, J. (2009). *The paradox of faculty voices: Online learning as a strategic asset* (Vol. 2). Washington, DC: Association of Public and Land-Grant Universities.

Skibba, K. (2011). *An investigation of how faculty members learn to teach adult students in blended program* (Doctoral dissertation). Available from ProQuest Dissertations and Theses database (UMI Number: 3492458).

SECTION IV

Studying Non-traditional Learners

15

VARIATION IN ADULT LEARNERS' EXPERIENCES OF BLENDED LEARNING IN HIGHER EDUCATION

Paige L. McDonald

Higher education serves an increasingly complex clientele. In the face of the worst economic downturn since the Great Depression, working Americans are turning to higher education to develop the knowledge and skills required in an increasingly competitive market (Soares, 2009). In 2010, of the undergraduates in the 16 to 24 age range, 40% worked full-time and 73% worked part-time (NCES, 2012b). Moreover, in recent years the percentage of adults over the age of 25 attending college increased at a rate exceeding the increase in enrollment of students under age 25. Between 2000 and 2010, enrollment rates for those 25 and older increased 42%, while enrollments for those under 25 increased only 34% (NCES, 2012a). Yet, the traditional model of higher education is ill-suited to the needs of these non-traditional learners. Barriers such as accessibility, affordability, accountability, program structure and duration, pedagogy and support, and poor alignment of learning institutions and systems pose challenges to the success of non-traditional learners in higher education (ACSFA, 2012). To promote adult learner success in higher education, institutions must adopt flexible delivery models supportive of learners who continually juggle work, learning, and a myriad of other social obligations (Soares, 2009).

Blended learning environments (Bonk & Graham, 2006; Garrison & Vaughan, 2008; Stacey & Gerbic, 2008) comprising a mixture of face-to-face and online learning experiences are gaining rapid popularity in higher education. Recent support for blended learning arises from a need to address learner isolation in online environments, while retaining the flexibility lacking in the traditional model of higher education. Blended environments can combine the best aspects of traditional face-to-face learning and online learning, while saving colleges money and offering learners increased access to higher education. Still, blended environments can pose challenges for learners with regard to time management, technological adaptation, and increased responsibility for their own learning (Garrison & Vaughan, 2008). To create blended environments supportive of adult learner success in postsecondary education we need to understand the various ways adult learners currently experience blended learning in higher education. This study identifies and describes three qualitatively different ways that adult learners experience blended learning in higher education (McDonald, 2012).

Literature Review

The literature indicates a lack of conceptual clarity regarding the term *blended learning*. Picciano's (2007) assertion that "blended learning means different things to different people" (p. 8) remains relevant. Some define blended learning according to *what* is blended: courses in which 30–79% online delivery is blended with face-to-face instruction (Allen, Seaman, & Garrett, 2007) or courses that combine "modern media, communication modes, times and places in a new kind of learning synthesis" (Norberg, Dziuban, & Moskal, 2011, p. 207). Others focus on *how* blending is achieved, defining blended learning as "[t]he thoughtful fusion of face-to-face and online learning experiences" (Garrison & Vaughan, 2008, p. 5). Absent from these conceptualizations is the perspective of the learner in blended courses. Because adult learners are participating in blended learning programs in higher education at an increasing rate, understanding the variation in their experiences may be valuable to adding the learner's perspective to future conceptualizations of blended learning.

A lack of conceptual clarity poses challenges to designing blended environments in higher education. In 2005, the Sloan Consortium adopted the defining characteristics of a blended environment as courses "that integrate online with traditional face-to-face class activities in a *planned*, *pedagogically valuable* manner in which a portion (institutionally defined) of face-to-face time is replaced by online activity" (p. 1). Garrison and Vaughan's (2008) emphasis on the "thoughtful fusion" (p. 5) of online and face-to-face learning echoes the need to carefully consider the design of blended courses. Yet Graham's (2006) discussion of critical differences in online and face-to-face learning environments highlights the difficulty in determining how to combine two seemingly divergent learning contexts. While traditional face-to-face learning occurs in a "teacher-directed environment" (p. 5) supportive of synchronous interaction in a high fidelity environment, distance learning systems have traditionally "emphasized self-paced learning" (p. 5) through asynchronous interaction in a low-fidelity environment. The noted differences raise questions as to how to design blended courses that emphasize the unique benefits of the different environments while integrating learning activities and interactions to maximize learning.

Course design influences both learner satisfaction and level of learning achieved in blended courses. A meta-analysis of 99 studies of online learning found that "blends of online and face-to-face instruction, on average, had stronger learning outcomes than did face-to-face instruction alone" (Means, Toyama, Murphy, Bakia, & Jones, 2009, p. 19). The report also indicated that course designs which promote reflection and self-monitoring support improved learning outcomes (Means et al., 2009). When course components are well organized and structured to support learning, students indicate a high level of satisfaction with blended courses (So & Brush, 2007). Moreover, learners' perceptions of the integration of online and face-to-face interaction lead to higher levels of learning (Bliuc, Goodyear, & Ellis, 2010). But determining how to effectively integrate online and face-to-face components of a blended course requires further understanding of how learners experience the various types of blends available in higher education.

Recent studies promote the benefits of blended learning in higher education: high levels of student and teacher satisfaction (Pearcy, 2009), student perceptions of increased connectedness and sense of community (Carter-Brown, 2009), student perceptions of improved analytical skills (Chen & Jones, 2010), student perceptions of increased ability to apply course concepts in the field (Chen & Jones, 2010), blended environments as supporting participation in course activities (Geçer & Dag, 2012), and higher levels of learning associated with the integration of online and face-to-face interaction (Bliuc et al., 2010). Few studies, however, focus on the unique experiences of adult learners in blended environments. In working toward a model of higher education suited to the needs of an increasingly complex demographic, greater consideration must be given to the experiences of adult learners in blended environments, particularly *Digital Immigrants* (Small, 2008) who must adapt to new technologies while simultaneously learning new concepts or skills.

Existing research also indicates the need to access learner readiness to participate in blended learning (Tabor, 2007), particularly with regard to ensuring learners have the time management skills required of blended environments (Tabor, 2007; Vaughan, 2007). Yet, more research is needed to identify unique challenges that adult learners experience in blended courses. Dziuban, Hartman, and Moskal (2004) argue that participation in blended courses requires learners to "relearn how to learn" (p. 9) because approaches they have used in other learning modalities may not be sufficient to the complexity of a blended environment. Understanding how adult learners currently experience blended learning will provide insight into how to prepare them to meet the specific requirements of learning in blended courses. To gain understanding of how adult leaders experienced blended learning in higher education, this study posed the following research question: *What are the qualitatively different ways adult learners experience blended learning in higher education?*

Research Approach

This study adopted a phenomenographic approach to qualitative research (Marton & Booth, 1997) to identify and describe variation in adult learners' experiences of blended learning in higher education. Phenomenography assumes that there are a limited, finite number of ways a phenomenon can be experienced or understood (Marton & Booth, 1997). Experiencing a phenomenon necessitates distinguishing *aspects* of its structure from the situational context and discerning the relationship among those aspects, which allows an individual to assign *meaning* to the phenomenon. Yet, individual experiences and understandings of a phenomenon present one aspect of a phenomenon at one point in time, rather than the totality of the experience of a phenomenon (Marton, 1981). Describing the totality of a phenomenon requires identification of the "the variation and the architecture of the variation in terms of the different aspects that define the phenomena" (Marton & Booth, 1997, p. 117). Variation in the collective experience of a phenomenon can be represented by patterns of experience, or categories of description, and the relationship among those patterns.

Data Collection

In phenomenography, interview data serve as the primary data source for identifying variation in experiences of a phenomenon (Marton & Booth, 1997). Interview transcripts form a collective pool of data from which patterns of experience can be identified. In this study, two in-depth, 1-hour interviews with each participant during the progression of a blended course served as the primary data source. The first interview used information from the pre-interview questionnaire to further explore participants' reasons for participating in blended courses. Additional questions explored experiences in current blended courses: activities, interactions with peers and faculty, interactions with technology, and the relationship between face-to-face and online sessions. The second interview posed questions about experiences in the course since the first interview, relying on similar questions. It also asked learners to define blended learning and to offer their opinions on participating in blended courses.

In this study a pre-interview questionnaire, document analysis, and observation were also used in data collection. The pre-interview questionnaire facilitated selection of 10 adult participants from four different blended courses of instruction. It queried each participant's age; current enrollment in a blended course; prior experience with face-to-face, online, and blended modes of delivery; preferred mode of delivery; comfort level with using technology in learning; goals within the current course; and relation of current course to personal and professional goals.

Document analysis and observation increased researcher understanding of the contexts in which blended learning was experienced by participants and allowed for verification of identified patterns of experience. The researcher reviewed program guidelines for blended courses, instructors' syllabi, and course materials to gain awareness of the contexts in which study participants experienced blended learning. Observations of synchronous face-to-face class sessions focused on variation in physical contexts, facilitation styles, use of technology in the classrooms, types of interaction present, and types of feedback provided. Online observations considered the degree to which faculty utilized online folders for posting materials, types of interactions present, types of feedback provided, and timing of interactions and responses to discussion questions.

Data Analysis

Phenomenographic analysis begins with an examination of individual descriptions of experiences of a phenomenon to identify structural *aspects* critical to various meanings ascribed to the phenomenon (Marton & Booth, 1997). In this study, analysis began by reviewing interview transcripts to identify various meanings learners ascribed to blended learning. The various meanings were then grouped into patterns based on similarities and differences by identifying *aspects* of the phenomenon signified as critical to each pattern of meaning and identifying a relationship among the aspects representative of the structure of the experience. Aspects contributing to the experience of blended learning were grouped as *components* of context, process, and learner. A pattern of experience comprised the meaning ascribed to blended learning and the corresponding relationship among components of context, process, and learner. The hierarchical relationship between aspects, components, and patterns is represented in Figure 15.1.

Research Site and Study Participants

The study was conducted within an adult degree completion program at a private liberal arts university designed to allow adult students to complete a

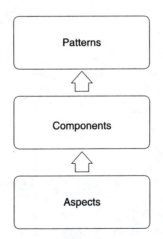

FIGURE 15.1   Relationship among Aspects, Components, and Patterns

Bachelor of Liberal Arts in Interdisciplinary Studies within a 2-year timeframe. All courses in the degree completion program are blended: students attend weekly face-to-face class sessions and also complete online assignments in Blackboard. Students participate in one 7-week course at a time, completing two courses in a semester. The program is also structured as a cohort: the same group of students proceeds through a prescribed course sequence together. In each school year, the university offers two cohorts on the main campus and one cohort at each of two satellite locations.

Course Variation

Courses in which study participants experienced blended learning varied with regard to course topic, course location, face-to-face contexts and frequency of meetings, online context and frequency of assignments, course syllabi, face-to-face facilitation, online facilitation, the relationship between the face-to-face and online components, and instructor feedback. Table 15.1 provides an overview of these context- and process-related differences by course.

Participant Variation

Study participants varied with regard to gender, age, type of prior college experience, preferred course modality, course goals, and level of comfort in using technology. Table 15.2 details the variation in participant characteristics.

Results

Phenomenographic analysis (Figure 15.1) revealed three different patterns representative of the qualitatively different ways that adult learners experience blended learning in higher education: Supplementary Learning, Interdependent Learning, and Adaptable Learning. Table 15.3 presents the critical aspects that combine to form components of context, process, and learner in each pattern. Shading within the table indicates the dominant component within each pattern. Descriptors included in the list of aspects indicate differences in the qualities of aspects across patterns.

Supplementary Learning

In this pattern of experience, learners ascribed meaning to blended learning based on the experience of two separate structural components, a face-to-face and an online component. Context was most emphasized in this pattern. The following discussion presents the aspects critical to components of context, process, and learner in this pattern of experience.

TABLE 15.1 Course Variation

	Course A	Course B	Course C	Course D
Topic	Human experience	Human experience	Global economics	Global economics
Location	Main	Satellite	Main	Satellite
Face-to-face context	U-shaped or two rows facing instructor, consistent room assignment, computer for instructor	Various arrangements, inconsistent room assignment, computers for instructor and students	U-shaped, facing instructor, consistent room assignment, computer for instructor	Rows of desks facing instructor, consistent room assignment, computer for instructor
Face-to-face frequency	Four Friday evenings, six Saturdays	Two Friday evenings, seven Saturdays	Three Friday evenings, six Saturdays	Seven Friday evenings, seven Saturdays
Online context	Materials posted in most folders, discussion questions posted before course start, instructor notes provided, syllabus posted online, announcements throughout course, grades available online	Materials posted in most folders, discussion questions posted progressively, instructor notes provided, syllabus posted online, announcements throughout course, grades available online	Discussion and announcement folders used, syllabus *not* posted online, discussion questions posted progressively, grades *not* available online	Materials post in several folders, discussion questions posted progressively, instructor notes provided, syllabus posted online, announcements *not* posted, grades *not* available online
Online frequency	Six weekly discussion questions, interaction *not* required, two internet assignments	Five weekly discussion questions, interaction required, two internet assignments	Four weekly discussion questions, interaction *not* required, two internet assignments	Two weekly discussion questions, interaction required, four internet assignments
Course syllabus	Standard inclusions, brief description of online component	Standard inclusions, brief description of online component	Standard inclusions, no mention of online component	Standard inclusions, detailed description of online component
Face-to-face facilitation	Lecture, discussion, activities, video	Note review, discussion	Lecture, discussion, video	Lecture, discussion, assignment review

(*Continued*)

TABLE 15.1 Continued

	Course A	Course B	Course C	Course D
Online facilitation	Instructor participation in discussions, announcements, Gradebook	Instructor participation in discussions, announcements, Gradebook	Administrative announcements	No online facilitation
Face-to-face/online relationship	Face-to-face discussion related to online discussion, most online questions completed prior to in class lecture, some after	Face-to-face discussion related to online discussion, online questions completed after in class lecture	Face-to-face discussion related to online discussion, online discussion responses completed before and after in class lecture	Face-to-face discussion related to online discussion, internet assignments discussed in class, online discussion responses completed before and after in class lecture
Instructor feedback	Verbal in face-to-face, written online	Verbal and written in face-to-face, written online	Verbal and written in face-to-face	Verbal and written in face-to-face

TABLE 15.2 Participant Variation

Course	Name	Gender	Age	Program year	Modality experienced	Modality preferred	Course goal	Technical comfort
A	Rebecca	Female	35–44	2	Traditional, online, blended	Blended	Content knowledge	High
	Ricky	Male	45–54	2	Traditional, online, blended	Blended	Applicable knowledge	High
B	Christy	Female	45–54	2	Online, blended	Blended	Become informed	Moderate
	Jean	Male	45–54	2	Traditional, blended	Blended	Become informed	High
	Sean	Male	35–44	2	Traditional, online, blended	Blended	Earn course grade	High
C	Darrin	Male	45–54	1	Traditional, online, blended	Blended	Degree	High
	Joy	Female	45–54	1	Traditional, online, blended	Blended	Knowledge	Moderate
	Patricia	Female	45–54	1	Traditional, online, blended	Traditional	Knowledge	High
D	Stephanie	Female	18–24	1	Traditional, online, blended	Blended	Knowledge	High
	Martin	Male	35–45	1	Traditional, online, blended	Traditional	Degree	High

TABLE 15.3 Aspects, Components, and Patterns of Experience

	Aspects	Supplementary learning pattern	Interdependent learning pattern	Adaptable learning pattern
Context component	Structure	Supplementary	Interdependent	Adaptable
	Instructor	Full control	Shared control	Not emphasized
	Time	Saved in face-to-face context	Saved in face-to-face context; Gained for assignment completion	Continual reflection on content
	Content delivery	Face-to-face emphasized	Not emphasized	Not emphasized
	Use of technology	Allows access to information outside classroom	Allows access to information both in the classroom and outside	Allows portable context, process, and knowledge
	Flexibility	Schedule; Work place/time	Schedule; Work place/time	Schedule; Work place/time
	Structuring	Common theme	Not emphasized	Not emphasized
Process component	Interacting	Face-to-face emphasized	Balance of face-to-face and online required	Face-to-face, online, and outside the learning environment
	Use of technology	Not emphasized	Increases agency in classroom; Augments content delivery	Not emphasized
	Structuring	Not emphasized	Promotes deeper understanding	Promotes layers of learning
	Applying	Personal/Professional	Personal/Professional; Online component as application	Personal/Professional; Multiple applications within course
	Reflecting	Not emphasized	Not emphasized	Continually thinking about content
Learner component	Learning increase	Not emphasized	Not emphasized	Results from layers of learning
	Understanding	Course content	Course content; Peers; Instructor	Course content; Peers; Instructor; Process of learning in blended courses
	Learner Preference	Face-to-face content delivery and interaction	Interaction face-to-face and online; Use of technology	Adaptable form; Learning increase

Learner Need	Schedule flexibility	Schedule flexibility; Use of technology	Not emphasized
Requisite skill	Time management; Use of technology; Self-motivation	Not emphasized	Not emphasized
Agency	Not emphasized	Due to use of technology	Due to use of technology; Adaptability of form
Change	Not emphasized	Not emphasized	Cognitive; Emotional; Behavioral

Context

Descriptions corresponding with this pattern indicated that some learners experienced the blended course structure as consisting of two separate components in which the online component supplemented a traditional face-to-face component: "The Internet and technology supplement the traditional setting in a very effective way" (Martin). Supplementing a face-to-face course with an online component saved learners time in the face-to-face context and allowed greater flexibility with regard to where and when learners completed course-related assignments. The supplementary relationship between components also supported increased content "absorption" (Patricia). Descriptions of experiences emphasized the instructor's control over course structure, content delivery, interacting, learner approach, and learner interest and understanding of course content. In this study, *structuring* refers to the experience of a purposive relationship between the face-to-face and online components of a course. Learners in this pattern experienced the least degree of structuring, noting merely a common "theme" (Ricky) across course components.

Process

Process aspects were emphasized least in this pattern of experience. Yet, interacting was experienced as critical to the learning process, specifically interacting face-to-face with the instructor: "I get more from communicating with somebody who is knowledgeable about the topic than I do from trying to pick the information out of other resources" (Martin). Immediacy of feedback influenced learners' preferences for face-to-face interaction. Interaction also increased learner interest in the course content and course context and proved critical to understanding course content. Experiences in this pattern indicated the application of learning content in personal and professional situations as an important result of participation in the blended learning process.

Learner

With regard to self-as learner, descriptions of experiences in this pattern indicated a tolerance for blended learning because of its ability to meet learner needs regarding time and flexibility, which permitted participation in higher education. Two of ten study participants indicated a preference for traditional courses, and the majority of their descriptions aligned with this pattern. While preferring traditional courses, they participated in blended courses because of the reduction in seat time and the retention of face-to-face interaction with the instructor and peers. Self-motivation, organization, discipline, time management, and experience with technology emerged as skills required of adult learners for participation in blended courses.

Interdependent Learning

In this pattern of experience, learners ascribed meaning to blended learning based on the experience of a complementary and interdependent relationship between the online and face-to-face components of blended courses. Process was most emphasized in this pattern. The following discussion considers the aspects critical to components of context, process, and learner in this pattern of experience.

Context

In this pattern, learners perceived the course structure as comprising two inter-dependent components, a face-to-face component and an online component, emphasizing the need for "balance" (Darrin) among them. The face-to-face class sessions imposed accountability, which complemented the flexibility of the online component. While experiences indicated instructors' influence over the learning context, they also stressed the influence of technology on the learning context. Technology allowed easy access to materials stored online and to online information in the face-to-face context. It also permitted supplementation of content delivery, allowing greater understanding of content. Learners noted time saved in the face-to-face context, yet they also stressed the additional time gained for assignment completion and reflecting on course content due to the online component.

Process

Descriptions of process in this pattern stressed the interdependence of activities and interactions in two different learning environments. Learners indicated the need for balance between interaction in the face-to-face context and the online context, as well as the need to interact with both peers and the instructor. Face-to-face interaction enabled content delivery, generated diverse view-points on course topics, and supported a level of familiarity necessary to promote understanding of online postings: "After meeting them, and spending time with them, their online interaction is just as effective as their face-to-face interaction" (Darrin). It also enabled clarification of misunderstandings resulting from the limitations of the online medium. Online discussion generated diverse viewpoints, allowed application of reviewed concepts, and empowered those not comfortable speaking in class to contribute: "I think the online portion allows the introverts to actually get to clarify their point without having to compete for time or resources" (Stephanie). Learners experienced a purposive relationship between online and classroom discussions, which fostered reflection and interaction and influenced their approaches to reviewing course content. They also noted applying course content from one course component to another. Use of technology, both in the classroom and outside of the classroom, enabled instant access to information critical to engaging in the process of learning: "If he's talking about something . . . I can look that up . . . so I use my iPad during class" (Darrin). Descriptions also indicated how learners used technology to augment course content delivery.

Learner

Experiences related to self-as learner in this pattern emphasized how blended courses met learners' needs for flexibility and the use of technology in order to participate in higher education. Learners indicated a preference for blended courses because they promoted increased familiarity with peers and the instructor, permitted interaction in two different environments, and allowed increased personal agency in the process of learning. Moreover, participation in two different learning environments yielded increased understanding of content as compared with other modes of learning delivery: "Searching for information gives me, I think, a *scope* that I wouldn't have otherwise, and the interaction with people online and in person gives me different perspectives and gives a *depth* to the material" (Rebecca).

Adaptable Learning

In this pattern of experience, learners assigned meaning to blended learning based on their perception of its adaptable form. Conceptualizations of structure were most complex in this pattern. The self-as learner was most heavily emphasized in descriptions related to this pattern; context and process were described in relation to their ability to meet the learner's needs and to support higher levels of learning.

Context

Context takes on a different meaning in Adaptable Learning as compared with the other two patterns of experience. Learners perceived the course structure as adaptable to both the needs of the learner and the needs of the learning situation: "To me it means changes, able to go from one form of learning to another form of learning at the will of the student or the will of the instructor" (Jean). The structuring of learning layers resulted in a form of learning "superior" (Martin) to either online learning or face-to-face learning in isolation. Use of technology enabled this adaptability and provided an extension of the course context beyond the boundaries of the online or face-to-face context. Learners experienced increased learning resulting from the integration of multiple forms of learning.

Process

In this pattern of experience, learners also perceived the blended learning process as adaptable to their needs and the needs of the learning situation. Integrated "layers" (Darrin) of various forms of learning ensured multiple types of interaction in which learners challenged diverse viewpoints, received feedback from peers and the instructor, reflected upon that feedback, and regulated their behavior according to that reflection. Learners noted continually thinking about course content as a result of the structuring of a relationship between online and face-to-face components and the increased opportunity for reflection upon peer responses to online discussion postings. Interaction regarding course content extended beyond exchanges with peers and the instructor to include family members and coworkers. Learners not only noted applying course content but also indicated how applying content facilitated learning. Descriptions focused less on how a blended course progressed and more on how the process of learning occurs in a blended course.

Learner

In Adaptable Learning, descriptions of experiences of blended learning indicated how blended courses aligned with the needs of learners. Participation in blended courses resulted in a "superior" (Martin) form of learning as compared with face-to-face or online modes of delivery in isolation by allowing continual engagement with course content, application of course content in multiple situations, and integration of information from a variety of sources: "It all intertwines, and I think you learn more, with each aspect of the blended" (Sean). Blended courses sustained learner interest: "Its various forms keep that student interested" (Jean). Blended courses also enabled increased control over the context and process of learning: "You're able to do whatever you want, whenever you want it" (Sean). Learners also experienced control over the level of learning they achieved: "It gives you an opportunity to soar . . . it's what you put in" (Christy). Understanding extended beyond understanding course content, peers, and the course instructor to an awareness of how interaction, reflection, and application facilitated learning. Use of technology dissolved context boundaries allowing for "portable knowledge" (Rebecca), enabling continual interaction with course content. As a result, learners felt empowered to adapt both the context and process of learning to their needs and indicated exceptional awareness of how to learn in blended courses.

Implications for Improved Practice and Future Research

Findings indicated that adult learners assigned different meanings to blended learning based on different experiences of context, different experiences of process, and different experiences of self-as learner in blended courses. In other words, because adult learners differ, because blended contexts differ, and because learners experience processes differently, experiences of blended learning in higher education will vary, eventuating variation in the meaning of the phenomenon. However, identification of variation in collective experiences of the phenomenon in higher education provides insight into improving the design of blended courses and into adopting practices supportive of learner success in blended courses in higher education. It also offers implications for future research on blended learning.

Course Design

Study findings revealed that structure matters to learners; more specifically, the degree of integration learners experience between online and face-to-face activities and discussion influences their perception of the level of learning they achieve. Moreover, learners who experienced the relationship between online and face-to-face components as a layering of learning opportunities noted not only an increased understanding of course content, their peers, and the instructor but also an acute awareness of the process of learning in blended courses. So, the online course components and face-to-face components should be balanced and integrated in an organic fashion, which promotes learner awareness of the relationship between components, activities, and interactions. Yet, further research is required to determine the appropriate sequencing of online and face-to-face activities and interactions to promote higher levels of learning and awareness of the process of learning in blended courses. Future research is also required to understand how many face-to-face sessions are required to promote the familiarity learners note as critical to understanding online communications and to ensuring accountability in the learning environment.

Findings indicated that learners in all patterns value interaction. In fact, in two patterns learners' descriptions emphasized that interaction must be required in both the online and face-to-face components of blended courses. In the face-to-face component, interaction generates immediate feedback critical to learners in discerning their own understanding of content and in gaining familiarity with the instructor and other learners. In the online component, it generates diverse viewpoints critical to reflection and self-regulation; the asynchronous, text-based environments allow learners increased time to reflect upon the responses of peers and the instructor and to, perhaps, modify their responses as their thought processes change. The relationship between online and face-to-face activities and discussions should be purposefully structured to allow for this type of reflection and self-regulation.

Study findings also conveyed that adult learners value the use of technology both in the classroom and outside the classroom, so it should be used in the face-to-face course sessions as well as online sessions. In blended courses, use of technology should be optimized by both the instructor and the learners in order to allow the full benefit of portable knowledge, including allowing learners access to the Internet during face-to-face class sessions.

Learner Success

In this study, adult learners differed with regard to their needs and preferences in a learning environment. In Supplementary Learning, adult learners valued blended learning for allowing participation in higher education, but they also emphasized the need for face-to-face interaction with the instructor and for sufficient face-to-face class sessions to impose accountability. In Interdependent Learning, learners emphasized the need to use technology in support of learning and the need to interact with peers and the instructor in both learning contexts to gain a broader and deeper understanding of course content. In Adaptable Learning, learners appreciated the increased control they gained over the context and process of learning and their ability to determine the level of learning they achieved. The variation in learner orientations toward participation in blended courses indicates the need to adopt a learner-centered approach to course design and delivery, which addresses the variety of adult learner needs and preferences and assists learners in becoming more engaged in the process of learning. Still, additional research is needed to understand how to design blended courses to meet a broad range of learning preferences and needs.

Findings also indicated that learners require a certain skill set in order to succeed in blended courses, notably skill in time management, the ability to self-motivate, and skill in using technology to support learning. Institutions of higher education should access learner competencies in these areas prior to enrolling learners in blended courses. They should also provide training in these skills prior to learner participation in blended courses to ensure that learners have the self-efficacy required to exercise control over their own learning processes. Initial courses should be designed to encourage development in time management skills and in the use of technology critical to learner success in blended courses. As participants noted, skill levels in these areas may vary, and faculty should not assume that all learners are competent in managing their own time and in managing technology to maximize their learning experiences.

Learners must also be made aware that the process of learning in blended courses is different from what they may have experienced in other modes of delivery. Faculty should endeavor to help learners recognize the relationship between online and face-to-face components, because findings suggested that this awareness promotes understanding of the process of learning in blended courses. However, further research is required to determine how to promote this awareness within blended curricula. Questions remain as to whether this type of awareness is most influenced by course design or by repeated experiences in blended environments. Moreover, findings also suggested that the degree of "blending" from course to course may influence the specific learning process required in each course. So, learners must recognize that they may be required to adapt their learning processes according to the demands of different types of "blends." A review of strategies for success in both face-to-face contexts and online contexts prior to and during learner participation in blended courses may help learners navigate the complexity of learning in a blended course. Yet, further research is needed to understand how to best prepare learners for the variation in blends they may experience in higher education.

Faculty Presence

In two of the three patterns of experience, descriptions stressed the critical influence of faculty in experiences of blended learning. Faculty presence in both the online and face-to-face components of blended courses proved critical to learners' understanding of course content, to their interest in course content, and to their awareness and comprehension of course concepts. Learners appreciated faculty lectures in the face-to-face context that related abstract constructs to real-world situations. This type of lecture/explication could also be provided in the online component of a course in the form of lecture notes or an introductory video. Faculty presence in the online discussion boards was experienced as critical for modeling the way in which learners could disagree with the contributions of peers without offending them. Feedback from faculty on online discussion responses proved critical in determining if learners' responses aligned with faculty expectations. This type of feedback can be crucial in the initial weeks of a blended course in which learners are trying to orient themselves to the expectations of a new teacher and the requirements of a new course. Faculty feedback in the face-to-face class sessions, particularly on the discussion questions posted online, demonstrates awareness of learner activity in the online component of the course and helps to integrate the face-to-face and online sessions of a course, so learners become more aware of the relationship between the two. In short, faculty presence and feedback in both the online and face-to-face sessions of a blended course are critical to the adult learner's experience of blended learning in higher education.

This study did not assess instructor development; however, descriptions in two patterns emphasized the importance of the instructor to experiences of blended learning. Given this emphasis, consideration must be given as to how to prepare instructors to facilitate blended courses, which differs from facilitation in other modes of delivery. For example, learners in this study described the importance of meeting with the instructor face-to-face to hear his or her experiences in relation to course content. They relied upon instructors to connect content from course readings to relevant, real-world situations and applications. However, in a blended course the online course components could also facilitate this type of interaction if instructors become engaged in the discussions and prepare lecture notes, presentations, or videos providing this type of information to learners. Institutions of higher education should provide training to instructors who have never participated in blended learning prior to their facilitation of a course, ensuring that they understand the importance of instructor presence in both the online and face-to-face class sessions. Also, the prospect of facilitating a more complicated learning environment requiring teaching responsibilities in multiple contexts may dissuade faculty from engaging in blended learning. So, further research is required to determine how to promote faculty participation in blended learning and how to prepare faculty to successfully facilitate blended courses.

References

Advisory Committee on Student Financial Assistance (ACSFA) (2012). Pathways to success: Integrating learning with life and work to increase national college completion. *Report to the U.S. Congress and Secretary of Education.* Retrieved from www.ed.gov

Allen, E., Seaman, J., & Garrett, R. (2007). Blending in: The extent and promise of blended education in the United States. *Proceedings of The Sloan Consortium.* Retrieved from www.sloanconsortium.org/publications/survey/pdf/Blending

Bliuc, A. M., Goodyear, P., & Ellis, R. (2010). Blended learning in higher education: How students perceive integration of face-to-face and online learning experiences in a foreign policy course. In *Higher Education Research and Development Society of Australasia (HERDSA) Conference, 2010.* Melbourne, 6–9 July 2010.

Bonk, C., & Graham, C. (2006). *Handbook of blended learning: Global perspectives and local designs.* San Francisco, CA: Pfeiffer Publishing.

Carter-Brown, C. B. (2009). *Building communities: The effects of offering face-to-face meetings to students studying at a distance.* (Doctoral Dissertation). Retrieved from Proquest.

Chen, C., & Jones, T. (2010). Blended learning vs. traditional classroom settings: Assessing effectiveness and student perceptions in an MBA accounting course. *The Scholarship of Teaching, 3*(1), pp. 16–21. Retrieved from www.umflint.edu/tclt/Scholarship_FA10_rev12_10.pdf ge=18

Dziuban, C. D., Hartman, J. L., & Moskal, P. D. (2004). Blended learning. *EDUCAUSE Center for Applied Research Bulletin, 7*, 2–12.

Garrison, D., & Vaughan, N. (2008). *Blended learning in higher education.* San Francisco: John Wiley & Sons.

Geçer, A., & Dag, F. (2012). A blended learning experience. *Educational Sciences: Theory and Practice, 12*(1), 438–442. Retrieved from http://akademikpersonel.kocaeli.edu.tr/akolburan/sci/akolburan18.10.2012_01.58.04sci.pdf

Graham, C. R. (2006). Blended learning systems: Definition, current trends, and future directions. In C. Bonk & C. Graham (Eds.), *The handbook of blended learning: Global perspective, local designs.* San Francisco: Pfeiffer Publishing.

Marton, F. (1981). Phenomenography – describing conceptions of the world around us. *Instructional Science, 10*, 177–200.

Marton, F., & Booth, S. (1997). *Learning and awareness*. Mahwah, NJ: Lawrence Erlbaum Associates.

McDonald, P. L. (2012). Adult learners and blended learning: A phenomenographic study of variation in adult learners' experiences of blended learning in higher education. (Doctoral Dissertation). Proquest.

Means, B., Toyama, Y., Murphy, R., Bakia, M., & Jones, K. (2009). Evaluation of evidence based practices in online learning: A meta-analysis and review of online learning studies. Washington, DC: U.S. Department of Education. Retrieved December 2, 2012 from www2.ed.gov/rschstat/eval/tech/evidence-based-practices/finalreport.pdf

National Center for Education Statistics (NCES) (2012a). *Fastfacts*. Retrieved from http://nces.ed.gov/fastfacts/display.asp?id=98

National Center for Education Statistics (NCESb) (2012). *The condition of education*. Retrieved from http://nces.ed.gov/programs/coe/indicator_cws.asp

Norberg, A., Dziuban, C. D., & Moskal, P. D. (2011). A time-based blended learning model. *On the Horizon, 19*(3), 207–216. Retrieved from http://search.proquest.com/docview/888254241

Pearcy, A. G. (2009). *Finding the perfect blend: A comparative study of online, face-to-face, and blended instruction*. (Doctoral Dissertation). Retrieved from Proquest.

Picciano, A. G. (2007). Introduction. In A. G. Picciano & C. D. Dziuban (Eds.), *Blended learning research perspectives* (pp. 5–17). Needham, MA: The Sloan Consortium.

The Sloan Consortium (2005). Blended learning: Sleeping giant. In *Sloan-C View: Perspectives on Quality Online Education, 4*(5), http://sloanconsortium.org/publications/views

Small, G. (2008). *iBrain: Surviving the technological alteration of the modern mind*. New York, NY: HarperCollins.

So, H. J., & Brush, T. A. (2007). Student perceptions of collaborative learning, social presence and satisfaction in a blended learning environment: Relationships and critical factors. *Computers and Education, 51*(1), 318–336. doi: 10.1016/j.compedu.2007.05.009

Soares, L. (2009). *Working learners: Educating our entire workforce for success in the 21st century*. Washington, DC: Center for American Progress.

Stacey, E., & Gerbic, P. (2008). Success factors for blended learning. In *Hello! Where are you in the landscape of educational technology? Proceedings ascilite Melbourne 2008*. Retrieved from http://www.ascilite.org.au/conferences/melbourne08/procs/stacey.pdf

Tabor, S. (2007). Narrowing the distance: Implementing a hybrid learning model for information security education. *The Quarterly Review of Distance Education, 8*(1), 47–57.

Vaughan, N. (2007). Perspectives on blended learning in higher education. *International Journal of ELearning, 6*(1), 81–94.

16

EDUCATING WARRIOR DIPLOMATS

Blended and Unconventional Learning for Special Operations Forces

Katherine M. Tyler and Kent C. Dolasky

Special operations forces, commonly referred to as SOF, are military service members who volunteer to become Navy SEALs, Army Special Forces and Rangers, Air Force Special Operations Aircrews and Special Tactics Personnel, and Marine Critical Skills Operators. To earn these elite designations, they acquire skills through a variety of service-specific training and education institutions.

The nature of special operations requires SOF to train and fight together as joint forces. The U.S. Special Operations Command created the Joint Special Operations Senior Enlisted Academy when the requirement for senior enlisted leaders of the special operations forces to learn together became necessary.

Traditional, professional military education for special operations and conventional forces generally follows a teaching format of lecture style face-to-face classroom sessions during a compressed schedule as a concentrated effort to prepare individuals for their next assignment. Military and civilian instructors teach classes as part of the scheduled workday, with students attending "in residence" for a prescribed duration from one week to one year. In many institutions a preponderant use of PowerPoint presentations illustrates lectures—likely stemming from their reliance during routine military information sessions and meetings referred to as "briefings."

When planning began for the first Academy course, therefore, designers, administrators, and instructors sought to move beyond the prosaic military education model and create a collaborative learning environment conducive to higher levels of critical thinking. Some argue that there is little rigor in professional military education (Barno, 2009; Johnson-Freese, 2012) and that assessments leave little room for failure—a type of grade inflation scenario without the grading—however, the mission of the Academy includes "the knowledge to think critically and lead successfully in the future operating environment" ("USSOCOM hosts first Joint Special Operations," 2010, p. 35). Designing for critical thinking within a collaborative learning community enables leaders to value the warrior diplomacy concept (Olson, 2008), which fosters cultural engagement within a holistic governmental approach as determined by the adversary. Olson (2008) [former commander of United States Special Operations Command] describes it as "agreeing to certain behaviors which will be of mutual benefit" (p. 26) within the U.S. War on Terrorism.

Pilot Class

A core group of subject matter experts, along with instructional designers, curriculum developers, and technical experts fashioned a blended learning curriculum with delivery over two phases—6 months of online learning followed by 2 months of face-to-face "resident" time culminating in a week-long capstone learning activity. To deliver the online content, the Academy purchased a learning management system and hired an administrator to manage the content collection, create passwords and permissions, and design navigational instructions.

While the online phase offered students the flexibility of anywhere, anytime learning—even for those deployed to remote areas—there were limitations in the level of interactive knowledge construction.

The pilot course instructors taught a nine-module sequential curriculum enabling students to learn at their own pace and participate as needed in discussion forums. Checks on learning were designed into the curriculum requiring students to submit assignments by posted deadlines. The course calendar gave students space for their continued daily work duties, as only the "resident seat time" can physically and mentally provide the benefit of full-time military student status. Students took a series of online end-of-module exams and prepared for the resident term by researching an assigned country of interest. They used discussion forums within each module throughout the 6 months of online learning and interacted with each other on introductory forums and in topic-related threads. Most discussion threads resulted in the required number of postings, giving students a surface level depth of familiarity and community.

Implementing a Better Blend

A robust evaluation program is the hallmark of rigorous curricula. After examining narrative feedback from the pilot class, the development team and staff implemented a program of continuous curriculum improvement to re-evaluate and determine if students are meeting the intended course objectives at every level. Subsequently, designers determine if the assessments remain in alignment with the content; and the course and module level instructional objectives (Quality Matters, 2012).

There were two goals in redesigning the curriculum: to allow students to achieve higher levels of critical thinking and to instill the concept of warrior diplomacy. Eschewing the traditional linear model, the designers redesigned the curriculum into four major integrated modules incorporating more active teaching and learning methods. Instead of introducing topics in a lock-step fashion, the designers used a more constructivist approach in assignments and learning activities requiring students to integrate prior knowledge, beliefs, and experiences to create new meaning.

Following the initial evaluation, the instructional team instituted several curricula modifications that frame the basis of this discussion and presented recommendations for similar evaluative inquiries. The authors propose two research questions:

1. Can senior enlisted leaders achieve a higher level of critical thinking with a learner-centered collaborative approach to teaching.
2. Is there a difference in students' affective level following a non-traditional (military) instructional style.

Community of Inquiry

The community of inquiry (Garrison, Anderson, & Archer, 2000) provides a model for interpretation and recognition of the evaluative improvements presented. Within the conceptual framework of a community of inquiry, Garrison et al. (2000) posit that learning occurs through the purposeful integrative design of cognitive, social, and teaching presence.

Cognitive Presence

Cognitive presence refers to "the extent to which the participants in any particular configuration of a community of inquiry are able to construct meaning through sustained communication" (Garrison et al., 2000, p. 89). According to cognitive and learning theories, students learn best when they are actively engaged in the course content (Schunk, Pintrich, & Meece, 2008). Similarly, a constructivist approach also supports critical thinking and a higher level of learning (Bloom, Engelhart, Furst, Hill, & Krathwohl, 1956; Garrison et al., 2000). Designing learning for cognitive presence, therefore, requires active learning strategies that are reflective and collaborative. Learning events that develop cognitive presence include case studies, debate, and problem-based learning activities requiring critical thinking and discourse (Stavredes, 2011).

Social Presence

Garrison et al. (2000) define social presence as "the ability of participants in a community of inquiry to project themselves socially and emotionally, as 'real people' (in essence their full personality), through the medium of communication being used" (p. 94). Emotional connectedness helps to build trust among learners. Stavredes (2011) develops the definition in the context of online facilitation, further adding that the process of building relationships promotes trust, and that trust allows students to feel more comfortable in sharing their thoughts and ideas. Students will be less inclined to share if they are concerned that their thoughts may be criticized; the process of emotional freedom of expression, therefore, establishes the necessary foundation for new construction of knowledge. Discourse is also essential if students are to understand the content and information presented.

Garrison et al. (2000) also argue that a cognitive presence in the learning community is dependent upon a successful social presence. Since learning does not occur in isolation (Vygotsky, 1978), creating opportunities for social interaction enables learner engagement. Successful intellectual exchanges support group cohesion in the creation of social presence. Stavredes (2011) suggests several ways to establish social presence by increasing learner-to-learner interaction in the online learning environment: discussion forums, team projects, and peer reviews.

Discussion in the online learning environment promotes collaboration, reduces learner isolation, promotes knowledge construction, and allows differing perspectives, shared discovery, and the development of critical thinking skills (Davidson-Shivers & Rasmussen, 2006; Stavredes, 2011). Facilitators, who proactively guide students toward desired learning outcomes, use active learning strategies; moderating online discussions, preparing concept summaries, and sharing new information with other students (Smith, 2008).

Teaching Presence

Successful forum management leads to open communication and group cohesion, both predicated on successful social presence (Garrison et al., 2000; Xin, 2012). Garrison et al. (2000) describe teaching presence as "the design of the educational experience" (p. 90). Teaching presence includes designing and developing learning activities and assessments and course facilitation, which is the responsibility of both the instructor and the students. Facilitation also includes modeling critical discourse and constructively critiquing students' contributions to discussion forums. A facilitator is "one who helps to bring about an outcome (as learning, productivity or communication) by providing indirect or unobtrusive assistance, guidance, or supervision" (Merriam-Webster, 2012, para. 1).

Stavredes (2011) suggests a communication checklist to ensure teaching presence online and to help learners develop critical thinking skills and construct knowledge. Her checklist includes:

- encourage participation
- encourage knowledge construction and critical thinking
- monitor progress
- communicate feedback on performance
- encourage self-directedness.

Strategies for these communication items include posting prompts to stimulate discussion, actively monitoring progress with checklists and rubrics, self-evaluation of performance, and asking learners to approach topics with alternative perspectives.

Learning Communities

Applying Vygotsky's (1978) theory of social constructivism, it is essential for students to gain knowledge through a community of practice or learning community. Bonk, Wisher, and Nigrelli (2004) find that online communities allow the distribution of expertise by fostering innovation and creativity amongst learners. Designing for instruction includes accommodation for students who have various levels of prior knowledge, and affording scaffolding for those with experience that is more limited; pre-assessment or planned communication strategies provide insightful recognition of such variables. Adapting the learning environment with advance organizers helps to lessen cognitive dissonance (Tileston, 2004) and provides knowledge sharing for those who are new to the subject.

In a learner-centered course, lecturers take on the role of facilitator or "guide on the side" and create active rather than passive learning activities. Inclusiveness in a learning community requires students to take active responsibility for their learning outcomes. Xin (2012) posits that learning communities in online classes are similar to a work group or team where interpersonal relationships form based on the task focus. Collaborative technologies and supporting activities play an important role in developing and maintaining a learning community. Bonk et al. (2004) suggest the use of chat rooms, bulletin boards, knowledge management portals, shared web links, online surveys of members, application sharing, site announcements, and annotation tools to support learners' community. Activities such as posting learner goal statements, social icebreakers, changes to the website based on member input, and reflections on job experiences assist in developing the learning community.

Critical Thinking

Paul and Elder (2006) define critical thinking as "the art of analyzing and evaluating thinking with a view to improving it" (p. 4). Critical thinking skills include the application of intellectual standards, which include clarity, accuracy, precision, relevance, depth, breadth, and logic (Paul & Elder, 2006). Applying the standards involves questioning in a consistent and innate manner and eventually "owning" the process so that it becomes routine—the student's intellectual standard. In designing instruction for critical thinking, Anderson et al. (2001) argue that learning objectives involve conceptual knowledge to analyze an issue followed by an evaluation of perspectives and the creation of a new defensible stance.

Instructor Improvements

Good teaching skills translate readily whether in the face-to-face classroom or online. Skills such as preparedness, dependability, subject matter expertise, concern for students' progress, and a positive attitude toward teaching and learning (Davidson-Shiver & Rasmussen, 2006) can make the difference in whether students attain desired learning outcomes. At the Academy, the instructor staff consists of civilian and active duty service members. In the normal rotation of active duty assignments, instructors are assigned to the Academy from 18 months to 3 years. Since most of the military instructors are also members of the special operations forces community, the instructor staff engages in a continuous program of cross-training to ensure that in the event of active duty instructor re-assignment there is an alternate knowledgeable instructor available.

A team of distance learning instructors coalesced to provide consistency for learners during the online phase. The team includes civilian and military instructors, and all are required to complete a faculty development Methods of Instruction Course taught through the Joint Special Operations University. The University offers ongoing faculty development opportunities throughout the year to improve online communication skills, integrate new technology, and maintain relevant knowledge of course content.

Curricular Improvements

Results shown are based on the instructor experiences delivering a curriculum to cohort classes in a professional military institution over 18 months. A range of post-module evaluation tools enabled the collection of qualitative and quantitative data. The community of inquiry model frames the practices instituted after the second cohort and through the present iteration of the Academy.

Cognitive Presence Improvements

Encouragement and ease of communication determine the extent of sustained cognitive presence in the mediated forum (Garrison et al., 2000)—and also within the traditional forum. Changes made to the instructional design of the online learning management system pages resulted in better navigation and fewer questions to the instructors about what to do next and where to find specific content. Instructors also began asking students more probing questions for each topic, requiring critical commentary based on a rubric; the rubric provides students with clear guidelines and expectations.

Students attending the Academy range from high-school graduates to those with graduate degrees, therefore the levels of writing skills vary tremendously. In the online phase of the Academy, an early writing assignment on miscommunication using the American Psychological Association (APA) format develops student awareness for clear communication and writing skills. Instructors also require students to post the body of their miscommunication paper to a discussion forum for peer-review critiques, resulting in peer feedback and improvement in both format and writing style.

During the resident phase, a refinement of the capstone exercise requires students to analyze real-world counter-terrorism campaign plans. Students form small groups and are assigned a geographic region. Each region has an existing counter-terrorism campaign plan, which the group reviews in detail, compares with doctrinal planning principles, and discusses in consideration of contemporary events. At the end of the project, the groups formally present their analyses, and are graded on individual and group rubrics.

Social Presence Improvements

Initially, several instructors led the online phase of instruction without a clearly defined work plan to respond to postings, grading, or providing feedback. An established distance learning instructor team now provides overall guidance for online student interactions, which has resulted in a greater social presence. All students' initial postings introduce themselves and the instructors contact those who fail to acknowledge these posts via email or a phone call. With the team approach came more individualized instructor-to-learner interactions, which include feedback, answers to content-related questions, and emails that support flexible due dates for deployed students.

Students are also required to post two additional papers: one on a historical SOF event and one on leadership (a major content module). The leadership paper generates discussion on the military promotion system, in which attaining the highest enlisted rank is difficult. Also, the posting of the miscommunication paper has generated comments about experiences as a community of practice, a possibility that might continue in their own units.

The instructors also implemented a generic Q&A forum, giving students the opportunity to have questions answered by their peers that subsequently reduce the need for redundant individual replies. Topics observed in the Q&A forum generally lead to changes to the online learning environment that include improvements in inadequate navigation or non-operational links, etc.

Teaching Presence Improvements

Garrison et al. (2000) note that the facilitator or instructor presence provides the bonding element of the critical community of inquiry. Stavredes (2011) expands on the importance of teaching presence, noting that learner satisfaction and student persistence are factors of the interaction strategies between learners and instructors. She writes, "the different ways you interact with learners can have a great impact on developing social presence, which affects cognitive presence" (p. 151).

Because of the development of a distance learning team, additional training, and a continuous program of evaluation, an improved blended learning experience exists at the JSOFSEA. Discussion forums' quantity and quality, resource awareness, and learning management system use have improved significantly.

Figure 16.1 shows the average number of discussion posts by individual students from Class 2 through to Class 8. The climb in the trend indicates the additional engagement provided by the formation of the distance learning team. The spike in Class 5 illustrates additional instructor staffing during that time period.

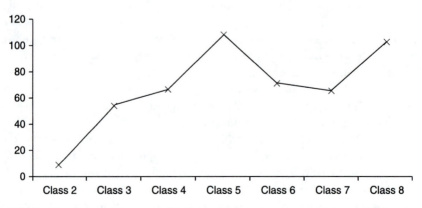

FIGURE 16.1   Average Number of Individual Discussion Forum Posts per Student by Class Number

Online learners find it helpful to have online library resources linked within the learning management system; however, students also need instructions for their access and successful use (Tyler, 2010). Information literacy cannot be assumed because students are digital natives or because they have enrolled in an online course of study. Designers added two resource links to the online course; one is a content collection providing students access to military publications pertinent to the joint operating environment and another access to ProQuest and EBSCOhost online research databases. During the resident phase, the university librarian teaches a session on database use, researching relevant topics, and determining appropriate materials.

Learning management system use continues throughout the resident phase of the Academy. Students submit papers and presentations within the appropriate modules, access resources, and review content as needed. Students also bring their laptops to class to enable just-in-time fact-finding on relevant discussion topics.

Maintaining a Community of Practice

Bonk et al. (2004) distinguish a learning community from a community of practice based on the objectives of the community while also acknowledging an overlap between the two. The essential difference is that of a dedicated learning environment versus the social networking importance in a community of practice where members share best practices or distribute information. Acknowledging the relationships formed at the Academy, technologists developed a reach-back component resulting in a community of practice through two venues to date: a Facebook page and an alumni site accessed via the learning management system. Through these two websites, staff and graduates foster continued learning through online interactions, and service members can find information and resources needed at the point of application (new assignments, missions, etc.). The Facebook page is quickly becoming a forum where graduates and current students share knowledge, network, and collaborate at times when their destinations or assignments converge. Efforts for maintaining the community (while building the community with each graduating class) are an important component to learner knowledge retention. Students share resources, stories, and experiences while they continue to build the relationships begun during their 8 months as a learning cohort. The communities of practice are also serving the Academy as an invaluable marketing tool among special operations forces.

Critical Thought in Action

Leaders at the highest levels of the United States Special Operations Command continue to set above average expectations for students selected for the Academy.

Poole (2011) describes special operators as "more mildly innovative in their problem solving style" (p. 87) than the general population, based on a case study of past and present special operators. Leaders expect graduates to move into advanced leadership positions requiring skills in strategic thinking, leadership, organizational management, and effective communication while maintaining proficiency in tactical and operational skills.

Faculty have developed authentic assessments, writing and public speaking assignments, and other collaborative performance-based or constructed response techniques for the advancement of each student. A research paper assignment requiring students to critically examine a country in terms of the United States' national security enables students to provide a comprehensive overview based on research data, in APA format, and to conclude with strategic recommendations for a course of action in conjunction with U.S. interests for national security. Dempsey (2012) describes strategy as an iterative process, one in which each choice provides context for the next. Specifically, he writes, "strategy is as much emergent as it is deliberate" (p. 2). This process, reflected in students' recommendations, determines learning modules' convergence and synthesis. A continuum of improvements in these research papers reflects the quality (subjectively determined by the instructors) and quantity (based on written word count) of papers submitted from Class 2 to the present. Based on the changes made to the Academy's cognitive, social, and teaching presence, instructors have found a marked improvement in the quality of strategic thought to the recommendations' sections. A quantitative analysis shown in Figure 16.2 indicates a 51% increase in the median word count of the recommendations sections in students' papers regarding strategic action for a given country. The recommendations are based on critical

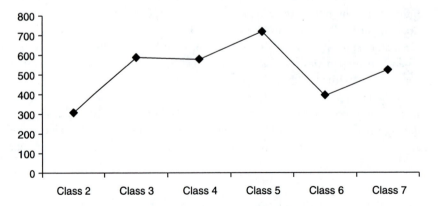

FIGURE 16.2   Median Word Count of Recommendation Section from Students' National Security Study and Assessment Papers Analyzing a Strategic Course of Action for a Given Country of Interest

analyses. The marked increase for Class 5 again reflects staff additions during that period.

Students' Evaluations

Improvements to discussions, papers, presentations, and speaking and writing skills indicate successful achievement in higher critical thinking levels—the diplomatic intent of assigned missions. Overall, improvements in critical thinking also affect morale and mission accomplishments; however, students provide the final word on instructional effectiveness when it impacts job performance on a holistic level. A representative sampling of their comments is shown below in a continuum from the earliest to the most recent class.

Student Comments

The investigators gathered comments following an evaluative survey that is sent to students 3 months after graduation; additional comments are found through non-traditional sources.

Class 1

This course far exceeded my expectations. It has given me the tools to be a relevant voice at the senior levels of leadership throughout SOF. As an Operations SGM, [Sergeant Major] it has provided me the tools to better prepare my Battalions in not only training but in the bigger picture of how SOF can influence national policy at the strategic, operational and tactical levels.

Class 2

. . . as recently as two weeks ago, the education I garnered while at the academy allowed me to converse with the CO [Commanding Officer] and PCO [Perspective Commanding Officer] and Commodore in regards to the Clausewitzian Trinity's influence on insurgencies. I feel so well equipped to aid and converse with my officers in a way that heretofore was not possible.

Class 3

As I stated when we graduated the course, the knowledge as well as the experience I received from JSOFSEA was well above my expectations. As I finished the course and moved to a joint position it has prepared me to not only look at it from a tactical and operational perspective but also from a strategic point of view. By far the best course SOF has to offer SR NCOs.

Class 4

It challenged me, I have never considered the stratigic [sic] level in my career and now I am able to communicate with the senior Officers on that level.

Class 5

The *JSOFSEA was one of the best leadership courses I have attended in the military. Since attending the course I have had many oppourtunites [sic] to brief what the course was about and how it is crucial that our up and coming SEA's go to this course to gain not only the education but to establish the contact with future SEA's throughout the community. Additionally the course has given me the ability [sic] to talk intelligently to my commandars [sic] and peers about future operational environments and things that are affecting our community now.*

Class 6

Learning the "*Big Picture" was something that had been missing for a long time. I finally understood where I fit into the big picture and can explain it to my youngest Airman. . . . I wish I could have spent another two months at the course, going deeper into some of the subjects.*

Summary

Analyses indicate significant improvements from the program's inception in both student engagement and critical analysis. Trends indicate a correlation between student engagement and the motivation to think strategically when additional staffing was available. While staffing is a challenge during times of reduced spending, the need to continue to evaluate and improve the program using learning analytics, student feedback, and research continues. These improvements in higher levels of critical thinking skills, analysis, and the motivation for students to employ those tools in strategic missions are affecting overall improvements in students' learning outcome and producing capable senior enlisted leaders in the joint operating environment.

Empowering senior enlisted leaders to think strategically maximizes the potential of the officer–enlisted leadership relationship and informs strategic decision-making within a given context, understanding the consequences of emergent second and third order effects. Brownhill (2012) neatly summarizes the need for continued joint enlisted education because the environment:

> can be generally characterized as a globalized, demographically emergent world with interdependent economies; shared and competing interests of developed and developing states; unpredictable failed states, rogue states, and nonstate actors; and ideologically based international terrorist networks fueled by dangerous historical animosities enhanced by technology.
>
> (p. 4)

Student papers and their narrative comments illustrate that the affective empowerment embodied in warrior diplomacy is reflected not only in their written assignments, but also in their narrative comments. As the Academy builds its own community of practice, creating a strong student network, the result is a high quality student experience that other institutions can employ to create curricular improvements for their blended courses or programs.

References

Anderson, L.W., Krathwohl, D. R., Airasian, P. W., Cruikshank, K. A., Mayer, R. E., Pintrich, P. R., Raths, J., & Wittrock, M. C. (Eds.) (2001). *A taxonomy for learning, teaching, and assessing: A revision of Bloom's taxonomy of educational objectives*. New York, NY: Longman.

Barno, D. W. (2009). *White paper*. House Armed Services Subcommittee on Investigations and Oversight. Near South Asia Center for Strategic Studies.

Bloom, B. S., Engelhart, M. D., Furst, F. J., Hill, W. H., & Krathwohl, D. R. (1956). *Taxonomy of educational objectives: The classification of educational goals. Handbook 1: Cognitive domain*. New York and Toronto: Longmans, Green.

Bonk, C., Wisher, R. A., & Nigrelli, M. L. (2004). Learning communities, communities of practice: Principles, technologies, and examples. In K. Littleton, D. Miell, & D. Faulkner (Eds.), *Learning to collaborate, collaborate to learn*. (pp. 199–219). Hauppauge, NY: NOVA Science. Retrieved from www.coursesites.com/bbcswebdav/pid-2451253-dt-content-rid-7508604_1/courses/bonkopen2012/Resources/Online%20Learning%20Communities%20and%20CoP%20Principles.pdf

Brownhill, C. L. (2012). Developing joint force officer-enlisted leadership capacity for the 21st century. *Joint Forces Quarterly, 66,* 4–5.

Davidson-Shivers, G. V., & Rasmussen, K. L. (2006). *Web-based learning: Design, implementation and evaluation*. Upper Saddle River, NJ: Pearson Education, Inc.

Dempsey, M. E. (2012). Making strategy work. *Joint Forces Quarterly, 66,* 2–3.

Garrison, D. R., Anderson, T., & Archer, W. (2000). Critical inquiry in a text-based environment: Computer conferencing in higher education. *The Internet and Higher Education, 2,* 87–105.

Johnson-Freese, J. (2012, July 3). Professional military education: Separate military requirements and academic degrees. *Small Wars Journal Blog*. [Web log comment]. Retrieved from http://smallwarsjournal.com/blog/professional-military-education-separate-military-requirements-and-academic-degrees

Merriam-Webster (2012). Merriam-Webster online dictionary. Retrieved from www.merriam-webster.com/dictionary/facilitator

Olson, E. T. (2008, March). Keynote Address. In R. Luman (Ed.), *Proceedings on Combating the Unrestricted Warfare Threat: Integrating Strategy, Analysis and Technology*. Symposium conducted at Johns Hopkins University APL SAIS, Maryland. Retrieved from www.jhuapl.edu/urw_symposium/proceedings/2008/Authors/Olson.pdf

Paul, R., & Elder, L. (2006). *Critical thinking: Concepts and tools*. Dillon Beach, CA: The Foundation for Critical Thinking. Retrieved from www.criticalthinking.org

Poole, K. H. (2011). *Understanding the cognitive style preferences of special operators both past and present*. (Doctoral dissertation, University of West Florida). Retrieved from http://library.uwf.edu

Quality Matters (2012). Quality matters rubric. Retrieved from www.qmprogram.org/rubric

Schunk, D. H., Pintrich, P. R., & Meece, J. (2008). *Motivation in education: Theory, research and applications* (3rd ed.). Upper Saddle River, NJ: Pearson Education, Inc.

Smith, R. M. (2008). *Conquering the content: A step-by-step guide to online course design.* San Francisco: Jossey-Bass.

Stavredes, T. (2011). *Effective online teaching: Foundation and strategies for student success.* San Franciso: Jossey-Bass.

Tileston, D.W. (2004). *What every teacher should know about effective teaching strategies.* Thousand Oaks, CA: Corwin Press.

Tyler, K. M. (2010). *Factors influencing virtual patron satisfaction with online library resources and services.* (Doctoral dissertation, University of West Florida). Retrieved from http://library.uwf.edu

USSOCOM hosts first Joint Special Operations Forces Senior Enlisted Academy (2010, August). *Tip of the Spear,* 34–35. Retrieved from www.socom.mil/News/Tip%20 of%20The%20Spear%20Archive/Tip%20Of%20The%20Spear%20Magazine%20 Archive%202010/August%202010.pdf

Vygotsky, L. (1978). *Mind in society: The development of higher psychological processes* (M. Cole et al., Eds.). Cambridge, MA: Harvard University Press.

Xin, C. (2012). A critique of the community of inquiry framework. *The Journal of Distance Education,* 26(1), Retrieved from www.jofde.ca/index.php/jde/article/ view/755/1333

SECTION V

International Perspectives

17

"ARE YOU WORKING IN THE KITCHEN?"

European Perspectives on Blended Learning

Anders Norberg and Isa Jahnke

Introduction

A European researcher instantly hit the reply button when he received our e-mail survey about blended learning (BL) and wrote, "Blended? Are you working in the kitchen?"

Had we mailed a non-expert by mistake? No, it was the right person. We already knew that there were many competing definitions of BL, but this image of the inspired educator in the kitchen was a fresh vision. Is BL a design concept for master chefs or just another easy take-away solution? Do we prefer different blends or dialects of BL in different parts of the world, and, if so, why? In this chapter we use mixed methods to specify some European perspectives about blended learning from European researchers and teachers.

Methods

Our main purpose is to create an overview of different understandings of BL in Europe. We applied mixed methods that include a literature review, website research about how universities use the term blended learning and an e-mail/online survey.

In June 2012 we conducted an e-mail survey regarding conceptions of blended learning to acquire an overview of the European perspective and "clues" about the European understanding of BL. Is it possible to identify something special about European BL approaches, or at least something non-American? The question was not whether European universities use new media and ICT-like communication technology in their mainstream educational offerings; Collis and van der Wende had already observed ICT as a part of a blend in higher education institutions in Europe in 2002 (Collis & van der Wende, 2002) and the hardware and Internet access is comparable to that of North America (OECD, 2010). However, how ICT is used in different countries, and with what results, is harder to measure. Our goal was to discover how European researchers approach the phenomenon of ICT integration.

We surveyed European researchers in the field of education: academic teachers, who published case studies about BL; and EU project managers with research and development (R&D) projects where BL was a key term. We chose experts from different European countries who had written about BL or technology in education because we knew them, had heard of them, or found them while doing Internet research. The questions also went to an International mailing list, JISCmail/SEDA (Staff & Educational Development Association) and the LinkedIn group "Higher Education Teaching and Learning, HETL." Some replied to our questions, others discussed replies. We had no ambitions to make a representative poll, but we were searching for clues, input, opinions, examples, and comments by European researchers.

We created the following three survey questions:

1. "What is *blended* in blended learning for you (e.g., components, type of blend, or just your definition)?" This first question is about the *blended* terminology or discourse itself.
2. "Could you possibly recommend a favorite paper on blended learning, or an author, conference or other favorite resource?" The second question is about the *European contribution* to the research about BL.
3. "Do you have any feeling or hypothesis about the differences between European and North American research on blended learning?" The third question is about mapping out *other general differences* regarding BL.

We sent the survey to 67 experts from 10 European countries, to the SEDA mailing list, and to the LinkedIn group HETL. A total of 33 experts answered: 21 experts from 9 countries answered at least 1 of our questions and 12 answered all 3. Of the 21 experts, we classified 15 as researchers in educational science or computer-human interaction and 6 as other academics, teachers, and development officers; none of the EU project managers replied. The experts discussed each other's answers, thus providing a total of 50 contributions.

With such a small set of voices, we did not create more statistics, but instead used the content as hints, citing part of the answers in our conclusions in the form of new questions.

When identifying a European perspective, we also were aware that Europe is a stretchable and diverse concept. The United Kingdom has much in common with the United States and Canada, and all are related by language and culture; German-speaking countries and Scandinavia have other traditions in common.

Furthermore, BL is not a concept with a clear main content with which to compare point by point. One expert commented: "Good luck with the can of worms that you are opening here."

Some Indicative Results

Use of The Blended Discourse

"What is Blended *in Blended Learning for You?" (Q1 of the email/online survey)*

From our survey, we collected a range of different answers with some typical replies, presented in Table 17.1.

The answers in Table 17.1 illustrate the discrepancies in "blended" terminology. While some refer to known definitions from North American authors, other regard "blended" discourse as confusing or useless, and researchers, teachers and education administrators use the term in different ways.

Sharpe, Benfield, Roberts, and Francis (2006) have found three ways in which the term BL was/is used in the UK:

1. BL describes a traditional course with supplementary resources in digital form—a common use of the term;
2. BL labels radical and innovative course designs, using digital media and communication; and
3. BL describes students with a holistic view of their learning, who use technology in new ways—a phenomenon that the authors say is both under reported and under researched.

TABLE 17.1 Quotes from Experts; "What is Blended in Blended Learning for You?"

* "Simply put, at the nine universities I have worked for, blended learning has meant that you have some face-to-face teaching and you have resources available online. Nothing more complex than that. Consequently, almost every programme in the UK is like that these days."
* "In the strictest sense, blended learning is where an instructor combines two methods in the delivery of instruction."
* "I never use the term—nor do I use the term e-learning any longer."
* ". . . many European researchers did not understand blended learning like I do. They mix many kinds of things in blended learning."
* "I find 'Blended learning' to be a completely useless term."
* ". . . it . . . goes without saying that all learning is blended, but that does not get us anywhere."
* "I always emphasize that blended learning is NOT a didactical concept."

We looked for the expression *blended learning* and its translations at the websites of the 20 highest ranked European universities in 2012 by Times World University to verify its daily use by European universities (www. timeshighereducation.co.uk/world-university-rankings/2012-13/world-ranking/region/europe). We also used Google site search, cleared the browser cache and checked results to ensure that counts from library catalogues were not included. Our results yielded an average of 208 instances per university website, varying from 0 to 1250, median 57. Three of these highly ranked university websites omitted BL.

We then searched the websites of randomly chosen universities or university colleges with the help of Wikipedia's country-wise listings, one from each of 47 countries, varying from 0 to 2490, resulting in an average of 186, median 11. Six university websites did not contain blended learning, 24 had 10 or more instances.

In general, higher counts come from classifying courses as blended learning. For a small comparison, a search at several US university websites in 2012 gives us these counts for "blended learning": 807 (suny.edu), 649 (cuny.edu), 213 (ucf.edu) and 189 (byu.edu). We conclude, therefore, that the extent of blended learning courses seems to be comparable both at European and North American institutions albeit mere diverse.

The different translations of BL in Table 17.2 reflect some national differences in interpretation.

European multi-national R&D projects and academic networks, mostly funded by the European Union, use BL discourse; e.g., COMBLE (www.

TABLE 17.2   Blended Learning in European Language

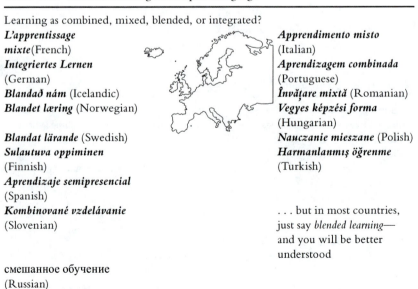

Learning as combined, mixed, blended, or integrated?

L'apprentissage mixte (French)

Integriertes Lernen (German)

Blandað nám (Icelandic)

Blandet læring (Norwegian)

Blandat lärande (Swedish)

Sulautuva oppiminen (Finnish)

Aprendizaje semipresencial (Spanish)

Kombinované vzdelávanie (Slovenian)

смешанное обучение (Russian)

Apprendimento misto (Italian)

Aprendizagem combinada (Portuguese)

Învățare mixtă (Romanian)

Vegyes képzési forma (Hungarian)

Nauczanie mieszane (Polish)

Harmanlanmış öğrenme (Turkish)

. . . but in most countries, just say *blended learning*— and you will be better understood

comble-project.eu/), Blend-XL (www.blend-xl.eu/), BLearning4all (http://
b-learning4all.eu/), Blinc (www.blinc-eu.org/), InnoEd (Page, Thorsteinsson,
& Niculescu, 2008), etc.

Research and development initiatives on BL are visible at a number of
European universities; in the UK, the University of Hertfordshire and the
University of Glamorgan have special initiatives in BL and a review of both
literature and practice of "blended e-learning" was published in 2006 (Sharpe
et al., 2006). In Finland, the Faculty of Social Sciences at the University of
Helsinki has BL initiatives and a yearly conference with international speakers
on BL and is cooperating with other higher education institutions in Finland
(Joutsenvirta & Myyry, 2011).

We also have found some *blended* terms that we seldom find in American
literature: "Blended e-learning" and "B-learning," probably from the
e-learning-period prior to 2005. When e-learning, often designed as content
provision for students or computer-based training, failed, any blend—
classroom sessions or synchronous teacher presence, for example—was a
welcome remediation. Driscoll (2002) describes BL as an introductory method
to initiate more effective e-learning in organizations, by adding technology to
traditional classrooms and moderating an asynchronous e-learning mix.

According to Sharpe et al. (2006), the often-criticized, unclear meaning of
blended learning is really a success factor because it allows teachers to negotiate
an appropriate meaning for the term (p. 4). Understood as a "boundary object"
by Laumakis, Graham, and Dziuban (2009), blended learning unites people in
imagining and developing the future, but not always in a coordinated way.

Blended Learning as a Research Term

*"Could you Possibly Recommend a Favourite Paper on Blended
Learning, or an Author, Conference or Other Favourite Resource?"
(Q2, Online Survey, 2012)*

The European experts provided many recommendations for reading about
blended learning: many cited their own papers; three recommended American
standard literature or books; and others recommended resources that described
the concept without using the term. This material, though fragmentary,
became a starting point.

We searched for books and published papers by European authors on blended
learning, "hybrid delivery," "mixed-mode delivery," etc. We found a few
European authors on a list of most cited papers and books on BL (Halverson,
Graham, Spring, & Drysdale, 2012), some of whom published together with
American researchers. The European authors, who are using the BL term, are
often computer scientists or teachers in various subjects doing case-based
research on results of implementing an IT tool or practice in their courses.

Computer scientists' relevant research fields include Technology-Enhanced Learning (TEL) or Computer-Supported Collaborative Learning (CSCL). TEL originates mainly from the educational sciences, while, according to Lonchamp (2010), CSCL is the combination of a CS segment (Computer Support or Computer Science) and a pedagogical or education element, CL (Collaborative Learning). CSCL focuses on collaborative learning and group cognition and includes different types of Computer Support, such as distance learning and collocated learning (face-to-face meetings using technology).

Moreover, we have found exclusively European expressions frequently used in research: "Blended learning arrangements," "blended learning scenarios," and "blended learning settings." This may reflect an attraction and a distance to the BL term at the same time.

Drysdale, Graham, Halverson, and Spring (2013) searched in the ProQuest Theses and Dissertation database for dissertations mentioning *blend*, *hybrid*, or *mixed mode* in the title or abstract (Drysdale et al., 2013) and found 205 American theses relevant for blended learning research registered until April 2012. The ProQuest database does not have the same coverage in Europe, but we found only three European dissertations during the same period when doing the same search, an indication that BL terminology is not central in European educational science-related teacher education, in which the terminology would be expected. European dissertations generally have titles and abstracts in English in parallel if they are not written in English.

According to a recent bibliographic study (Halverson et al., 2012), the most cited European paper on blended learning, number six globally, is "Can Blended Learning be Redeemed?" by Martin Oliver and Keith Trigwell (2005) with 287 citations to date, according to Google Scholar. The paper challenges conventional understandings of the BL term. The authors argue that the concept of a "blend" does not add anything meaningful or constructive when we think of blending environments, media, and pedagogies, etc. in education. Trigwell and Oliver (2005) argue that there is no general theory of blending in use, nor exists any defined example of unblended learning. Instead they ask: Isn't all learning a result of blends? Is "blending" the best word to use when describing technology implementation in teaching? Cannot pedagogical variation theory be more suitable (Runesson, 2005)? The variation theory states that what is being taught is not identical with what is learned by the students, but a learner needs a variation of teaching input to learn.

We also found a number of research papers that do not ignore blended learning, but propose new meanings and adapt the term to European educational research. We discuss six examples:

1. German researchers, Mandl and Kopp (2006) say that BL is an ambiguous term and propose ways to make the term more meaningful. The concept of BL needs to be considered in a broader didactical framework in which

the teacher has to prepare the different elements (methods, media) to improve the quality of the teaching–learning arrangements (Kerres & Jechle, 2002). The combination of presence and e-learning phases can be done in different ways and different conceptual models (Mandl & Winkler, 2004). They conclude that inconsistency of the term requires a stronger focus on the learner and the learning processes (Reinmann-Rothmeier & Mandl, 2001): Learning is an *active* process of construction (social construction of new knowledge); a *constructive* process (knowledge is constructed by integrating into the own existing knowledge); an *emotional* process (positive feelings instead of fear and negative feelings); a *self-controlled/-organized* process; a *social* process (learning takes place during interaction with others); and a *situational* process (learning is connected to a special context/situation). How should those six learning elements and BL be put together? They do not provide a solution, but, rather, create four aspects to formulate an appropriate frame for BL, an authentic context that allows/ triggers multiple perspectives, has a social context, and needs instruction/ support—very similar to Lave and Wenger's (1991) "situated learning approach."

2. The Norwegian researchers, Kudrik, Lahn, and Morch (2009), studied blended learning in a large, multinational company, also recognizing definition problems and lack of literature on BL, noting it as "practice oriented, but seldom informed by theory" (Kudrik et al., 2009, p. 2). They argue Vygotsky's idea (1978) that there is a duality of learning, one socially oriented, the other individual; both interdependent. Based on this duality, we now have new means to enhance both collaborative and individual learning with a richer set of available technology and media that helps both modes of learning.

3. In their book, *Preparing for blended e-learning* (2007), Allison Littlejohn and Chris Pegler perceive the blending of activities and blending of media in teaching and learning as commonplace; the newer aspect of e-learning adds the blend of place and time dimension. Successful, fully online courses are still rare, yet blended e-learning offers a step-by-step model to increase the use of e-learning, hence the expression "blended e-learning." Littlejohn and Pegler reflect on this from both teacher and student perspectives and present a planning tool, LD_lite (Learning Design_lite), a combination of three earlier existing frameworks that can be used separately, together, or in sequence for planning sustainable sequences of learning.

4. Aleksej Heinze and Chris Procter (2006) argue that four European earlier defined theories can contribute considerably to the concept of BL, although they do not use the term. They construct their BL model for use in a part-time Computer Science program solely from the combination of these four European theories:

i.   Vygotsky's *Zone of Proximal Development* (1986) addresses the difference or distance between what a student can learn individually and what s/he can learn under capable teacher guidance and social interaction with peers. The learning process should be focused on this zone.

ii.   Lave and Wenger's *Community of Practice* (1998) builds on Vygotsky's (1962) emphasis on social interaction among peers for deep learning, but concentrates on learning as a function of a group of learners, communicating shared needs, interests, and problems, and not as a transfer of knowledge from the teacher to the group of learners.

iii.   Laudrillard's *Conversational Framework* (2002) describes the communication between teacher and student as an iterative dialogue game in three cycles that support the student's on-going learning process. There is no one right media for this; the progress prioritized is the dialogue.

iv.   Salmon's *E-moderating Model* (2000) builds on Maslow's hierarchy of human needs (1943) and describes five consecutive steps for introducing student to web-based course work.

5.   Derntl and Motschnig-Pitrik (2005) argue that blended learning is very complex and in a case-based experimental phase, lacking theory support, structure, and models of social interaction to combine with e-learning content, etc. They propose a Blended Learning Systems Structure (BLESS) model that understands, organizes, and streamlines BL into something more useful. They tested the model in a computer-science course.

6.   Kerres and de Witt (2003) find that blended learning arrangements use both combinations of delivery media formats, didactical models and a constructive component. They present a framework to handle didactical design decisions, but conclude that it is difficult to find a single guiding didactical model.

These European researchers have a common interest for a blended learning discourse, but pursue an understanding to deepen and connect it to theory, existing didactical models, and pedagogical research. They are not only theorists, but also provide models and guidance for practice.

Are there General Differences Between Europe and North America Concerning Research on Blended Learning?

The last question was "Do you have any feeling or hypothesis about the differences between European and North American research on blended learning?" (Q3, online survey 2012). Table 17.3 demonstrates the range of answers to the question: Is there a European understanding of blended learning that differs from the North American?

TABLE 17.3   Quotes from Experts

• "A major obstacle in the German research is firstly the gap between pedagogues in schools and researchers from the field of E-learning/Blended learning and the lack of reference between Higher education didactics and the area of E-learning/Blended learning. This seems to be different in the USA."

• "The hypotheses on both sides of the Atlantic seem ill defined, and largely unhelpful in bringing about any meaningful change in education or learning. This could be because the area has become largely development-focused, lacking analytical rigour."

• "Since in Europe as well as in N. America people share the same technology to support the learning process, I suppose that there are no significant differences in this research."

• "No. I consider the diversity in blended learning is already very important among universities in the same country, and the main factor is the fact that blended learning is developed as a top-down learning methodology or as a complementary model that has developed after the f2f model in the organisation."

• "I have not looked specifically at differences between European and North American research on blended learning. However, everything comes to the same point: How do academics understand the term 'Pedagogy'?"

• "I guess it means the same" (in Europe and the US).

• "No idea."

Some respondents assert that the blended learning concept is global because of using the same global technologies. Others remark that differences within countries and between them can be as big as between continents, while others observe differing understandings of and approaches to pedagogy and education in Europe and North America. Additional factors can be a) the global dominance of North American books and other publications and b) the necessity to use current discourse to become understood and to become published in prestigious journals (Öhrn & Weiner, 2009).

In the next section, we examine these differences between Europe and North America by widening the context and formulate some questions, which are useful for reflection on the varying use of BL discourse in Europe and North America, rather than making clear propositions.

Implications—Widening the Context

Based on our experiences and studies, we derive implications by formulating some questions aiming for reflection on the use of blended learning in research.

a) Who are the Educational Researchers and do they Teach Themselves?

We have sorted globally relevant, blended-learning education researchers into four categories and as a framework to enhance understanding of European and North American writing on blended learning.

Researchers on education have "education" as a study object and experiment field; work on accepted scientific platforms; and study change in education. These researchers include sociologists, statisticians, psychologists, historians, philosophers, and computer scientists, and in North America, researchers in instructional technology and design. We do not find huge differences between European researchers and North Americans in this group, although European researchers discuss blended learning with some reservation, using expressions such as "blended learning arrangements" or "blended learning scenarios" instead of just BL.

Educational researchers work within a framework of "education" as an academic discipline in German-speaking countries and in Scandinavia (Biesta, 2011). Education is not only an object for study, but an academic subject in development. The basic direction is to develop theory to describe and enhance practice, often in connection to teacher education. The UK and the US do not have this framework. Since IT integration in teaching and learning is not a very central theme or focus for European educational research, it is not surprising that blended learning is not either. A common criticism is that blended learning is not theory-based, not well defined, and is only a superficial and popular description of development.

Researchers on educational practices and change are teachers of any subject, who conduct personal research on teaching and learning practices they are involved in. The typical paper is the case study. Their direction is to improve education and perform interventions, experiments, and studies in the process. These researchers, common in many countries, are likely to use modern and not yet fully defined concepts such as blended learning that appear to be an attractive concept for ambitious teachers. American books, research publications, conferences, and websites also dominate Europe. Most European teachers have English as a well-developed second language, and relevant publications in their own language can be hard to find. If they find anything, however, it may be theoretical and not written primarily for them.

Education developers and educational technologists support active academic teachers in the change process. In the US, they are rooted in academic disciplines of their own instructional technology and design; in other countries, they are a small group randomly composed of technicians, former or active teachers, and pedagogical coaches, etc., and have a varied and unclear status, if the group exists at all (Hudson, 2009). They support change of practice and they have a good overview of what is current in their field. They often get the theory that they need from instructional technology and design from overseas, since European countries do not have this discipline, although some universities implement positions in research in higher education, Didaktik, and institutional research. Blended learning feels much more open to negotiate new designs and teaching/learning concepts in educational development processes, than Didaktik does.

Furthermore, some new variables across these groups need to be considered. Interest for the blended learning discourse can be more likely if the researchers are themselves involved in teaching, supporting, or organizing undergraduate courses, and if the researchers work at an expanding university (widening of access, coping with upscaling of enrolment, struggling to establish their courses on new markets, etc.). In both cases, "BL" offers a framework for communication about change.

b) How much is a Course Seen as a Product on a Market, Needing Labels and Product Descriptions?

A course in higher education can be seen as either or both a "product" in an education market trying to attract students (it does not matter if the individual or a state pays the tuition) and/or a "public good" for the upbringing of well-educated democratic citizens. If we imagine a scale between these two, university marketing people would emphasize one and national politicians perhaps another. Recently, MOOC courses have caused a debate on "McDonaldization" of higher education (http://chronicle.com/blogs/ worldwise/moocs-mass-education-and-the-mcdonaldization-of-higher- education/30536). Is a course in the US seen more as a product than a course in Europe, needing attractive product design, accurate labelling and definition? Is *blended* one such product label to be understood within a business context? Or do European researchers on the other hand care too little about higher education teaching and learning, its student-perceived quality, usefulness, and attractiveness?

c) Can Varying Pedagogic Traditions Play a Role in the Varying use of Blended Learning as a Research Term?

Instructional design and instructional technology are important backgrounds to e-learning and blended learning research in the US and Canada. Since technology is central in these science fields, the term *blended* is suitable for general descriptions of technology implementations in course design. These theories and models are not much known at European universities, but more so in company-based education sectors. In Europe, a background in Didaktik is more common, at least in German-speaking countries and in Scandinavia. However, in the UK, Didaktik can mean teaching methods in general. For Anglo-Americans, Didaktik sounds authoritarian, formal, and dull. But Didaktik is both old and young and must be understood from the academic ideal of "Bildung," which is difficult to translate into English; proposed translations include formation and erudition. The European approach to Didaktik combines the development of teaching/learning with academic staff and curriculum development. "The art of teaching" is a simple definition.

Didaktik deals with what to learn and why—corresponding somewhat to academic staff development and curriculum theory (Wildt & Jahnke, 2010). Didaktik, as the art of teaching, has traditionally not been much about the "how" of teaching and learning. Instead, the Humboldt concept of academic freedom (Humboldt, 1970) fits in the same tradition, giving the learner the freedom (Lernfreiheit) to learn from any teacher that suits him and according to his own liking, but with the knowledge of what he must learn to pass his exam. The free academic must both research and teach, but he can chose when, to whom, what, and how to teach (Lehrfreiheit).

At many European universities, the teachers today must develop the digital versions of their courses themselves in their preparation time, while teachers at American universities more frequently receive help from professional instructional, pedagogical, and graphic designers.

The Fachdidaktik (subject didactics) deals with the how of teaching related to the subject (e.g., Engineering, Education, Social Sciences) regarding the special properties of the subject. Here, the BL models can fit in more naturally, such as the TPACK model for understanding relationships between content, pedagogy, and technology (Koehler & Mishra, 2009). Hamilton argues that the European discourse of didactics is essentially identical to the Anglo-American "Pedagogics" (Hamilton, 1999): "Only their language divides them" (p. 135).

d) Are some Important Questions in Education Research Left Unattended if the Word "Blended" is not Used?

Do European educational researchers risk missing something important if the perspective that "blended" stands for is not used? We would answer, "Yes, maybe."

The blended discourse seems, by its openness, to constitute a pragmatically *understandable concept* for teachers and policy-makers in the change process by functioning as a *negotiable third way* between the traditional education practices and something new, unknown, techno-driven, and extreme, and points at possible, gradual, generic change instead of disruptive change. The blended perspective further points at the *shifting* between place and time modalities inside the learning process as something important to study (Norberg, Dziuban, & Moskal, 2011).

e) Are Instructional Design and Didactical Design coming closer and how do They Approach BL?

The integration of ICT in education can be developed and studied within frameworks of Instructional design or Didactical design. We think blended learning by itself is not yet a sufficient didactical or instructional design approach, although BL has given rise to many good practices. We argue that the North American model of The Instructional Design (ID) and the European model of Didaktik (Didactical Design) are quite similar today; they have just been developed differently but can work together on technology integration in teaching and learning, with the help of BL and beyond.

The instructional design by Gagné, in *The conditions of learning and theory of instruction* (1965), uses the behaviorist learning approaches for understanding how learners learn, the basis for instructional design. Therefore, it is not a surprise when ID in its earlier understanding is seen as the practice of producing instructions for learners to allow them to create experiences that make the acquisition of knowledge and skill more efficient, effective, and appealing (Merrill, Drake, Lacy, & Pratt, 1996). An instructional design was seen as a classroom approach to create a "goal–mean relation" and to assist in the selection of methods to support teaching and learning (Winn & Snyder, 1996). To summarize, the instructional design was reduced to *methods* to support learning. Today, the understanding of instructional design is far broader; it includes the design of student–teacher interaction to support learning (IRMA, 2011) and combines educational and instructional experiences (see Zierer & Seel, 2012 for an overview).

The didactical design, Didaktik, started at a broader frame and focused on the relation between *student, teacher,* and *content*. This triangle is the main foundation for a didactical design. In addition, HochschulDidaktik (University-Didaktik) does not only focus on course development, but also on curriculum and academic development (Wildt & Jahnke, 2010). The term "didactical design" follows the German concept of Didaktik by Klafki (1963, 1997) and is inspired by Hudson (2008), by Fink's course design (2005), and Lund and Hauge (2011), who stress the differences of teaching concepts and learning activities and differentiate designs for teaching *and* designs for learning. Coming from this background, a didactical design includes teaching objectives, the *plan* of *how to* achieve those objectives in such a way that the learners are able to develop competencies and skills that the teachers have in mind, and different forms of feedback and assessment to assess the learning progress of the students (Biggs & Tang, 2007). The theoretical foundation of Didactics is based on two main concepts. First, the shift from a teacher-centered teaching to a learner-centered learning (Barr & Tagg, 1995) and second, the idea that learning does not follow a behaviorist concept, but is more a knowledge construction: a co-creation of new knowledge among a group of people that is "an active process of constructing rather than acquiring knowledge" (Duffy & Cunningham, 1996, p. 171).

The teaching objectives today are specified as *learning outcomes* and *competence development* that the students should develop over time. The didactical design asks how to make this possible, so that the learners are able to develop those skills. The didactical design is the *enabler* so that learning can take place (Jahnke & Kumar, 2013). The idea of the design is first to name the competencies (teaching/learning goals) and then to design how the students could achieve and develop those skills. In Europe, there are often the four main levels of focus: professional knowledge competency, method competency, social competency, and personal competency.

Conclusion

Blended is an open term. When teachers saw that a) the understanding of e-learning as a total disruption in both teaching and learning was a mistake, and b) much of their earlier experience and knowledge of teaching is still valid, relevant, and useful in a world of new technology, then it is obvious why they like the word *blend*. What is more natural than to call the new IT integration a *blend* between old and new when communicating about it? The closer we come to an actual teaching situation description, the more natural the term seems to be for communication and educational development purposes. But is the *blend* metaphor really a suitable tool for a deeper analysis of what is happening when forming general theories? Do we have meanings that are defined well enough? Many European researchers seem to doubt that, and see the *blended* discourse as too superficial, in need of clarification and theory support. However, it seems that we are approaching a more global discussion on this when didactics, pedagogics, and instructional design, etc. converge.

At the end of the day, learning still takes time and effort, and teacher guidance in a community of reflecting peers takes us further than merely access to content—as before.

References

Barr, R., & Tagg, J. (1995). From teaching to learning. A new paradigm for undergraduate education. *Change: The Magazine of Higher Learning, 27*(6), 12–26.

Biesta, G. (2011). Disciplines and theory in the academic study of education: A comparative analysis of the Anglo-American and Continental construction of the field. *Pedagogy, Culture & Society, 19*(2), 175–192. Doi:10.1080/14681366.2011.582255

Biggs, J., & Tang, C. (2007). *Teaching for quality learning at university* (3rd ed.), New York, NY: Open University Press.

Collis, B., & van der Wende, M. (2002). *Models of technology and change in higher education – An international comparative survey on the current and future use of ICT in higher education*. Report from Higher Education Policy Studies, University of Twente. Retrieved from http://doc.utwente.nl/44610/1/ictrapport.pdf

Derntl, M., & Motschnig-Pitrik, R. (2005). The role of structure, patterns, and people in blended learning. *The Internet and Higher Education, 8*(2), 111–130. Doi:10.1016/j.ihe-duc.2005.03.002

Driscoll, M. (2002). Blended learning: Let's get beyond the hype. *E-Learning*, *3*(3), 54.

Drysdale, J. S., Graham, C. R., Halverson, L. R., & Spring, K. J. (2013). Analysis of research trends in dissertations and theses studying blended learning. *Internet and Higher Education*, *17*(1), 90–100.

Duffy, T. M., & Cunningham, D. J. (1996). Constructivism: Implications for the design and delivery of instruction. In D. H. Jonassen (Ed.), *Handbook of research for educational communications and technology* (pp. 170–199). New York, NY: Simon & Schuster Macmillan.

Fink, D. L. (2005). Integrated Course Design. *Idea paper #42*. Idea Center, Kansas. Retrieved from www.theideacenter.org/sites/default/files/Idea_Paper_42.pdf

Gagné, R. (1965). *The conditions of learning and theory of instruction*. New York, NY: Holt, Rinehart & Winston.

Halverson, L. R., Graham, C. R., Spring, K. J., & Drysdale, J. S. (2012). An analysis of high impact scholarship and publication trends in blended learning. *Distance Education*, *33*(3), 381–413. Doi:10.1080/01587919.2012.723166

Hamilton, D. (1999). The pedagogic paradox (or why no didactics in England?). *Pedagogy, Culture and Society*, *7*(1), 135–152. Retrieved from www.tandfonline.com/doi/pdf/10.1080/14681369900200048

Heinze, A., & Procter, C. (2006). Online communication and information technology education, *Journal of Information Technology Education*, *5*, 235–249.

Hudson, A. (2009). *New professionals and new technologies in new higher education? Conceptualising struggles in the field*. Umea, Sweden: Umeå University, Department of Interactive Media and Learning (IML), SE-901 87. Retrieved from: www.diva-portal.org/smash/get/diva2:236168/FULLTEXT01

Hudson, B. (2008). A didactical design perspective on teacher presence in an international online learning community. *Journal of Research in Teacher Education Umeå University*, *15*(3–4), 93–112.

Humboldt, W. von (1970). On the spirit and the organizational framework of intellectual institutions in Berlin. *Minerva*, *8*(2), 242–250.

IRMA, Information Resources Management Association (2011). *Instructional Design: Concepts, Methodologies, Tools and Applications*. Information Science Reference, 1-2074. Doi:10.4018/978-1-60960-503-2

Jahnke, I., & Kumar, S. (2013, in press). iPad-didactics—Didactical designs for iPad-classrooms: Experiences from Danish schools and a Swedish university. In C. Miller & A. Doering (Eds.), *The new landscape of mobile learning: Redesigning education in an App-based world*. New York, NY: Routledge.

Joutsenvirta, T., & Myyry, L. (Eds.) (2010). *Blended Learning in Finland*, Faculty of Social Sciences, University of Helsinki. Retrieved from www.helsinki.fi/valtiotieteellinen/julkaisut/blended_learning_Finland.pdf

Kerres, M., & De Witt, C. (2003). A didactical framework for the design of blended learning arrangements. *Journal of Educational Media*, *28*, 101–114.

Kerres, M., & Jechle, Th. (2002). Didaktische Konzeption des Telelernens. (Didactical conception of distance learning). In L. Issing (Ed.), *Information und Lernen mit Multimedia und Internet* (pp. 266–281). Munich: Publisher Internat. Psychoanalyse.

Klafki, W. (1963). *Studien zur Bildungstheorie und Didaktik*. Weinheim: Beltz.

Klafki, W. (1997). Critical-constructive didactics. In M. Uljens (Ed.), *Didaktik* (pp. 215–228). Lund, Sweden: Studentlitteratur.

Koehler, M. J., & Mishra, P. (2009). Introducing TPCK. . . In AACTE Committee on Innovation and Technology (Ed.), *Handbook of Technological Pedagogical Content Knowledge (TPCK) for Educators* (pp. 3–29). New York, NY: Routledge.

Kudrik, Y., Lahn, L., & Morch, A. (2009). *A case study of blended learning in a Nordic insurance company: Three issues for e-learning.* Conference paper at The International Conference on E-Learning in the Workplace 2009, June 10–12, New York, NY. Retrieved from www.academia.edu/374223/A_Case_Study_of_Blended_Learning_In_a_Nordic_Insurance_Company_Three_Issues_for_E-Learning

Laudrillard, D. (2002). *Rethinking university teaching: A framework for the effective use of educational technology* (2nd ed.). London: Routledge/Falmer.

Laumakis, M., Graham, C., & Dziuban, C. (2009). The Sloan-C pillar and boundary objects as a framework for evaluating blended learning. *Journal of Asynchronous Learning Networks, 13*(1), 75–87. Retrieved from www.bartfennemore.com/edt6040/images/9/99/Laumakis_1.pdf

Lave, J., & Wenger, E. (1991). *Situated learning. Legitimate peripheral participation.* Cambridge: Cambridge University Press.

Lave, J., & Wenger, E. (1998). *Communities of practice: Learning, meaning, and identity.* Cambridge: Cambridge University Press.

Littlejohn, A., & Pegler, C. (2007). *Preparing for blended e-learning.* London: Routledge.

Lonchamp, J. (2010). CS in CSCL. In *13th International Conference on Interactive Computer aided Learning-ICL 2010.* Retrieved from www.loria.fr/~jloncham/ICL2010.pdf

Lund, A. & Hauge, T. E. (2011). Designs for teaching and learning in technology-rich learning environments. *Digital Kompetanse – Nordic Journal of Digital Literacy, 4,* 258–272.

Mandl, H. & Kopp, B. (2006). *Blended learning: Forschungsfragen und perspektiven* (Forschungsbericht Nr. 182). Munich: Ludwig-Maximilians-Universität, Department Psychologie, Institut für Padagogische Psychologie. Retrieved from http://epub.ub.uni-muenchen.de/905/1/Forschungsbericht182.pdf

Mandl, H., & Winkler, K. (2004). E-Learning – Trends und zukünftige Entwicklungen. In K. Rebensburg (Ed.), *Grundfragen Multimedialen Lehrens und Lernens* (pp. 17–29). Norderstedt: Books on Demand.

Maslow, A. H. (1943). A theory of human motivation. *Psychological Review, 50*(4), 370–396. Retrieved from http://psychclassics.yorku.ca/Maslow/motivation.htm

Merrill, M. D., Drake, L., Lacy, M. J., & Pratt, J. (1996). Reclaiming instructional design. *Educational Technology, 36*(5), 5–7. Retrieved from http://mdavidmerrill.com/Papers/Reclaiming.PDF

Norberg, A., Dziuban C. D., & Moskal, P. D. (2011). A time-based blended learning model, *On The Horizon, 19*(3), 207–216, Emerald Group Publishing. Doi 10.1108/10748121111163913

OECD (2010). *Are the new millennium learners making the grade? Technology use and educational performance in PISA.* OECD Publishing.

Öhrn, E., & Weiner, G. (2009). The sound of silence! Reflections on inclusion and exclusion in the field of gender and education. *Gender and Education, 21*(4), 423–430. New York, NY: Routledge.

Oliver, M., & Trigwell, K. (2005). Can "blended learning" be redeemed? *E-Learning and Digital Media, 2*(1), 17–26.

Page, T., Thorsteinsson G., & Niculescu, A. (2008). A blended learning approach to enhancing innovation. *Studies in Informatics and Control, 17*(3), 297–304.

Reinmann-Rothmeier, G., & Mandl, H. (2001). Unterrichten und Lernumgebungen gestalten. In A. Krapp & B. Weidenmann (Eds.), *Pädagogische Psychologie* (pp. 601–646). Weinheim: Beltz.

Runesson, U. (2005). Beyond discourse and interaction. Variation: A critical aspect for teaching and learning mathematics. *The Cambridge Journal of Education, 35*(1), 69–87.

Salmon, G. (2000). *E-moderating: The key to teaching and learning online.* London: Kogan Page Limited.

Sharpe, R., Benfield, G., Roberts, G., & Francis, R. (2006). The undergraduate experience of blended e-learning: A review of UK literature and practice. *The Higher Education Academy.* Retrieved from www.heacademy.ac.uk/resources/detail/teachingandresearch/Undergraduate_Experience

Vygotsky, L. (1978). *Mind in society: Development of higher psychological processes.* Cambridge, MA: Harvard University Press.

Vygotsky, L. (1986). *Thought and language.* Cambridge: MIT Press.

Wildt, J., & Jahnke, I. (2010). Konturen und strukturen hochschuldidaktischer hochschulforschung – ein rahmenmodell (Shapes and structures of research on didactics in higher education). In *Journal Hochschuldidaktik*, 4–8.

Winn, W., & Snyder, D. (1996). Cognitive perspectives in psychology. In D. H. Jonassen (Ed.), *Handbook for research for educational communications and technology* (pp. 112–142). New York, NY: Simon and Schuster.

Zierer, K., & Seel, N. (2012). General didactics and instructional design: Eyes like twins—A transatlantic dialogue about similarities and differences, about the past and the future of two sciences of learning and teaching. *SpringerPlus, 1*(1), 15.

18

OUT OF HOURS

Online and Blended Learning Workload in Australian Universities

Yoni Ryan, Belinda Tynan, and Andrea Lamont-Mills

Context

Australian universities have, since the mid-1990s, adopted a blended or hybrid teaching approach to "delivery" of their programs. After a national university system was mandated by the federal government in the late 1980s (Cunningham et al., 1998) and major distance education universities adopted early digital technologies such as CDs and videoconferencing, attention quickly turned to the use of Web 1.0 for off-campus students, and its potential for providing "flexibility" to on-campus students was soon recognized.

Most Australian universities are commuter campuses with few residential students. James, Krause, and Jennings (2010) summarized their longitudinal data of the experience of first-year students in a range of institutions to reveal that on-campus students were often not attending classes, in part because they were obliged to work hours that conflicted with their class timetables. They reported that 61% of full-time first-year students have paid employment. Furthermore, they spend just over 15 hours per week in class contact, and even less in private study (10.6 hours per week). This contrasts with the recommendation of 12 hours of class contact per week (over four subjects) and 30 hours per week in private study suggested in many universities. A growing number of academics confronted the apparent need for more flexible access to education for employed students, and saw the potential of digital technologies to address the issue of non-attendance by offering lectures in alternative web-mounted formats such as PowerPoint slides, interactive multimedia and recordings of their lectures. Online materials would allow students "anytime, anywhere" access. Distance programs were the first to benefit, but financial officers were persuaded of the potential for labor cost savings through online delivery to both remote students and those who were more simply "time poor" and found attendance inconvenient, through a new emphasis on independent and asynchronous learning outside class and a reduction in class time. By 2007, the Australian version of the US NSSE, the AUSSE, was reporting that 43% of all students spent fewer than 15 hours per week on-campus, including their class time, with the result that over one third were undertaking 50% of their study online (AUSSE Research Briefing, 2008). The report argued that online delivery was clearly substituting for class time.

Hence, from the mid-1990s, Australian universities adopted, to varying degrees, an educational approach in which "blended," "hybrid," or "flexible" learning became the norm, to the point where by 2010, universities that had a primarily distance student cohort made no distinction between on- and off-campus delivery. All students were to be provided with the same online materials; on-campus students had the additional benefit of face-to-face teaching if they so chose. Unlike the situation in many public universities in the US, where pay incentives were given to instructors to adopt online teaching, Australian academics were expected to incorporate digital delivery as a routine pedagogical approach.

The Research Issues

The present authors, academic/educational/staff developers, had observed that staff at their institutions were complaining not only about increased research and administrative burdens, but the high demands consequent on e-teaching: the "24/7" email requests, the need to develop materials in foreshortened time-frames for upload to course websites, and the frequent changes to Learning Management Systems (LMS) that have characterized Australian universities in the first decade of this century. With a grant from the Australian Learning and Teaching Council (ALTC), now the Office for Learning and Teaching (OLT), we undertook a study in four universities that addressed, inter alia, the following research questions:

What research is available on how workload is allocated in online and blended learning environments through Workload Allocation Models (WAMs)?

1. How do staff perceive the validity of their institutional WAMs with respect to teaching time?
2. How do academic staff "manage" workload in blended and online teaching?

This chapter reports on some findings of that project. We discuss the current literature on workload and WAMs, outline the more intensive task profiles of blended teaching, report on staff perceptions of increased workload and their strategies to manage workload while maintaining quality, and explore the implications of increased workload for the future of university teaching.

Methodology

We conducted semi-structured interviews with a purposefully selected sample of 25 academic (faculty) and professional (support) staff at each of our four universities: the University of New England (UNE), the Australian Catholic University (ACU), the University of Southern Queensland (USQ), and Central Queensland University (CQU). Three are predominantly distance universities but with sizable on-campus numbers at several campuses and ACU is primarily campus-based but nationally distributed and is moving rapidly to online delivery to combine small class size numbers at the various campuses. Interviews produced 88 valid responses, after eliminating corrupted voice files. Interviewees were selected on the basis that they had taught or were teaching in online and blended modes, with a wide range of years of experience, and differing levels of seniority. A small number of those interviewed (3 out of 88) who had taught but were now designated as support staff were included, to give some perspective on how academics were managing their online delivery. Descriptive themes were analyzed using N-Vivo, and sub-themes were subsequently generated. A literature search was undertaken pre-interview of the research and "gray" or non-peer reviewed literature, including education media such as *The Chronicle of Higher Education*, on workloads and costs associated with online-only and blended learning, drawing on US, Canadian, UK, and Australian studies, and the workload policies of the four universities, which are listed in the References below. Ethics clearance was obtained under the standard Australian research protocols, allowing for anonymized quotations by interviewees.

Research on Academic Workload

The "gray literature," reports, blogs and opinion pieces in educational media, have long reported the time demands of e-teaching. Yet research thus far has focused little on this aspect of contemporary academic work. In their contribution to a world-wide study of the academic profession in the twenty-first century, Coates, Dobson, Friedman, Goedegebuure, and Meek (2009) found that Australian academics' average hours were reported as 50.6 per week throughout the year, amongst the highest in the world. The study indicated that there are many pressures on academic staff that have increased workload, stress and "work–life imbalance"; they must win grant income, publish, and deal with increased administrative tasks associated with accreditation—quality regimes and student appeals—for example. It should be noted that in the Australian context, almost all faculty staff are expected to undertake research, teaching, and "service" work in both community and institutional arenas, historically in the proportions of 40:40:20, although there is a growing trend to "teaching only" positions. Bexley, James, and Arkoudis (2011), in their survey of 5000+ Australian academics, reveal that just under half reported unmanageable workloads. A recent study by Strachan et al., reported by Rowbotham (2012), blamed escalated research and administration expectations as the predominant workload issues.

Yet it was apparent to the present authors that a further cause of excessive load was the result of moves to pervasive digital environments as academics prepare for both face-to-face classes and for digital delivery, introducing changes in the composition of teaching tasks (as will be described below) and a reconfiguration of academic labor. In those institutions with a distance program, specialist editing teams and web and graphics developers were available to develop materials using the affordances of digital technologies. However, with the migration of more and more technical and word-processing applications to the desktop, teaching staff assumed many of the tasks once undertaken by specialist staff. In particular, the editing staff, "typing pools" and graphic artists typical of the print-based distance university were largely dismantled. The result has been that Australian academics typically develop, teach, and grade their own online courses, generally without the benefit of the development teams prescribed in the large PEW projects (Twigg, 2003).

Contemporary Work Allocation Models (WAMs)

While all Australian universities have broad guidelines on workloads, few have comprehensive WAMs that take account of the variety of task profiles demanded by the use of new technologies in teaching. The literature on WAMs is scant and reports of evaluation of their effectiveness even scarcer. The available literature mostly provides descriptions of newly developed models (Bitzer, 2006; Ringwood et al., 2005) or the development process for WAMs (Bitzer, 2006) and associated workload policies (Paewai, Meyer, & Houston, 2007). Key factors for satisfactory WAMs would appear to be staff collaboration in model development, transparency, equitable loads, and provision for regular review of the model (Stevens, 2008).

In the Australian context, workload is negotiated through a national union of university staff; the sector is moderately unionized with over 25,000 members, with a majority of staff belonging to the Union, although direct action has declined markedly over the past 15 years (Ryan, 2012). The National Tertiary Education Union (NTEU, www.nteu.org.au) covers both academic and professional staff and, while it develops Australia-wide broad policies on industrial matters, Enterprise Bargaining Agreements (EBAs) are negotiated at the local institutional level. As with HR policies at individual institutions, the NTEU has not yet specifically focused on the workload contingent on e-teaching, although it has successfully imposed a 37¼-hour week as the "standard" work week, with a notional cap of 1735–1750 hours per year. Professional staff in most institutions can be recognized and paid for additional work over this allocation, but academic staff cannot: it is assumed that academics need to work over that set amount if they are to progress their career, and the self-reported evidence is that they do (Coates et al., 2009).

Detailed and accurate financial and workload data are not readily available for Australian university teaching. Operating grants are allocated by the federal department, based on student enrolments at two "census dates" during the calendar year, with loadings for specified disadvantaged groups. Universities are free to determine teaching funding within their set envelope of funds. Hence institutional workload policies are generally developed on the basis of student load or Equivalent Full Time Student Load (EFTSL) per teacher, with the general assumption being that each student in a fully online program in particular is added at low marginal cost, producing economies of scale. However, actual institutional workload policies vary: Vardi (2009) describes three models operating at her institution: a contact hours model based on actual teaching time; an actual hours model, which attempts to allocate time for various activities; and a points-based model, which ascribes relative points to a range of activities, although the EFTSL model is not used at her institution. Kenny, Fluck, and Jetson (2012) describe the efforts to negotiate workload policies at the University of Tasmania, and argue for a hybrid model that combines actual activities with actual student numbers (not EFTSL). These approaches contrast with load allocations reported in the US, where actual student numbers or "headcount" seems to prevail.

Headcount Model

Allocations in purely US online tutoring are generally based on a maximum actual headcount per class; at the University of Phoenix Online, for example, in the late 1990s numbers were capped at 12–15 per class section, although this has now increased to a maximum of 25. Instructors are also limited to a maximum number of sections per period of study. Moreover, online-only providers such as Capella and University of Maryland University College (UMUC) pay a fixed US$3000 (in 2010) per class/semester, and monitor both facilitator time online and contribution to LMS activities, which is not routinely done for Australian instructors, especially those using hybrid modes. UMUC also has dedicated technology and administrative support staff for each program, another staff member for student advising, and embedded writing support. Such support does not characterize online or hybrid teaching in Australia, with the result that instructors develop, maintain, and teach, as well as providing additional comprehensive student support to retain and engage students (Tynan, Ryan, Hinton, & Lamont-Mills, 2012).

Class size research is important to educational policy development. Setting class-size limits is a budget-related matter for administrators (Parker, 2003). They must determine an optimal class size to balance the cost–benefit relationship, while maintaining manageable faculty workloads without impinging upon quality education. Little research has been reported regarding class sizes for online courses (Boettcher & Conrad, 2004; Simonson, 2004) and most of the class sizes recommended in the literature for distance education are based on anecdotal evidence (Simonson, 2004). Mupinga and Maughan's review (2008) of practices in the US found that the number of students in online classes varies with institutions. From 16 colleges in Texas that supplied information on their workload policies, the majority (60%) equated the sizes of online courses to traditional face-to-face courses (Virtual College of Texas, 2004). Hence no distinction was made in their workload allocation models between online and face-to-face classes.

Actual Hours Model

Tomei (2004) compared the amount of contact time required for a traditional face-to-face class with that for an online class, and found the latter required 14% more hours than face-to-face teaching. Although his findings suggest ideal class sizes for online (n=12) and face-to-face situations (n=17), his figures are simply an extrapolation from his measured workload to a full-time load situation and therefore would vary depending on the number of teaching hours expected in a semester. This includes taking care of content delivery and facilitation, counseling, and assessment. His study only considers a subset of the many online teacher roles (no course design and preparation, management or administration included), clearly omitting the tasks that an Australian academic would routinely undertake. Cavanaugh (2005) argues that teaching online requires one and a half to two times the work for face-to-face classes.

Due to the perceived higher demands of student–teacher interaction in online courses, many (e.g., Ko & Rossen, 2004; Sellani & Harrington, 2002; Cavanaugh, 2005) have argued that academic workload increases with class size. Overall, research findings, practical guidelines and standards, and anecdotal evidence suggest that productive staff–student interaction is reduced by larger class size, since the critical element in online (as in face-to-face) teaching is constructive feedback (Boud & Falchikov, 2007; Espasa & Meneses, 2010).

Administrative tasks obviously increase with class size. Discussion groups appear to function best with class sizes of 12–25, depending on the complexity of the issues canvassed. Even establishing separate discussion groups for classes over that size takes time, and intra-class dynamics require customized responses to each group. Orellana (2006) presents the evidence for students' experiences in large classes negatively impacting on student–faculty interaction. Instructors also believe that quality of online instruction is questionable for large class sizes (Olson, as cited in Olson, 2002; Parker, 2003). Yet O'Hare (2011) reports a standard Curtin University (Australia) B.Ed course with staff:student ratios of 1:75, to be undertaken by part-time online tutors within a 12 hour per week paid time allowance, which translates to less than 10 minutes per week per student.

Orellana (2006) focused on different levels of interactivity in relation to class size, although results indicated no straightforward relationship between online courses' class sizes and their actual level of interaction. This suggests that other factors are affecting interactivity, such as instructor time commitment and administrative and teaching workload, course content, student characteristics, and technological limitations. The present study confirms these variables as major contributors to the quality of learning outcomes for students, and the professional satisfaction of teachers, most especially in relation to the time commitment in responding to students online.

EFTSL Model

Because of the government funding model for Australian universities, EFTSL is the standard administrative model adopted for teaching costs, as described above. Under this model, actual headcount in a class is divided by eight, to represent a full-time student enrolment status of four subjects/courses each semester, or eight courses per year for overall funding purposes. However, as we have seen above, headcount more accurately reflects real workload, as staff–student interaction is a critical element of contemporary pedagogies. The present study would suggest that actual headcount may be necessary because staff–student interaction is a critical element of contemporary pedagogies.

Activities Model

Vardi (2009) reports on the activities model of workload, which differentiates between the different activities required for teaching; broadly, preparation/development time, actual teaching time (predicated on 3–4 hours face-to-face per week in most courses), and marking time. This model does not account for the significantly increased number of tasks now needed in e-teaching. Table 18.1 was compiled from a list of the tasks required for fully online teachers, drawing on Position Descriptions from exclusively online institutions from the US, such as the UoP Online, Capella University, Penn State World Campus, and Ragan's (2007) paper, as well as the online literature. The right-hand column details these; the left-hand column indicates those that must also be undertaken by the teacher in a blended course. A generous assignment of tasks to "online only" demonstrates that 31 of the 35 are also required for blended units, demonstrating that blended teaching intensifies workload as well as changing the nature of instructor tasks.

Clearly, blended teaching *increases* and *intensifies* teaching activities through an increase in the number of tasks and the daily time commitment to communication with students, as well as changing the *nature of instructor tasks*. Indeed,

TABLE 18.1 Task Profiles for Online Only and Hybrid/Mixed Model/Web-Enhanced Teaching

Tasks	Blended online/ class tasks	Online tasks
Prepare for class		
Design course for online presentation	✓	✓
Edit/revise material	✓	✓
Upload content to LMS/submit to QA staff before upload and respond to QA queries	✓	✓
Research for updated information	✓	✓
Ensure that ancillary materials are mailed (if required)	x	✓
Create discussion questions	✓	✓
Write netiquette	✓	✓
Set up CMS	✓	✓
Prepare students for online study (orientation)	✓	✓
Coordinate with instructional design/QA staff	✓	✓
Read materials	✓	✓
Present information		
Monitor and contribute to discussion board	✓	✓
Post material (if required)	x	✓
Post discussion questions	✓	✓
Practice and guidance		
Answer emails	✓	✓
Post to discussion boards	✓	✓
Online live sessions (if used)		
Provide technical support	✓	✓
Provide practice quizzes	✓	✓
Deal with conflicts promptly	✓	✓
Model effective online interaction	✓	✓
Monitor progress and encourage lagging students	✓	✓
Testing and assessment		
Grade assignments	✓	✓
Setup online tests	✓	✓
Grade tests (automatic)	✓	✓
Provide feedback on assignments	✓	✓
Develop test content	✓	✓
Develop exams	✓	✓
Assess messages in online discussions	✓	✓
Test online testing process	✓	✓
Provide feedback		
Email	✓	✓
Class announcements	✓	✓
Discussion question responses	✓	✓
Automated responses to study quizzes	✓	✓
Create feedback rubric for common questions	✓	✓

no less than the then Australian Universities Quality Agency (AUQA), in its audit of Charles Darwin University, explicitly notes that calculations of load based on the old paradigm of classroom teaching "are no longer appropriate" (Audit of Charles Darwin University, 2011, p. 24). The following section broadly describes workload policies at the four universities examined here.

Workload Policies for Blended Learning

Analysis of the WAMs at each of the universities reveals that three, the primarily distance institutions, have no "allowance" for the additional tasks undertaken by teachers in a blended environment, nor is there consideration of the time needed to develop rich online learning environments, certainly nothing like the 810 hours Rumble (2011) recommends. He quotes US studies' estimates for development time for a wholly web-based course, citing typical "release time" of 180–200 hours for the development phase. As we have seen in Table 18.1, however, the tasks required for development, delivery, interaction, and grading components of a blended subject are almost as numerous as those for a wholly online subject.

At ACU, which had adopted mandated blended models, and after intense pressure from the local union, some allowance for online development was made; however, it was assumed that once developed, there was little or no updating of materials for each new offer of the subject. Rumble (2011) argued that once materials are developed, they may not be redeveloped for 8 or 10 years, with an overall reduction in staff time. However, at ACU, "redevelopment" had to be designated "major" to warrant a work allocation, and this was at the discretion of the supervisor of staff, normally a Head of Department. Further, hourly allocation was reduced for small enrolment courses, considered to be fewer than 20 EFTSL or 160 students by headcount. By contrast, in the three predominantly distance institutions, online-only and blended teaching development and delivery were assumed to be equivalent, with "redevelopment" conducted at 5-yearly intervals for accreditation purposes. Hence there was no allowance for the inevitable updates needed for weblinks that have disappeared, and the "warp speed" at which new discoveries alter "content."

WAMs simply did not reflect the new realities of e-teaching, in terms of student numbers, or preparation time.

Staff Perceptions of Workload Models

Staff across the four institutions expressed limited understanding of their local WAM, apart from those actively involved in their local union branch. When they did demonstrate an accurate knowledge of the WAM, they reported that the accepted method of allocating load, EFTSL of itself was inadequate in reflecting the amount of time each individual student required in a blended or wholly online environment:

> So enrolments, it's a really messy thing, enrolments still work off the EFTSL model but in terms of how we see or perceive students as the rank and file staff here is by the hourly basis . . . we're still stuck in terms of seeing teaching as an on-campus mode.
>
> I think it comes out to 20 minutes per student (over the full semester if the instructor "worked to rule").
>
> The EFTSL load, the workload that is based on EFTSL, is built around the notion of student numbers. And that does not equate to the hours that you put in, either in face-to-face teaching or preparation, or mixed mode teaching, online time, individual consultation with students. Clearly if you've got huge numbers, the amount of time that you would spend with student assistance and individual consultation must inevitably increase, as would marking and those sorts of things. But it doesn't alter things such as preparation, face-to-face teaching hours or online BlackBoard work. Where you would do the same amount of work for one student as you would for a hundred.

Just over 52% of all participants stated that there was no specific allowance for online-only teaching; just over 20% responded that there *was* such an allocation—with staff from ACU and USQ more likely to nominate a specific allocation for wholly online teaching. Responses thus reflect lack of detailed awareness of WAMs, and a lack of clear policy guidelines on workload in an increasingly blended delivery environment. They also reveal the limited attention individual students would receive under current workload models, were staff to follow them to the letter. As demonstrated in Table 18.1, staff face a more demanding task list for their teaching activities in the blended environment: "If I were to jot down all the extra things that I do that I would not have to do individually if I did them all in a face-to-face meeting, I think it would be a lot more."

As will be outlined below, most staff "do the hours" to ensure students receive more than this parsimonious allowance, but they do so "out of hours," in the belief that students would be shortchanged by allocated nominal hours, and that the overall quality of education would decline if they strictly observed their allocation. Staff also believed that students demanded a high level of attention, partly because they now conceived of their educational experience as a service activity similar to other online services such as banking, and partly because they lived in a 24/7 world, and expected their teachers did too. Student expectations for personal or prompt responses to queries were correlated with the ease with which students could contact staff in an online environment:

> One of the things about online is that people see it as a personal service.
> You say—yes, there's the Blackboard discussions and so on. That means
> that every day you go into it and you service that Discussion group—
> every day. If I'm running a lecture group—like face-to-face stuff—I'm
> not servicing those classes every day. And then of course students
> decide—oh well, they're a bit diffident about putting up a stupid
> question, so they email you or ring you.

Yet the apparent ease and speed of email communication for students were
countered by staff concerns about misunderstanding:

> I think it takes a lot longer for me to form a suitable reply online than it
> does for me to just spit out an answer. Because I spend a lot of time
> thinking "how should I say it? Have I said that OK? Is someone going to
> take that the wrong way?" And I'll spend half an hour on a five minute
> question.

Moreover, tasks not included in Table 18.1 include professional learning in new
LMS and newer applications such as podcasting:

> In terms of first—learning—working out the technology around it,
> because—you know whether I could stream it, capture it and stream it on
> . . . And that was problematic. Just the size of the files and working out
> all the logistics of how to use it—took a really long time.

In summary, staff overwhelmingly believed that their institutional models for
work allocation did not reflect the reality of their actual teaching activities in
digital environments, that EFTSL numbers were an inappropriate basis for
work calculation, that student expectations of 24/7 service teaching was
an additional burden of e-teaching, and that simply working in the online
environment, including learning new applications, swallowed time. There are
also workload and policy issues that limit the capacity of staff to engage in
innovation in learning and teaching. For some, there are inadequate incentives
to devote additional time to teaching, compared with the perceived career
benefits of research (Chalmers, 2011).

Staff Management of E-Teaching Workload

When asked about their most common online activities, participants identified
discussions as the most common teaching activity (73 of 88), followed by "traditional learning resources" (e.g., PowerPoint lecture slides, readings—63 of 88),
podcasts (51 of 88), and then assessment (42 of 88). This is an interesting result,
as discussion boards commonly feature as time-intensive and therefore likely to

be avoided by those concerned to minimize load. Discussion topics introduced to ensure some interactivity in the blended learning "space," are time-consuming, yet are recognized as a significant learning activity. The majority of staff believed that quality would suffer if they reduced their online activities:

> To be honest, what I would have to do is to provide a sub-quality service. So you're looking at no feedback on assignments—all those sorts of things. So to me, that's sub-quality service.
>
> Some of the things I could do (to reduce work time) would be move to quizzes instead of assignments. That can be marked electronically. Other activities that would count toward assessment that could be somehow marked electronically. It seems to me, I think there are clever ways to use technology.

As the last quotation indicates, staff have considered a number of strategies that might help reduce workload, including setting assignments that allowed automated marking. However, they were conscious that quizzes were often low-level tasks that did not "test" the skills needed in today's professional workforce, such as analytic and persuasive writing, and aural and visual communication. They conceded that many staff managed workload by not revising materials, but expressed concern that the lack of up-to-date materials disadvantaged and de-motivated students:

> If I was to teach to the workload, there would be minimal updating of the course, so they'd get very stale very fast and problems wouldn't be dealt with.
>
> I would need to make the assessment task almost non-existent. You know, when you're the only lecturer and you have—this coming semester I'm going to have 120 students—and if you give them two assessments to do—you know, you can't spend 15 minutes on 2,500 words. So I think you'd need to probably almost cut out assessments.
>
> I've been thinking about getting rid of discussion boards, as an assess-able task. But then I'm really loathe to do that, because that's where the learning happens and that's where the students are supported by me. And questioned by me and challenged and challenged by each other—other students—if you can really get that happening well, that's really fantastic. And that's where they learn.

It is of interest that so few participants (14/88) nominated email as one of their teaching tasks when, for many academics, as well as other professionals, it is the bane of their work lives.

Although staff rarely confessed to this themselves, except through an occasional acknowledgement that they should have reviewed materials once more before upload, those interviewed believed some staff failed to update materials as a strategy to manage workload. They reported that they needed more professional development assistance on how to become more efficient in their online work, but felt they could not "spare the time" to attend scheduled workshops. They adduced a range of potentially deleterious effects on student learning if they were to reduce their hours. However, in the main, they have simply accepted that e-teaching takes more time than current WAMs prescribe. Moreover, they generally cannot devise strategies that might reduce workload without compromising the quality of student learning. They would have to avoid updating materials, leading to irrelevance, or avoid discussion forums "where the real learning occurs."

Summary of Findings

Australian academic staff in this study overwhelmingly perceived that their workload allocation did not sufficiently account for the additional workload engendered by e-teaching, whether in fully online or web-supplemented modes. Consistent with other research (Coates et al., 2009), they believed they had excessive workloads. This study could not quantify work hours in e-teaching—one of 88 participants was prepared to estimate that blended learning added 20% to classroom instruction time; another posited it consumed double a face-to-face workload. However, the study provides a new insight into high reported work hours as a direct result of the new technology tasks and communication modalities in teaching. The study also points to the inadequacy of Australian university WAMs to account for academic roles that routinely include more students, more tasks, and constant reskilling. This study would indicate that, as Larkins (2011; 2012) argues, "student person numbers (not EFTSL) more accurately reflect academic staff workload issues." On that basis, Larkins has established that the Student to Staff Ratio averages 34:1 across the Australian sector. It demonstrates that notwithstanding the valorisation of research over teaching (Chalmers, 2011; Bexley et al., 2011), for the academics interviewed here, deliberately reducing their teaching time to lower load would negatively impact on student learning. They accepted, albeit reluctantly, they would continue to teach "out of hours."

Implications for Teaching Futures

Given the findings reported here, amid concerns about the sustainability of e-teaching practices, we might posit a scenario that would reduce the workload of individual academics by eliminating much resource development time and the time taken to learn new technical applications. The recent development of MOOCs by elite US scholars as well as lower-end commercial publishers and providers, while currently lacking a viable business model, could point to the inevitability of world-wide common content in "Maths 101," with minimal modification for local contexts. Instructors could then concentrate on facilitation of learning in the digital space and in reduced class time through blended learning. Indeed, a similar model is already established in large US for-profit enterprises such as UoP (Ryan, 2004). However, moves toward this future may not be the panacea for institutional budgets that many envisage, if smaller class sizes of 25 are adopted to follow the US model of more individualized attention and greater staff–student interaction, thereby reducing the typically large classes in Australian universities. ·

Acknowledgements

Support for the original work was provided by the Australian Learning and Teaching Council Ltd, an initiative of the Australian Government Department of Education, Employment and Workplace Relations (Since renamed Office of Learning and Teaching). The project team would like to thank the following people for their contributions to the project and support of the team: Professor Grant Harman (Adjunct Professor, University of New England); Dr Deborah Vale (Project Officer); Dr Alan Smith (previously University of Southern Queensland); Dr Rosalind James (University of New England); and Dr Leone Hinton (Project partner Central Queensland University).

Notes

The four institutional work models that form the documentation can be retrieved from: www.usq.edu.au/hr/empcond/ea2010; www.acu.edu.au/__data/assets/pdf_file/0005/380984/Academic_Workloads_Guidelines_October_2011.pdf; www.cqu.edu.au/_data/assets/pdf_file/0016/5047/CQUniversity-Enterpise-Agreement-2009-FINAL-signature-version-v2-130111-changes-to-salary-rates.pdf; and www.une.edu.au/hrs/eb/academic-agreement.pdf

References

AUSSE Research Briefing No. 3 (2008). Enhancing the engagement of distributed learners. Retrieved from http://research.acer.edu.au/cgi/viewcontent.cgi?article=1008&context=ausse

Australian Universities Quality Agency (2011). Audit of Charles Darwin University Retrieved from www.auqa.edu.au

Bexley, E., James, R., & Arkoudis, S. (2011). *The Australian academic profession in transition*. Melbourne: Centre for the Study of Higher Education.

Bitzer, E. M. (2006). Attempting a fair and equitable academic workload distribution in a faculty of education, EASA/Kenton International Conference, Wilderness, South Africa.

Boettcher, J.V. & Conrad, R. (2004). Faculty guide for moving teaching and learning to the web, League for Innovation in the Community College, Phoenix, AZ.

Boud, D. & Falchikov, N. (2007). *Rethinking assessment in higher education: Learning for the longer term*. London: Routledge.

Cavanaugh, J. (2005). Teaching online—A time comparison, *Online Journal of Distance Learning Administration*, *8*(1). Retrieved from www.westga.edu/ distance/ojdla/ spring81/cavanaugh81.htm

Chalmers, D. (2011). Progress and challenges to the recognition of the scholarship of teaching in higher education, *HERD*, *30*(1), 25–38.

Coates, H., Dobson, I., Friedman, T., Goedegebuure, L., & Meek, L. (2009). *The attractiveness of the Australian academic profession: A comparative analysis*. Melbourne: L.H. Martin Institute.

Cunningham, S., Tapsall, S., Ryan, Y., Stedman, L., Flew, T., & Bagdon, K. (1998). *New media and borderless education*. Canberra: AGPS.

Espasa, A. & Meneses, J. (2010). Analysing feedback processes in an online teaching and learning environment: An exploratory study. *Higher Education*, *59*, 277–292.

James, R., Krause, K-L., & Jennings, C. (2010). *The first year experience in Australian universities: Findings from 1994–2009*. Retrieved from www.griffith.edu.au/gihe/ staff/klkrause-publications/FYE_Report_1994_to_2009-opt.pdf

Kenny, J., Fluck, A., & Jetson, T. (2012). Placing a value on academic work: The development and implementation of a time-based workload model. *Australian Universities' Review*, *54*(2) 50–60.

Ko, S. & Rossen, S. (2004). *Teaching online: A practical guide*. Boston: Houghton Mifflin.

Larkins, F. (2011). Academic staffing trends: At what cost to teaching and learning excellence? Retrieved from www.lhmartininstitute.edu.au/insights-blog/2011/10/ 65-academic-staffing-trends-at-what-cost-to-teaching-and-learning-excellence

Larkins, F. (2012). How should academic staffing trends be analysed? Retrieved from www.lhmartininstitute.edu.au/insights-blog/2012/02/75-how-should-academic- staffing-trends-be-analysed

Mupinga, D. M. & Maughan, G. R. (2008). Web-based instruction and community college faculty workload, *College Teaching*, *56*(1), 17–21.

O'Hare, S. (2011). The role of the tutor in online learning. In G. Williams, C. Statham, N. Brown, & B. Cleland (Eds.). *Proceedings of Changing Demands, Changing Directions, ASCILITE Conference*, Hobart 4–7 December, 909–918.

Olson, C. (2002). Leadership in online education: Strategies for effective online administration and governance. In K. Rudestam & J. Schoenholtz-Read (Eds.), *Handbook of online learning: Innovations in higher education and corporate training*, (pp. 237–256), Thousand Oaks, CA: Sage.

Orellana, A. (2006). Class size and interaction in online classes, *The Quarterly Review of Distance Education*, 7(3), 229–248.

Paewai, S., Meyer, L. H., & Houston, D. (2007). Problem solving academic workloads management: A university response, *Higher Education Quarterly*, *61*(3), 375–390.

Parker, A. (2003). Motivation and incentives for distance faculty, *Online Journal of Distance Learning Administration*, *6*(3). Retrieved from www.westga.edu/~distance/ ojdla/fall63/parker63.htm

Ragan, L. (2007). *Best practices in online teaching*. Retrieved from http://cnx.org/ content/col10453/1.2/

Ringwood, J. V., Devitt, F., Doherty, S., Farrell, R., Lawlor, B., McLoone, S., Rogers, A., Villing, R., & Ward, T. (2005). A resource management tool for implementing strategic direction in an academic department, *Journal of Higher Education Policy and Management*, *27*(2), 273–283.

Rowbotham, J. (2012). Shady hollows a stumbling block to gender equity, *The Australian Higher Education Supplement*, November 7, 29.

Rumble, G. (2011). Flexing costs and reflecting on methods. In L. Burge, C. Gibson, & T. Gibson (Eds.), *Flexible pedagogy, flexible practice: Notes from the trenches of distance education* (pp. 243–255). Athabasca: Athabasca University Press.

Ryan, S. (2012). Academic zombies: A failure of resistance or a means of survival?, *Australian Universities' Review, 54*(2), 3–11.

Ryan, Y. (2004). Taking it to the world: The US private sector model. In L. Moran & G. Rumble (Eds.), *Vocational Education and Training Through Open and Distance Learning, World Review of Distance Education and Open Learning, 5,* 147–163.

Sammons, M., & Ruth, S. (2007). The invisible professor and the future of virtual faculty, *Journal of Educators Online.* Retrieved from www.itdl.org/Journal/Jan_07/article01.htm

Sellani, R. & Harrington, W. (2002). Addressing administrator/faculty conflict in an academic online environment, *The Internet and Higher Education, 5*(2), 131–145.

Simonson, M. (2004). Class size: Where is the research? *Distance Learning, 1*(4), 56.

Stevens, M. (2008). Workload management in social work services: What, why and how? *Practice, 20*(4), 207–221.

Tomei, L. (2004). The impact of online teaching on faculty load, *International Journal of Instructional Technology and Distance Learning, 1*(1), 3–45.

Tynan, B., Ryan, Y. Hinton, L., & Lamont-Mills, A. (2012). *Out of Hours: Final Report.* Sydney: Office for Learning and Teaching.

Twigg, C. (2003). Improving learning and reducing costs: New models for online learning, *EDUCAUSE,* Sept/Oct, 28–38.

Vardi, I. (2009). The impacts of different types of workload allocation modes on academic satisfaction and working life, *Higher Education, 57*(4), 499–508.

Virtual College of Texas. (2004). Faculty compensation and course sizes for online/VCT courses statewide.

Blended Learning in K–12 Environments

19

BLENDED LEARNING IN THE K–12 EDUCATION SECTOR

Heather Staker and Michael B. Horn

The study of blended learning in postsecondary environments has a longer history and more scholarship than the study of blended learning in K–12 settings. For many years, the K–12 community generally assumed that blended learning was roughly equivalent in both sectors and that the K–12 field could piggyback on postsecondary research. New findings about how blended learning is developing in the K–12 sector reveal, however, that although blended learning is similar in many aspects at both levels, it also differs in significant ways.

Several aspects of blended learning are the same in both sectors. For decades, neither sector had a technological innovation that allowed it to serve substantially more students without proportionally multiplying its costs. But online learning—and some forms of blended learning, online learning's offshoot—have changed the equation for both the higher education and K–12 systems. Online and blended learning introduce the possibility of delivering a broader course catalog with more customized instruction to vastly more students—without necessarily building larger campuses, hiring more instructors, or printing more textbooks. In this way, some models of online and blended learning bear the hallmarks of a classic disruptive innovation, an innovation that transforms a complicated, expensive, inaccessible, and centralized sector into one that is simpler and more affordable, accessible, convenient, and customizable (Christensen, 1997).

This chapter focuses on the development of blended learning in the K–12 sector. Between 2010 and 2012, researchers at the Clayton Christensen Institute collected information from roughly 100 education experts and 80 organizations to understand what blended learning looks like for K–12 education and how it is expanding into blended learning schools. This chapter summarizes that research and draws the following conclusions:

- The postsecondary and K–12 sectors define blended learning differently. At the K–12 level, blended learning is a formal education program in which a student learns at least in part through online learning, with some element of student control over time, place, path, and/or pace; at least in part in a supervised brick-and-mortar location away from home; and the modalities along each student's learning path within a course or subject are connected to provide an integrated learning experience.
- Four models of blended learning are the most prevalent in the K–12 sector: the Rotation, Flex, A La Carte, and Enriched Virtual models. As the practice of blended learning evolves, these models are likely to shift and expand.
- Most of the Rotation models are examples of sustaining innovations; they improve the performance of the established classroom model along the dimensions that society has historically valued. The Flex, A La Carte, and Enriched Virtual models, in contrast, offer a very different value proposition, and one that could be disruptive to the traditional classroom. Over time, the more disruptive models are likely to play a larger role in transforming secondary education.
- Policymakers, particularly at the state level, are in the best position to remove regulatory barriers that thwart important blended learning innovations from emerging and to create new regulations that channel blended learning to its highest-quality potential.

Defining Blended Learning: Postsecondary and K–12 Comparison

The postsecondary and K–12 sectors are undergoing a simultaneous transformation as they confront online and blended learning models, although postsecondary institutions are farther along than their K–12 counterparts. Among college students, only 10 percent took at least one online course in 2002. That fraction grew to just under 25 percent in 2008 and hit 31 percent in 2010 (Allen & Seaman, 2011). At least one projection shows it hitting 50 percent in 2014 (Christensen, Horn, Caldera, & Soares, 2011). Although the numbers are not tracked as well at the K–12 level, one estimate suggests that 300,000 students were taking at least one online course in K–12 in 2002—roughly half a percent of students; that number increased to roughly 1 million students—or nearly 2 percent—in 2007, and some estimates now suggest the number of K–12 students engaged in online learning is over 4 million students—or roughly 7 percent of the schooling population (Christensen, Horn, & Johnson, 2010). Notwithstanding the postsecondary lead, both sectors are now experiencing an inflection point where, after a long period of incubation, their worlds are beginning to flip rapidly to highly scalable online technology.

The two sectors share a similar history for how these technologies entered their systems. Disruptive innovations often first gain traction in areas of "nonconsumption," meaning among consumers whose alternative to using the new technology is not taking part in the system at all. True to pattern, many of the early online learners at the college level were students who could not attend a traditional brick-and-mortar institution because of work or family obligations during the day. Online learning offered the opportunity to learn at any time of the day or night and at any time of the year. In that light many regarded it as clearly better than nothing (Christensen et al., 2011). In similar fashion, early adopters of online learning in the K–12 sector were students who had dropped out of school, needed to recover credits, or wanted to take courses that their traditional schools did not offer. They turned to online learning as their only accessible alternative (Christensen et al., 2010).

Despite these congruities in overall direction, pace of change, and starting points, the postsecondary and K–12 sectors have structural differences that affect the path that online learning is taking as it migrates from serving pockets of nonconsumption toward serving the mainstream. In particular, the phenomenon of blended learning for the K–12 sector must be defined differently from the phenomenon of higher education. Scholars at the postsecondary level often use a continuum to define blended learning, with traditional face-to-face instruction on the left and online learning on the right. Blended learning is somewhere in between. Researchers at Babson College, for example, said that postsecondary blended learning courses and programs "are defined as having between 30 percent and 79 percent of the course content delivered online." They also stated that any course or program with more than 80 percent of the content delivered online is an example of an online course or program, not blended (Allen & Seamen, 2006). Figure 19.1 depicts a conceptualization of this definition.

At first, many people ported this postsecondary definition to the K–12 level and assumed that the linear continuum would work there as well. But over time researchers found that the definition was lopping off a significant segment of K–12 blended learning implementations. It was too narrow to describe the complete universe of K–12 blended learning possibilities. In particular, the postsecondary definition ruled out instances when students were attending a brick-and-mortar classroom for the entire school day, perhaps participating in homeroom, band practice, and the like, but were receiving more than 79 percent of their content and instruction online in a classroom or computer lab. From the students' perspective, they felt like blended learners. They did not see

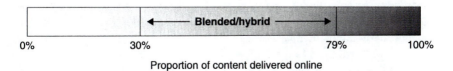

| 0% | 30% | 79% | 100% |

Proportion of content delivered online

FIGURE 19.1 Blended Learning Continuum for Postsecondary Education

themselves as full-time virtual-school students, and neither did anyone else at the brick-and-mortar school. The K–12 sector needed a definition of blended learning that included these students.

The reason that the K–12 sector needed a broader definition is because K–12 schools perform a different job from postsecondary institutions. One of the main jobs that society "hires" K–12 schools to do is purely custodial; the majority of children need a safe place to be during the day outside of the home while their parents are busy. Although postsecondary institutions arguably play a custodial role, too, both the purpose and solution are quite different from those in K–12 education. K–12 students, who attend school in the traditional, brick-and-mortar sense, except that the Internet delivers most of their instruction, are still fully participating in the school's custodial function. They are experiencing a blend of the traditional with the online, but in their case, it is not a blend of *traditional face-to-face instruction* with online learning. Rather, it is a blend of the *traditional custodial role of the school* with online learning.

In many cases blended learning programs include both custodial supervision and face-to-face-instruction. But in *all* cases they include at least the former, and so that is the element that must be part of the definition. The Clayton Christensen Institute has found that the common components across the wide range of K–12 blended learning programs are first, students engaged in online learning, and second, a supervised brick-and-mortar experience away from home. Accordingly, it has defined blended learning as:

> A formal education program in which a student learns at least in part through online learning, with some element of student control over time, place, path, and/or pace; at least in part in a supervised brick-and-mortar location away from home; and the modalities along each student's learning path within a course or subject are connected to provide an integrated learning experience.
>
> (Staker & Horn, 2012)

One important aspect of the Clayton Christensen Institute definition is that blended learning involves at least some "element of student control over time, place, path, and/or pace." This specification is to distinguish blended learning from the more common K–12 practice of technology-rich instruction, which takes place when a teacher uses technology-based enhancements, such as electronic whiteboards, broad access to Internet devices, document cameras, digital textbooks, Internet tools, and online lesson plans, but the students continue to learn in a mostly unified, monolithic way as a class (Staker & Horn, 2012). The authors of the annual *Keeping Pace with K–12 Online Learning* report comment that

> the main reason we like this definition is because of what it defines out; i.e. not within the definition of blended learning, including all sorts of

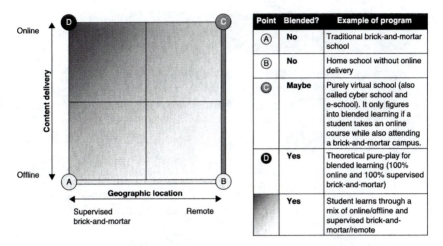

Point	Blended?	Example of program
(A)	No	Traditional brick-and-mortar school
(B)	No	Home school without online delivery
(C)	Maybe	Purely virtual school (also called cyber school and e-school). It only figures into blended learning if a student takes an online course while also attending a brick-and-mortar campus.
(D)	Yes	Theoretical pure-play for blended learning (100% online and 100% supervised brick-and-mortar)
	Yes	Student learns through a mix of online/offline and supervised brick-and-mortar/remote

FIGURE 19.2 Blended Learning Matrix and Examples of Points on the Matrix

Source: Adapted from 'The risk of K–12 blended learning: Profiles of emerging models,' by Heather Staker, 2011, p. 6. Copyright 2011 by Clayton Christensen Institute. Adapted with permission.

> educational technology applications that are layered onto a classroom or school without changing the instructional model.
>
> (Watson, Murin, Vashaw, Gemin, & Rapp, 2012, p. 15)

In contrast to blended learning at the postsecondary level, the phenomenon of blended learning at the K–12 level is best conceptualized as a matrix rather than a linear continuum. On the X-axis of the matrix is the geographic location of a typical student in the blended program, which ranges from 100 percent supervised brick-and-mortar to 100 percent remote—either at home, or some other place. On the Y-axis is the percent of time that a typical student in the program learns online, which ranges from 100 percent online learning to 100 percent offline. Figure 19.2 depicts this conceptualization and examples of different points on the matrix (Staker & Horn, 2012).

Models of K–12 Blended Learning[1]

The taxonomy in Figure 19.3 depicts a categorization scheme for the K–12 blended learning landscape as it currently exists based upon the Clayton Christensen Institute's analysis of programs that either are preparing to launch or are already in existence. The roughly 80 programs included in the study are highly varied in the way that students experienced their learning across several dimensions, including teacher roles, scheduling, physical space, and delivery methods. Their models fell into four distinct clusters, however, with each sharing design elements that distinguish them from

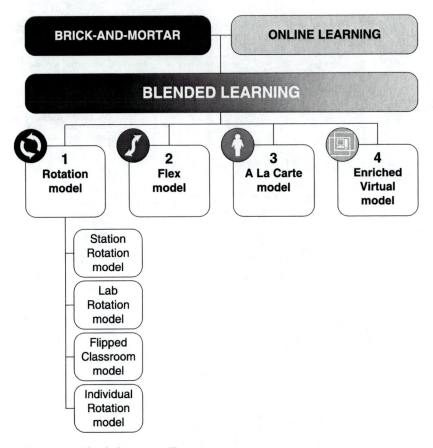

FIGURE 19.3   Blended Learning Taxonomy

Source: Adapted from 'Classifying K-12 blended learning,' by Heather Staker and Michael B. Horn, 2012, p. 2. Copyright 2012 by Clayton Christensen Institute. Adapted with permission.

the others. It is important to note that many school operators have implemented more than one blended learning model for their students. Accordingly, the models represent particular programs within a school, not a typology for whole-school design.

The first blended learning model that is beginning to appear with increasing frequency across the K–12 sector is the Rotation model, a program in which, within a given course or subject (e.g., math), students rotate *on a fixed schedule or at the teacher's discretion* between learning modalities, at least one of which is online learning. Other modalities might include activities such as small-group or full-class instruction, group projects, individual tutoring, and pencil-and-paper assignments. The Rotation model is now common enough that at least four different versions of it are evident. These four sub-models are:

1. *Station Rotation*—a Rotation-model implementation in which within a given course or subject (e.g., math), students rotate *on a fixed schedule or at the teacher's discretion* among classroom-based learning modalities. The rotation includes at least one station for online learning. Other stations might include activities such as small-group or full-class instruction, group projects, individual tutoring, and pencil-and-paper assignments. Some implementations involve the entire class alternating among activities together, whereas others divide the class into small-group or one-by-one rotations. The Station Rotation model differs from the Individual Rotation model because students rotate through all of the stations, not only those on their custom schedules.

    An example of the Station Rotation model is the KIPP Empower Academy, which in 2011–12 served roughly 230 kindergarten and first-grade students in South Los Angeles. Empower places its kindergarten students into heterogeneous, 28-student classes. Throughout the day the students rotate on a fixed schedule among online learning, small-group instruction with Lead Teachers, and small-group instruction with Intervention Teachers (Bernatek, Cohen, Hanlon, & Wilka, 2012).

2. *Lab Rotation*—a Rotation model implementation in which within a given course or subject (e.g., math), students rotate *on a fixed schedule or at the teacher's discretion* among locations on the brick-and-mortar campus. At least one of these spaces is a learning lab for predominantly online learning, while the additional classroom(s) house other learning modalities. The Lab Rotation model differs from the Station Rotation model because students rotate among locations on the campus instead of staying in one classroom for the blended course or subject.

    An example of the Lab Rotation model takes place at Rocketship Education, a network of five schools serving 2,400 K–5 students in San Jose, California. Up to four classes of students together cycle into a Learning Lab for 100-minute blocks. They spend 60 to 80 minutes of that time engaged in self-directed online learning under the supervision of a team of five Individualized Learning Specialists. They cycle to other classrooms for literacy, social studies, math, and science instruction with face-to-face teachers (Bernatek et al., 2012).

3. *Flipped Classroom*—a Rotation-model implementation in which within a given course or subject (e.g., math), students rotate *on a fixed schedule* between face-to-face teacher-guided practice (or projects) on campus during the standard school day and online delivery of content and instruc-tion of the same subject from a remote location (often home) after school. The primary delivery of content and instruction is online, which differen-tiates a Flipped Classroom from students who are merely doing homework practice online at night. The Flipped Classroom model accords with the idea that blended learning includes some element of student control over

time, place, path, and/or pace because the model allows students to choose the location where they receive content and instruction online.

An example of the Flipped Classroom takes place at Stillwater Area Public Schools along the St. Croix River in Minnesota, where students in grades 4–6 math classes use Internet-connected devices after school at the location of their choice to watch 10- to 15-minute asynchronous instruction videos and complete comprehension questions on Moodle. At school they practice and apply their learning with a face-to-face teacher.

4. *Individual Rotation*—a Rotation-model implementation in which within a given course or subject (e.g., math), students rotate on an *individually customized, fixed schedule* among learning modalities, at least one of which is online learning. An algorithm or teacher(s) sets individual student schedules. The Individual Rotation model differs from the other Rotation models because students do not necessarily rotate to each available station or modality.

An example of the Individual Rotation model takes place at Carpe Diem Collegiate High School and Middle School. There, the faculty assigns each student a specific schedule that rotates them between online learning in the learning center and offline learning. Each rotation lasts 35 minutes.

The second blended learning model depicted in Figure 19.3 is the Flex model. This model describes a program in which online learning is the backbone of student learning, even if it directs students to offline activities at times. Students move on an *individually customized, fluid schedule* among learning modalities, and the teacher of record is on-site. The teacher of record or other adults provide face-to-face support on a flexible and adaptive as-needed basis through activities such as small-group instruction, group projects, and individual tutoring. Some implementations have substantial face-to-face support, whereas others have minimal support. For example, some Flex models may have face-to-face certified teachers who supplement the online learning on a daily basis, whereas others may provide little face-to-face enrichment. Still others may have different staffing combinations. These variations are useful modifiers to describe a particular Flex model.

One example of a Flex-model implementation is the San Francisco Flex Academy, one of California's first full-time, 5-days-a-week blended learning high schools. At this chartered school, K12, Inc. delivers its catalog of online curriculum and instruction, while face-to-face teachers use a data dashboard to offer targeted interventions and supplementation throughout the day for core courses. The teachers of record for the core courses are the face-to-face teachers.

The third blended learning model from Figure 19.3 is the A La Carte model. This model describes a scenario in which students choose to take one or more courses entirely online to supplement their traditional courses and the teacher of record is the online teacher. Students may take the online courses either on the brick-and-mortar campus or off-site. This differs from full-time online learning and the Enriched Virtual model (see the next definition) because it is not a full-school experience. Students take some individual online courses and other courses at a brick-and-mortar campus with face-to-face teachers. The courses themselves in this example are of course not blended learning, but the overall student experience is.

Quakertown Community School District (QCSD) in Pennsylvania has reorganized its facilities and staffing to facilitate the A La Carte model. QCSD offers students in grades 6 through 12 the option of taking one or more online courses. All students complete a cyber orientation course prior to enrollment. Courses are asynchronous and students can work on them any time during the day. QCSD has created "cyber lounges" where students can work on their online courses at school, but they are also free to complete the courses remotely if they prefer. The teachers of record for the courses are the online teachers, most of whom also teach face to face courses for QCSD.

The fourth blended learning model from Figure 19.3 is the Enriched Virtual model. This model describes a full-school experience in which within each course (e.g., math), students divide their time between attending a brick-and-mortar campus and learning remotely using online delivery of content and instruction. Many Enriched Virtual programs began as full-time online schools and then developed blended programs to provide students with brick-and-mortar school experiences. The Enriched Virtual model differs from the Flipped Classroom because in Enriched Virtual programs, students seldom attend the brick-and-mortar campus every weekday. It differs from the A La Carte model because it is a full-school experience, not a course-by-course model.

For example, at the Albuquerque eCADEMY, students in grades 8–12 meet face-to-face with teachers for their first course meeting at a brick-and-mortar location. They can complete the rest of their coursework remotely, if they prefer, as long as they maintain at least a "C" grade point average in the program.

The Clayton Christensen Institute's taxonomy represents an early categorization scheme for the emerging K–12 blended learning landscape. It is certain to require an update as the field continues to improve upon the models and develop new approaches.

Blended Learning—A Disruptive Innovation?[2]

Few dispute that emerging blended learning models are bringing about significant changes for the K–12 sector. The questions arise, however, of which models are the most transformative? Which will have the most lasting impact? Which should be pursued most enthusiastically?

Professor Clayton M. Christensen of Harvard Business School developed a set of theories about innovation that can shine a light on those questions. He found that most innovations fall within one of two categories: those that sustain the established system, and those that disrupt it. The purpose of some innovations is to improve the performance of established products along the dimensions of performance that mainstream customers in major markets have historically valued. Christensen calls these *sustaining innovations*. Commercial enterprises pursue sustaining innovations so that they can sell them for better profits to their best customers (Christensen, 1997). Airplanes that fly farther, computers that process faster, cellular phone batteries that last longer, and televisions with clearer images are all examples of sustaining innovations (Christensen, Horn, & Johnson, 2010).

Public agencies consistently pursue sustaining innovations as well. They are motivated by political and social priorities instead of by profit, but they engage in the upward march nonetheless. Sustaining innovations have left a profound mark on postsecondary institutions, which compete to deliver better sports teams, publish more acclaimed research, and recruit the most elite students (Christensen & Eyring, 2011). K–12 public schools have likewise pursued sustaining innovations aggressively. Today public schools deliver countless programs and services that rarely existed before the mid-twentieth century, including physical education, health education, summer school, school lunch programs, counselors, and medical and dental care (Christensen, Horn, & Johnson, 2010).

Whereas sustaining innovations help established organizations improve their ability to serve mainstream customers, another type of innovation— *disruptive innovation*—presents an even more powerful force in transforming industries. Disruptive innovations tend to be simpler and more affordable than existing products. This allows them to take root in simple, undemanding applications within a new market or arena of competition. Little by little, disruptions predictably improve. At some point, disruptive innovations become good enough to handle more complicated problems—and then they take over and supplant the old way of doing things (Christensen, 1997).

The introduction of the personal computer is a clear example of the power of disruptive innovation. Prior to the introduction of the personal computer, the least expensive computer was the minicomputer. It cost well over $200,000, was the size of a filing cabinet, and essentially required an engineering degree to operate. The personal computer entered the scene in the 1970s and 1980s, but mainstream customers, as well as minicomputer companies, paid little attention to it because its processing power was so inferior to that of minicomputers. Apple, one of the pioneers in personal computing, originally sold their early computers as a toy to children. Children had been nonconsumers of computers before, so they did not care that the product was not as good as minicomputers (Christensen, Horn, & Johnson, 2010).

But little by little the disruption improved. Apple, Dell, and other personal computer makers introduced what for them were sustaining innovations and eventually, the personal computer became capable of doing work that previously required minicomputers. This made computing widespread and cheaper. It left almost everyone—except minicomputer companies—better off (Christensen, Horn, & Johnson, 2010).

Which are better, disruptive or sustaining innovations? The answer, arguably, is neither. Minicomputer companies performed a vital function as they invested in sustaining innovations to make their computers bigger and more powerful for their best customers. Meanwhile, the inventors of the personal computer performed a great service to other customers, who needed something smaller, cheaper, and easier to use. Sustaining innovations are absolutely vital to a healthy and robust sector, and disruptive innovations are crucial for bringing into reach different value propositions for new markets.

To return to the topic of K–12 blended learning, is the appearance of blended learning across the K–12 landscape indicative of a disruptive or sustaining innovation? Christensen has helped answer that question with his observations about hybrid technologies. He noted that whenever a disruptive technology emerges, the leading firms in the field often do attempt to adopt it, but they do so as a *sustaining innovation*, generally by creating a hybrid solution that marries the old technology with the new to create something that performs better along the initial definition of performance to serve their existing customers (Christensen, 1997).

The history of excavators provides an illuminating example from an admittedly very different industry. Prior to World War II, huge excavators that dug holes and trenches relied on a system of pulleys, cables, and drums to manipulate their big buckets. But in 1947, a new mechanism emerged for extending and lifting the bucket: hydraulically actuated systems. The first hydraulic excavators had limited power and strength, they could only move a limited amount of earth with each scoop, and they had minimal reach. Because their capacity was so small and their reach so short, hydraulic excavators were of no use for general excavation and mining. As a result, the entrant firms had to find new applications for their products. To their delight, they found that small residential contractors actually preferred the new machines. The smaller machines allowed them to dig narrow ditches for water and sewer lines for houses under construction. Cable-actuated excavators were much too large and imprecise for the job, so before the arrival of hydraulic excavators, residential contractors had to dig trenches by hand. The hydraulic excavators offered a welcomed solution to nonconsumers (Christensen, 1997).

Meanwhile, Bucyrus Erie, the leading cable shovel maker, was aware of the emergence of the hydraulic excavating technology, but faced a predicament. Its most important mainstream customers, the general excavators and miners, had no use for a weak, low capacity, short-reach hydraulic excavator. Bucyrus's response was to try to offer "the best of both worlds"—the power, capacity, and reach of a cable-actuated system, blended with the precision and maneuverability of a hydraulic excavator. In 1951 it introduced the "Hydrahoe." This new machine featured hydraulic cylinders to curl and draw the shovel, and at the same time, a cable mechanism to lift the shovel. The Hydrahoe was a *hybrid* of the two technologies (Christensen, 1997).

Other excavator companies also experimented with using hydraulics to serve their existing customers. Over the long-term, however, the new entrants who developed pure hydraulic excavators for residential contractors improved upon their technology enough that the hydraulic excavators were able to address the needs of mainstream excavation contractors. The established firms and hybrid machines lost the contest. Today, hydraulic systems have replaced cable-actuated excavators entirely (Christensen, 1997).

Bucyrus had two options when it wanted to participate in the hydraulics opportunity. The *sustaining* option was to invent a hybrid product that would allow it to market hydraulics to its existing customers while continuing to deliver the performance that cable-actuated machines offered. The *disruptive* option was to find a new market that would value the pure-play hydraulic technology for what it was—smaller, simpler, and more maneuverable. Bucyrus chose the sustaining, hybrid strategy. As a result, it missed the larger disruption that eventually occurred in the industry as pure hydraulic technology became good enough to meet the needs of mainstream general excavators and miners (Christensen, Horn, & Staker, 2013).

A similar choice may be confronting those who are interested in bringing online learning to the schoolhouse. The analogy goes like this: online learning is like hydraulics and the traditional classroom is like the old cable-actuated system. The *sustaining* option is to invent a hybrid solution that gives educators "the best of both worlds"—the advantages of online learning combined with all the benefits of the traditional classroom. The *disruptive* option is to deploy pure-play online learning in new models that depart from the traditional classroom and target nonconsumers who value the new technology for what it is—more customizable, affordable, and convenient. The decision is important because in the end disruptions almost always become good enough to meet the needs of mainstream customers. In other words, the disruptive models almost always overtake the sustaining models over the very long term (Christensen, Horn, & Staker, 2013).

The gray box in Figure 19.4 represents the *hybrid zone of blended learning*. The models that fall within this zone bear many of the traits of both online learning and the traditional classroom. When viewed through the lens of Disruptive Innovation Theory, the models in the hybrid zone appear to be sustaining innovations relative to the traditional classroom.

Most of the Rotation models fall within the hybrid zone because they continue to do the job of the traditional classroom. They help to keep students in their seats in the classroom for the prescribed number of minutes, and they preserve the general structure of facilities, staffing, and school operations.

For example, the Station Rotation model uses the same concept of station rotation that has existed in primary schools for decades, and then merely

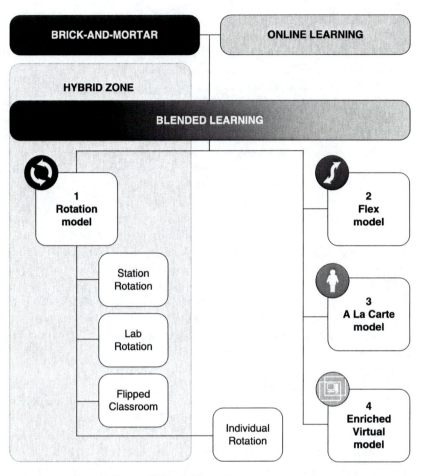

FIGURE 19.4   Hybrid Zone of Blended Learning

Source: Adapted from 'Is K-12 blended learning disruptive?,' by Clayton M. Christensen, Michael B. Horn, and Heather Staker, 2013, p. 29. Copyright 2013 by Clayton Christensen Institute. Adapted with permission.

adds an online station. At KIPP Empower, blended learning facilitates a marginal increase in the student–teacher ratio, but the traditional structure of age-based cohorts, the number and size of classrooms, and the role of face-to-face instruction remain largely intact. Similarly, the Lab Rotation model starts with the traditional classroom and then merely adds a rotation to a computer or learning lab. At Rocketship, students cycle to the Learning Labs for 100 minutes, but the rest of their program hinges on direct classroom instruction. Its rotations may drive operational efficiency and facilitate personalized instruction, but they do not replace the emphasis on "traditional" instruction in the classroom. The Flipped Classroom model also continues to do the job of the traditional classroom. Although teachers are implementing it in different ways, in general the Flipped Classroom is emerging as a technique that traditional teachers can use to improve student engagement, rather than an innovation that upends school operations.

Indicative of their sustaining nature, the Station Rotation, Lab Rotation, and Flipped Classroom models can all be implemented without major revisions to the resource allocations or processes already in place at a school. None of the models requires significant changes to physical facilities, staffing, or scheduling (although several, like Rocketship, do use the Lab Rotation model to make some significant changes to these elements, it is not a requisite of the model). Each introduces a hybrid solution that marries the traditional classroom with a new technology—online learning—to create something that performs better along the initial definition of what a good classroom is meant to do.

In contrast, the Flex, A La Carte, and Enriched Virtual models, as well as the Individual Rotation model, each have the potential to be disruptive relative to the traditional classroom, particularly at the secondary school level. They come at blended learning from a fundamentally different vantage point. Instead of beginning with the basic classroom and then asking how online learning can improve it, these models do the reverse. They start with the online courses and then look at how classroom experiences can enhance the virtual. Many of the traditional constructs of schooling are irrelevant in these models. Students in Flex programs have no need for age-based cohorts because all are moving through courses and modules at their own paces and on their own schedules. Students in Enriched Virtual programs divide their time between learning at a brick-and-mortar location and learning remotely online. They seldom visit the classroom every weekday, and that untethering from their seats has all sorts of implications for facility and faculty utilization. Students in the A La Carte model dispense with the traditional classroom altogether for certain courses. Theirs is the clearest case of pure disruption.

The Individual Rotation model is the one Rotation model that has disruptive rather than sustaining characteristics. It differs from other Rotation models because students do not necessarily rotate to each available station or modality. Some students might learn completely online if that method works best for them. To implement an Individual Rotation model requires a fundamental redesign of staffing, facilities, and scheduling. Interestingly enough, two of the most visible Individual Rotation models—that used at Carpe Diem schools and in School of One (now called New Classrooms)—literally do away with the traditional classroom altogether and create a significantly larger open learning space as the main room for students.

As disruptive models of blended learning become better and better, the fascinating question is this: what is to become of the school and classroom? The majority of students in America need school—or a supervised place to learn. Various societal stakeholders "hire" schools to do many things for their children, just one of which is learning. A custodial job—keeping children safe—is equally important for many. Schools provide important social services, which range from counseling and mentoring to health services and free meals—and in the years ahead, schools will likely provide more of these services, not fewer, for some students. From the perspective of children, having a place to have fun with friends is also vital. In the future, the importance of the traditional classroom will likely diminish. But schools will still play an essential function in delivering other important jobs. Over the long-term, they will have the luxury of focusing their resources on truly nailing those jobs while online learning takes on more of the responsibility of managing the delivery of content and instruction.

Policy Suggestions from Blended Learning Operators

As stated earlier, both sustaining and disruptive innovations are vital to a healthy and robust education sector. Several Rotation-model implementations that are sustaining the traditional classroom are beginning to produce improved state test scores and cost savings, which the schools can then reinvest in other parts of their models. These innovations are breakthrough improvements. Meanwhile, disruptive models of blended learning are introducing new value propositions to the K12 sector, such as the ability to offer Advanced Placement and elective courses for little cost to rural schools; access to 24/7 learning for students who have work and family obligations; and credit-recovery options for students who must retake a course or unit to graduate. Society benefits from allowing the force of disruption to distribute more affordable, accessible education options to those without a realistic alternative. Disruptive innovations are singularly capable of inciting a transformation.

The most significant barrier to encouraging high-quality innovation in the K–12 sector is a regulatory environment that does not incentivize the right experiments. In May 2011 the Clayton Christensen Institute (formerly named Innosight Institute) published profiles of 40 early blended learning programs that are emerging across the United States. Along with those profiles, the report summarized feedback from the program operators about how to improve regulation to allow them to implement their models more effectively (Staker, 2011). Interestingly, the leaders of programs with more disruptive blended learning models were much more vocal about desired policy changes to advance their programs than were their counterparts with sustaining models. The following example illustrates one operator's struggles to build a transformative program in the current policy environment.

Carpe Diem (CDCHS) is a charter school serving grades 6 through 12 in Yuma, Ariz. It began in 2000 as a traditional high school that served nearly 300 students in face-to-face classrooms. In 2005, the owners of the facility that CDCHS was renting decided to sell the property. Without a building, Executive Director Rick Ogston and his team felt they had no option but to resort to online learning to stay within budget. Within a few months, school leaders put in place an Individual Rotation model that had the hallmarks of a disruptive innovation. Instead of traditional classrooms, CDCHS's new building featured 300 cubicles housed in a central learning center. CDCHS only retained six certified teachers, along with several paraprofessionals. Students rotated between e2020 software at their computer workstations and direct instruction with face-to-face teachers (Staker, 2011).

By 2010, CDCHS ranked first in its county in student performance in math and reading and ranked among the top 10 percent of Arizona charter schools. *Businessweek* recognized CDCHS as one of the top high schools in America in its 2009 report, and *U.S. News & World Report* gave CDCHS the same recognition in its 2010 report (Staker, 2011).

Despite his success, Ogston said that policy hurdles were compromising CDCHS's effectiveness. His biggest concern was with funding. He said that because state funding allocations for schools were unpredictable and unstable, his school administrators were unnecessarily crippled in their budgeting and planning abilities. He also said that federal stimulus funding often has replaced—not added to—education allocations from the states, and these federal monies usually carry more restrictive, time intensive, and unwieldy auditing and compliance mandates, thus leaving schools with less money than before the stimulus funds were offered. Finally, Ogston said that federal requirements about the "highly qualified teacher" designation are preventing him from hiring knowledgeable content experts (Staker, 2011).

Other operators listed dozens of additional laws and regulations that hindered their ability to restructure their classrooms to leverage the positive aspects of blended learning. They asked policymakers, state boards of education, and state departments of education to encourage the upgrade of the K–12 education system by taking measures to withdraw policies that no longer fit the new classroom structures that online learning enables. One leader summed up the consensus when he said that any policy about procedure, rather than performance, undermines the creation of a child-centered system (Staker, 2011).

Even if policymakers do nothing, disruptive innovations have a way of transforming industries. Mail delivery in the United States has forever changed because of email, without any reregulation of the U.S. Postal Service. Online learning already has begun to transform K–12 education, and it is starting to blend into brick-and-mortar schools. Blended learning models in the hybrid zone of blended learning will likely sustain the traditional classroom for years to come. They provide important new methods for schools to improve operational efficiency and boost outcomes. Meanwhile, the more disruptive blended learning models will get better and better. If they continue to follow the disruptive pattern, they have the potential to overtake the traditional classroom structure over the longer term, particularly at the secondary school level.

Notes

1 This section is mostly extracted from *Classifying K–12 blended learning* (Staker & Horn, 2012).
2 This section is mostly extracted from *Is K–12 blended learning disruptive?* (Christensen, Horn, & Staker, 2013).

References

Allen, I. E., & Seaman, J. (2006). *Making the grade: Online education in the United States, 2006.* Needham, MA: The Sloan Consortium. Retrieved from http://sloanconsortium.org/publications/survey/making_the_grade_2006

Allen, I., & Seaman, J. (2011). *Going the distance: Online education in the United States, 2011.* Wellesley, MA: Babson Survey Research Group. Retrieved from www.onlinelearningsurvey.com/reports/goingthedistance.pdf

Bernatek, B., Cohen, J., Hanlon, J., & Wilka, M. (2012). *Blended learning in practice: Case studies from leading schools, featuring Kipp Empower Academy.* Austin, TX: Michael & Susan Dell Foundation. Retrieved from http://5a03f68e230384a218e0-938ec019df699e606c950a5614b999bd.r33.cf2.rackcdn.com/Blended_Learning_Kipp_083012.pdf

Bernatek, B., Cohen, J., Hanlon, J., & Wilka, M. (2012). *Blended learning in practice: Case studies from leading schools, featuring Rocketship Education.* Austin, TX: Michael & Susan Dell Foundation. Retrieved from http://5a03f68e230384a218e0-938ec019df699e606c950a5614b999bd.r33.cf2.rackcdn.com/msdf-rocketship_04.pdf

Christensen, C. M. (1997). *The innovator's dilemma.* New York, NY: Collins Business Essentials.

Christensen, C. M. & Eyring, J. (2011). *The innovative university: Changing the DNA of higher education from the inside out.* San Francisco: Jossey-Bass.

Christensen, C. M., Horn, M. B., Caldera, L., & Soares, L. (2011). *Disrupting college: How disruptive innovation can deliver quality and affordability to postsecondary education.* Washington, DC: Center for American Progress. Retrieved from www.americanprogress.org/wp-content/uploads/issues/2011/02/pdf/disrupting_college.pdf

Christensen, C. M., Horn, M. B., & Johnson, C. W. (2010). *Disrupting class: How disruptive innovation will change the way the world learns* (updated ed.). New York, NY: McGraw Hill.

Christensen, C. M., Horn, M. B., & Staker, H. (2013). *Is K–12 blended learning disruptive?* San Mateo, CA: Clayton Christensen Institute.

Staker, H. (2011). *The rise of K–12 blended learning: Profiles of emerging models.* Mountain View, CA: Clayton Christensen Institute.

Staker, H. & Horn, M. B. (2012). *Classifying K–12 blended learning.* Mountain View, CA: Clayton Christensen Institute.

Watson, J., Murin, A., Vashaw, L., Gemin, B., & Rapp, C. (2012). *Keeping pace with K–12 online learning: An annual review of policy and practice, 2012.* Durango, CO: Evergreen Education Group. Retrieved from http://kpk12.com/cms/wp-content/uploads/KeepingPace2012.pdf

20

BLENDED LEARNING IN NEW YORK CITY

The iLearnNYC Program

Anne-Marie Hoxie, Jennifer Stillman, and Kara Chesal

Blended learning—a hybrid of online and face-to-face learning—has the potential to better personalize learning for students, as computer algorithms can potentially differentiate learning in a way that is practically impossible for a single teacher in a room full of 34 children. In a high poverty school district like New York City, where approximately 75% of the students receive free or reduced lunch, blended learning's potential becomes even more important. Urban communities tend to have students with greater needs than their more affluent suburban counterparts, as well as students who vary widely in ability level, circumstances that blended learning pedagogies can possibly support.

Blended learning is, in some respects, the modern incarnation of mastery learning (Bloom, 1968). With a mastery learning approach, teachers don't move on until all students master a concept, and teachers ensure this happens through instructional variation. Research suggests that there are positive effects from mastery learning on cognitive and achievement outcomes, students' confidence in learning situations, school attendance rates, involvement in class sessions, students' attitude toward learning, and a variety of other affective measures (Guskey, 2007, pp. 23–24). Despite these positive results, mastery learning is difficult to implement, and is not widely practiced. Blended learning, with its regular use of online learning courseware that can potentially help teachers differentiate student assignments, combined with face-to-face teacher instruction, might be able to help teachers more easily vary instruction to the degree necessary for mastery learning to succeed on a wide scale.

Because of this potential, blended learning has become increasingly prevalent in schools around the country (Barbour et al., 2012). Despite higher levels of implementation, however, blended learning remains an imprecise and evolving concept, making it difficult to research its effectiveness. The Innosight

Institute is a leader in attempting to codify blended learning, and they have been tweaking their definition over the past couple of years. Their most recent definition states:

> Blended learning is a formal education program in which a student learns at least in part through online delivery of content and instruction with some element of student control over time, place, path, and/or pace *and* at least in part at a supervised brick-and-mortar location away from home.
>
> (Staker & Horn, 2012, p. 3)

They further define different types of blended learning in terms of where students do their online learning, and how often they are engaged in online learning versus face-to-face learning.

This chapter will focus on how schools within the New York City Department of Education's Innovation Zone (iZone) are implementing blended learning, using the Innosight Institute's blended learning typology to examine teacher survey data about blended learning's perceived impact on student learning and on their own practice. Our analysis explores whether some approaches to blended learning are better than others, from the teacher perspective, as well as whether teachers' choices around online content impact their perceptions of blended learning's effectiveness, an aspect of blended learning that has been only minimally explored in the existing blended learning literature. Additionally, we use student survey data to explore blended learning's impact on student intrinsic motivation and self-directed learning, as well as student satisfaction with blended learning's ability to meet their learning needs. Specifically, this chapter seeks to answer the following research questions:

1. Flex v. Rotation Teachers: Are there differences in teachers' sense of efficacy and their perceptions of blended learning's impact on students between those who use a "Flex" versus a "Rotation" approach to blended learning?
2. Creator v. Utilizer Teachers: Are there differences in teachers' sense of efficacy and their perceptions of blended learning's impact on students between teachers who create their own course content, the "Creators," and those who use vendor created content, the "Utilizers"?
3. Student impact: How do students describe their experience with blended learning? What impact has participation in blended courses had on students' academic motivation and self-directed learning?

Context

The New York City Department of Education (NYCDOE) is the largest public school system in the United States, serving over 1.1 million students in nearly 1,700 schools. The NYCDOE employs approximately 75,000 teachers, and has a highly diverse student population: 40% of students are Hispanic, 32% are black, 14% white, and 13% Asian. Roughly 40% of NYC students live in homes with a primary language other than English, and 75% of students receive free or reduced lunch.

Such a large school system creates both challenges and opportunities to maximize classroom resourcing and student performance. Politically, a mayor-appointed chancellor leads the NYCDOE, overseeing 32 community school districts, each with a superintendent responsible for management, principal appointments, and tenure decisions. Despite this centralized infrastructure, most of the NYCDOE system is based on the principle of localized decision-making. Within the larger DOE, there are 60 school support networks, known as Children First Networks (CFNs), that serve as an instructional and leadership support system for schools. Schools review their needs and budgetary priorities, and select the most appropriate CFN to join.

An overarching goal of the NYCDOE is to prepare students to graduate from high school career and college ready. After consulting with schools, CFNs, and a wide variety of innovative education thinkers, the NYCDOE determined that a critical lever to achieving this goal is shifting schools away from the current, standardized way of teaching and learning to a much more personalized approach that meets the needs, strengths, and motivations of each individual student. The NYCDOE created the Innovation Zone (iZone) to pioneer this new way of organizing the education experience for NYC students. The following four principles comprise the iZone Framework:

- Next Generation Curriculum and Assessment—Schools and staff design and implement engaging competency-based curricula and rigorous performance tasks to help understand each student's strengths and meet their needs.
- Personalized Learning Plans and Progress—Teachers, advisors, students, and parents manage a personalized learning plan that accounts for each student's learning pace and preferred learning methods. Personalized Learning Plans transform the roles of students and staff to increase student ownership and engagement.
- Flexible and Real-World Learning Environments—Students learn in the way they learn best—be it independently, one-on-one with a coach, collaboratively in small groups, online, or beyond school in real-world contexts, such as internships or early college courses. Teachers incorporate learning settings that use space, scheduling, and technology flexibly in order to meet each student's needs.
- New Staff and Student Roles—School staff and teacher teams adopt new roles as learning coaches, advisors, content experts, and assessment experts. Students take on new roles planning and managing their own learning in

a variety of modalities. As a result, students have more ownership of and are more engaged in their learning process, and schools have greater flexibility in scheduling appropriate learning supports based on students' personalized learning plans and staff talent.

While all iZone schools and CFNs are broadly organized around the strategies listed above, the iZone differentiates strategies based on the readiness, interest, and capability of individual schools and CFNs. iZone schools thus participate in one or more of three initiatives in the iZone's current portfolio:

- iZone360: iZone360 CFNs and schools commit to reorganizing all of their resources and school practice areas, including budgets, staff, space, instruction, scheduling, and technology, around meeting the needs of individual students. These CFNs and schools are supported by a full-time Innovation Coach and are working with partners with expertise in student-centered school design and development.
- InnovateNYC: InnovateNYC manages the iZone's portfolio of early-stage innovations with high potential for transforming schools toward more personalized, student-centered models. InnovateNYC recruits schools with the capacity to pilot innovations, evaluates impact on practice and student outcomes, and provides feedback to partners on product design. Promising innovations are expanded through other iZone initiatives or scaled system wide. The portfolio includes School of One, several personalized learning systems for elementary school students that use adaptive learning algorithms to personalize learning progressions, and the construction of an innovation ecosystem to match software developers with educators for rapid prototyping and research.
- iLearnNYC: iLearnNYC, which is New York City's blended learning initiative and the focus of this chapter, supports schools interested in using blended learning models to better personalize learning to the needs, motivations, and strengths of individual students. iLearnNYC gives teachers access to a wide variety of online tools to help them better vary instruction to meet each student at his/her level, something that can be a challenge in a large, diverse classroom.

In the 2011–2012 school year, the iLearnNYC program provided 124 schools with access to the Desire2Learn (D2L) learning management system (LMS), and online content from a wide variety of vendors. Vendors were chosen by an iLearnNYC selection committee that reviewed the content using both International Association of K–12 Online Learning (iNACOL) and Southern Regional Education Board (SREB) guidelines. The Request for Proposals (RFP) selection process accounted for the following:

- Quality and type of content
- Quality of user experience
- Ability to meet specifications for integrating into the iLearnNYC online learning platform
- Value of content and supporting services
- Program plan
- Organizational capacity
- Past demonstrated effectiveness
- Submitted price

The committee also did extensive testing with two courses from each vendor, and then further narrowed the pool based on which vendors met technical criteria established by the NYCDOE's Division of Instructional and Information Technology. Implementation managers were centrally hired to troubleshoot technical and pedagogical issues and support iLearnNYC schools. Teachers in iLearnNYC schools were also invited to attend summer professional development sessions and additional training throughout the school year with D2L, vendors, and iLearnNYC pedagogical experts.

iLearnNYC is a non-prescriptive program, operating on the premise that schools should be empowered to use online learning tools for blended learning in a way that makes the most sense for their unique student populations and school culture. This open playing field has facilitated a wide variety of implementation strategies, and iLearnNYC blended classrooms vary widely in the time students spend learning online versus how much time they spend learning face to face, and in the content choices made by iLearnNYC teachers. Variation in teachers' approaches allowed us to explore how different blended choices affect teacher perceptions of what blended learning can do for students and teachers. Our findings, presented below, provide an early indicator that some blended learning approaches might have greater potential to improve education than others.

Data and Methods

Participants

This study uses teacher and student survey data, captured from New York City middle- and high-school teachers and students who participated in the iLearnNYC blended learning program during the 2011–2012 school year. All 125 schools that participated in the iLearnNYC program were asked to complete surveys in both the Fall and Spring as part of a larger evaluation study of the New York City Department of Education's iZone. There were 38 middle schools and 87 high schools that participated in the iLearnNYC initiative. Each school typically had only a handful of teachers who implemented blended learning; this was decided at the school level and varied school by school. Teacher data in this study are drawn from teachers' Spring survey: 197 teachers in 54 schools completed surveys through an online survey tool. Student data in this study are drawn from both Fall *and* Spring surveys. A total of 799 students in 33 schools completed Fall and Spring surveys, providing change data on a series of student scales. Surveys were open for one month to allow teachers and students ample time to complete the online surveys.

Teacher Measures

Teacher survey questions were crafted using qualitative data collected during extensive observations of blended classrooms, through interviews with teachers about their blended learning experience, and through evaluating the existing literature on blended learning. Each specific measure is described below.

Flex v. Rotation

The Spring 2012 iLearnNYC survey asked teachers to indicate their approach to blended learning from a list of choices. We developed these choices using our own observational data and by building upon the work already done by *The Innosight Institute*, whose four models are as follows:

1. Rotation: students rotate between learning activities, one of which is online learning;
2. Flex: students primarily learn online, but work individually with a teacher based on the data generated online;
3. Self-Blend: students choose to take online courses as a supplement to their traditional schooling; and
4. Enriched Virtual: students primarily take all of their courses online, but congregate periodically at a school site for supplemental learning and connection.

In New York City, models 3 and 4 are not currently an option, so our teacher survey questions honed in on just Rotation and Flex. We offered the Rotation model as three different choices, because our classroom observations and teacher interviews indicated that there was wide variation in how teachers approached a Rotation model, and we hoped to capture this variation for analysis. While the Innosight Institute also further refines the Rotation model, our surveys were in the field prior to their most recent release of model definitions, and thus there is minor variation between their language and ours. Our final survey choices for teachers were as follows:

1. Flex—My students work in the iLearnNYC platform, using vendor content all class period in a lab or with laptops. My students are all working on different courses or on the same course at their own pace. My main role is a facilitator and mentor.
2. Rotation: Online Dominant—I use the iLearnNYC platform/vendor content as the primary driver of class instruction. I introduce the day's lesson at the beginning of class with some kind of activity, and conclude class with a group discussion based on what students were doing online with vendor content, but students spend most of their time in the iLearnNYC platform.
3. Rotation: Online Supplement—I use the iLearnNYC platform/vendor content to enhance my lessons, and my students rotate between classroom experiences. The rotation includes at least one segment for online learning, and then other segment(s) for activities such as teacher-led small-group or full-class instruction, group projects, and pencil-and-paper assignments. This can include the entire class alternating among activities together, small groups rotating among stations, or the classroom moving between a lab and a face-to-face setting.
4. Rotation: Flipped—I use the iLearnNYC platform/vendor content for flipped instruction, where students watch video lessons or independently learn new skills and content at home. When students come to class, I can work with them on practice problems, small group instruction, and projects based on prior learning.

For our final analysis, all teachers who selected one of the three Rotation models described above were coded as "Rotation teachers," as there was not a large enough sample size for each sub-categorization to conduct analysis. Teachers who selected the Flex description were labeled as "Flex teachers."

Creator v. Utilizer

Our classroom observations and interviews with blended teachers indicated that there was wide variation in the way that teachers approached online content. While many were selecting the vendor content they found most appropriate and useful for their students, others were creating their own content, devoting a great deal of time to developing an online space of their own creation. These different approaches appeared worthy of further analysis. The Spring 2012 iLearnNYC survey asked teachers to indicate their level of use—often, sometimes, or never—in response to the following questions:

1. "I use vendor content 'chunks' that I choose and curate";
2. "I use vendor content as it is presented and sequenced"; and
3. "I use my own content embedded in an online platform."

Teachers who created their own content either some or all of the time were coded as "Creators." Teachers who never created their own content, and instead relied upon the materials supplied by online learning vendors, were coded as "Utilizers."

Perceptions of Blended Learning's Impact on Students

The Spring 2012 iLearn NYC survey included a series of questions designed to measure teacher perceptions of how blended learning is impacting their students. Questions focused on those areas where the architects of the iLearnNYC program think blended learning should make a difference: student engagement, student motivation, higher-order thinking, self-regulation, personalization, and college and career readiness. Teachers were asked to rate their agreement with a series of statements about blended learning's impact on students on a five-point scale (1—Strongly Disagree, 2—Disagree, 3—Neutral, 4—Agree, 5—Strongly Agree). Responses were re-coded into a four-point scale, with those who were neutral filtered out of the data set. Mean effect sizes in Table 20.1 and 20.4 refer to this scale where 3 is now equal to Agree, and 4 is now equal to Strongly Agree.

Perceptions of Blended Learning's Impact on Teacher Efficacy

The Spring 2012 iLearn NYC survey also included a series of questions designed to measure teacher perceptions of how blended learning is impacting their own practice, such as their ability to meet every student's learning needs, and their feelings of satisfaction, success, and efficiency. Teachers were asked to rate their agreement with a series of statements about blended learning's impact on their own practice on a four-point scale (1—Strongly Disagree, 2—Disagree, 3—Agree, 4—Strongly Agree). Mean effect sizes in Table 20.2 and 20.5 refer to this scale.

Teachers were also given the Teacher Efficacy Scale (Tschannen-Moran & Woolfolk-Hoy, 2001), which asks teachers 12 questions about what they think they can do in the classroom to influence a variety of classroom variables, such as controlling disruptive behavior, crafting good questions, motivating students to value learning, and providing alternative explanations when students are confused. Choices for questions are: 1—Nothing, 2—Very Little, 3—Some Influence, 4—Quite a Bit, 5—A Great Deal. All answers are averaged into a single efficacy score that ranges between 1 and 5.

Student Measures

Student survey questions were designed to gauge student satisfaction with the iLearnNYC experience, and to measure college and career readiness outcomes that the iLearnNYC program seeks to impact. Each measure is described below.

Academic Motivation

Student motivation was assessed using the Academic Motivation Scale (Vallerand et al., 1992), a 28-item instrument grounded in Self-Determination Theory to gauge student extrinsic, intrinsic, and amotivation factors. The Academic Motivation Scale generates a motivational "score," indicating the comparative level of student motivation from internal and external factors. Because of iLearnNYC's focus on boosting student independence in the online space, our analysis focused on the intrinsic motivation subscale, which consists of four questions that capture a student's intrinsic motivation to know, four questions that capture a student's intrinsic motivation toward accomplishment, and four questions that capture a student's intrinsic motivation to experience stimulation. All questions are prefaced with: "Why do you go to school?" This phrase is then followed by a series of answers that students must rank on a 1 to 7 scale; 1 is "Does not correspond at all," 7 is "Corresponds exactly." A sample intrinsic motivation to know answer is, "Because I experience pleasure and satisfaction while learning new things."

Self-Directed Learning

A student's ability to direct his or her own learning was measured using the Self-Directed Learning Scale (Lounsbury, Levy, Park, Gibson, & Smith, 2009). According to the scale's authors, self-directed learning is "a disposition to engage in learning activities where the individual takes personal responsibility for developing and carrying out learning endeavors in an autonomous manner without being prompted or guided by other people." The Self-Directed Learning Scale is a 10-item instrument, with responses made on a five-point Likert scale (1— Strongly Disagree, 2—Disagree, 3—Neutral/Undecided, 4—Agree, 5—Strongly agree). Students are asked about the extent to which they regularly learn things on their own outside of class, set goals for themselves, and find the resources they need to help themselves answer questions.

Student Learning Needs met by Blended Learning

To determine the extent to which blended learning better meets students' needs, from their perspective, the iLearnNYC Spring survey asked students to indicate whether they were more likely to get assignments that are at the right level for them in their iLearnNYC blended courses than in their non-iLearnNYC courses. Answer choices were "sometimes," "yes," or "no," and students were left in these three categories for analysis.

Student Satisfaction with Blended Learning

The level of satisfaction students had with their blended experience was measured by asking students how likely they were to take a blended course again during the next school year. Answer choices were "very likely," "somewhat likely," and "not at all likely," and students were grouped by these responses for analysis.

Data Analysis

We used different data analysis methodology for each of our research questions. Methods for each are described in detail below.

Flex v. Rotation Teachers

*   Are there differences in teachers' sense of efficacy and their perceptions of blended learning's impact on students between those who use a "Flex" versus a "Rotation" approach to blended learning?

To explore whether there is a relationship between teacher approaches to blended learning, and their perceptions of how blended learning is impacting both students and their own craft, we used an independent samples T-Test to compare the mean responses of Flex teachers with the mean responses of Rotation teachers to the survey questions that ask teachers about how they perceive blended learning's impact.

Creator v. Utilizer Teachers

*   Are there differences in teachers' sense of efficacy and their perceptions of blended learning's impact on students between teachers who create their own course content, the "Creators," and those who use vendor created content, the "Utilizers"?

To explore whether there is a relationship between teacher content decisions in a blended class and their perceptions of how blended learning is impacting students, we used an independent samples T-Test to compare the mean responses of Creators with the mean responses of Utilizers to the survey questions that ask teachers about how they perceive blended learning's impact.

Student Impact

*   How do students describe their experience with blended learning? What impact has participation in blended courses had on students' academic motivation and self-directed learning?

Two sets of ANOVAs were conducted to answer these questions. In the first set, two between-subjects ANOVAs were calculated with intrinsic motivation as the dependent variable. In the first analysis, students' self-reported learning needs being met was the independent variable and in the second, students' satisfaction with blended learning was the independent variable. In the second set of ANOVAs, self-directed learning was the dependent variable with students' self-reported learning needs being met as the first independent variable and students' satisfaction with blended learning as the second.

Findings

Flex v. Rotation Teachers

- Are there differences in teachers' sense of efficacy and their perceptions of blended learning's impact on students between those who use a "Flex" versus a "Rotation" approach to blended learning?

Our analysis suggests that teachers who used a Rotation approach to blended learning compared with those who used a Flex approach showed significant difference in their attitudes toward what blended learning can do for students (Table 20.1).

On average, teachers who used a Rotation approach have a more positive opinion of what blended learning is doing for their students than do the teachers who were implementing a Flex approach. Rotation teachers were more likely to agree or strongly agree that blended learning makes students more engaged with content (M = 3.15, SD = .77) than Flex teachers (M = 2.79, SD = .65); t(103) = −2.60, $p < .01$. Rotation teachers also saw a greater increase in student motivation for low performing students (M = 3.01, SD = .80) compared with Flex teachers (M = 2.62, SD = .77); t(104) = −2.61, $p < .01$, as well as a greater increase in motivation for average performing students (M = 3.14, SD = .68) compared with Flex (M = 2.84, SD = .59); t(102) = −2.46, $p < .05$. Rotation teachers were also more likely to view blended learning as creating opportunities for students to self-regulate their learning (M = 3.42, SD = .65) compared with Flex (M=3.00, SD=.68); t(119) = −3.44, $p < .001$, and creating a learning experience that is more personalized for each student (M = 3.39, SD = .65) compared with Flex (M = 2.98, SD = .78); t(103) = −3.08, $p < .01$.

These findings on self-regulation and personalization are in some ways counter-intuitive to what might be expected when comparing Rotation v. Flex. In a Flex approach, students are much more in control on a day-to-day basis over what they are doing online (controlling the pace, deciding which aspects of the course to engage with) as their course is primarily delivered online, with the teacher pulling students out for individual and small group instruction as needed. Yet, Rotation teachers are more likely to view blended

TABLE 20.1 Comparing Rotation Approach Teachers' (n=62) and Flex Approach Teachers' (n=64) Perceptions of the Impact of Blended Learning on Students

Question	Rotation mean (SD)	Flex mean (SD)	t	df	p	ES
Blended learning makes students more engaged with content	3.15** (0.77)	2.79 (0.65)	-2.60	103	.011	.37
Blended learning has improved my relationship with my students	2.88 (0.83)	2.73 (0.69)	-.93	84	.35	.15
Blended learning increases motivation to learn for low performing students	3.01** (0.80)	2.62 (0.77)	-2.61	104	.010	.40
Blended learning increases motivation to learn for average performing students	3.14* (0.68)	2.84 (0.59)	-2.46	102	.015	.31
Blended learning increases motivation to learn for high performing students	3.24 (0.71)	3.08 (0.68)	-1.17	104	.247	.16
Blended learning pushes students to engage in higher order thinking	3.03 (0.71)	2.75 (0.79)	-1.96	103	.053	.29
Blended learning creates opportunities for students to self regulate their learning	3.42*** (0.65)	3.00 (0.68)	-3.44	119	.001	.41
Blended learning creates a learning experience that is more personalized to each student	3.39** (0.65)	2.98 (0.78)	-3.08	103	.003	.41
Blended learning helps students gain skills they need to be successful in college and career	3.25 (0.67)	3.00 (0.69)	-1.88	100	.063	.25

(Scale: 1=Strongly Disagree, 2=Disagree, 3=Agree, 4=Strongly Agree)
$\star$ $p < 0.05$; $\star\star$ $p < 0.01$; $\star\star\star$ $p < 0.001$

learning as offering opportunities for self-regulation than Flex teachers, and also more likely to view Rotation as being personalized, despite the fact that Flex students are experiencing a course that is, at least in theory, personalized to their level and pace.

Rotation teachers retain more control over content and pedagogical decisions than do Flex teachers, and this contrast may be what is driving the different perceptions of blended learning implementation. Rotation hews much more closely to the traditional idea of the teacher being in charge of the classroom, and does not go as far as Flex in challenging teachers to rethink their role as educators. Teachers new to blended learning might simply feel more positive about experimenting with a Rotation approach than a Flex approach because it is more incremental in altering their role in the classroom.

We also explored teacher perceptions of how they benefited from being blended instructors, inquiring as to how it impacts their own efficacy. Table 20.2 and 20.3 present subgroup means for Rotation and Flex blenders for the 2011–2012 school year.

Teachers using the Rotation approach perceived, on average, that they were benefiting more from being a blended teacher than did Flex teachers. Rotation

TABLE 20.2 Comparing Rotation Approach Teachers' (n=62) and Flex Approach Teachers' (n=64) Perceptions of the Impact of Blended Learning on Their Own Efficacy

Question	Rotation mean (SD)	Flex mean (SD)	t	df	p	ES
Participating in iLearnNYC has made my job as a teacher more satisfying	2.75 (0.74)	2.61 (0.75)	−1.12	124	.26	.15
Participating in iLearnNYC has made my job as a teacher more efficient	2.94* (0.70)	2.63 (0.70)	−2.49	124	.014	.31
Participating in iLearnNYC has made me feel more successful as a teacher	2.77 (0.77)	2.53 (0.73)	−1.81	124	.074	.24
Participating in iLearnNYC has made it easier for me to meet every student's learning needs	3.00* (0.75)	2.69 (0.75)	−2.34	124	.021	.31
Participating in iLearnNYC has increased my students' performance	2.92* (0.75)	2.66 (0.72)	−2.01	124	.047	.26

(Scale: 1=Strongly Disagree, 2=Disagree, 3=Agree, 4=Strongly Agree)
* $p < 0.05$; ** $p < 0.01$; *** $p < 0.001$

TABLE 20.3   Comparing Rotation Approach Teachers' (n=62) and Flex Approach Teachers' (n=64) "Sense of Efficacy" Scale Scores. Teachers Were Asked a Series of Questions About What They Thought They Could Do in the Classroom to Influence a Variety of Classroom Variables

	Rotation mean (SD)	Flex mean (SD)	t	df	p	ES
Teacher "Sense of Efficacy" Spring scale score	4.27* (0.51)	4.03 (0.54)	−2.45	120	.016	.23

(Scale: 1=Nothing, 2=Very Little, 3=Some Influence, 4=Quite a Bit, 5 =A Great Deal). All Answers Were Averaged into an Efficacy Score
* $p < 0.05$

teachers were more likely to agree that participating in iLearnNYC has made their jobs more efficient (M = 2.94, SD = .70) than Flex teachers (M = 2.63, SD = .70); t(124) = −2.49, $p < .05$, has made it easier for them to meet every student's learning needs (M = 3.00, SD = .75) than Flex teachers (M = 2.69, SD = .75) t(124) = −2.34, $p < .05$, and has increased their students' performance (M = 2.92, SD = .75), more so than did Flex teachers (M = 2.66, SD = .72) t(124) = −2.01, $p < .05$. Rotation teachers also had slightly higher *Teacher Efficacy Scale* scores (M = 4.27, SD = .51) than Flex teachers (M = 4.03, SD = .54); t(120) = −2.45, $p < .05$. Again, teachers maintain more control of content and delivery in a Rotation model compared with a Flex model, likely driving teacher attitudes toward blended learning.

Creator v. Utilizer Teachers

• Are there differences in teachers' sense of efficacy and their perceptions of blended learning's impact on students between teachers who create their own course content, the "Creators," and those who use vendor created content, the "Utilizers"?

Our findings (see Table 20.4) suggest that Creators, on average, have a much more positive view of blended learning than Utilizers. On six out of the nine questions where teachers were asked about their perceptions of how blended learning impacts students, the Creators were more likely to agree that blended learning is having a positive effect. The Creators saw greater benefit in terms of student engagement (M = 3.15, SD = .67) than did Utilizers (M = 2.78, SD = .70); t(105) = −2.73, $p < .01$, as well as perceiving stronger student–teacher relationships (M = 2.98, SD = .68) than did Utilizers (M = 2.56, SD = .83); t(86) = −2.09, $p < .05$. Creators were also more likely to agree that blended

TABLE 20.4 Comparing Creator and Utilizer Perceptions of the Impact of Blended Learning on Students

Question	Creator mean (SD) (n=70)	Utilizer mean (SD) (n=60)	t	df	p	ES
Blended learning makes students more engaged with content	3.15** (0.67)	2.78 (0.70)	−2.73	105	.008	.37
Blended learning has improved my relationship with my students	2.98* (0.68)	2.56 (0.83)	−2.09	86	.040	.32
Blended learning increases motivation to learn for low performing students	3.05*** (0.66)	2.53 (0.82)	−3.46	107	.001	.49
Blended learning increases motivation to learn for average performing students	3.19*** (0.58)	2.79 (0.65)	−3.34	104	.001	.40
Blended learning increases motivation to learn for high performing students	3.28 (0.58)	3.04 (0.77)	−1.83	107	.070	.24
Blended learning pushes students to engage in higher order thinking	3.02 (0.61)	2.76 (0.86)	−1.83	105	.070	.26
Blended learning creates opportunities for students to self regulate their learning	3.40** (0.52)	3.07 (0.69)	−3.03	122	.003	.33
Blended learning creates a learning experience that is more personalized to each student	3.29 (0.62)	3.11 (0.77)	−1.37	106	.174	.18
Blended learning helps students gain skills they need to be successful in college and career	3.27* (0.55)	2.98 (0.75)	−2.28	103	.025	.29

(Scale: 1=Strongly Disagree, 2=Disagree, 3=Agree, 4=Strongly Agree)
* $p < 0.05$; ** $p < 0.01$; *** $p < 0.001$

learning increased motivation for low performing students (M = 3.05, SD = .66) compared with Utilizers (M = 2.53, SD = .82); t(107) = −3.46, $p < .001$, as well as motivation for average performing students (M = 3.19, SD = .58) compared with Utilizers (M = 2.79, SD = .65); t(104) = −3.34, $p < .001$. Creators also perceived greater benefit in terms of student self-regulation (M =

3.40, SD = .52) than did Utilizers (M = 3.07, SD = .69); $t(122) = -3.03$, $p <$ .01, and increased college and career readiness (M = 3.27, SD = .55) compared with Utilizers (M = 2.98, SD = .75); $t(103) = -2.28$, $p < .05$.

The statement that revealed the biggest difference in perception between the Creators and Utilizers is, "Blended learning increases motivation to learn for low performing students." Creators, on average, agree that blended increases motivation for these students, while the Utilizers, on average, lean toward disagreement. Our qualitative research pointed us to the difficulty of motivating students through blended learning if the students are not already motivated to begin with, and this finding is promising for teachers struggling to figure out how to implement blended learning in a way that reaches their lowest performing students.

Similar to our analysis of Flex v. Rotation teachers, we also examined subgroups' means on perceptions of increased teacher efficacy for Creators and Utilizers. While Creators are more likely than Utilizers to agree that blended learning is benefiting their students, as described above, both groups are similar in their attitudes toward whether blended learning is benefiting them. There were no statistically significant differences between Creators and Utilizers in their answers to survey questions about whether participating in iLearnNYC has made their jobs more satisfying, more efficient, more successful, or has made them better able to meet their students' learning needs ($p > .05$). Nor was there any difference in Teacher Efficacy Scale scores ($p > .05$).

Overlapping Constructs?

To ensure that we are measuring two separate constructs when comparing Creators with Utilizers and Rotation teachers with Flex teachers, we looked at the overlap between Creators and Rotation teachers, and Utilizers and Flex teachers (see Table 20.5). Our analyses revealed that, while there is some overlap between these groups, they are not the same exact teachers. Rotation teachers were more than twice as likely to be Creators, and Flex teachers were somewhat more likely to be Utilizers, but the groups were not a one-to-one match.

- Student impact: How do students describe their experience with blended learning? What impact has participation in blended courses had on students' academic motivation and self-directed learning?

iLearnNYC is designed to personalize the learning experience for students and push them toward greater independence. Our data suggest that blended learning is having its intended effect (see Table 20.6). Students reported higher intrinsic motivation: $t(729) = 3.05$, $p < .01$ and self-directed learning

TABLE 20.5 Crosstabulation to Confirm Different Constructs are Being Measured

	Utilizer	Creator
Flex	38	24
Rotation	18	43

(756) = 2.16, $p < .05$ at the end of the school year than the beginning of the school year. Students also responded positively to questions about their satisfaction with blended learning and whether their academic needs were met by blended learning. Nearly one-half of students in the program reported that they are definitely more likely to receive assignments at their level in their iLearnNYC courses, and another 39.5% stated that this is true some of the time. Only 11% of students reported that they do not receive assignments at their level in iLearnNYC courses. Students also reported how likely they were to take another blended course in the next school year. Only 18% said that they were not likely to take another blended course next year.

We investigated whether students who reported greater satisfaction with the program were more likely to report increases in intrinsic motivation and self-directed learning than those who reported less satisfaction in their iLearnNYC courses. Specifically, to determine if students who reported that they were likely to take another blended course were also benefiting more from their iLearnNYC program, we compared students who said they were likely to take another with those who were unsure and those who did not plan to take another in terms of reported changes in intrinsic motivation and self-directed learning. In addition, we compared how students report about the likelihood of receiving

TABLE 20.6 Student Satisfaction with Blended Courses

More likely to get assignments that are at the right level for you, not too easy and not too hard, in your iLearnNYC blended and online courses

	(n=2002)	%
Yes	992	49.6
Sometimes	790	39.5
No	220	11.0

If given a choice how likely are you to take iLearnNYC blended and online classes next year?

	(n=2002)	%
Very likely	668	33.4
Somewhat likely	974	48.7
Not likely	360	18.0

assignments at the right level for them in their iLearnNYC blended courses in their intrinsic motivation and their self-directed learning.

Two sets of ANOVAs (see Table 20.7 and 20.8) were conducted to uncover the trends. In the first set, two between-subjects ANOVAs were calculated with change in intrinsic motivation as the dependent variable. In the first analysis, students' self-reported learning needs being met was the independent variable. There was a significant effect of met needs on change in motivation, $F (2, 620) = 4.60$, $p < .010$. LSD post hoc analyses revealed that the group that reported "Yes, they were more likely to receive assignments at the right level for their needs" obtained scores that were significantly higher than the other the group that reported "No, they were not more likely to receive assignments at the right level" ("Yes" $M = 2.94$, "No" $M = -2.19$). There was no significant

TABLE 20.7 Assignments That Are at the Right Level for You

Summary of ANOVA: Intrinsic motivation	Sum of squares	df	Mean square	F
Between groups	1910.41	2	955.20	4.60
Within groups	128804.40	620	207.75	
Total	130714.80	622		

* $p < 0.05$

Summary of ANOVA: Self-directed learning	Sum of squares	df	Mean square	F
Between groups	387.39	2	193.69	4.22
Within groups	29503.60	643	45.88	
Total	29890.99	645		

* $p < 0.05$

TABLE 20.8 Likely to Take Blended Course Next Year

Summary of ANOVA: Intrinsic motivation	Sum of squares	df	Mean square	F
Between groups	2255.51	2	1127.76	5.44
Within groups	128459.29	620	207.19	
Total	130714.80	622		

* $p < 0.05$

Summary of ANOVA: Self-directed learning	Sum of squares	df	Mean square	F
Between groups	300.62	2	150.31	3.27
Within groups	29590.36	643	46.02	
Total	29890.99	645		

* $p < 0.05$

difference between the "Yes" or the "No" group and the group of students who reported that they "Sometimes were more likely to receive assignments as the right level for their needs." In the second, students' satisfaction with blended learning was the independent variable. There was a significant effect of satisfaction on motivation, $F (2, 620) = 3.27, p < .039$. LSD post hoc analyses revealed that the group that reported being *not* at all likely to take another blended course obtained scores that were significantly lower than the other two groups (very likely, and somewhat likely) (Not at all $M = -2.18$, Somewhat $M = 1.36$, Very $M = 3.35$).

A second set of between-subjects ANOVAS were calculated with self-directed learning as the dependent variable. In the first analysis, students' self-reported learning needs being met was the independent variable. There was a significant effect of met needs on change in self-directed learning, $F (2, 643) = 4.22, p < .015$. LSD post hoc analyses revealed that the group reporting that "Yes, they were more likely to receive assignments at the right level for their needs" obtained scores that were significantly higher than the other two groups that reported "No, they were not more likely to receive assignments at the right level" and "Sometimes they receive assignments at the right level" ("Yes" $M = 1.21$, "No" $M = -.79$, "Sometimes" $M = -0.11$). In the second, students' satisfaction with blended learning was the independent variable. There was a significant effect of satisfaction on self-directed learning, $F (2, 643) = 3.27, p < .039$. LSD post hoc analyses showed that the students who reported being very likely to take another blended course scored higher than the group somewhat likely and the not likely at all group (Very $M = 1.37$, Somewhat $M = .08$, Not at all $M = -.37$).

In summary, students generally reported being satisfied with their blended courses. Students who participated in the iLearnNYC blended program reported becoming more intrinsically motivated in their academics and more self-directed in their learning from the beginning of the school year to the end. This was most evident among students who felt that their course was a better fit for them than their non-iLearnNYC courses, and also among students who were interested in pursuing more blended courses in the future.

The findings point to the importance of personalization in blended learning classrooms. These are preliminary findings and do not include a comparison group of students who did not take a blended course; however, the data support the notion that blended courses are a viable method for students to get more personalized support, and that such support may lead to greater growth in the important constructs of motivation and self-directed learning.

Conclusion and Discussion

As school districts pilot and scale blended learning, there are two primary groups that will test blended learning's potential, and help establish what benefits it might make over more traditional methods: 1) teachers, whose perceptions of blended learning this study explores, and 2) the individuals creating the technological tools and educational content for the blended learning marketplace. Each will play an important role in determining whether blended learning fulfills its potential to be a pedagogical framework that makes mastery-based learning a real possibility for all students in any classroom. The implications of our early research findings for each of these two groups and their interplay are explored in detail below.

Teachers who take on the challenge of becoming blended instructors must make many decisions about how to combine online and face-to-face learning, including crucial decisions about what the online content will be, and how often to use it. These decisions, however, are clearly impacted by what is available in the blended learning marketplace, thus complicating our findings. While our research suggests that choosing to use online learning as only one element that students rotate through, and choosing to create one's own online learning content both have important positive associations with teachers' perceived effectiveness as blended instructors, these choices are undoubtedly driven, in part, by a marketplace that is constrained in two major ways. First, much of the online courseware that is available cannot be easily modularized, and teachers are not free to easily pick and choose the parts of an online course that work for them in the context of their own classroom. Accordingly, they may choose not to use vendor content at all, creating their own, or they may only choose those vendors that do provide easy modularity of content. Thus, the higher satisfaction rates of teachers who used a Rotation approach compared with a Flex approach and of the Creators compared with the Utilizers could be a comparison of this: those who have found a happy modular medium compared with those who took the plunge in an all or nothing situation, and now have lingering doubts about the usefulness of their courseware.

The second major blended learning marketplace constraint impacting teacher perceptions of its effectiveness is that some of the online choices available to teachers resemble online textbooks, and do not fundamentally shift what the teacher is able to do in terms of differentiating instruction and implementing a mastery-based learning system. If the choices in the educational courseware marketplace were more revolutionary, the Creators might be Utilizers, and those who use a Rotation approach might take a Flex approach instead. In other words, when vendors create options that make mastery based learning imminently doable, by easily giving each student the freedom and tools to engage with material that excites their interests and is appropriate for their individual learning level and style, the conversation about blended learning will necessarily take on a much different tone. Some of our student data foreshadow this future conversation about blended learning. Students who reported that they were more likely to receive assignments at the right level for them in their iLearnNYC blended courses reported significantly greater improvements in their intrinsic motivation and their self-directed learning from the beginning to the end of the school year compared with surveyed students who reported that they "did not" or only "sometimes" receive assignments at the right level. We were unable to match student answers with their teachers' approaches to blended learning, but students who perceive the online space as better meeting their own learning needs will be the voice that will help teachers to make informed choices about how to implement blended learning in their own classrooms. Student voice will also drive the marketplace as vendors struggle to create demand for their educational products, hoping to appeal to teachers and school leaders through the testimonials of engaged students who are thriving in their online learning space.

This research does not yet warrant driving teachers to use one blended learning approach over another, and currently suggests that teachers who do not relinquish too much of their responsibility to technology perceive more benefit for themselves and their students. But if education technologies advance to a state where there is a clear benefit to students who learn certain types of material in the online space, and education courseware easily supports differentiated instruction for mastery based learning, teachers will have an easier time navigating the use of blended learning in the classroom and have the potential to improve greatly upon traditional approaches.

References

Barbour, M., Brown, R., Waters, L. H., Hoey, R., Hunt, J. L., Kennedy, K., Ounsworth, C., Powell, A., & Trimm, T. (2011). *Online and blended learning: A survey of policy and practice of K–12 schools around the world.* Vienna, VA: International Association of K–12 Online Learning.

Bloom, B. S. (1968). Learning for mastery. *Evaluation Comments, 1*(2), 1–14.

Guskey, T. R. (2007, Fall). Closing achievement gaps: Revisiting Benjamin S. Bloom's "Learning for Mastery". *Journal of Advanced Academics, 19*(1), 8–31.

Lounsbury, J. W., Levy, J. J., Park, S.-H., Gibson, L. W., & Smith, R. (2009). An investigation of the construct validity of the personality trait of self-directed learning. *Learning and Individual Differences, 19*(4), 411–418.

Staker, H., & Horn, M. B. (2012). *Classifying K-12 blended learning.* Mountain View, CA: Innosight Institute.

Tshannen-Moran, M., & Woolfolk-Hoy, A. (2001). Teacher efficacy: Capturing an elusive construct. *Teaching and Teacher Education, 17,* 783–805.

Vallerand, R. J., Pelletier, L. G., Blais, M. R., Briere, N. M., Senecal, C., & Vallieres, E. F. (1992). The academic motivation scale: A measure of intrinsic, extrinsic, and amotivation in education. *Educational and Psychological Measurement, 52*(4), 1003–1017.

21

BLENDING IT ALL TOGETHER

Charles D. Dziuban, Joel L. Hartman,
and George L. Mehaffy[1]

As this volume concludes, we wanted to review some of what we think are the major elements in the story of blended learning. This chapter focuses in particular on four key issues: research findings and conclusions; core values; the recurring issue of definition, and the opportunities that lie ahead. Researchers in this volume report a variety of conclusions about the evolution of the blended modality and present trends for its momentum in education and its potential for transforming all levels of teaching and learning. At the same time, blended learning's potential for change comes with some opportunity costs that require our attention. Discussion of those costs leads us to conclude that that there are four core values associated with blending both teaching and learning. A third issue is the continuing struggle by educators and researchers over the past decade to formulate a functional definition of blending for pedagogy and research. Therefore we attempt to resolve definitional issues by reconsidering how we approach that problem through several theoretical perspectives. Finally, we consider the road ahead. Blended learning as a pedagogical model has paved the way for many cutting edge educational innovations; one in particular offers the possibility of reaching untold numbers of students throughout the world. However, that innovative approach begs several important issues that have yet to be resolved. Our discussion considers the potential and the unanticipated side effects of offering learning on a massive scale. We also propose an alternative model for large scale blending that involves faculty from multiple campuses in the design process while still allowing individual instructors to offer their own campus based classes. Because blended learning pushes the boundaries of traditional education, we consider the impact of this on traditional research

---

1 Authors in alphabetical order.

methods and information exchange. We conclude with three admonitions about the conduct of research to realize its potential, maximize its success, and make it valuable to practitioners.

Blended Learning Research Findings and Conclusions

The authors of these chapters use several effective approaches to inquiry that develop a series of important findings. For instance, blended teaching and learning can be scaled effectively across multiple institutions as long as that scaling is based on established best practices and strong support mechanisms. However, one of the problems with widespread adoption involves the loss of granularity in evaluation data. Another finding from the research reported here shows that students involve themselves in the blending process informally by using multiple course modalities to design individualized programs of study, thereby potentially decreasing their time to completion. Class interaction patterns become significantly altered in the blended learning environment where student engagement reflects not only involvement with peers and instructors but course content and the learning platform as well. Blended course models are impacted significantly by the community of inquiry model—cognitive, social and teaching presence influencing students' perceptions of their learning environment. Other findings demonstrate that engagement benchmark data can be evaluated by multiple cohorts in the redesign of effective field-based learning experiences for students. Research suggests that over the long run, blended learning is sustainable, reducing the importance of course modality because concentration focuses on learning rather than tools or format. Many studies directly state or imply that research designs in blended learning must be updated continually, based on double feedback loops emanating from several rounds of data collection making the case for design-based research. The findings make a clear case that blended courses provide a superior environment for students to develop their skills and concept of understanding through multiple reinforcing study opportunities. In order to be effective and meaningful, research conducted at the institutional level should be augmented with the scholarship of teaching and learning within specific disciplines conducted by both faculty and students. Conclusively, the data show that high quality faculty development is the cornerstone of effective blended programs. However, demographic characteristics of the student population should be considered in professional development activities, with the caveat that teaching and learning in the blended environment runs the risk of overburdening both faculty and students. Looking across several studies in this book it becomes clear that blended learning offers potential for improving educational practice over a wide range of educational settings as long as the instructional design attends to the learning characteristics of student cohorts. Instructor interaction with technology is also critically important. The teacher who is able to design an effective balance between their instructional techniques and the learning tools produces much more effective learning opportunities for students. Taken as a collective, these studies demonstrate that high quality research in blended learning is being conducted throughout the world. In addition virtually every author, to some degree, has intimated that it is time to move on to a second generation research agenda in blended learning. Some issues are well understood, such as student success, withdrawal, and satisfaction for both instructors and learners. However, other questions remain unanswered. How will we address the quality issue? Will there be a prototype model for blended learning? Is blended learning the right term or would some other metaphor be more appropriate? How are we to help students deal with the overwhelming amount of information available to them and discern that which is valid form that which is flawed? How do we best place critical thinking into the blended environment? Can blended learning diminish the growing equity gap in American education? How are social networking and mobile learning impacting the blended environment? Of course, this list is far from comprehensive but answers to these questions will move us forward and raise new questions (and opportunities) that will demand our attention.

Blended Learning is Not New

In the rapidly changing landscape of American education, technology offers new possibilities not previously imagined. Of all these many developments, the unbundling of higher education is perhaps the most profound transformation. Technology not only challenges traditional institutions, but also empowers students to take those courses from a variety of sources thereby assembling their own programs of study. Suddenly, learning opportunities are available everywhere, threatening the former dominance of the traditional way of doing things. For example, results from the tenth annual survey of online learning in the United States by the Babson Survey Research Group (Allen & Seaman, 2013) served as a reminder that online and blended learning are not new phenomena in the United States, and the adoption of technology-mediated teaching and learning practices by institutions of all types and sizes continues to make steady progress on most fronts. Looking back across the past decade, the annual survey reports have documented an increase of five million students taking at least one online course per year (from 1,602,970 to 6,714,792), a 22.4% increase (from 9.6% to 32%), and a 19.7% increase in the proportion of academic leaders rating online learning outcomes the same as or superior to face-to-face instruction (from 57.2% to 76.9%). These figures remind us that the transformation of higher education has been underway for some time.

Blended Learning is a Good Idea

The authors in this book have incorporated several new approaches to exploring the impact of blended learning ranging across scaling, evaluation models, faculty and student perspectives, and nontraditional environments, in K–12 and higher education settings. They adopted innovative methodologies that attune to changing educational settings where more traditional research procedures can be increasingly ineffective. One justification for this blending of methods comes from what Jenkins (2006) describes as the convergence culture where emerging technologies such as blended learning interact with more traditional face-to-face pedagogy in complex learning environments. One does not replace the other, but rather they coalesce into new hybrid learning modalities. By combining traditional and technology-enhanced instruction, blended learning forces researchers to respond with innovative and flexible methods that produce usable—and useful—information. Virtually everyone who worked on this book believes that blended learning is a transformational force in education and understands that effective inquiry is vital to assessing its potential for repositioning education in cultures throughout the world. Blended learning, therefore, demands blended research.

Blending is a good idea; however, good ideas come at a cost. We cannot cling to traditional approaches. Steven Johnson (2010) tells us that for innovation (including research) to happen, it needs an environment that allows all ideas to compete in an open interchange. He describes this phenomenon as a liquid network, where ideas swarm around each other identifying the adjacent possible: the creative next step that will move us forward. Robin Sloan, in his book *Mr. Penumbra's 24-Hour Bookstore* (2012), approaches Johnson's adjacent possible from a different perspective, which he labels "the maximum happy imagination" that represents the next possible step in the progress of society. Clay, the protagonist of the book, is asked to project the future as far as he possibly can. The conversation goes as follows:

> Okay: "World government . . . no cancer . . . hover-boards."
> "Go further: What's the good future after that?"
> "Spaceships. Party on Mars."
> "Further."
> "Star Trek. Transporters. You can go anywhere."
> "Further."
> I pause a moment and realize: "I can't."
> ". . . It's really hard. . . . We probably just imagine things based on what we already know, and we run out of analogies."
>
> (Sloan, 2012, p. 60)

Effective research requires a systematic and incremental improvement of methods, data collection, analysis, results presentation, and even reconsideration of what constitutes usable data if we are to advance our knowledge about effective learning. Further, this reconsideration has to take place in an open environment that can respond to the needs of the students, faculty, and administrators in classes, disciplines, departments, colleges, across institutions, across consortia, and even across continents. Approaching outcomes from multiple perspectives is the best means for reaching consensus about effectiveness and moving to that next creative step. This seems particularly important for blended classes that appear to be prototype liquid learning networks where students have much more freedom to design their learning strategies.

Core Values of Blended Learning

At its core, blended learning has four critical values. The modality involves both human intervention and technology, confronting the faculty member with the powerful question: What are the things that I can do best, and what are the things that I should relegate to technology? Answering this question challenges faculty members to grapple with the most profound question of all: What is the unique value that only I can add? Increasingly, that question will apply not only to faculty thinking about their own courses but to entire institutions, as courses become available from anywhere on earth, and where one faculty member can teach hundreds of thousands of students. Jeff Selingo (2003), editor at large of the Chronicle of Higher Education, predicts, for example, that introductory courses (the ones that are the easiest to commodify) will become free or nearly free. In this environment, perhaps every institution will have to make a fundamental set of decisions about the unique value that it adds, and the unique services and programs that only it can provide.

A second core value of blended learning is that it shifts substantial attention from the faculty member to a focus on students and pedagogical approaches from instructivist to constructivist methods. In the traditional classroom, faculty reside at the center of the enterprise, particularly in lecture contexts. In blended learning course models, faculty have to think about how students will operate, for a portion of the course, with substantially less faculty direction. The course requires elements and materials with which students interact apart from the class. In blended learning design, the portion of time that students spend working outside of class is much more interactive than homework assignments. The time spent out of class in the blended learning model is in fact time that is spent in class; it simply means that the definition "in class" has been substantially broadened.

Despite the irony, a third value of blended learning is the focus on faculty. Far too often, transformations in teaching and learning have tried to eliminate faculty roles (Doyle & Ponder 1977) at times with the so-called "teacher-proof" curricula. However, faculty members have a critical role at the center of teaching and learning that always has been a profoundly human enterprise. Issues of encouragement, persistence, and responding to complexity and confusion are still primarily roles that human teachers do best (Weigert, 1991).

Finally, the value of blended learning comes when an instructor moves a portion of a course to a technology-mediated environment, producing substantial quantities of data for analysis. In the world of data and learning analytics, most findings depend on data derived from student behavior, the so-called "click-stream data" (Ciaramita, Murdock, & Plachouras, 2008). Currently, information systems are being developed that can gather those data, link them to the institutions' other databases, and build highly informative and predictive systems. In fact, at a conference recently, it was suggested that once faculty saw how much information they could obtain about their students from the online environment, they would be increasingly attracted to teaching entirely online (Mehaffy, 2011). Perhaps blended learning is a "gateway drug" to online teaching.

The Issue of Definition

In an article entitled "Can Blended Learning Be Redeemed?" that has been cited hundreds of times in the literature, Oliver and Trigwell (2005) contend that the term "blended"—when associated with learning—should be abandoned or reconceived. Insightfully, they show us that what is really implied by the term "blended learning" is more accurately blended instruction, teaching, or pedagogy and that all learning is individual. Further, they contend that the multiple definitions in the literature are not at all helpful, but rather quite confusing and redundant. They summarize the crux of their argument as follows:

> *The term "blended learning" is ill-defined and inconsistently used. Whilst its popularity is increasing, its clarity is not. Under any current definition, it is either incoherent or redundant as a concept. Building a tradition of research around the term becomes an impossible project, since without a common conception of its meaning, there can be no coherent way of synthesizing the findings of the studies, let alone developing a consistent theoretical framework with which to interpret data.*
>
> (Oliver & Trigwell, 2005, p. 24)

Our inability to form a precise and commonly accepted definition of "blended learning" (or even see the need for one) is probably best explained by Bowker and Starr (1989):

> *Boundary objects are objects which are both plastic enough to adapt to the local needs and constraints of several parties employing them, yet robust enough to maintain a common identity across sites. They are weakly structured in common use, and become strongly structured in individual-site use. They have different meanings in different social worlds but their structure is common enough to more than one world to make them recognizable, a means of translation. The creation and management of boundary objects is key in developing and maintaining coherence across social worlds.*
>
> (p. 297)

Perhaps Oliver and Trigwell's (2005) emphasis on definitional requirements might be reconsidered through the boundary object concept. In doing so, blended learning becomes more responsive to multiple organic and evolving learning environments where students tend to build personal learning geographies (Harmon, 2004). In the first chapter of this book, Tony Picciano makes it clear that an administrative framework is a prerequisite for any effective definitional work. Charles Graham (2013) speculates that this vague definition of blended learning may be a strength because it allows institutions to adopt and use the term in the context of their particular institutions. Oliver and Trigwell (2005) go on to assert that blended learning realizes success because of its ability to establish a varied environment in what is or can be learned. One might reasonably infer that because blended learning may be a boundary object that learning variation is inherent in its underlying properties. The more fundamental research problem may not be one of definition, but rather of designing research methods that respond properly to a generalized construct.

An excellent example of blended learning as a boundary object may be found in the recent EDUCAUSE report on the Next Generation Learning Challenges program wave one funding cycle on blended learning. In that report, Millichap and Vogt (2012) found, in many pre-proposals, vastly differing definitions of "blended learning" depending on the context of the institution from which the submission originated. Because blended learning demands the convergence of so many varied educational cultures, developing a common definition becomes daunting and quite possibly nonproductive. Bowker and Starr (1989) state: "Like a blackboard, a boundary object 'sits in the middle' of a group of actors with divergent viewpoints" (p. 46).

New Applications and New Opportunities

You would have had to have spent the past year in a cave to miss the news about the latest development in online learning: MOOCS, or Massive Open Online Courses. Analysts following the phenomenon have described it as everything from a force that will transform higher education as we know it to a passing fad—and nearly everything in between.

However, these courses, despite all of the press coverage, have not yet become a threat to most institutions, particularly those that enroll students in the middle ability ranges. Successful participation in a MOOC requires a substantial amount of self-motivation, probably a fairly advanced level of academic preparation, and undoubtedly learner self-confidence. Currently, the majority of MOOCs are not for credit except through third-party assessors. However, there is evidence of the potential for strong student-to-student interaction, including the formation of spontaneous study groups, development and contribution of software modules, and even translation of course materials into other languages (Bennett, 2012). Most likely, their real impact will come 3 to

5 years from now when these courses become vastly more interactive, personalized, and responsive to individual students.

Ironically, the same technologies that allow for disruptive strategies like MOOCs also enable a variety of blended learning models. Technology uncouples students from being continually present in the classroom. In the best of circumstances, technology allows professors to offload responsibilities that can be taken up by technology. As Cathy Davidson (CathyNDavidson, 2012) famously observed: "if we can be replaced by a computer screen, we should be." Her point was simple; we ought to let technology do what technology can do, reserving for us the human interactions and activities that are (at least so far) not able to be done effectively through technology. For example, technology can record a lecture and make it available anywhere, thus encouraging the development of the flipped classroom, popularized by Salman Khan (2011). Suddenly the lecture becomes available anywhere, at any time, on many different devices. This relieves the professor of the responsibility of providing the same lecture semester after semester, and instead encourages the development of highly interactive and collaborative activities that can be accomplished only by a faculty member in a mediated setting. The combination of technology and human intervention defines the critical difference. John Naisbitt (1988) was right, in his award-winning book *Megatrends*, when he predicted that as technology becomes increasingly prevalent, there will be a need for mediating human engagement. The result, he argued, would be a process he referred to as "high-tech, high-touch." Now, 30 years later, that prediction seems to be particularly apropos in the world of technology-mediated learning. Blended learning, in all of its various representations, has as its fundamental premise a simple idea: link the best technological solutions for teaching and learning with the best human resources.

Reconsidering Traditional Methods

By definition, blended learning research is messy, leaving many people frustrated with our inability to develop robust cause-and-effect relationships through experimental research. Going back to Oliver and Trigwell's (2005) points about its definition, we may have to acknowledge that blended learning is not as clear cut as other modalities. According to Taleb (2012), "We just cannot isolate a causal relationship in a complex system" (p. 58). At this stage of distributed learning, in general, we may be entering what Cavanagh (2012) calls the post-modality era, where students and faculty no longer make substantial decisions about their learning environment based on class modality. Agreeing with Meyer (2005), who early on warned of the limiting nature of metaphors and labels, Cavanagh contends that distance, online, and blended learning will simply become learning. Studies at the University of Central Florida have shown that class modality does very little to predict student success

(Dziuban, Moskal, Cavanagh, & Watts, 2012) and that students make no distinction in how they evaluate their courses based on modality at the empirical level (Dziuban & Moskal, 2011). However it remains to be seen if careful qualitative analysis can validate these seemingly counterintuitive conclusions.

Because it is loosely configured, designating blended learning as a treatment effect in comparative studies can be problematic, and because there is no one specific model of blended learning, when investigators present their hypothesis test results, we often have no way of knowing just what was involved in the blend. Therefore, investigators have a growing responsibility to be very specific about the teaching environments in various class modalities. Another growing problem is that the traditionally labeled face-to-face class is rapidly disappearing with the incursion of technology into almost every learning situation, making comparative studies increasingly problematic. There are so many confounding variables in these situations that it is nearly impossible to determine what impacted what.

Second, in this new arena, we have to carefully reconsider how we use statistical hypothesis tests and the assumption that p-values are an objective measure. Consider the following statement by Matthews (2005):

> Scientists, in contrast, thought of the p-values as an objective test of whether a theory was right or not. Until the early 1960s and onwards, top statisticians tried to warn scientists about the dangers of misunderstanding p-values without success. For most scientists p-values seemed objective and easy to use and, most important of all, top journals demanded p-values as evidence that the findings were worth publishing.
>
> (p. 88)

Historically, most researchers conduct experimental and comparison group studies by arbitrarily picking a significance level and then obtaining the largest possible sample size to run the study. The consequence is that by pre-choosing a significance level and sample size, the comparison difference that will be significant is fixed, essentially giving up control of the study. These hypothesis tests are much more effective when the investigator gives some careful thought to the process by deciding about effect size prior to running the analysis (Walster & Cleary, 1970). Silver (2012) best stated the rationale for the value of such a process: "The key to making a good forecast is not limiting yourself to quantitative information. Rather, it's having a good process for weighing the information appropriately" (p. 100).

Blended learning presents many opportunities for research that incorporates modern innovations for data collection, data analysis, presentation, and interpretation of results, and the incorporation of findings into decisions about effective pedagogy and policy. However, this area of inquiry is also fraught with forces that cause us to reexamine staid traditions about what constitutes evidence. On the positive side, our ability to collect and analyze data is amazing. The newfound ability to mine big data allows us to find information and decision rules that were previously unattainable. However, big data contain big noise, so thoughtful researchers must be on guard to ensure their results are based on the signal in the data and not that random noise (Silver, 2012).

Promise for the Future

There is much to be excited about in blended learning. However, the modality will only achieve its full potential when course design is paired with faculty crowdsourcing, challenging the cottage industry model of an individually designed course. We need structural designs that combine the best of blended learning with the best of faculty crowdsourcing. The American Association of State Colleges and Universities (www.aascu.org), is working on such a model. They have gathered scholars together from a variety of campuses and disciplines to create an interdisciplinary blended learning course entitled Global Challenges (www.aascu.org/GlobalChallenges/). The goal of the course, often presented in the first year of college, is to produce globally competent American citizens. Faculty members who teach the course on the separate campuses have their own students, typical of a blended learning model. However, they share in the development of course design, content, student activities, exercises, tests, and other assessments. This new course has been described as a Massive Collaboratively Designed Course, or MCDC.

In the typical course, the quality of the design, delivery, and assessment rests solely with one individual faculty member. Therefore, the quality of the course varies widely from individual to individual, depending on the background, capability, and motivation of that individual faculty member. In addition, in the typical course, the classroom metaphor is a black box: only one faculty member knows what works best (if indeed they can discern that) and no one else is likely to learn about what works best from that course context. The collaboratively designed blended learning course maximizes the potential to improve over time through the collective wisdom of the instructors who participate, as well as the feedback from students. Equally important, the data derived are collective data, across many individual sections, which allows for comprehensive analysis, not only at the macro level but in various kinds of disaggregation and subunit analysis. Perhaps equally important, the massive collaboratively designed course allows faculty members to keep their own students and for institutions to maintain a traditional business model. One has little difficulty imagining that institutions of higher education will change dramatically in the years ahead. But most likely the transformation will be purposefully incremental. Using massive collaboratively designed courses that continue to allow students to register on individual campuses, and institutions to continue to have a revenue stream, promises a more evolutionary than revolutionary change for existing institutions.

John Naisbitt's (1988) concept of high-tech, high-touch, despite the enthusiasm of some that education in the future will be technology-based and substantially automated, presents us with the challenge in the coming century of finding a balance between rapidly advancing technology and the unique capabilities of individual human teachers. Clearly the model of the last century, which is in many respects a model of earlier centuries, will have difficulty persisting in the twenty-first century. We need both high-tech and high-touch. We also need the most sophisticated and technologically advanced ways of engaging students in a world in which lifelong learning will become a reality, not simply an expression of hope. At the same time, however, the vast majority of students will continue to need human intervention, particularly in the form of caring, creative, and reflective practitioners who are able to encourage and inspire the coming generation of students. Blended learning gives us the opportunity to think critically about the boundary between high-tech and high-touch, and offer the best from each.

Conclusion

Let us end with three admonitions. First, as researchers, we must learn that there is nothing wrong with being wrong. Error is an inherent part of research and can be very informative. By being open to the likelihood of errors in our research, we can accumulate verifiable data that Schulz (2010) contends permits us to manage by fact and not anecdote. Investigators have a great responsibility because data cannot speak for themselves. We must give the data a voice and we cannot do so through a filter of *everything blended is good*. Second, we should remember that progress is best made in those bite-sized chunks of the adjacent possible and that simple is really better. Third, researchers have a prime responsibility to make their findings relevant to the worlds of those who make decisions based on the information we give them about blended learning. An exciting world of possibilities opens up before us with the arrival of blended learning models and practices. But the story is a complicated one, and deserves to be told with all of its nuances and complexity.

References

Allen, I. E., & Seaman, J. (2013). *Changing course: Ten years of tracking online education in the United States.* Babson Survey Research Group and Quahog Research Group, LLC.

Bennett, W. J. (2012). Is Sebastian Thrun's Udacity the future of higher education? Downloaded February 10, 2013 from www.cnn.com/2012/07/05/opinion/bennett-udacity-education

Bowker, G. C., & Starr, S. L. (1989). *Sorting things out: Classification and its consequences.* Cambridge, MA: MIT Press.

CathyNDavidson (2012, July 23). Exactly! That's why I think IF we can be replaced by computer screen, we should be—if we cannot, then do something amazing! [Twitter post]. Retrieved from https://twitter.com/CathyNDavidson/status/227557151831388160

Cavanagh, T. B. (2012). The postmodality era: How "online learning" is becoming "learning". In D. G. Oblinger (Ed.), *Game changers: Education and information technology* (pp. 215–228). Boulder, CO: EDUCAUSE.

Ciaramita, M., Murdock, V., & Plachouras, V. (2008, April). Online learning from click data for sponsored search. In *Proceedings of the 17th international conference on World Wide Web* (pp. 227–236).

Doyle, W., & Ponder, G. A. (1977). The practicality ethic in teacher decision-making. *Interchange, 8*(3), 1–12.

Dziuban, C., & Moskal, P. (2011). A course is a course is a course: Factor invariance in student evaluation of online blended and face-to-face learning environments. *Internet and Higher Education, 14*(1), 236–241.

Dziuban, C., Moskal, P, Cavanagh, T. B., & Watts, A. (2012). Analytics that inform the university: Using data you already have. *Journal of Asynchronous Learning Networks, 16*(3), 21–38.

Graham, C. R. (2013). Emerging practice and research in blended learning. In M. G. Moore (Ed.), *Handbook of distance education* (3rd ed., pp. 333–350). New York, NY: Routledge.

Harmon, K. (2004). *You are here: Personal geographies and other maps of the imagination.* New York, NY: Princeton Architectural Press.

Jenkins, H. (2006). *Convergence culture: Where old and new media collide.* New York, NY: NYU Press.

Johnson, S. (2010). *Where good ideas come from: The natural history of innovation.* New York, NY: The Penguin Group.

Khan, S. (2011). Let's use video to reinvent education: Salman Khan on TED.com. Video retrieved from http://blog.ted.com/2011/03/09/lets-use-video-to-reinvent-education-salman-khan-on-ted-com/ (last accessed: 04.15.2011).

Matthews, R. (2005). *25 big ideas: The science that's changing our world.* New York, NY: MJF Books.

Mehaffy, G. (2011, September). *The shifting policy landscape.* Presented at the Future of Online Learning Summit, Chicago, Illinois.

Meyer, K. A. (2005). Common metaphors and their impact on distance education: What they tell us and what they hide. *Teachers College Record, 107*(8), 1601–1625.

Millichap, N., & Vogt, K. (2012, December 11). *Building blocks for college completion: Blended learning.* Next Generation Learning Challenges.

Naisbitt, J. (1988). Megatrends: Ten new directions transforming our lives. New York, NY: Grand Central Publishing.

Oliver, M., & Trigwell, K. (2005). Can "blended learning" be redeemed? *E-Learning, 2*(1), 17–26.

Schulz, K. (2010). *Being wrong: Adventures in the margin of error.* New York, NY: HarperCollins Publishers.

Selingo, J. (2003). The disappearing state in public higher education. *Chronicle of Higher Education, 49*(25), A22.

Silver, N. (2012). *The signal and the noise: Why so many predictions fail – but some don't.* New York, NY: The Penguin Press.

Sloan, R. (2012). *Mr. Penumbra's 24-hour bookstore: A novel.* New York, NY: Farrar, Straus and Giroux.

Taleb, N. N. (2012). *Antifragile: Things that gain from disorder.* New York: Random House.
Walster, W., & Cleary, T. A. (1970). Statistical significance as a decision rule. *Social Methodology, 2*(1), 246–254.
Weigert, A. J. (1991). *Mixed emotions.* Albany, NY: State University of New York Press.

INDEX